The Rhetoric of Suffering

The Rhetoric of Suffering

Reading the Book of Job in the Eighteenth Century

JONATHAN LAMB

CLARENDON PRESS · OXFORD
1995

Oxford University Press, Walton Street, Oxford OX2 6DP

Oxford New York
Athens Auckland Bangkok Bombay
Calcutta Cape Town Dar es Salaam Delhi
Florence Hong Kong Istanbul Karachi
Kuala Lumpur Madras Madrid Melbourne
Mexico City Nairobi Paris Singapore
Taipei Tokyo Toronto
and associated companies in
Berlin Ibadan

Oxford is a trade mark of Oxford University Press

Published in the United States
by Oxford University Press Inc., New York

© Jonathan Lamb 1995

British Library Cataloguing in Publication Data
Data available

Library of Congress Cataloging in Publication Data
Lamb, Jonathan, 1945–
The rhetoric of suffering: reading the book of Job in the
eighteenth century / Jonathan Lamb.
Includes bibliographical references (p.   ) and index.
1. Bible. O.T. Job—Criticism, interpretation, etc.—
History—18th century. 2. Bible. O.T. Job—Criticism,
interpretation, etc.—Great Britain. I. Title.
BS1415.2.L26 1995
223'.106'094109033—dc20   94-48439
ISBN 0-19-818264-3

1 3 5 7 9 10 8 6 4 2

Typeset by Best-set Typesetter Ltd., Hong Kong
Printed in Great Britain
on acid-free paper by
Bookcraft Ltd,
Midsomer Norton, Avon

For Bridget

We set up a word at the point at which our ignorance begins, at which we can see no further, e.g. the word 'I', the word 'do', the word 'suffer':—these are perhaps the horizon of our knowledge, but not 'truths'.

Friedrich Nietzsche, *The Will to Power*

Was I an imitator and a fool that I needed to introduce a third person in order to describe the fate of two human beings who made life hard for one another? . . . I ought to have known that this third person who pervades all life and literature, this ghost of a third person who has never existed, has no significance and must be disavowed.

Rainer Maria Rilke, *The Notebooks of Malte Laurids Brigge*

Acknowledgements

I began work on this book in 1988, and since then have contracted more debts in the researching and writing of it than I can ever properly acknowledge. There are, however, several institutions to whom I am deeply grateful. First, the University of Auckland, where I worked for twenty-five years, and which generously funded two periods of paid leave, and granted me one of unpaid leave, during the six years it took me to write the book. The bulk of my research was completed while on a fellowship at the National Humanities Center in North Carolina in 1991–2: the combination of a munificent stipend, a roomy study, tirelessly considerate staff, and stimulating colleagues induced in me a calm intensity which was so productive that I have often wished I could recover it. That period ended with a bout of frenzied writing at the Huntington Library, out of which the core of the book emerged; and I am grateful to the staff of the library for the encouragement and assistance they gave me for that month. It is with great affection as well as gratitude that I mention the Clark Library and the Yale Center for British Art. Short-term fellowships were given me by these institutions at the very beginning of the project, when I myself was unsure of its value or point: people patiently listened and gently pointed me in the right directions, and I am glad I can offer them something to show for their kindness. The William Goodenough Trust has ensured that the last lap of the race has been run in great comfort, and very close to the British Library. I am grateful to the staff of the British Library, the Beinecke Library, and the Sterling Library at Yale for their help. I want particularly to thank Hazel Mannion and Sheryl Baster of the University of Auckland Library and Susan Bennett of the Royal Society of Arts for their kindness.

Three colleagues in the New Zealand academy have given me considerable support: Jocelyn Harris of Otago, Mark Williams of Canterbury, and Warwick Slinn of Massey University. Simon During of the University of Melbourne has been a steady friend and a stimulating companion.

Among my colleagues at Auckland, I want to thank Alex Calder, Wystan Curnow, Michael Neill, Robert Nola, Terry Sturm, Don Smith, Andrew Sharp, Bridget McPhail, and Elisabeth Wilson for suggestions and ideas. I owe much to Roger Nicholson on a broad front, but particularly for his prompt and cheerful help with computing and printing; likewise I thank Harry Leder for his setting up my travelling software. Annie Goldson, Paul Stone, and the students of papers 18.306 and 18.308 listened to my ideas at different stages of their development; and the Friday 'reading group' in its various manifestations (Stephen Zepke, Hester Joyce, Brigid Shadbolt, Leonie Reynolds, Catherine Dale) broke and re-set my ideas about the sublime. Ross Jenner and Laurence Simmons have been invaluable company and challenging seminarians. Sebastian Black has seen me through numerous official channels, and always with the best results. Claudia Marquis has fed and indulged me. I owe more to Bridget Orr, my partner and my co-worker in the field of the eighteenth century, than I am able to record.

There are some American friends and colleagues who have been very helpful to this project: I want to mention Michael Seidel, Annabel Patterson, Susan Green, John Bender, Claude Rawson, Margaret Doody, Sylvia Tomasch, Neil Hertz, Jim Gill, Allen Dunn, Jerry Christenson, and Mark Seltzer. Gib Bogle has provided me with shelter and warmth in Pasadena. In England I have depended on David Ellis, Malcolm Andrews, and Rod Edmond for encouragement and good humour. Jane Duncan and Ian Duncan have been hospitable, patient, and expert by turns; and Mel Humphreys and Richard Wallace have reminded me that there is more to life than writing books.

My daughters, who have not felt much of the benefit of this exercise, have nevertheless unselfishly cheered me on, and helped me where they could. I want to thank Esther Lamb and Rebecca Lamb; and also Susan Lamb, who helped shoulder the burden through the first stages.

Acknowledgements are due to the Dulwich Picture Gallery for permission to reproduce Poussin's *Rinaldo and Armida*; to the Auckland City Art Gallery Collection for permission to reproduce plates 10 and 11 of Blake's *Job*; to the Crawford Municipal Art Gallery, Cork, for permission to reproduce James Barry's *Ulysses and a Companion*; to the British Museum's Department of Prints and Drawings for permission to reproduce James Barry's aquatints, *The Earl of Chatham* and *The Conversion of Polemon*; to the Yale Center of British Art for permission to reproduce James Barry's *Job Reproved by his Friends*; to the Brooklyn Museum for permission to reproduce Joseph Wright's *The Dead Soldier*; and to Annie Goldson for permission to reproduce the photograph of the tomb of Penelope Boothby. Portions of Chapters 6 and 12 first appeared in *Eighteenth-Century Studies* and *Eighteenth-Century Fiction* respectively.

Princeton   J.L.
December 1994

Contents

List of Illustrations

PART I

Stories of Job

1 *Introduction*

All men can skill to complayne with Job. Wherefore is it that the
faythfull speake so? It seemeth that they be nice and womanish.

(John Calvin, *Sermons on Job*)

This study is not intended to be a literary history, tracing the evolution
of readings of the book of Job from the neoclassical and providentialist
to the Enlightenment or rationalist, and thence to the Romantic and
sublime. The confidence needed for such a narrative is exactly what the
book of Job undermines, being the story of a man who becomes
womanish in refusing to sacrifice the particularities of his woes to the
symmetry his friends claim to see in them. It is a story destructive not
only of the connections which Job's comforters (and perhaps many of
his readers) expect to be binding causes to effects, but also of any theory
of verisimilitude which assumes an interpretable meaning or moral to be
embedded in a representation of events. For connections it substitutes
interruptions, and for meanings repetitions. This has raised much debate
about its genre—whether it is epic, allegory, or history—and about its
status as theodicy—whether it is in fact intended to justify God's ways
to humankind. There is no dispute pursued inside the story of Job's
sufferings that is not capable of being renewed on the outside by readers
trying to make sense of that very dispute. It is a story that provokes
imitations of itself by resisting what interpreting readers want it to say,
and by inviting the less prescriptive to inhabit its strange indiscipline. It
is as impossible to define as it is to get quit of it.

Instead of constructing a developmental model of the changing tastes
and priorities of eighteenth-century readers, therefore, this study offers
to treat Job as a figure and a name for a recurrent cultural antinomy that
emerges in fields as diverse as monumental sculpture and voyages of
discovery, as well as in politics and literature, whenever the interpretation and the point of first-person testimonies are at stake. This
antinomy is always recognizable in its basic form as a conflict between
the law—in its broadest sense of principle, rule, and precedent as well as
of statute—and those elements of a personal history, usually painful, for
which there is no prescription or parallel. Job refuses to be read as an
example, or as a case with wider significance: he voices doubts about all
the available forms of narrative. When Job is quoted or gestured at, he

will not, therefore, behave as a positive instance; he will signpost a border dispute between the public and the private spheres in which he is already engaged. It is a dispute pursued in terms neither side can fully understand over infringements and injustices neither side will acknowledge as such.

As the epigraph from Calvin suggests, gender constitutes such a borderline, especially at the frontier of articulate grief. The extravagance of a womanish complaint, expelled so often to the noiseless rim of the protocols and rites of mourning, runs alongside other unstudied reactions to emergencies which the upholders of rules and norms construe as misbehaviour. Felons at certain critical junctures on their road to the gallows, members of a parliamentary opposition when the distinction between public spirit and ambition gets blurred, navigators at the limit of the known world, and people with a taste for the sublime, reject the normative discourse of principle and precedent as inadequate for the expression of what they feel, or else deliberately misapply it. Whether it is consolation they refuse, or the maxims of party or state, or the received wisdom concerning the discovery of territory, or the bounded symmetries of the beautiful, when they put aside the language which makes experience generally predictable, exemplary, probable, and narratable, the cost of such neglect is a conflict with the defenders of the normal that is often keyed to a citation or a replay of Job's story. The debates surrounding Warburton's fierce and ingenious interpretation of Job during the mid-eighteenth century were notable for the occasions when polemical divines consciously (and more often unconsciously) re-enacted the unnegotiable collisions between Job and the comforters, keeping open and extending by virtue of their interpretative zeal the very scandal they wished to remove. At the other extreme, a woman such as Martha Bilson, whose story will end this chapter, has no other resource when her miseries are routinized by a Job-quoting clergyman than to quote Job back at him in a desperate effort to reclaim the particularity of her sufferings and the authenticity of her complaint.

It is no coincidence that the bitterest theological disputes about Job should occur during the same decades which saw the first experiments with the novel. The crisis of exegesis and the question of genre back onto each other; and to the degree that Fielding, Richardson, Sterne, and Goldsmith are drawn to examine the problems of representation, so they are tempted to rewrite portions of Job's story. Their difficulties with the intransigent particulars of the passages of private life extend to the incorrigible feelings incident to moments of suffering and grief, so that the questions of what kind of narrative is being written, and what kind of reading such writing deserves, form as prominent a part of their narratives as the debate about the generic legitimacy of complaint in the dialogues of Job. In all of these texts, writing about the problems of writing involves reading about the problems of reading.

The line of Joban imitations runs as far as the late twentieth-century reader, inured since the advent of modernism to the reordering of assumptions about narrative structure and interpretation, and further sensitized to the implausibility of large narratives by postmodernist and poststructuralist critiques of periodization, the subject, genre, textuality, and history. I want to instance these factors no further than to point to some of their results in recent work on the eighteenth century, such as John Bender's *Imagining the Penitentiary*, Peter de Bolla's *The Discourse of the Sublime*, and Terry Castle's *Masquerade and Civilisation*, where the developmental model is exchanged for a trope formed from one specific aspect of cultural activity: the architecture of prisons, the discourse of debt, the protocol of a masquerade ball. These tropes are not adduced as indices of the regularity of social behaviour, or as symbols of the coherence of cultural production, but as sites of recurrent contradictions between the norms proposed by society for its own government and the sum of individual anomalies it accommodates and tolerates. In its most specific form the trope labels a contradiction between the rules of representation and actual practice which is observed to extend in unforeseen ways to a variety of representational forms (buildings, clothes, novels, aesthetics, oratory, and optics) which preserve the modality of the basic contradiction. And as it is a contradiction that invades the very methods used by a culture to record and transmit its own priorities to itself, the trope functions as a catch-all for everything that is excessive, oblique, or inconsistent in this self-representation.

I am going to use Job as this sort of trope. He will link the fundamental contradiction between the rules of representation and the actualities of practice to the heterogeneous contexts in which that contradiction is capable of surfacing, sharpening its paradoxes and complicating its circular and reflexive formations. He will provide a name and a local habitation for all that is surplus to the exemplary economy of norms and precedents; and he will problematize the methods of exemplary interpretation and allegorical exegesis that are customarily used to retrieve anomalies and pronounce them orthodox. This disturbance of representational technique, named Job, will bring excess into the open, and make articulate the agitated and complaining voice of the first person singular. I am interested in identifying the energy or power of this complaint, unabated by orthodox interpretation and unocculted as delinquent nicety. It is an energy which, when it is free to fight with law or authority, provokes an open-ended series of scandals, both unforgiving and endlessly recurrent.

Job is this sort of energetic and scandalous delinquent. His strong sense of the futility of his affliction causes him to raise fundamental doubts about order, providence, justice, and meaning. A quarrel ensues with his friends, who want to stand up for the principles of justice and intelligibility flouted by his complaint. His impatience increases with his isolation, and although he falls silent after God's intervention, there is no sign that the feelings of confusion and despair he has been trying to communicate have been removed or even diverted. The story of Job is remarkable for its concentration on this single and recurrent aspect of the crisis of normative language, taking it through as many as five phases (the three rounds with the comforters, followed by another with Elihu and a final contest with God) which deepen and complicate the issues of complaint, until they reach a limit (the doors of heaven, the furthest reaches of language and thought) at which the idiom of explanation ceases to function other than as an apodictic echo or a tautology, and where complaint itself can only be iterated as a hollow paradox. Even more remarkable is the fact that a narrative form has been found capable of representing this crisis of representation. The book of Job delivers in dramatic and moving terms a confrontation so much in excess of the available means of accounting for it, that it is a miracle, or a scandal, it has been delivered at all.

The second-order scandal of Job is at the level of reading. If the contest is not to stall on the tautologies of authority and the paradoxes of delinquent complaint, it needs to find among its readers an audience more flexible than the comforters and less peremptory than God. Readers have often observed the paradoxes of Job's story: that it is a parable of patience consisting in nothing but symptoms of impatience; that it is a justification of providence which calls clearly and persistently into doubt the justice of providence; that Job contrives to prophesy the redeemer and the resurrection without believing in an afterlife, and so on. These paradoxes are the effects of the unresolved questions raised in a story which can never advance to new ground, but only interrupt and repeat itself. They issue a challenge to its readers, however, to enter into its want of logic, and to find the evil or the good of it. To the same degree that this challenge is met, the story of Job moves into the next stage of its telling, which is the record of its reception and use by readers. The history of the reading of Job is strewn with crises mimetic of those it describes, recurring at the same level of intensity as often as the book and its options are taken up.

The testing of normative language goes on, then, at the two levels of narrative delivery and active reading, unrolling as an indefinite series. Readers repeat the same repetitions, and interrupt themselves with the same interruptions that they have been reading about. A scandal that endlessly outruns the methods for containing and dismantling it has a certain appeal for the British during the eighteenth century, despite the destruction it causes to structures of belief and theories of pedagogy. Suspicion of system and what Burke called speculative reasoning, whose ill consequences were evident to him alike in French politics and philosophy, and hospitality to a pragmatism whose inquisitiveness and initiative derive from the glorious revolutionary interruption of a line of authoritative descent, are the distinguishing features of Whiggism. Bolingbroke contrasts the inductive and enquiring cast of British thought with the abstract ontologies fashionable on the Continent. The *a priori*, whether as the *sine qua non* of a deduction, or as the unquestioned principle or rule which commands implicit obedience, stands in contrast to the *a posteriori*, which involves a curiosity about effects unhindered by any allegiance to a governing cause, or indeed to any principle of investigation not coincident with the activity of finding things out. Those embarked on the libertarian exploitation of contingencies are actively sceptical of the indefeasible authority of any idea or precedent. Tristram Shandy—a comic Job adrift in an apocryphal genre of narrative—makes this plain in his vehement defence of the impulsive and constitutive nature of his work: 'A pretty story! is a man to follow rules——or rules to follow him?'[1]

The triumphs of this pragmatic bent, such as common law, the novel, taste, public spirit, Newtonian physics, and associationist psychology, tend to circle round the questions of standards and originary forms, producing elaborate and endless substitutions of effects for causes, and outcomes for validations, that are destined after a century to harden into Podsnappery. Even before then, upholders of the Revolution Settlement are inclined to transform the constitutive terms of party, philosophy, criticism, or belief into peremptory and irrefragable doctrine; but the difference between these adaptive positions of the British and the arguments *a priori* drawn out, according to Bolingbroke, in a Europe enslaved to the authority of first principles, is that they are much more vulnerable to shock. Supported by nothing more substantial than custom or iteration, the self-evidence of favourite British notions is subject to sudden collapses or contradictions which shatter the illusion of ideo-

---

[1] *The Life and Opinions of Tristram Shandy, Gentleman*, ed. Melvyn New and Joan New, 3 vols. (Florida: Univ. Presses of Florida, 1978), i. 337.

logical consistency that habit has given them. Such emergencies are experienced with sharper pain for being uninsured by any explanation or justification at a level higher than practice. Hume discloses the astounding singularities that lie behind customary modes of thought, just as Newton opens up behind the regularities of gravitation a gap in the plenum (the hollow medium of action taking place over a distance) for which he can offer no adequate account. Pitt's patriotic eloquence brings up the question of sheer ambition, and the efficacy of protestations of disinterestedness in satisfying it. The law of the 1750s—especially criminal law—exhibits the haphazardry of an unformulated body of cases, founded on immemorial usage, and constitutive of the judgements and sentences of further cases. Although the law aims by this accumulation of practical wisdom to privilege the customary and the usual, in practice it fosters the bare possibilities and the incalculable chances that Fielding uses as the material of his fiction. Likewise the discourse of taste makes room for subjective caprice and contingency while trying to frame the consensual basis of choices and evaluations. On a broad front the differences between what is commonly done or believed in and what it is possible to do or to feel, breaches the regulative function of ideas of the probable. The decade in which these risks are felt most acutely coincides with Warburton's battle over the interpretation of Job. It is a decade that includes the Lisbon earthquake, an unprecedented event involving misery on such a colossal scale that Voltaire finds he can respond only by personifying the ruined city as Job.

The scandalous possibilities of a pragmatic culture, whose norms are easily assailable by singular and personal experiences of chances, and which is defended solely by the authority of custom, chime with the scandals of Job. In his plight the British recognize the anxiety endured whenever the familiar pulse of custom is interrupted by an unpredictable event, or by a phenomenon that corresponds to no model or purpose. Job offers an intuition of a life immune to the common ways of generating meaning—a life peculiarly sensitive to the unhinged particularity of each passing moment, whose nearest approximation to form is recurrence and repetition, and which, in narrative terms, ought not to have been delivered, or ought not to have happened in the first place.

Although these issues in Job are always entangled with the circumstances of their delivery, and cannot therefore be cleanly unravelled by a metadiscourse, there are three theoretical positions which I have found helpful in considering the scandalous particularity of individual practice within a system of permeable norms. They are the discourses of the sublime, of practice, and of self-reference. The grounds of their relation to each other consists in the following: an unremitting testing of rules and axioms; an awareness of the tautologous form of justification; an interest in the instrumentality of 'unfolded' tautologies, and the indication this provides of an unregulated access to power; a highly provisional notion of subjectivity and identity; and an acknowledgement that the limit case (no matter how extreme or isolated) has no reference beyond the system of communication itself, and that the auditor or reader is therefore the co-producer of differences and modifications within that system.

The sublime is in many ways the aptest of these three discourses in so far as it thrives in the eighteenth century, is frequently illustrated with reference to Job, and persists within postmodernist aesthetics as a buoyant and (some would say) an urgent matter of debate. In eighteenth-century Britain Longinus was admired (especially by Whig readers) for his irregularity, and his contempt for any authority not stamped with the mark of genius. Hence his refusal to define the sublime according to precept, and his delight in citing not the rules of the sublime, but the sublime itself. 'But tho' Longinus does not directly tell us what the sublime is, yet in the first six of seven chapters of his Book, he takes a great deal of Pains to set before us the Effects which it produces in the Minds of Men.'[2] Longinus' refusal to measure his delivery of the sublime against a standard or rule has a number of fascinating consequences. The first is that it can only be known by making it happen again. Longinus' criticism is not descriptive but mimetic: he '*is himself* that great Sublime he draws'.[3] Owing to its lack of formal precedent the discourse of the sublime must express the quality it aims to convey, and act indistinguishably from the action it reveals. It means being sublime on the sublime.

This necessity drives readers no less peremptorily than it drives Longinus to reproduce the intensities of the sublime, forcing them to abandon the more sedate pleasures of interpretation and commentary for passionate identification. To scrutinize Job's complaints or the experience of the sublime for a meaning or moral behind the vehemence of each successive instant is to assume a difference between the inside and outside of expressive language that both Job and Longinus energetically deny. Longinus detests allegory as heartily as those who were to defend Job against Warburton. The sublime can only mean doing it, again and again, as Jonathan Swift observes in his *On Poetry: A Rhapsody*, where the rising critic is to read Longinus in a translation of a translation, and

---

[2] John Dennis, *The Advancement and Reformation of Poetry* (1701), in *The Critical Works of John Dennis*, ed. Edward Niles Hooker, 2 vols. (Baltimore: Johns Hopkins Univ. Press, 1939), i. 223.
[3] Alexander Pope, *An Essay on Criticism* in *Poems*, ed. John Butt (London: Methuen, 1963), i. 680.

to learn to quote quotation on quotation.⁴ Whether mimesis is cast as this barren series or as the swelling and triumph of the mind when it claims to itself 'some part of the dignity and importance of the things which it contemplates',⁵ it constitutes the sublimity of absorbing the sublime. When Job wishes his complaint were a message carved on a rock and supposes a reader capable of speaking it out loud, he defines his own redemption as the possibility of this mimetic sequence: a face-to-face encounter with himself. The reader appropriates the force of the original and glories in it as an event of his or her own creation. As John Dennis points out, the modern critic must imitate the Greek one, 'and when he treats of a Subject which is sublime, treat of it sublimely' (*Reflections on An Essay on Criticism* [1711] i. 409). The power of the sublime is never vested, therefore, in an authority defined by a text, but is available to anyone capable of responding to its intensities, internalizing them, and then expressing them as one's own.

The second consequence of a sublime which reproduces its intensities in the vacuum left by the rules of good composition is that it no sooner wins power for the reader than it questions and destabilizes the ground of this agency. The moment of the sublime is a usurpation of power, achieved by projecting the critical ego into the place of the force it contemplates: 'Hence proceeds what Longinus has observed of that glorying and sense of inward greatness, that always fills the reader of such passages in poets and orators as are sublime'.⁶ But this glamorous sense of competence is bordered on the one side by the shameful experience of personal inferiority preceding it, when 'the Sublime . . . with the rapid force of Lightning has born down all before it, and shewn at one stroke the compacted Might of Genius';⁷ and on the other by inevitable transfusion of appropriated 'compacted Might' to the next reader, who will absorb it and claim it, 'as if what was only heard had been the Product of [his] own Invention' (*On the Sublime*, 14).

The recurrence of the sublime at the same level of intensity along a chain of readers may weaken the claim for subjective continuity, but it ensures that the sublime is never mistaken for a force independent of this subjective exchange of energy. The third consequence of a sublime turning perpetually on itself is that nothing can ever be construed as sublime outside this series of communicative moves. Despite the frequent assertion to the contrary by eighteenth-century landscape special-

---

⁴ *The Poems of Jonathan Swift*, ed. Harold Williams, 3 vols. (Oxford: Clarendon Press, 1937; repr. 1958), ii. 648–9.
⁵ Edmund Burke, *A Philosophical Enquiry into the Origin of our Ideas of the Sublime and the Beautiful*, ed. James T. Boulton (London: Routledge and Kegan Paul, 1958; repr. Oxford: Blackwell, 1987), 50–1.
⁶ Ibid. 51.   ⁷ *On the Sublime*, trans. William Smith (London, 1739), 3.

ists, there is no sublime environment, no phenomenon in nature that can claim an intrinsic part in these intensities, or pretend to be a cause or end of them. As Kant points out, they are bounded by the subject, and by the crises it faces in winning agency. 'Thus the broad ocean agitated by storms cannot be called sublime. . . . All we can say is that the object lends itself to presentation of a sublimity discoverable in the mind. For the sublime, in the strict sense of the word, cannot be contained in any sensuous form.'[8] The mimesis involved in the sublime event is not representational, therefore, according to the classical definition of mimesis as the construction of an image of things in the world; rather it is a struggle between two subject-positions competing for the right to speak forcefully in the first person. This is precisely the structure of the dialogues of Job and the dynamic of reading them.

In many ways the sublime can be produced as a specimen of practice, since it is shy of the metalanguage that can account for the production of adequate examples according to definite rules and models, resolving instead to render the sublime according to itself: sublimely. Similarly, Job's rejection of consolation displaces exemplary grief with the activity of suffering: 'Therefore I will not refrain my mouth; I will speak in the anguish of my spirit; I will complain in the bitterness of my soul' (7: 11). Like Longinus, he opts for a mode of expression unmediated by standards of propriety and accuracy: his lamentation is continuous with the sharpness of his feelings, it does not describe, cite, or universalize them. The Joban subject and the subject of sublimity do not present themselves as exemplars fulfilling the requirements of a pre-established norm, but as personal, excessive, and singular cases consisting in nothing but loose particulars whose articulation will constitute a passionate event, not an object of understanding, evaluation, or interpretation.

I take practice to be the opposite of what Pierre Bourdieu calls 'learned ignorance'. If learned ignorance depends on a facility in handling the norms and rules designed to nominate and control practical outcomes, practice itself is a skill or competence that knows itself solely in its activity, 'a mode of practical knowledge not comprising knowledge of its own principles'. When a skilled practitioner tries to explain the grounds of the art to a curious observer, the explanation will be made badly because it will substitute citations of rules for the 'silences, ellipses, and lacunae of the language of familiarity',[9] and either hide or forget what is really known. Bourdieu instances the Sophists as the last

---

[8] Immanuel Kant, *Critique of Judgment*, trans. James Creed Meredith (Oxford: Clarendon Press, 1991), 92.
[9] Pievre Bourdieu, *Outline of a Theory of Practice* (Cambridge: Cambridge University Press, 1977; repr. 1990), p. 18.

practitioners of such knowledge in Western philosophy, because they taught their pupils with nothing but the rhetoric they used. Their *technai* were collections of fragments of oratory, passed on for free improvisation and adaptation, not conceptualized as representations, or measured against extrinsic criteria of truth or verisimilitude (*Outline*, 20). Longinus, writing in the second Sophistic, offers his treatise on the sublime as just such a *techne*, filled with bits of poems and speeches that will be animated, and animate, only on condition that the practice of the pupil-reader equal that of the master-writer. Longinus points to Isocrates as learnedly ignorant in his reliance upon the virtues of metalanguage: thus his 'ill-timed Encomium of Eloquence is an inadvertent Admonition to the Audience not to listen or give credit to what he says' (*On the Sublime* xxxvii. 1).[10] Job accuses his comforters of causing to be ignored what they are learnedly explaining, namely his own pain.

Those who invoke the law (in its broadest sense) against a practice ignorant of its own principles, blinding themselves to the more serious and destructive ignorance involved in trying to govern an activity bound to wither under such invocations, are denied the examples and illustrations that practice is supposed to produce in justification of the law. Practice is diminished precisely to the extent that it is instanced in this way, indicating that the law is not justified by events (as the comforters finally concede to Job), but only by itself. The law is the law, a tautology that demands obedience regardless of its inefficiencies and inequities. Michel de Certeau has expanded Bourdieu's critique of critique into an exploration of the various tactics adopted on the side of practice when it is menaced by the tautologies of the law. He applies the Greek word *metis* to the clandestine defence of practice, naming a kind of agility he associates equally with rope-dancers and gamblers that allows them to take advantage of immediate circumstances in order to seize the initiative. According to de Certeau the practical subject acts in defence of the particularity of personal experience, and of the rhetorical flair of the voice that alone is fit to speak of it. However, it acts from a position of real weakness, with a body already submitted to the intrumentality of the law and inscribed with its sentences. 'Every power, including the power of law, is written first of all on the backs of its subjects. . . . Books are only metaphors of the body. But in times of crisis, paper is no longer enough for the law, and it writes itself again on the bodies themselves.'[11] Scarred with these marks of regulation, and condemned to have the

---

[10] This point is handled more at large in Jonathan Lamb, 'Longinus, the Dialectic, and the Practice of Mastery', *ELH* 60 (1993), 545–67.

[11] Michel de Certeau, *The Practice of Everyday Life*, trans. Steven Rendall (Berkeley, Calif.: Univ. of California Press, 1984), 140.

specificities of complaint dismissed as improbabilities, the practical subject resorts to counter-memory, to a species of recall prompted by fresh circumstances, a vigilant serendipity that exploits the occasionality of events in order to upset the authority of the past, and to proclaim the injuries it has suffered. *Metis* finds a home for the singular detail in the network of conventional doctrine, just as a cuckoo finds a place for its egg in an alien nest. It is a restoration of practical pertinence, a surprise that was expected without being foreseen, 'a flash repartee' (88). The leading effect of this counter-memory is a recovery of voice, not the voice that might be assumed originally to be coincident with practice (Bourdieu's 'language of familiarity'), but the voice that has been cleverly substituted for its written supplement. It is the voice of subverted writing: 'The sound of the body becomes an imitation of this part of itself that is produced and reproduced by the media—i.e. a copy of its own artefact' (132).

To restore the copy of a copy to practical vocality is to take advantage of the same sublime seriality Swift disparages as the quotation of quotation upon quotation. It is to bring the reading of the written fragment to a level of intensity equal to that of the original expression. The sublime of practice is the recovery of voice through the ventriloquization of the written medium. In mounting sublimity upon sublimity, or copy upon artefact, not in the blind insistence upon authority or in an ever-fading print of the authentic thing, but in the resourceful modification of priority, textuality, and cruelty implicit in a word such as prescription, the empowered subject seizes from behind the pseudo-legitimacy of the written word a phonographic skill which needs no justification but its exercise. The sterile circularity of the law's self-authorization is transformed into a sort of fruitful pleonasm (translation of translation, quotation on quotation, sublimity on sublimity) whose point is the power-shift, the moment of exchange between author and reader, reader and speaker, 'I' and 'I'. In the book of Job this moment is conceived by the hero as a writing upon writing, an inscription upon stone of the disastrous effects of being written on by God, a complaint about the humiliation of being reduced to a byword or proverb: 'Oh that my words were now written! oh that they were printed in a book! That they were graven with an iron pen and lead in the rock for ever' (19: 23–4). Then Job foretells the reading of this writing as a redemptive act, in which agency will be won, and vindication achieved, by the reading aloud of a newly empowered 'I': 'For I know that my redeemer liveth, and that he shall stand at the latter day upon the earth: And though after my skin worms destroy this body, yet in my flesh shall I see God: Whom I shall see for myself, and mine eyes shall behold, and not another' (19: 25–7).

In the discourses of the sublime and of practice the excessive feelings of the subject, although they may appear to overflow all bounds and to run in channels altogether foreign to the communicative regime which seeks to legislate and code their flow, in fact re-enter it, but on terms much more suitable to the vocal first person. Rather than breaching the system of signs, expressive practice makes a difference within it, widening its possibilities and extending its life. According to systems theory, communication suffers from the limitations of any system which cannot account for itself by adopting a position above or beyond itself. 'There is no place within differentiated systems . . . from which the entire system [can] be observed'; or, as another specialist on this topic puts it, 'There is no place from which you photograph the whole thing'.[12] Consequently its drift is determined by a series of differences which redistribute power within the system, similar to those I have observed in the reception of the sublime and in the *metis* of practice. These redistributions occur across a line drawn not between system and non-system, but between the conservative and radical forces within the system itself, summarized by Niklas Luhmann as those assumptions and preferences clustering on the one hand around tautology (simplicity, probability, predictability, low risk) and around paradox on the other (complexity, improbability, low predictability, high risk).

Tautology is itself the simplest expression of a circular logic on which all justifications within a system are forced to rely, since they cannot seek it outside. Tautology is used to protect the authority of the norm, which is in turn nothing but the sum of chances reduced to its most probable and expectable form. 'Society is what it is', 'the law is valid because it is valid', 'art consists of works of art, and what a work of art is, is determined by art', and so on.[13] 'Tautologies are distinctions that do not distinguish. . . . They are always based on a dual observation scheme: something is what it is' (*Self-Reference*, 136). A paradox, on the other hand, is a radical distinction that aims to carry difference beyond the limits of circularity constituted by the system: 'Society is what it is not', 'The book of Job is a theodicy that denies theodicy'. Paradox disturbs the normative framework of tautology with a contradiction unimprovable within the system as a difference. In fact when paradox stands in a sheer opposition to tautology, it sets up the blockage of the dialogues of Job, where the comforters' assertion of law as law is contradicted by Job's assertion of the law as not law, again and again, without any possibility of re-entry or of a power-shift.

[12] Niklas Luhmann, *Political Theory and the Welfare State*, trans. John Bednarz (Berlin: Walter de Gruyter, 1990), 51; J. F. Lyotard and J. L. Thebaud, *Just Gaming*, trans. Wlad Godzich (Minneapolis: Univ. of Minnesota Press, 1985), 43.

[13] See Niklas Luhmann, *Essays on Self-Reference* (New York: Columbia Univ. Press, 1990), 125, 193; *Political Theory*, 191.

The unfolding of tautology and the instrumentalization of paradox occurs when the level of improbability generated by a difference is held to a point consistent with the capacity of that difference to make a difference. In fact, among his numerous definitions of power, Luhmann includes this one: 'Power is an opportunity to increase the probability of realising improbable selection combinations'.[14] In the discourses of practice and the sublime, this is where one would expect to see a quotation of a quotation, a copy of a copy, writing on writing, or sublimity upon sublimity. In systems theory it is where self-reference becomes both the means and index of a power-shift, and of a difference that has the impact of an event. Self-reference is articulated as a pleonasm, such as the expectation of expectations, the distinction of distinctions, the observation of observations, and finally the difference of differences; as practice it involves the same double-take de Certeau associates with *metis*, a dual observation which squints at practical possibilities and restores a routine gesture to pertinence by means of the parallax figured in the pleonasm. Instead of dividing itself up to affirm itself of itself, an activity takes itself to the second power to see what can be done. Another definition of power states, 'Power has to be seen as selection based on selection'.[15]

The *locus classicus* of the unfolded tautology is the reflexive position of the subject answered by the gaze of its other, the *alter ego*—Job face to face with God or with his reader—where self-reference culminates in self-reflection. The period that most dramatically exhibits the adaptation and improvement of this position is the eighteenth century. Luhmann takes Adam Smith's scene of sympathy—the 'recognition of the other *as another*'—as his paradigm within a epoch notable for the liberation of 'new, risky, and one might say "unsocial" selective procedures'. The subject acts in defiance of the laws of probability and the norms of social behaviour: '*Curiosity* became a legitimate motive for pursuing knowledge, *profit* became something like income without a contractual base (i.e. without social legitimation), *raison d'état* became a political maxim, and *empassioned love* became a sufficient basis for choosing a partner'.[16]

Luhmann's liberated eighteenth-century subject is determined, like Job, practically to engage the complexities of experience in the first person. The 'improbability of highly personal communication' can result in blockage under the coercion of the law's servants, who may be inclined (like the comforters) to ignore the law's primary function as a facilitator of expectations in an effort simply to compel obedience from

---

[14] *Trust and Power* (Chichester: John Wiley, 1979), 114.
[15] See *Political Theory*, 55, 168; *The Differentiation of Society* (New York: Columbia Univ. Press, 1982), 151.   [16] Ibid. 5, 267.

loquacious complainants.[17] Luhmann explores the more fruitful alternative that presents itself when 'I see others as another I'—that is to say, when the projection of the first person singular into the place of power occupied by a mirrored 'I' encourages power to circulate in a non-transitive way.[18] Such a scene is imagined by Job as the delivery of the improbabilities of his complaint to a substitute, or redeemer, which will bring him face to face with an other whom he calls God, and activate the circuit of mimetic intensities. Although he concedes that this adoption of a stranger's perspective is an extremely unreliable position, consisting as it does of doubled contingency and mutual improbability, Luhmann points out that in so far as it invites the subject to calculate the chances of satisfaction (that is, the possibilities of realizing improbable selection combinations), selections become possible in the light of other selections. At this stage, power (the selection of selections) is available as a first-person option within the circuit.

After the third and last round fought between Job and his mockers, he makes his astounding oath of clearance, liberating himself from the law as coercive instrument, and daring everyone, even God, to deny the plausibility of his words. The reader who liberates Job's voice imitates this usurpation by releasing power in an unreliable but vivid form. Imitations of the book of Job never fade because they are already forecast in the text as events, making it impossible not to render the reading as an intense and loaded reaction to its own mirror-image. Readers who do not shun the scandal, and who respond to the challenge of being the reader Job wants, find the opportunity to make selections of selections. Practice on both sides of the page is a matter of taking an unprecedented initiative. Just as Job equals himself to God by defying all justifications of divine power, so readers equal themselves to Job by inhabiting the intensity of such an improbable selection combination. In this respect mimesis is precisely not what Terry Eagleton proposes when he says of sympathetic imitation in the eighteenth century, 'To mime is to submit to a law'.[19]

This leaves Job finally in the hands of an actual reader who cannot be blind to the bid for personal power into which s/he has been recruited. Job's is not a speech on behalf of universal misery, being strongly inflected with the desires and choices of a unique and unparalleled subject, a first person singularly himself. Job is not about to confound his case with a cause of public concern or with an enterprise of social

---

[17] *Love as Passion: The Codification of Intimacy*, trans. Jeremy Gaines and Doris Jones (Cambridge, Mass.: Harvard Univ. Press, 1986), 22; *Trust and Power*, 112.

[18] *A Sociological Theory of the Law* (London: Routledge and Kegan Paul, 1985), 26.

[19] *The Ideology of the Aesthetic* (Oxford: Basil Blackwell, 1990), 53.

legitimation. But in order to see eye to eye with God he needs to be 'I' to 'I' with the reader, his redeemer—a mutuality that is pragmatic, self-interested, and short-lived. The usurpations of sublime mimesis and the redoublings of practice ensure that this is not a governable or stable presentation either of the written or the readerly 'I', but a calculation of expectations and chances that will urge power along a chain of subject positions for the sake of the current selector of selections. Although such an arrangement of wilful egoism conforms to the scene of sympathy Luhmann finds outlined by Adam Smith, it is a long way from the altruism and sociable coherence with which the impulses of sensibility are generally credited in the eighteenth century. I want to trace this circuit in two readings of Job.

The Stories of Sitis and Martha

These two stories are rewritings of Job that emerge from resistant readings, both intended to eliminate the scandal of the original and to put a clear moral in the place of its ambiguous outcome. The sole result of the attempt to minimize the scandal of Job's refusal of instruction is a faithful replay of the unnegotiable positions his refusal entails, leaving the complaint of injustice and meaninglessness as buoyant as ever and the comfort as mealy-mouthed. Inconvenient material from the old story protrudes into the new one in a direct ratio to the desire to expel it. The re-presentation of Job's tribulations says exactly what its author wishes it not to say, a failure which merely repeats the defect of the original instead of erasing it. In the second of these two stories, the Job-figure achieves a counter-reading remarkably like Job's outline of a redemptive reading that turns (as his does) on a tautology which unfolds in a face-to-face encounter.

The first story is the pseudepigraphic *Testament of Job*, a popular medieval way of handling the lives of secular and scriptural heroes as a bequest to the reader, comprising a deathbed summary of leading traits (Job's patience, Cresseid's wantonness, and so on), together with an appropriate moral. The second is a story taken from John Warton's collection of episodes of rural misery, *Death-bed Scenes and Pastoral Conversations*, where he tells us how he used the book of Job to correct the excessive complaints of one of his parishioners.

The Job of the *Testament* has very little to worry about, since he has been assured privately by God that his torments will have an end, and that he will be restored to wealth and power. Indeed he is suffering only for having done God's business—purging the temple of idols—and it is a matter simply of weathering the effects of Satan's revenge. With undisturbed confidence he inhabits the sort of world that the other Job's comforters describe, where good men are rewarded and evil ones perish. The terror and excess of the scriptural Job are transferred to his wife, here called Sitis, who is assigned a much larger and more undignified role than the nameless woman who simply tells the first Job to curse God and die. In reducing the testamentary Job to the clear outline of a patient and pious patriarch, the writer finds Sitis a convenient bin for all the excesses of passion and language which characterized the original, but which are surplus to the dainty plot of the present interpretation. In Sitis are gathered the defects of temper and body which an exemplary Job will reprove.

Sitis's faults are a want of physical dignity, a noisy grief for her lost children, and a preoccupation with burials and memorials. While Job is being pious on the dunghill, she ventilates her sorrows and begs for food. Disguised as a baker, Satan tricks her into selling her hair for bread. As she gives her husband the loaves paid for with her humiliation, she cries, 'Job! Job! Although many things have been said in general, I speak to you in brief. In the weakness of my heart, my bones are crushed'.[20] Here in very abbreviated form is a transition from mute abjection to a vocal particularity, centred on the body and delivered in the first person singular, typical of the other Job. And just as he joins the circumstantial rhetoric of anguish to a demand for writing and a reader, so Sitis laments the want of a memorial. Had her children lived, they would have borne the family name into the future ('Your memorial has been wiped away from the earth—my sons and daughters of my womb for whom I toiled with hardship in vain' [i. 849]). But even these shattered memorials lack a memorial of their own to mark where their bodies lie. She pleads with the comforters to help her disinter the corpses of her offspring from the ruins of the house that fell in on them: 'Let us see them, even if it is only their bones. Have I the womb of cattle or a wild animal that my ten children have died and I have not arranged the burial?' (i. 859). This passionate challenge, womanish but nice only in the sense of being exceedingly circumstantial, resituates the question of memorials, and of compensatory marks or records, within a matriarchal and bodily economy, rather than the genealogical and patrilineal argument she first put to her husband. This suggests that it is the recovery of a personal voice of complaint, not the instrument of tribal memory, that she has in mind for her vindication. Here she is actuated by the same terror of an unmarked grave as Job—'O earth, cover not thou my blood, and let my cry have no place' (16: 18)—and, like him, she seeks a tomb

---

[20] *The Testament of Job*, in James H. Charlesworth (ed.), *The Old Testament Pseudepigraphia* (New York: Doubleday, 1983), i. 850.

that will function as an epitaph: 'Oh, that my words were now written . . . that they were graven with an iron pen and lead in the rock forever' (19: 23–4).

In the event, she is not to see her children's bones nor to have a memorial, either to them or to her own voice, because her husband, still faithful to the iconoclastic principles which caused his downfall in the first place, sternly rejects her proposal. He needs no tomb, he says, to remind him that his children dwell in heaven, at which proof of his imperturbable virtue Sitis dies, 'sprawled out dead' in the cowshed (i. 860), unmourned, unremembered, her womb now literally on a level with animals. Plainly the materiality of her desires and her immersion in the particularity of bodily existence are found at first ridiculous and at last contemptible by the author of the *Testament*, who is quite as keen as Satan to insult her womb in order to test an ideal of transcendental constancy. He finds it convenient to elaborate the distinction between Job's piety and Sitis's turbulence along these misogynist lines, so that his dunghill turns out to be altogether a cleaner and more ascetic place than her cowshed.

She is a great deal more readable than her husband, however, owing to her re-assembly of the scandalous circumstances of the original under the pressure of a Job who has, like his author, taken up the attitudes of the comforters. That is to say, the *Testament* is founded on a reading of Job that elevates the exiguities of faith at the expense of the passionate physicality that makes interesting the very distinctions it is seeking to draw. Sitis functions as the waste material of her author's interpretation of the original text, the sum of everything excessive to the clear meaning he has drawn from it, and everything exorbitant to the norm. However, her complaint refurbishes the unmoralizable sharpness of the original. Her demand for a memorial crudely mimics Job's call for an inscription and a redeemer. She outlines, although she does not live to exploit, the possibilities of a relationship to writing and reading that would allow her to overcome the improbability of highly personal communication. In any event, to read Sitis is vividly to be reminded of injuries the author of the *Testament* wanted forgotten.

Late in the eighteenth century or early in the nineteenth, in a rural parish in England, a keen young housemaid called Martha Bilson met a man at chapel with whom she fell in love. She married him and became pregnant. It should have been a short and happy story, but unfortunately her husband was both a bigamist and a swindler. Having plundered her of her virginity and her savings, he told her of another wife and decamped, leaving her the task of coping with her pregnancy on her own, in a strange village without money or friends. As it turned out, she miscarried and soon afterwards was immobilized by a fistula; but her rage and despair at the unjust treatment she had received from the man she thought she had married seems to have caused her more exquisite agony than her bodily infirmities.

The story is told by John Warton in his compilation of modern testaments under the heading 'Martha Bilson—Impatience'. He organizes it in three sections. The first deals with Martha's unrestrained grief and outrageous lamentations; the second is devoted to reading and reflecting on the book of Job; the third is the scene of a Christian deathbed, where a transformed Martha submissively and humbly recommends herself to the mercy of a God she now knows to be neither arbitrary nor cruel. This at least is how Warton would like to tell the story, except that it rather runs away from him at the end.

From the outset he is struck by the extraordinary vehemence of Martha's sense of injustice and her refusal to moderate it. The first he hears of her is a shriek. She cries out from the upstairs bedroom during a visit he is paying her landlady, old Mrs Clayton: 'The voice of a woman, exclaiming with mingled grief and anger, "Ah, the villain! ah, the wicked wretch: he will be the cause of my death! he has ruined and undone me!" ' Mrs Clayton tells Mrs Warton that the woman has just miscarried, and, 'When her dreadful pain comes on she cannot bear it, Madam, and she screams out in this manner'.[21] When Warton goes upstairs to ask her if she has no comfort from religion, she responds simply, 'I have been used barbarously, and I have done nothing to deserve it, and my troubles are greater than what I can bear'. And when he asks her about the hereafter, she demands in turn, 'Is not God very cruel to suffer me to be afflicted in this manner, when I have done nothing to offend him?'(2: 7, 9). After he hears of her fistula and of her desire for death ('I longed for it much more than life', she tells him later) he finds the parallels between her complaint and Job's too strong to be ignored; so he begins to tell her Job's story so that she can try to imitate his exemplary patience, and be consoled.

It is clear from the start that he and Martha have widely different reasons for their interest in Job. He attracts her attention to the story by giving a picture of abjection with which she can identify: 'Remember how Job behaved in his misery; bereaved of all his children, riches, and glory; from the crown of his head to the sole of his foot covered and tormented with painful and loathsome sores; lying prostrate on the hearth, and his venerable hoary hair and beard defiled with ashes' (ii. 50). Excitedly she asks, 'But what did Job do, Sir? You did not tell me

---

[21] John Warton, *Death-bed Scenes and Pastoral Conversations*, 3 vols. (4th edn., London: John Murray, 1830), ii. 7.

that,' and he notices how 'an energy, new and unknown in her before, seemed now to actuate her whole mind and frame' (ii. 51). It doesn't take him long to realize that she wishes to model herself on a Job whose afflictions she believes are, like her own, not chastisements of a sinful creature but the opportunity for an afflicted innocent to exhibit hidden strengths, including the power of revenge. But that is not what Warton has in mind. He insists Martha understand the wide difference between Job's singular uprightness and superlative faith and her passionate and wilful commitment to her own cause.

This leads to a pattern of involuntary imitations of the original. Warton takes up the role of a Job's comforter, asking questions such as, 'Must I go on speaking to the winds, or shall I leave you to your own fancies?', and, 'Do you think that God ever does harm to anybody merely to show his strength?' (ii. 9, 17). For her part Martha acquires the sentiments and the language of Job: 'I see no reason why he should bring these evils upon me,' and (talking of her pitiless lover), 'I must be a stock or a stone not to hate the wretch' (ii. 9, 69).[22] Indeed the pleasure she takes in Job's denunciations of the wicked carries her into readings of the Psalms, particularly the seventy-third, where she finds 'very strong expressions against the wicked, and every kind of bad wish against enemies' (ii. 88). Warton tries to explain that in the original Hebrew predictions are often rendered as wishes; and Martha seems charmed with these finer points of the discourse of excess, 'I hope I shall be able in future to explain some of these texts for myself, without any danger of mistaking them' (ii. 101).

Once again, the equality of readerly opportunity naïvely supposed by Martha is not part of Warton's plan. Like Walter Shandy with uncle Toby, the aim is to get his respondent to hold, not weigh, the grains and scruples of wisdom. As he tells her, the literal meanings of the scriptures 'are, after all, not to be understood, but with a great many limits and qualifications, which will give them a quite different meaning from what *you* suppose' (ii. 96). He begins to sound like Warburton exploring an allegory; and so he continues, combining an extremely partial reading of Job with an analysis of Martha's faults. As in the displacements and editings of *The Testament of Job*, what goes missing from the original book reappears as the physical and emotional disqualifications of a marginal female. Warton's Job is indomitably patient and faithful: at the very lowest extremity of his affliction he declares his trust in God; he likewise swears that he has never cursed his enemies; but principally he believes in the equity of providence as an aspect of the soul's immor-

---

[22] Job 8: 2, 'How long shall the words of thy mouth be like a strong wind?' and 6: 12, 'Is my strength the strength of stones? or is my flesh of brass?'

tality, manifest in 19: 25, 'For I know that my redeemer liveth', a verse Warton is to quote several times in the story and always with remarkable effect. In every significant disagreement with Martha, he cites a textual crux, and passes it off to her as an unequivocal proof of Job's piety. By 'trust' Job does not mean necessarily positive faith, involving an implicit reliance on the goodness of God, as Warton argues, but more probably the paralysis of terror that makes him incapable of withstanding an irresistible force. The 'redeemer' verses are used to Christianize this trust-as-faith, and likewise the lines concerning the forgiveness of enemies, taken most disingenuously by Warton from Job's oath of clearance (31: 29–30), whose temerity he sedulously ignores. The paradoxes of the original are suppressed in favour of a consistent interpretation. In the oath, for example, Job stakes the innocence of his life against the pointlessness of what has happened to him; and when he talks of a redeemer he means a substitute or stand-in (a reader, as I have argued), who will vindicate him, not a saviour.

Because Warton is reading Job across and against Martha's will to identify with him, his blindness to the range of the text corresponds with a remorseless acuity about her faults. 'She was too much buried in present sensible things' (ii. 30) he remarks, after one of her many failures to match her own case with the symmetry of his doctrine; she is prone to be 'prolific in the description of [her] sorrowful circumstances' (ii. 142). As he positions the weight of his authority against her sense of the singularity of her condition and the particularity of her accounts of her extreme pain, he knows what she would say in defence of them, were she capable of a critical estimate of her pragmatism: 'She would have said, perhaps, if she had known how to do so, "Your theory is right, but it is overthrown by facts;" but then her facts were merely assumptions, and not founded in truth' (ii. 33). It is an insidious distinction, not least for the private concession it makes to the empirical weight of the particulars of her case. She tells him that he cannot sympathize with her fully because he doesn't know all the details of her story, but for his own part he takes a grim amusement in watching the physical symptoms of her failure to resist his doctrinal strength: 'Poor Martha could bear me no longer. The clouds had for some time been gathering, and now at length, when she was called upon so pointedly to answer for her present state, the torrent burst forth and overwhelmed everything' (ii. 84).

His alertness to this distinction between the shapeless materiality of facts on one side, and the pure outlines of faithful instruction on the other, accounts for one of the odder scenes in the narrative. He comes across Martha seated with two friends in the churchyard, and she hails him pleasantly and tells him they have just had their dinner on a tombstone; at which he suddenly associates the ideas of food and corpses and makes (to himself) this astounding riposte: 'Well, thought I, the worms that are under it will soon dine upon you all three' (ii. 115). It is as if he is overcome with an urge to bury her and her appetite for 'present sensible things', as the *Testament* buries Sitis in the mud of the byre.

This ripple in Warton's confidence, which is signalled several times in the course of his story by evidence of a wish to hide Martha in the earth and give her voice no place, seems to be owing to his consciousness of how unfairly he is treating her over the interpretation of Job, and how heavily he is having to rely on his entitlement as clergyman to textual mastery. He knows that Martha's complaints are as authentic as Job's, were each to be charitably interpreted, and that they are faithful to the original especially in the stringency of the questions she poses about the place of evil within a providential dispensation. He must be equally alive to the parallel between his own responses and the mockery of the comforters. His efforts to clear a difficult text through his stern handling of her misery are nowhere more apparent than in his readings of 19: 25, prompted by Martha's astute commentary on Job's trust in God. She says that Job must have believed in an afterlife to have behaved with such confidence in the depth of his afflictions; and Warton, who, as an Anglican divine, was well aware that most commentators take Job at his word when he denies a life after the grave, plays with a hypothesis that Martha is right for once, and proceeds to interpret 'redeemer' as saviour, which again he knows to be a contested meaning. As if aware that these two verses are crucial to his exegetical triumph over Martha, and that potentially they allow a refuge for her particularized agony that he would prefer it not to have, he returns to them compulsively to protect his interpretation. Here, for example, he combines Bildad's comparison between men and worms (25: 6) and Job's claim of wormy kindred (17: 14), with his own interpretation of redemption: 'And though after my skin worms destroy this body, yet in my flesh shall I see God' (19: 26). Worms work on everything about Martha he would prefer to disappear, leaving the core of ungendered spirit to be saved.

He returns to the redemption text when he hears Martha pray to Christ to spare her false husband, 'for thou hast redeemed *him* too'. But this triumph is followed by two remarkable solecisms, both committed while reciting this crucial text. The first takes place at Martha's sickbed, when it is clear she is not going to recover: 'I began almost involuntarily the service for the burial of the dead. In a common case, this would have been strikingly ill-timed; but here, the two first, at least, of the introductory sentences suited me admirably' (ii. 122). He means John 11: 25–27 and Job 19: 25–27, which begin the order for the burial of the dead. And they suit admirably only assuming that Martha is perfectly prepared to die in the belief that the redeemer is Christ, and that all her own readings of Job have been a mistake. The second is even more embarrassing, and occurs when he reads the same verses over Martha's pauper's coffin without realizing that it is hers. Not until he sees her father and the two friends from the tombstone standing by the trench, is he aware that he has absent-mindedly buried her in an unmarked grave: 'Not a particle of doubt any longer remained; I had buried Martha, and I had disregarded her last injunctions, which were, "to bury her decently" ' (ii. 147).

How are these breaches of clerical charity to be explained? In the dualist terms Warton has been using, Martha's worst characteristics—her tendency to mire herself in the little circumstances and minute particulars of singular and corporeal existence—belong with the worms beneath the slab, just as her spirit belongs above, in the doctrine of redemption his consolations have defined. His impatience with her impatience goes a little further. Her counterpart is good old Mrs Clayton, who dies much more beautifully than Martha, having delivered herself of sentiments of such primitive simplicity they deserve, he says, 'to be recorded in letters of gold, or rather in some imperishable material, for a pattern to generations' (ii. 72). Mrs Clayton's words may be 'graven with an iron pen, and lead in the rock for ever' because her redeemer is Warton's redeemer. Who then might Martha's be? Warton has intended him to be the same, but three times he has invoked him not to redeem but to bury Martha. Her redeemer has to be responsible for the inscription and scrutiny of memorials that Warton wishes to banish from the grave so as not to disturb the silence of Martha's buried voice. By displacing this redeemer, and substituting the Christ of the Prayer-book, her last wish for a carved stone, or at least one with some short written account of her life, goes ungranted. *Her* redeemer would have to be a writer and reader of memorials such as William Wordsworth, attentive to the 'matters of fact in their intensity' which rural epitaphs are peculiarly adapted to commemorate. But for Warton such matters of fact constitute the rubbish he has had to chip away from Job in order to represent Martha Bilson as his faithful imitator. In the process he prompts an imitation of quite the opposite kind.

The striking thematic parallels between the stories of Sitis and Martha indicate how much their narrators have staked on dualist readings that expel from the account of suffering the reinscription of details needed to make it interesting. All that is left of Job worth reading about is embodied in the excessive feminine counterpart, and in her struggle against a piety so uninflected as to be narratively valueless, considered on its own. The narrow interpretation is designed to produce an exemplary tale based on the absolute distinction between the social and spiritual economy of virtue and the sprawl of surplus particulars, between circumstances that illustrate the moral of the story and instruct the reader, and loose and flying facts that attach to nothing of significance. But it is owing precisely to the disparagement of excessive circumstances that neither story ends with the moral *éclat* its author desired, for in the end there is no material support for the moral, nothing by means of which it may be inscribed, other than what is held up as quite antithetic to it. In forgetting to commemorate the fleshly remains of Martha, Warton has, in spite of his best intentions, damaged his narrative, and restored the parallel with Job in a form he cannot govern or approve of. Before he gets to the scene of the pauper's grave, he says, 'Here this history should terminate, that I might neither blame myself nor lower another . . . in the good opinion of the reader. But I prefer truth to all false embellishments, and must therefore risk his displeasure by spoiling my story' (ii. 145). Is the displeasure of his reader the pleasure of Martha's? Certainly *truth* here is something different from the 'truth' that overthrew the facts of Martha's case; in fact it has become implicated in those facts. The loss of Sitis from the *Testament* likewise makes an abyss in the tale no amount of patriarchal imperturbability will compensate. The sacrifice of closure is, paradoxically, the necessary consequence of getting rid of openness. But in that necessity the re-entry of the reader is accomplished, and Sitis and Martha move into position as readable readers of Job—the Job ripe in physical affliction who brandishes his sores before his justifiers—while their authors assume the forbidding and culpable piety of his mockers.

It is significant that Warton's story should begin in the schoolroom, where infant minds are being impressed with the hierarchies of knowledge by the worthy Mrs Clayton, so that they will know who was the meekest man, the wisest, the hardest of heart, and so on. It is also interesting that he and Mrs Warton find it difficult to keep straight faces as Mrs Clayton demonstrates the success of her teaching. The fissure opened up here between seriousness of pedagogic purpose and triviality of outcome is continuous with the chasm which consumes the last act of Warton's tragedy, and defrauds (or relieves) the reader of a decisive ending. In that space Mrs Warton takes up the position of Martha's reader-redeemer. When she visits the dying woman, and leans over her to say, 'You might now teach your teacher . . . you would now teach *me* the practice of the thing itself', she replaces the simple assertions and derivations of Mrs Clayton's schoolroom with a tautology that unfolds in the intentness of an *ego* looking at its other, and discovering in that reflection how to realize an improbable selection combination, as Luhmann might say. The teaching of teachers is like the selection of selections, sublimity on sublimity, and writing on writing in its shifting of power from a single agency to a reflexive encounter between two first persons. It is remarkable too how confidently Mrs Warton sets this access of self-reference in the context of practice, where action supplants interpretation, and authority tutelage. She has found the answer to Martha's question, 'But what did Job do?'; it is to double up the index of torment (writing, teaching, reading) until the 'I' acquires agency in a dual observation of practical possibilities. The energy generated by unfolding the tautology of teaching as teaching makes tears fall from Mrs Warton's eyes directly onto Martha's face, which she cons with all the concentration that Job reserves for the sight of God, or a reader for a phonographic sign. Intensity recurs not as the blockage of Warton's barren standoffs with his pupil, but as a recurrent and intense mimesis that shifts power along a line of redeemers: from Job to Martha, from Martha to Mrs Warton, and from Mrs Warton to me, the next reader.

2 *Job and the Practice of Writing*

> Conscious unhappiness is not a delusion of the mind's vanity but something inherent in the mind, the one authentic dignity it has received in its separation from the body. This dignity is the mind's negative reminder of its physical aspect; its capability of that aspect is the only source of whatever hope the mind can have. The smallest trace of senseless suffering in the empirical world belies all the identitarian philosophy that would talk us out of that suffering.
>
> (Theodor Adorno, *Negative Dialectics*)

The stories of Sitis and Martha exhibit the arrogance of systems of doctrine and interpretation towards the emergencies faced by individuals. The system wants to display private distress as a public example and an accountable event; the individual prefers to regard distress as a shock, unexpectable and therefore beyond the scope of prescription, exemplification, and consolation. These women propose alternative methods of making sudden pain tolerable that depend on practical adaptations of Job's story suitable to complaints made in the first person singular. Such adaptations ignore or undermine the universality of official consolation by developing a relation of the complaining voice to a redeeming voice capable of doing justice to the particulars of the case. They make no gestures towards the fulfilment of norms or law; they accumulate the circumstances of a private and personal grief in an effort of practical vocality determined by self-reference and the unfolding of tautologies. The successful relation of voice to voice and 'I' to 'I' depends not upon a recovery of innocence and identity but on a redoubled writing, a superscript or a writing upon writing. This is how improbable selection combinations are going to be realized, how the improbability of complaint is to be overcome, and how access to power may be obtained by the victim of power. Authority loses its pretext in proportion as energy is exchanged between first persons singular whose voices may sound alike, but whose interests in power are urgent and peculiar to themselves, and therefore socially illegitimate. Beyond the recurrent intensities punctuating the flow of energy from one subject to another, there is no wisdom or lore to rely on but the skill for adapting the improbabilities of complaint to an imitating and imitable form, and for turning barren seriality into a range of practical options. It is a skill for

concentrating energy and then releasing it in the pleonastic form characteristic of an unfolded tautology. Neither the concentration nor the
release can take place without the medium of writing—writing studied
not as prescription but as *techne*, a fragment that can be read with such
absorption that it vibrates to the echo of a voice. Job's imagined epitaph,
Sitis's memorial, and Martha's gravestone are the yearnings for this
writing, the cry of the blood sealed in lettered stones, and then redeemed
by the reader who, in spelling it out, lets the cry be heard again. The
book of Job and the printed stories of Sitis and Martha are the realities
of that writing, consulted by the reader who has the option of
revocalizing the inscribed complaint. From neither side is this simply
writing, but writing upon writing, a redoubling of the grievous script
copied by the law, according to Kafka and de Certeau, upon the skin of
its victims.[1] De Certeau shows that the voice which the suffering party
aims to recover is not a simple cry coincident with the activity of
suffering, but a sound arising from the cunning substitution of inscription for inscription: 'The sound of the body becomes an imitation of this
part of itself that is produced and reproduced by the media—i.e. a copy
of its own artefact' (132).

The simplest case of painful muteness is the body marked by a self-
justifying authority. Gilles Deleuze and Felix Guattari call this savage
inscription, a mode of tribal filiation and territorialization used to
declare, suddenly and arbitrarily, what is owned and owed—the graphic
system of an oral culture of infinite debt that extends to existence itself:
'A voice that speaks or intones, a sign marked in bare flesh, an eye that
extracts enjoyment from the pain'. The composite of the speaking voice,
the marked body, and the enjoying eye imposes and certifies unconditional obligation. 'All the stupidity and the arbitrariness of the laws, all
the pain of the initiations, the . . . red-hot irons, and the atrocious procedures have only this meaning . . . to mark [man] in the flesh, to render
him capable of alliance, to form him within the debtor-creditor relation.'[2] For Elaine Scarry, the scene of torture provides the same spectacle of the body subdued by pain, although it disguises itself as an
exercise in communication. Under the remorseless prompting of the
torturer, speech disintegrates first into the pointless rapidities of confession, and then into inarticulate cries: 'The prisoner becomes a colossal
body with no voice and the torturer a colossal voice . . . with no body.'[3]
For Scarry the equivalent of the torture chamber in the Old Testament

[1]   Michel de Certeau, *The Practice of Everyday Life*, trans. Steven Rendall (Berkeley, Calif.: Univ.
of California Press, 1984), 140.
[2]   Gilles Deleuze and Felix Guattari, *Anti-Oedipus*, trans. Robert Hurly, Mark Seem, and Helen
Lane (London: Athlone Press, 1983), 188–90.
[3]   Elaine Scarry, *The Body in Pain: The Making and Unmaking of the World* (Oxford: Oxford
Univ. Press, 1985), 57.

is the problematic moment shared by God and his creature when their relation must be materialized as torment of the flesh: 'God's invisible presence is asserted, made visible, in the perceivable alterations he brings about in the human body . . . in the leprous sores and rows of boils that alter the surface of the skin' (183). Opening up between the creature on the one hand, dumb with agony and bounded by the limits of its skin, and on the other the boundless self-substantiating and self-authorizing voice of the creator, is an abyss unbridgeable by concepts of justice, punishment, or even vengeance; it can be bridged only by an act of substitution.

Scarry gives a number of examples, all relevant in one way or another to Job: the begetting of children (where a body is lent to one who has no body); the reinscription of God's writing on the body as a law carved on stone; the investment by the wounded creature in a memorial or narrative of suffering; the substitutive gesture of sympathy or its equivalent in 'the shape of perceived-pain-wished-gone' (290); or the trial, which sets up a contest between law-as-sentence and complaint-as-plea that will be resolved on one side or the other as the empowerment of a voice (298). Deleuze and Guattari are interested particularly in the second of these substitutions: the replacement of the inscribed body with writing in stone. This memorial to the process of being marked (writing on writing) coincides with the supplanting of the orality of savage debtorship by the graphism of the next stage of writing, which introduces a system of exchange they call barbarian or imperial inscription. This involves 'the creation of a second inscription . . . immobile, monumental, immutable. . . . The old inscription remains, but is bricked over by and in the inscription of the State'.[4] Although such writing privileges the voice, and subordinates tablets, stones, and books to its sonority, its substitutive technique ensures the despotic authority of script: 'The subordination of graphism to the voice induces a fictitious voice from on high which, inversely, no longer expresses itself except through the writing signs that it emits' *(Anti-Oedipus,* 205).

The practical advantages of substituting a written orality for an oral writing (graphophony for phonography), and the revision such a substitution entails in the relations of the body to power, are the themes of the book of Job. God has written painfully on the body of his servant for no reason but to prove obligation, and he speaks to the viewers of the spectacle, demanding they be edified and pleased by it. Job is all body and no voice until he utters his complaint, when he declares several times that his words might be better for being written rather than spoken. Whereupon God condescends to speak directly to Job, and

---

4   *Anti-Oedipus,* 198, 196.

propels him back into the silence which preceded his complaint. According to Scarry's argument, Job's wish for a writing fit to render the pain of being written upon by the divine voice is what she calls 'a remaking of making', an unfolded pleonasm which, like de Certeau's copy of a copy, is the index and vehicle of a counter-artifice and a counter-memory (320). It is the monument to a personal injury that may in the future be redeemed as voice by its reader even though the story terminates in silence. According to Deleuze and Guattari, the shift is more complex. God alone enjoys the advantages that accrue to the despot in substituting the written orality of the imperium for savage or oral writing, just as before he enjoyed watching the living body as he was writing upon it: his is the spectacle of voice incarnated as sign, his the voice from on high that eliminates vocality while seeming to vindicate it. If Job is not to be a dumb pawn in this rapid switch from a phonographic to a graphophonic power-play, it must be assumed that he has acquired enough of despotic intuition to conceive a substitutive or pleonastic way of renouncing the debts which caused his spectacular suffering; at the same time he must be supposed sufficiently tenacious of oral formations to skirt or to oppose the proclamations *de haut en bas* that put vocality under the dominion of an absolute or universalized writing. That is to say, he must be imagined still to be invested in the voice, despite using techniques of voice-suppression in order to reacquire it.[5]

There is None Like Him in the Earth

The story of Job is divided roughly into three parts. The first tells how God boasted of Job's integrity, and how Satan, citing the maxim that nobody is good for nothing, tempted God to test Job by destroying his property, corrupting his body, and disturbing his mind. The second comprises the dialogues of Job and his comforters, an irascible exchange of views between a man stuck in the particulars of his plight, and three friends who wish to universalize it in terms of the moral law and the principle of an equal providence. The second section is terminated by the theophany, in which God addresses Job in the first person, silencing his questions by invoking and reproducing in a series of mighty interrogations the unquestionable wonder and self-identity of his creation. The third section—partly an overflow of the speech from the whirlwind—tells of Job's restoration, how he is rewarded for his constancy by being re-endowed in health, progeny, and goods, and how the comforters are

---

[5] Cf. de Certeau: 'Voices can no longer be heard except within the interior of the scriptural systems where they recur.' *The Practice of Everday Life*, 131.

reproved for speaking foolishly. It is commonly supposed that the first scene in heaven and the final picture of restoration are prose additions, derived from an ancient fable and designed to give a perfunctory symmetry to the turbulent but inconclusive poetry of the dialogues. However, the tripartite structure serves to emphasise the three distinct levels at which the theodicy of Job is conceived, and to challenge the reader with the difficult task of tracing the connections between them.

In the court of heaven God takes a bet on Job's strength of will by staking the man's body against anything Satan can do to harm it, short of death. The prize is power: either the power of having the divine work coincide at all points and at all times with the determinations of God's will; or the power of having identified the unpredictable element that renders what is made to a degree independent of its maker, and colonizable from another quarter. The contest resembles the temptation of Adam and Eve, where the issue of predestination comes into potential conflict with the freedom of the creature to choose. The aleatory terms in which Job's ordeal is cast, however, derogate considerably from the range and efficacy of God's will. If he is truly taking a chance on an outcome he has not determined, then Satan has in effect already won the bet, for the margin of doubt between creator and creation already exists. On the other hand, if he is not taking a chance, why is Job submitted to such gruesome torment simply to fool Satan? Furthermore, is the Job that survives this ordeal the same as the one who was bet upon, the man so perfect and upright 'that there is none like him in the earth'? (1: 8) If Job's sufferings have changed him to the degree that he is no longer quite like what he was (less certain, for example, more wealthy—certainly more conscious of himself as an object of attention), then again Satan wins, having correctly predicted that circumstances alter cases, and that the integrity on which the wager was made is no longer what it was. The answer to these quibbles is given by William Sherlock, who quotes Job and then declares, 'The Sum is this; Infinite Wisdom is and must be unaccountable; her ways are unsearchable and past finding out'.[6] This is the theodicy of an unequal providence, where the dispensation may look like chance or caprice because its purpose will unfold only in the dimension of eternity. The gamble is a metaphor of our uncertainty, not God's; for 'Chance acts by no Rule, nor with any Counsel or Design' (Sherlock, 3).

The comforters are not at all diffident about these matters, however, and make very confident judgements about how they are ordered. Although they pay occasional lip-service to the invisibility of divine inten-

---

[6] William Sherlock, *A Discourse Concerning the Divine Providence* (William Rogers: London, 1694), 91.

tions, they claim to know exactly on what principles God is working. The medium in which they operate is that of the maxim or precept, and the bid they are making is for the reputation of wisdom. Eliphaz opens his consolation by asking Job to remember how formerly he applied the same wisdom to difficult cases: 'Behold, thou hast instructed many, and thou hast strengthened the weak hand' (4: 3). He proceeds to cite the master principles of their joint creed, 'Remember, I pray thee, who ever perished, being innocent?' (4: 7). Even if the righteous are afflicted, trust in God will soothe all their anxieties; and in any event it will not do to seem to murmur against providence: 'Shall mortal man be more just than God?' (4: 17). In less emollient language Bildad and Zophar reiterate these positions, insisting on the equity of God's dealings with respect to the guilty ('the hypocrite's hope shall perish' [8: 13]) and the pure in heart ('he shall deliver the island of the innocent' [22: 30]), at the same time as declaring, rather paradoxically, the incommensurability of providence and human judgement: 'The measure thereof is longer than the earth, and broader than the sea' (11: 9).

They go on to interpret Job's obstinate refusal of consolation as forgetfulness: a failure to remember the instructive consolations he used to dispense, the result of a larger amnesia concerning the history of his own transgressions. They remind him of breaches of the law that have slipped his mind: 'Thou hast sent widows away empty, and the arms of the fatherless have been broken. . . . Receive, I pray thee, the law' (22: 9, 22). It is an easy step from remembering Job's forgotten sins to reading his present misery as apt punishment for them. Since he recalcitrates against the role of the good exemplar—the righteous man called upon to prove his faith in adversity—they cast him as a bad example, an object lesson in the requital of the wicked. By one shift or the other they mean to tailor Job's afflictions to the formulaic dimensions of received wisdom, and to make his plight authenticate their precepts. This is the violence of comfort, the corollary of a theodicy of temporal equity, defined by Voltaire as assigning priority to the universality of a doctrinal proposition over the urgency and particularity of the pain it is meant to soothe.[7]

The theophany presents an opportunity to bridge the gap between the providence of unsearchable purposes and the doctrine of particular providence preached by the comforters. In the speech from the whirlwind, God vouchsafes not to explain his work to Job, but simply to

---

[7] He paraphrases Bildad, then reproves such pitiless consolations: '*Dieu vous voit du même œil que les vils vermisseaux | Dont vous serez la proie au fond de vos tombeaux. | A des infortunes quel horrible langage! | Cruels, a mes douleurs n'ajouter point l'outrage.*' 'Poème sur le desastre de Lisbonne, ou examen de cet axiom, tout est bien', *Œuvres Complètes* (Paris: La Société Littéraire-Typographique, 1785), xii. 119.

instance it as a sequence of wonders in whose presence astonishment must supplant diffidence and doubt. God shifts the metaphor from the game of chance to the standard of taste. Rather than a gamble confirming him in his power to predict, he now offers the marvels of nature as continuous with the stunning unfathomability of his own being: their self-subsistence is the measure of the worship he commands. Instead of the phenomenal poverty attaching to the pure doctrine of impenetrable providence, which offers nothing for the mind or imagination to seize on, God gives his inscrutability the form of the world and asks Job to confirm his faith by beholding the splendour and self-evidence of everything in it. At the conclusion of this replay of the creation, with each thing presented as a miracle, God rejects the theodicy of the comforters, saying that only Job in his terror spoke of him 'the thing that is right' (42: 7).

In a sense, the comforters present Satan's challenge over again, since like him they approach God armed with the wisdom of their maxims, and desire him to submit to the laws adduced from what he himself has made. The theophany ought therefore to open a way between the sheer arbitrariness of the divine rejoinder to Satan ('Do what you want') and the vacuum arising from an unqualified repudiation of the comforters ('You know nothing'). By supplanting problems of intelligibility with questions of taste, so that the attention of the questioner is commanded by the sight and noise of natural phenomena rather than by the unpredictability of events, inscrutability is compounded with delight. This is the theodicy of the sublime.

In fact, the upshot of the story is a compromise, inevitable once Job is restored on the grounds of having said something *right* about God. All Job can recollect saying is that he has understood nothing of what has happened to him (42: 3). Even if that means he submitted entirely to the unsearchable ways of God, his ignorance returns to him in the form of wisdom to the extent that he is rewarded for saying something right, while the comforters, who tried themselves to affirm the unsearchable nature of the divine dispensation, are punished for saying something wrong. In other words, if false submission to providence is accompanied by a metalanguage which declares wrongly that what has transpired is what is true, while true submission is right simply because its blind terror is its truth, then Job is restored not to equity but to the arbitrary terms of the wager which first undid him. What Job thinks he has said is that anything could happen to him, that he is at the mercy of an arbitrary force he cannot resist or understand, just like any stake in a bet. To find that you win when you lose, and that you are wise only when you say you are ignorant, discloses a rule in the game that makes the statement of ignorance both true and false, and that operates rather like Bourdieu's theory of *docta ignorantia*. Actually to be ignorant and to confess it is right; but to state it as doctrine is wrong: however, to *reward* the confession of ignorance for being right is to bring ignorance within the terms of a doctrinal rule ('talk of vulnerability and you become less vulnerable') which necessarily falsifies it. Renewed in the judgement of the error of the comforters is the same error. The interesting alternative of wonder is set aside in favour of two apparently irreconcileable positions: a statement or narrative of ignorance, and the mere experience of being ignorant. As Sherlock says, the reader eventually knows the whole story of Job (i.e. that his patience was rewarded) and knowledgeably appreciates the value of ignorance; but until that knowledge is acquired, it is not sublime wonder but unlimited terror that supervenes: 'The Story of Job's Afflictions strikes Terror and Astonishment into all that hear them' (*Discourse of Providence*, 114).

It is possible to consider the incompatibilities of these theodicies not as vicious circles but as narrative programmes. God, Satan, and the comforters each invest in Job as a fully moralizable or interpretable story. God's wager predicts a tale of strength and fidelity; Satan imagines one of impatience and blasphemy; while the comforters recite to Job's face a history of hidden transgressions, now exposed in his miserable plight. These investments depend on setting a future Job in an exemplary relation to some maxim, precedent, or prophecy lodged in the past. Satan and the comforters intend him to illustrate their maxims of human fallibility; God wants to instance Job as the perfect product of his will. Apart from Job himself, accused of forgetfulness because he is locked into a cluster of painful particularities which prevent him from constructing a bridge between his current circumstances and the past, or from predicting himself a likely future, the theophany is apparently the only intervention dedicated to saying how things are, rather than how they have been or ought to be. The wild ass, the unicorn, and the war-horse are presented for their own sakes as inherently marvellous because they are without parallel or precedent.

As in the field of theodicy, however, where the sublimity of providence is dissipated within a system of reward and punishment that reconstructs a history of arbitrary moves tied to statements of certainty and the sensation of terror, so in the field of narrative the sublimity of the whirlwind speech is absorbed into the effort of producing the unique thing as exemplary. The suffering of Job begins because God wants to instance him to Satan in precisely the same way that he instances the unicorn, wild ass, and war-horse to Job; that is as an independent existence which will nevertheless act as a proof of issues external and heterogeneous to itself. What is proposed as wonderful because it is comparable to nothing but itself ('none like him in the earth') is then forced to operate as a sign of what it is not, and to risk terror and destruction by being made to do so. Unparalleled integrity is cited to demonstrate how perfectly divine intentions meet in divine products. It is not Job that Job stands for, or leviathan that is manifest in leviathan, but the efficacy of another will in respect of the appearance of self-identity. Leaving aside the question of whether it is possible to use integrity as a sign and still preserve it as itself, it is clear that Job, in representing both more and possibly less than himself, is a measure of divine performance; and that the creatures cited in the theophany likewise do more than simply gloriously subsist; they *mean* something extra about the force of the deity who is, in the process of instancing them, about to bring the story of Job to an exemplary end and a moral point.[8]

If, as the comforters suggest, Job's failure to tell his own story is owing to forgetfulness, it might be said that his adversaries have too much memory. There is nothing in world history which they forget when it comes to showing why Job's pain is necessary and consonant with all rules of right, according to a circular logic which equalizes all pain with punishment. Their narratives tautologize pain. The theophany, God's citation of his own creation, tautologizes everything. Everything is because it is; the unique is instanced as unique, put in parallel with itself as an unparalleled phenomenon.[9] Job himself is instanced in this kind of way, a nonpareil representing his own uniqueness. Why God, the most unique of all, should need to buttress his self-manifestations in this way is another enigma arising from supererogatory feats of recall, for it seems that his absolute authority needs some sort of authorization, cited from a fund of instances of his absolute authority.[10]

Job takes his own singularity much more seriously than those who want to make stories out of it, or to treat it as a representative form of

---

[8] Cf. Jorge Luis Borges' commentary on Max Brod's opinion that leviathan and behemoth are the axis of an ancient attempt to think in abstract terms: 'The true, though possibly unconscious purpose of the Book of Job is to underline the inexplicability and inscrutability of God. God doesn't justify himself: He declares his power.' 'The Book of Job', in Edna Aizenberg (ed.), *Borges and his Contemporaries* (Columbia, Mo.: Univ. of Missouri Press, 1990), 274.

[9] Voltaire believes that Genesis is in fact an imitation of Job, a much older text in his opinion. *Dictionnaire Philosophique*, article 'Job', *Œuvres Complètes*, xxxxi. 129.

[10] On the mirror-structure of the story see Alan Cooper, 'Narrative Theory and the Book of Job', *Studies in Religion*, 11 (1982), 35–44. I am indebted to Stanley Fish, 'Spectacle and Evidence in *Samson Agonistes*', *Critical Inquiry*, 15 (1989), 556–86 for an account of how the disfigurements of a suffering individual constitute a scandalous breach of continuity for any witness of them, until such time as they can be produced as instances of larger and more regular patterns by means of narrative: 'The effect is to make the present into something that has already happened,' so that the 'unparalleled' may function as an example (558–60).

the unparalleled. He wants to insist on the local, present, unprecedented, and intense particularity of his experiences, and as it were to reclaim the negative side of being like no other. His last resource is to avoid words altogether. The silence he lapses into at the beginning and the end of the dialogues—'The words of Job are ended'—and into which he retreats at the conclusion of the theophany, may be taken either as the 'asymbolia of mourning,' the symbolic collapse which occurs when it is no longer possible to translate loss into a communicable form, or as the refuge chosen by someone unhappy with the definitions of words.[11] But when Job uses words, his first aim is to represent in as much detail as possible the afflictions that have overtaken him. 'My flesh is clothed with worms and clods of dust; my skin is broken, and become loathsome' (7: 5); 'Thou hast filled me with wrinkles' (16: 8), 'My face is foul with weeping' (16: 16), 'My breath is corrupt' (17: 1), and so on. The information is specific enough for commentators to make informed guesses about his skin disease.[12]

The specificity of these self-descriptions is probably derived from one of the Babylonian archetypes of the book of Job, which not only lists the symptoms of physical decay but also personifies maladies such as Headache, Cough, and Cramp.[13] But it is seized on very happily by the Job poet, as Philippe Nemo points out, as a sort of zero-degree speech symptomatic of 'un phénomène inouï'.[14] Complaint reduced to the minimal articulation of a list of disfigurements stands in fundamental opposition to the narratives and explanations of his friends, who wish to interpret what Job merely shows. He collects all that is left of himself in a gesture of unprecedented misery. To the extent that this abjection is unique, no matter how painful or negative, it participates in the sublimity that would belong to the creatures of the theophany in their uncited, unparalleled being. As Job speaks in the ruins of his body his complaint rises, principally because it allows (like the theophany at its best) a local and sensible habitation for extreme feelings. Robert Lowth, one of the book's finest readers in the eighteenth century, says, 'The imagery . . . which is taken from the parts and members of the human body, is found to be much nobler and more magnificent in effect, than that which is taken from the passions of the mind'.[15]

---

[11] Julia Kristeva, *Black Sun: Depression and Melancholia*, trans. Leon S. Roudiez (New York: Columbia Univ. Press, 1989), 42.

[12] Marvin H. Pope, *The Anchor Bible Job* (New York: Doubleday, 1965; repr. 1974), 142 n. 17. Hereafter cited as Pope.

[13] Pope, p. lvi.   [14] Philippe Nemo, *Job et l'exces du mal* (Paris: Grasset, 1978), 43.

[15] Robert Lowth, *Lectures on the Sacred Poetry of the Hebrews*, 2 vols. (London: J. Johnson, 1787), i. 361. The potential of the disfigured body, subject to 'wounds, plagues, and carbuncles', especially in its relation to the kingly 'body-of-power', is the theme of Louis Marin, 'The Body-of-Power and Incarnation at Port Royal and in Pascal', in Michel Feher (ed.), *Fragments for a History of the Human Body III* (New York: Zone, 1989), 412–47.

There is, however, a psychology as well as an aesthetics of abjection. It has been shown that the exaggerated lucidity with which despairing people speak of the disintegration of their physical links with their environment constitutes a last-ditch practice of phylogenetic signalling. When Job speaks of his extremity in terms of 'the skin of his teeth' (19: 20), what he speaks of, and how he speaks of it, are intimately connected, as they are in the case of the woman with a skin disease who reported under analysis, 'I speak as if at the edge of words, and I have the feeling of being at the edge of my skin, but the bottom of my sorrow remains unreachable'.[16]

The epiphany of Job's broken body is a complaint only in the sense that a cry of pain or a symptom of sickness is a complaint. It is not a discourse or analysis, but a practice. That is to say, it is exactly what the language of the comforters is not. Despite what they suspect, Job is not claiming justice under a known precedent or law; nor is he measuring his ruin inside a narrative of success and failure. He is not normalizing his experience, nor attempting to render it in a probable form. Kierkegaard says there is no philosophy in Job's suffering: he does not 'tranquillize like a hero of faith' but unleashes instead 'the prodigious insurrection of the wild and bellicose powers of passion'.[17] Deleuze and Guattari call this a schizo-flow, desire in its singular and uncoded form which threatens to scramble the axiomatic system (*Anti-Oedipus*, 176). His impassioned voice is insurrectionary because it leaves no room for precedent, or 'any explanation at second hand' (Kierkegaard). As Lowth points out, Job's language is 'single and unparalleled in the sacred volume'.[18] But when Job says his grief is without example, his comforters think that he is offering himself as a measurable instance of singular injustice, blasphemously citing his condition as a failure of the law. They think he is trying to construct a scandalous narrative which impeaches the justice of God. Now it may well be that Job disfigured, and demanding that his friends see what he is showing them, constitutes the same impossible object of vision as Milton's Samson, and that he is accused of impiety simply because he arouses extreme disgust. Or it may be that the book of Job is testing the language of sense-certainty on a broad front, and that the particularization of Job's griefs constitutes part of a pattern of collisions between historicized universals and unparalleled particulars. Either way, Job breaches the continuity of the proper, erupting as an anomaly whether he is produced as an example or as a unique being. Therefore his practice of complaint is not supposed to be audible. It is

---

[16] Kristeva, *Black Sun*, 56.
[17] Søren Kierkegaard, *Repetition: an Essay in Experimental Psychology*, trans. Walter Lowrie (New York: Harper Row, 1941), 115.
[18] Lowth, *Lectures*, ii. 347.

silenced by the theophany, which sinks his uniqueness within a citational structure, and by the charge of blasphemous self-righteousness, which incorporates his case into exemplary narratives and histories. On either side Job confronts rhetoric designed to make him renounce his singularity, and he discovers that the frustration of trying to deliver in words the terror and astonishment of here and now causes him more pain than his body. Eliphaz jeers at him for trying to talk of his singularity, 'Thine own lips testify against thee. Art thou the first man that was born?' (15: 6–7).

'Answer Thou Me'

At this point Job is forced out of practice, and what Bourdieu would call the familiar language of suffering, into analysis and metalanguage. He is obliged to understand what he is being accused of, and to rebut it in its own terms. Instead of his words coinciding with his pain ('I will speak in the anguish of my spirit; I will complain in the bitterness of my soul' [7: 11]), he must now speak of words themselves, what they are capable of, and how egregiously they can fail. The more heated his exchanges with the comforters become, the more likely he is to refer to the language of what has just been said: 'Shall vain words have an end?' (16: 3); 'How long will ye vex my soul, and break me in pieces with words?' (19: 2); 'Hast thou plentifully declared the thing as it is? To whom hast thou uttered words?' (26: 3–4). These are partly *tu quoques* delivered in the face of similar criticisms from the comforters; but, more importantly, they express his diffidence about a language that denies any constitutive relation to its theme, or any vulnerability to the weaknesses it names. As an unwilling entrant into *docta ignorantia*, he knows that the reflexive gesture most important to the discourse of universals is not to be ignorant of the ignorance metalanguage entails. What use is it for Bildad to declare that man is a worm, and the son of man too? Where is he speaking from, and does he include himself in the judgement? If so, can worms talk adequately of their worminess, plentifully declare the thing as it is?

For his own part, Job is uneasily aware that as soon as his groaning is no longer an immediate response to the strokes he receives, and when his speech ceases to belong to the activity it names, his words go from him, and attach themselves to other objects, or start meaning what he never intended them to mean. 'If I speak of strength, lo, he is strong. . . . If I justify myself, mine own mouth shall condemn me; if I say, I am perfect, it shall also prove me perverse' (9: 19). Here Job anticipates the criticism Eliphaz is to make at 15: 6: his own mouth does condemn him because it is not demonstrating but explaining and justifying the uniqueness of his case. He is trying to know and communicate his belief that he is without parallel: a declaration necessarily unplentiful once the shift has been made from active complaint to learned ignorance. As soon as Job accepts the challenge of wisdom, that is, of knowing what he is about and stating the principles upon which he proceeds, his failures demonstrate the arguments of the others, and he turns himself into an example at his own expense. He provides the sign of the strength that inheres in some other agent; with his tongue he offers the specimen of perversity that is the theme of someone else's speech. The perfection he wants to proclaim in himself dissolves in the act of instancing it, and he is condemned to say the opposite of what he wants to say.

He is bitterly accurate in his estimates of how his practice has been transformed into instructive narrative. He is 'a byword to the people' (17: 6). Like Samson, he is sung and proverbed: 'And now I am their song, yea, I am their by-word' (30: 9). He has entered the narrative pedagogy of wisdom, pointing its morals and illustrating its legends. He grows aware that the vanity and emptiness he identifies in words applies only to his own uneasy descent from active speech into the metalanguage of justification. Although he would like to think that critical terms are as empty in the mouths of his antagonists as they are in his own, he knows that consolation has the power to wound as well as to exasperate him because it mediates between the painful particulars of the moment and the models and archetypes which his pain-as-pain denies, but which his pain-as-sign requires and exemplifies. By a logic both tight and circular the boils on his body utter the law that makes their eruption necessary; they represent the lesson of the lesion, the point of a fable of wickedness, and the meat of a proverb about vanity. He senses that the closer his case gets to one of these alien narratives, the more completely he will be destroyed from his own point of view, because he will have have been universalized in a message he will not be able to acknowledge or understand. He will be a probable item in a hostile *vraisemblance*, he will be the shadow of a form he cannot recognize, the object of a citation whose source he cannot read and therefore cannot question. 'The greatest difficulty in all he suffered was, that he could not possibly understand what God meant and intended in bringing all those Calamities on him.'[19]

Mockery is his name for the narrative spun by the comforters out of the matter of his unique suffering. He understands this mockery to include God as well as himself. When he asks, 'Are there not mockers

----

[19] Sherlock, *Discourse of Providence*, 109.

with me?' (17: 2), and requests, 'Suffer me that I may speak, and after that I have spoken, mock on' (21: 3), he defends the difference between the words of practical demonstration, dead level with the circumstances of their enunciation, and the normative resonance that allows the comforters to detect behind present circumstances the ancient authority that turns them into lessons. There is nothing odd or contingent that can survive this mimicry, for it reduces everything to a mnemonic of the law. This mockery is heard in their confident assertions, in the face of Job's terror, of the mystery and the strength of God. They enclose the referent of incalculability within the reference to the incalculable, trivializing not only Job's pains but also the providence they impersonate, as if their echo of what they take to be God's voice were the password of the elect. 'As one man mocketh another, do ye so mock him? . . . Your remembrances are like unto ashes' (13: 9, 12).

While the dialogues last Job mocks back, but he finds it impossible to contradict their mockery or to forget their ashen remembrances. He has to consider divine intentions within the quantum of antecedent wisdom of which the comforters say they are reminded as they read the marks on his body. So when he talks of his wounds, he conceives them as a medium between the inscription and interpretation of this wisdom, a medium which (like his language) used to be part of him but is now alien, generating meanings he himself cannot construe. He imagines the decay of his flesh as an array of testimonies against him: 'And thou hast filled me with wrinkles, which is a witness against me: and my leanness rising up in me, beareth witness to my face' (16: 8). And he is quite certain that the breaching of his body is a form of inscription. 'Thou markest me,' he says to God, 'Thou settest a print upon the heels of my feet' (10: 14; 13: 27); 'Thou writest bitter things against me' (13: 26). When he thinks of the pains of interpretation he switches the metaphor to archery. His body is a target, and the interpretative gesture of pointing (so well stressed by Blake in the thicket of fingers darted against the patriarch's torso in the tenth plate of his Job series [Fig. 1]), is the shooting of the arrow. 'Why hast thou set me as a mark against thee?' (7: 20). 'He hath broken me asunder . . . shaken me to pieces and set me up for his mark' (16: 12).

To the comforters, Job cries out that they are breaking him in pieces with words—shooting at the mark, interpreting the sign, citing the wisdom that is inscribed in his bodily disintegration—and he asks why they could not be satisfied simply with abusing his body (literally sodomizing him) rather than subjecting him to this ruin-by-interpretation: 'Why do ye persecute me as God, and are not satisfied with my flesh?' (19: 22).[20] As God's butt, Job's weakness is exploited at a distance, beyond touch, so that his humiliation is worse than a slave's because he cannot even gauge its limit, or the nature of the power that inflicts it. All he knows is his ignorance of the telegraphy taking place through the surface of his skin. As a process cognate with mockery, this targetting depends on the division of the formerly unparallelled creature. It requires a margin for the doubling of the signs that it articulates, a gap equivalent to the distance between the 'mark' and the unique person who has been broken in pieces to construct it, or between the target and the alleged sins of Job the eyes of the archers detect behind it. As such a sign, parallel but not identical with itself, Job has none of the privileges of a symbol or a hieroglyphic, or of other motivated signs which share the quality of their referents. Stranger to the meanings others impose and derive from his punctured skin, he experiences the arbitrariness of his function. His flesh materializes the difference between speech as practice and the historicized, exemplary writing whose meaning lies hidden, as far as he is concerned, in the gulf separating the particular ulcer or boil (the sign of strength) from the remembered law (the meaning of strength).[21]

Job's resistance to the violence by which his body is represented as text at first takes the form of counter-mockery. He makes his own speech resonate with parodies and ironic quotations. The twelfth chapter begins with a sardonic encomium on the attainments of his comforters, 'No doubt but ye are the people, and wisdom shall die with you' (12: 2). He goes on to ventriloquize their lore, reciting every pious apothegm he can think of in order to show how trite they are, and how little they say about absolute power. 'He increaseth the nations, and destroyeth them: he enlargeth the nations, and straiteneth them again' (12: 23). If they can trot out this sort of stuff, so can he, except that he will not call it wisdom. Dhormé calls it a satire against moralists who delude themselves that they alone are the heirs of true doctrine.[22] Zuckerman suggests that the parody is a device hit upon by the poet to allow 'Job the Silent' to find his tongue; and Warner too finds the dialogic improvisation on cultic and generic forms to be expressive of unsteady moods that

[20] See e.g. N. H. Tur-Sinai, *The Book of Job: A New Commentary* (Jerusalem: Kiryath Sepher, 1957), 302, 445; and Pope, 236 n. 31a. Job uses the same phrase in the oath of clearance (31: 31): 'Oh, that we had of his flesh! We cannot be satisfied', and is referring again to the custom of sexually abusing captured enemies.

[21] This distinction between symbol and sign is made by Hegel, *Aesthetics*, i. 304–5, and elaborated by Jacques Derrida, *The Margins of Philosophy*, trans. Alan Bass (Chicago: Univ. of Chicago Press, 1982), 81–7. Its implications for the practical voice are fully drawn out by de Certeau, *The Practice of Everyday Life*, 139–50.

[22] Paul Dhormé, *Le livre de Job* (Paris: Victor Lecoffre, 1926), p. cviii.

otherwise would be inexpressible.[23] Paul Sanders prefers to call this device quotation, designed to give 'density of texture' to the dialogues.[24] It seems to be a more urgent, and in de Certeau's sense, a more *metic* tactic. Sensing the gap between the proverbial phrase and its referent, divine power, his parody aims to sever the links between the two. If the words of the comforters can be made to sound like nonsense, then their readings of the text on his skin are weakened and he stands a chance of reclaiming his afflictions as proper to himself. To empty out the words of mock-wisdom is to recover his own case—his integument and his plea—from their system of precedents and examples, and to dodge whatever of almighty wrath is being processed through it. This tactic is not particularly successful, however, since his mockery fails entirely to embarrass or silence his opponents. They treat it in much the same way as his practice of grief; that is, as a further symptom of self-righteousness. If mockery is to work it has to build on, not ironize, the structures that are oppressing him.

Instead of seeing himself as the powerless medium of writing, with his wounds standing witness against him, Job starts to demand his own writing, or writing on his own account. He decides to take Eliphaz's advice to receive the law (22: 22), so he asserts the rights of an accused man to a full juridical process. Instead of mocking the mockery of the comforters, he imagines their talk of precedents, judgements, and punishments materializing as a trial. He will have the law by putting his case before a tribunal; he will have witness, judge, counsel, plaintiff, and defendant fulfil their roles in the process of arraignment.[25] He wants mediators, sureties, pledges, indictments—anything that will traverse the space between sign and meaning and declare to him the grounds of their relation. He talks of a daysman or umpire (9: 33), a witness (16: 19), and a vindicator or redeemer who will represent him before God's tribunal (19: 25). He imagines how it would be if only his unknown accuser had drawn up a bill of indictment: 'Surely I would take it upon my shoulder, and bind it as a crown to me' (31: 36). In an authoritative modern translation of the previous verse Job fancies himself confronting this written charge not as God's sign but as an individual bearing the mark of his proper name: 'Behold my signature, let Shaddai answer me'.[26] This is at the end of his last speech, where Job pronounces the

---

[23] Bruce Zuckerman, *Job the Silent: A Study in Historical Counterpoint* (Oxford: Oxford Univ. Press, 1991), 97–100; Martin Warner, *Philosophical Finesse* (Oxford: Clarendon Press, 1989), 114–23.

[24] Paul Sanders (ed.), *Twentieth-Century Interpretations of the Book of Job* (New Jersey: Prentice-Hall, 1968), 14.

[25] For a list of these terms in the book of Job, see Saadiah ben Joseph al-Fayyumi, *The Book of Theodicy*, trans. with commentary by L. E. Goodman (New Haven, Conn.: Yale Univ. Press, 1988), 35 n. 8; also Nemo, *Job et l'exces du mal*, 177.   [26] Pope, 199, 209 n. 35b.

great oath of clearance, formally placing his sworn word between himself and God.

By virtue of this move, which calls law out of its invisible lurking-place in the memories of his comforters to make it morally as well as juridically reponsible for deciding his specific case in the light of day, Job abstracts his body from the exemplary economy of hidden statutes and from the esoteric script which, under their authority, has functioned equally unanswerably as charge, witness, and punishment. And in claiming his right to the meaning of whatever is inscribed or testified against him, he rearranges the temporality of memory. Instead of a law occulted by its own primordial authority, whose edicts have always already taken effect in a past unreachable except by the sonorities of the comforters' mockery, he supposes a *practice* of the law, occurring on the borderline between the present moment, when the actual case is measured against the statute, and the moment in the future, when it will be decided. Such a temporality resists exemplary narrativization, for its most interesting development has not yet happened; and it privileges a vigilance in the face of particulars whose significance is not decided, only imminent. 'The action of the trial is incomplete . . . the jury is empowered to in some sense reverse it, and it is *only* because this possibility exists that the story is being retold.'[27] Verisimilitude ceases automatically to favour the remembered universal, and may incline towards the immediate future of a highly personal and heavily particularized communication.[28]

Job's hypotheses of written charges and a scrutable law constitute the resourcefulness praised by de Certeau. They are interjections that situate the objects of memory on a new spatio-temporal axis. Remembering is now an intuitive use of details whose pertinence is suddenly manifest— a surprise expected (because the balance of the tightrope-walker and the optimism of the gambler are being regained indefatigably from moment to moment) without being foreseen (because what is recalled is not the pre-established law, but that which might test, disturb, or evade it). For this effect of a reminder that operates in advance of itself, Kierkegaard coins the term 'recollection forwards',[29] a species of repetition that reverses the valency of the precedent. Instead of subjects governing their

---

[27] Elaine Scarry, *The Body in Pain*, 298.

[28] Discussing the asymmetry of individual practice and its formal maxims in communications systems, Niklas Luhmann accounts for it in these terms: 'Successful communication becomes increasingly improbable, given conditions in which the person's view of the world is increasingly individualised and yet the world is still held to be anonymously constituted'. *Love as Passion: the Codification of Intimacy*, trans. Jeremy Gaines and Doris Jones (Cambridge, Mass.: Harvard Univ. Press, 1986), 23. By placing the rule within the same time as the particulars it is to determine, Job rescues not only his body but also the credibility of personal complaint.

[29] *Repetition*, 35. Compare Deleuze and Guattari on the debtor-creditor relation of savage inscription, 'which on both sides turns out to be a matter of memory—a memory straining towards the future'. *Anti-Oedipus*, 190.

actions according to those rules which make familiar narratives out of them, such as the young man in his essay who has fallen in love and ought to follow all the customary moves of a bourgeois inamorato, one makes a bid for the recognition of the other possibilities of that narrative, to be found in an unimaginable future and in some outrageous dereliction of prerequisites (the young man abandons the young woman). Kierkegaard argues that Job performs the same sort of outrage on the narrative category of 'trial'. Precedent is banished from the very purlieu of precedent, leaving no room for 'any explanation at second hand' (115). In requiring that God himself be his judge, Job embarks on a contest that is adapted to no prior form, generating an infinitely nuanced dialectic 'by which the exception breaks away from the universal' (132). Kierkegaard adds that this counter-narrative of the practice of a counter-memory is indescribably consoling (118), meaning that it is in some degree recollected, like the recognition of something that had been known and then forgotten.

Repetition, Self-Reference, and Redemption

Up till now we have seen Job and God joined more or less in common cause, in so far as they prefer to talk a familiar and particularizing language of here and now—this Job, this body, this leviathan—as opposed to the comforters, who operate in the dialectic of universals in order to point a moral, regardless of the self-identity of the thing itself. With their overweening faith in the value of prescription, the comforters fall to the side of the despotic system of graphophony outlined by Deleuze and Guattari; while God and Job, still attached to vocalized instances, fall to the side of the phonography of savage representation.

Under the stress of interrogation, Job learns the lesson Hegel teaches in the *Phenomenology* and of which God's deixis is the proof; namely, that it is impossible plentifully to declare the thing as it is. To assert that this or that sense-object has absolute truth for consciousness 'is not to know what one is saying, to be unaware that one is saying the opposite of what one wants to say'.[30] What is posited as the being of a tree, a house, a leviathan, or a Job is precisely what the experience of such sense-objects conceals; for even *this* piece of paper *now* is not always this present piece of paper unless one can abstract the plurality of thises and nows from the specific articles being gestured at. To ignore this truth, says Hegel, is to be condemned to a perpetually recurrent forgetfulness: 'The natural consciousness is always . . . learning from experi-

[30] G. W. F. Hegel, *Phenomenology of Spirit*, trans. A. V. Miller (Oxford: Oxford Univ. Press, 1977), 65.

ence what is true in it; but equally it is always forgetting it and starting the movement all over again' (64). Although Job learns his lesson well enough to know that if he mentions strength it is not his own strength he can talk of, and that if he tries justifying himself, he will end up doing the very opposite, his attainments give him no satisfaction. If he is to be denied the familiar language of practice, then forgetfulness is more eligible than learned ignorance, and repetition is preferable to the decisive judgments of his companions.[31]

If one were to imagine Hegelian repetition operating in a more promising sequence than the perpetual cycles of remembering and forgetting, perhaps one would suppose something like the clairvoyance of de Certeau's expected surprise; or the recognition of the unprecedented in Kierkegaard's forward recollection; or the suspense of awaiting a verdict that Scarry says makes the outcome of the retold tales of a trial so exciting; or the straining of the memory as it reaches into the future, mentioned by Deleuze and Guattari; or the passionate mimesis of the Longinian sublime, which converts past intensities into the surprise of their recurrence. Excitement is always to be renewed because nothing is known or remembered so definitely as to spoil the pleasure of disclosure: the past has no authority over what is about to happen, and consciousness is liberated from the tyranny of its previous experience. To make this supposition plausible, however, it is necessary further to suppose that repetition as a practice is possible only when the mind is conscious—conscious not of what it forgets, but of the fact that it is forgetting. In the book of Job it is finally this degree of reflexive deliberation that will distinguish Job's declarations from God's.

Kierkegaard wants to see the collaboration between God and Job continue to the end, with Job's dream of a trial realized in the oath of clearance—the direct challenge to God—and, in God's reply from the whirlwind, the final, just, and satisfying sentence. I would rather argue that Job's practice, revolving around his impassioned and enigmatic appeal for writing, depends on that self-referential engagement with universalizing techniques that Scarry calls the remaking of making, de Certeau the copy of the artefact, Deleuze and Guattari the overwriting of the written, Boileau the sublime of the sublime, and Luhmann the selection of selections. Job will resort to a mockery of mockery that will usurp the power God claims in positing or performing the thing itself. Job will unfold the tautologies of the law by conceiving practice as a writing of the written. 'Oh, that my words were now written; oh, that

---

[31] Of the non-exemplary structure of the book of Job, Richard Grey offers the following explanation: ' 'Tis only Repetition of the same Things over and over again; poetically amplified and exaggerated'. *An Answer to Mr Warburton's Remarks* (London, 1744), 53.

they were printed in a book! That they were graven with an iron pen and lead in the rock for ever!' (19: 23–4).

These remarkable lines are different from the oath of clearance. There Job exploits the form of legal deposition in order to break back into voice, graphophonically declaring himself as he is by delivering a writ with a signature whose performative weight is meant to retrieve the vocal force of his patriarchy, when 'men gave ear, and waited . . . after my words they spake not again' (29: 21–2). Here in the nineteenth chapter he is not delivering himself as a finished history with a name, or bidding for the restoration of his reputation and his voice, but presenting himself as an issue capable of recurring by means of the interaction of two substitutes or delegates: the text in the rock, and the redeemer who will release its message and vindicate its author: 'For I know that my Redeemer liveth, and that he shall stand at the latter day upon the earth' (19: 25). The resuscitative virtue of written fragments suggests itself to Job in the metaphor he uses for the lenitive effect of an affidavit or an indictment: 'Surely I would take it upon my shoulder: and bind it as a crown to me' [31: 36]. This writing will act as a bandage to soothe, or as a garment to hide, the pain of the other writing, whose message he will never understand, which is inscribed in his boils and ulcers. It will be writing upon writing, a phylactery worn over the marks on his skin, whose efficacy will transpire as a future event taking place as the redeemer's mediation between Job and God.

To enter fully into this textual-redemptive event, it is necessary closely to consider those verses where Job numbers four steps towards a dialogue with God: incarnate sign, writing, epitaph, and redeemer (in Hebrew *go'el*, meaning legal champion or representative). The graphemes in the book and on the rock are imagined as a palimpsest which will cover and rebut the meaning of the under-text on his body. They will be wrapped around his broken body like a second skin, and he will wear them (as the first phase of his vindication) like a cloak or a hat. Job's double relation to writing is represented in a woodcut in a seventeenth-century German rebus Bible, where his story is inscribed upon his body in a mixture of hieroglyphics and words, like a vast tattoo.[32] Whether the combination of icon and letter in the composition is intended to figure the two sorts of writing—the mark violently imprinted and the alphabetic sign worn protectively like a garment—the placing of Job next to a stone, over which runs the same mixed script, suggests that the artist has in mind the third if not the second step of Job's sequence, namely the epitaph, where inscription finds a home on the pillar or

---

[32] Reproduced in Bo Lindberg, William Blake's *Illustrations of Job* (Abo: Abo Akademi, 1973), pl. 110.

cenotaph that stands in for the absent body of the person to whom it is raised. At any rate, the German artist seizes on the substitutive relation of flesh to script, and script to stone, so important in this section of the poem.

When Job says earlier of God, 'He breaketh me with breach upon breach' (16: 14), the pleonasm rehearses the double cut that constitutes the desired writing—that is, a mark upon the mark, writing upon the written, the copy of the artefact, the remaking of what is already made—and it prompts Job's first conception of how epitaph and *go'el* belong to the scheme of redemption:

O earth, cover not thou my blood, and let my cry have no place. Also now, behold, my witness is in heaven, and my record is on high. . . . O that one might plead for a man with God, as a man pleadeth for his neighbour! (16: 18–21)

The apostrophe to the earth is an oblique plea to God to allow him a document (or record) of his voice (or cry). The earth takes the place of the missing witness who is, in turn, to take the place of Job on the earth in a plea before God. The midpoint between these two substitutions is taken by a tomb, the marker of Job's blood, which will carry a version of the record the witness is to deliver. However, Job's anxiety about whether he will be allowed such a memorial (recurring again at 30: 24, where he fears that God will stretch his hand out against his grave and annihilate it) means that it is less a definite objective in itself than a hinge between the cry that has a place and a mark in the ground, and the record on high that will in the future be witnessed and redeemed on earth. Whatever there may be of graphophonic ambition in Job's plan for a monumental writing, capable of activating an imperial voice *de haut en bas*, is controlled by his phonographic placement of the voice and its substitutes in the ground and on the earth. This is where the witness of writing on writing and the overwriting despot will have it out.

The same pattern is followed in the nineteenth chapter. The desire for an inscription or record leads to an hypothesis of the witness or *go'el*, except that the middle term of the tomb is more distinct. Job imagines his words incised on a stele, 'O . . . that they were graven with an iron pen and lead in the rock for ever' (19: 24). His relationship to the *go'el* is correspondingly more elaborate, for it involves both his own physical destruction and a personal view of God ('And though after my skin worms destroy this body, yet in my flesh shall I see God' [19: 26]). These lines have been celebrated as a type of prophecy of Christ and as a vision of the Day of Judgement, despite Job's reservations elsewhere in the poem (at 7: 9 for instance). Some recent interpretations argue that the verses indicate a transition from Job's subjection under a violent and arbitrary God (he of the prologue) to his restoration by a deity filled with mercy (the God of victims who rescues him in the epilogue). Others maintain that the redeemer is a spiritual agent, something like the personal god of the Sumerian cults. At the other extreme, some scholars stress the temporal function of the redeemer, and Job's necessarily literal expectation that it will be in his flesh (i.e. while he is still alive) that he will see God, leading them to suppose that the memorial and the redeemer are empty speculations: Job really wants to speak with God, and his wish is gratified in the theophany.[33]

There is no doubt that the lines are difficult; as Dhormé says, they articulate a desire for writing that has provoked a great deal of writing. Only if the temptation to narrativize the advent of the redeemer is resisted will the sequence of substitutions—mark for flesh, book for mark, engraved rock for book, redeemer for rock, Job for redeemer— reconcile the various agencies mentioned and the times in which they are supposed to operate. Each substitutive item is like a detail of forward recollection, an index of vigilant expectation of the next stage in the successive preparation of expectable surprises. It is a mistake to see the sequence culminating in the last surprise of Job appearing once again in the flesh, face to face with a materialized God. However, the buoyant and ever-imminent possibility of speaking powerfully 'I' to 'I' is what redemption is all about.

This scene with God is determined by a line of conjectures, made in the certainty that plain speaking is not possible and reflecting Job's struggle with the manifold combinations of crying, dying, writing, and witnessing. It is not a confrontation, therefore, between two agents, or a creator and his creature, so much as two possibilities or mirror-images of agency, each arising from over-writing, and dependent on the function of the redeemer if the tautology of writing is to be unfolded. The practice of redemption cannot do without this delegate standing between the creature ruined in its body and wanting a voice, and the vocal creator who prints his authority upon the body. Nor can it be imagined within the definite temporal limits of a decisive outcome and a completed narrative, since the tautology of law as law, that which is written as that which is written, is unfolded in repeated acts of forgetting and

---

[33] On the 'dédoublement de Dieu' see Nemo, *Job et l'excès du mal*, 187–98, and René Girard, *Job the Victim of his People*, trans. Yvonne Freccero (London: Athlone Press, 1987), 139–41. The redeemer-god is proposed by Pope 134 n. 25a, and Dhormé, 256. For the redeemer's temporal function, see M. L. Barre, 'A Note on Job 19: 25', *Vetus Testamentum*, 29 (1979), 109; and James K. Kink, 'Impatient Job: An Interpretation of Job 19: 25–27', *Journal of Biblical Literature*, 84 (1965), 150; and on the redeemer as the object of a pointless hypothesis, see Tur-Sinai, 303–6, and Zuckerman, 134.

remembering which depend upon a presentation of an unprecedented and therefore unrecognizable complaint in a recognizable way. Negative repetition is the arbitrary delivery of discrete messages in the iterated gesture of coercive legalism: 'Who would wish to be a tablet upon which time writes every instant a new inscription?' asks Kierkegaard (35). The hinge on which Job's practical response to absolute power turns, then, must be supposed to be repetition based on writing and its availability to future readers in some durable medium, just as it is in 16: 18. Writing in stone about writing on the body avoids the arbitrary pulse of negative repetition by materializing and exploiting the paradox of forgetting by remembering, 'betokening forgetfulness' in Thomas Hardy's happy phrase, and transforming the failure of anamnesis and prescription into an expectably unpredictable triumph.[34] The inscribed monument suspends the past, neutralizes the primordial law that causes messages to be inscribed in bodies, and urges a voice to arise from an overwritten text that will speak of and in the victims of writing. It sets the point of determination in the future when matters of fact will be read with intensity, and when the force of an event arrived at by reading will be deeply and suddenly familiar. The impersonation of the voice of the stone will be equal to its unprecedented and particular message, paralleling what is unparalleled. To unfold this tautology successfully it is necessary that the reader understand that writing upon writing involves the continuity of the business of reading with the text in which that reading is specified as redemptive. To be reading the book of Job at all is to be implicated in the practice of self-reference embodied in the counter-memorial of the stone: it is to be edging always forward to some intensity that will renew a sense of what went before.

Stones

A stele called the Job Stone once stood at Qarnayim, near the Sea of Galilee, bearing the figures of a god and a worshipper in relief, with a dedication in hieroglyphics.[35] It seems likely therefore that what Job intends by his engraved rock is a monument along these lines. Surviving memorials from this time, such as the Moabite Stone (850 BCE), or the Hadad Stone (c. 800 BCE), carry detailed chronicles of the kings they commemorate, inscribed (in the case of the latter) on a colossal statue of the deity to whom it is dedicated.[36] It is possible that these memorial

---

[34] 'Here stood this aspiring piece of masonry, erected as the most conspicuous and ineffaceable reminder of a man that could be thought of; and yet the whole aspect of the memorial betokened forgetfulness.' *Two on a Tower* (London: Macmillan, 1975), 34.

[35] See Pope 4 n. 1.

[36] See G. A. Cooke, *A Text-Book of North Semitic Inscriptions* (Oxford: Clarendon Press, 1903),

stones represent for Job the same double relation of writing to body as that caught by the German engraver who set out his story as an overlapping tattoo. Certain colossi, erected by the gates and along the walls of Assyrian palaces, were inscribed with encomiums of their owners whose texts ran right over the figures of the lions, bulls, or other mythical creatures that were carved beside them in the stone.[37] In these examples power, muted by death, makes a colossal pretence to voice. The sovereign body proclaims itself in a tale of might so extensive that it overflows everything in its vicinity, preserving by writing the extensive territory that belongs really only to vocalized commands. For Job the appeal of such an excessively marked body lies in the potentially delinquent configuration it suggests. It is not the power of commanding everything with a factitious voice, but the petrified outlines of what is overflowed—the adjacent creatures and the stone itself—that intrigues him. He wants to exploit the supplements of power that a dead king is forced to rely on if he is still to seem to rule. The double shift from flesh to mark, and mark to inscribed rock, is what power has to stoop to if it is to be remembered; but in stooping it risks being usurped and forgotten.

Like Greek columns and steles made before 500 BCE, these stones of the Semitic regions speak in the first person: 'I am Mesha, son of Kemosh', or 'I am Panammu, son of QRL'. The stone itself takes the place of the missing body; the words take the place of voice, which is heard as soon as the witness or reader stands in front of the stone to spell them out. No inscribed stone can speak, even in the first person, without a reader lending it a voice.[38] The stone may say, 'I am Job', but what it asks is, 'I am the text of Job; read it as if you were me'.[39] Even the name Job, intended to appear as the signature warranting the oath of clearance, is onomastically denied the propriety of a pure name, because it bears a meaning continuous with the texts of his complaint. It means

---

1–4, 161–3. Cooke also mentions lead tablets, inscribed with messages to the gods, which were posted through special tubes into sepulchres and necropoli (135). Since the art of filling engraved inscriptions with lead post-dates the age of Job, Pope speculates that he refers to these lead-letters as an alternative to the engraved stone (134 n. 24a).

[37] G. R. Driver, *Semitic Writing: From Pictograph to Alphabet* (London: British Academy, 1948), 15.

[38] Autoglyphs, self-engraved stone images of the mother of the gods endowed with remarkable powers of speech and agency, are discussed by Roger Caillois in *Pierres* (Paris: Gallimard, 1966), 20. Shelley's poem *On the Medusa of Leonardo* describes a female figure in stone armed with similar powers of self-production: 'Yet it is less the horror than the grace | Which turns the gazer's spirit into stone, | Whereon the lineaments of that dead face | Are graven, till the characters be grown | Into itself, and thought no more can trace.' Quoted in Carol Jacobs, 'On looking At Shelley's Medusa,' *Yale French Studies*, 69 (1985), 165.

[39] This and the following remarks on ancient funerary monuments are indebted to J.-P. Vernant, *Myth and Thought among the Greeks* (London: Routlege and Kegan Paul, 1983), 306–11, and (immensely useful) Jesper Svenbro, *Phrasikleia: anthropologie de la lecture en Grèce ancienne* (Paris: Éditions La Decouverte, 1988), 13–73.

'Where is my father?' and so repeats in abbreviated form the theme of all his perplexed questioning of authority and of God.[40]

The carved words, then, keep the possibility of vocalization within the line of substitutions, specifically of the tropes of prosopopeia (the reader will ventriloquize the voice and the name of the stone) and of apostrophe (the stone, thus animated, will address itself to the traveller who has paused to read). Job's reader (and the reader of any epitaph which is not, in Wordsworth's phrase, 'a proud writing'[41]) completes the circle by standing before the stone to lend it a voice, and then staying to hear what it has to say. Stone and inscribed sign are joined in an immemorial pun that anticipates this double office of the reader. The Old Babylonian word *abnu*, like the Greek homonym *sema* and the closely resembling English words *muniment* and *monument*, comprehends both stele and sign.[42] The stone is both dumb and eloquent, mutely appeals and also makes itself heard, just as its readers, in transferring their voice to the stone, are struck dumb and petrified by words they themselves are the means of articulating. The gesture of reading is punnable as the gesture of sympathetic grief, for in turning to a stone to read they are turned to stone, changing places and qualities with it.[43] Edward Young makes this euphonious paradox of gravestone-reading: 'We read their monuments, we sigh, and while | We sigh, we sink; and are what we deplore'.[44]

Instead of existing as a silent trophy of the boundless empire of the subject who speaks, and whose words cover everything he rules, the first-person memorial to a forgetful and forgettable victim appropriates power according to the usurpational pattern of the sublime, projecting the 'I' first into the mouth of the reader, then into the place of the force that menaced it. In each phase it is 'as if what was only heard had been the Product of its own Invention'.[45] Or, as de Certeau puts it, 'The sound

---

[40] See Pope 6 n. 1. Tur-Sinai places Job's name in a homiletic tradition where it means 'one who is hated, one who has an enemy', i.e. the adversary, Satan (pp. lxxi–ii). Dhormé says it means 'he who attacks' or 'he who repents' (p. xiv); and Alexander Cruden renders it also as two possibilities: 'he that weeps', and 'he that speaks out of an hollow place'. *A Complete Concordance to the Holy Scriptures* (London: J. Rivington, 1834), 843.

[41] *Essay on Epitaphs i, Prose Works of William Wordsworth*, ed. W. J. B. Owen and Jane Worthington Smyser (Oxford: Clarendon Press, 1974), ii. 59.

[42] See Svenbro, *Phrasikleia*, 23, and Driver, *Semitic Writing*, 14 n. 1.

[43] The authoritative discussion of the rhetoric of mutual substitution that takes place between the reader and the inscribed stone is Paul de Man, 'Autobiography as Defacement', *MLN* 94 (1979), 919–30. For an exploration of the pun on *sema* see Jacques Derrida, 'The Pit and the Pyramid', in *Margins of Philosophy*, trans. Alan Bass (Chicago: Univ. of Chicago Press, 1982), 82–99; and for a detailed handling of the relations between body, stone, and spectator, see J.-P. Vernant, 'Dim Body, Dazzling Body', in *Fragments for a History of the Human Body*, ed. Michel Feher (3 parts, New York: Zone, 1989), i. 21–38.

[44] *Night Thoughts*, ed. Stephen Cornford (Oxford: Oxford Univ. Press, 1989), 'Second Night', ll. 362–3; p. 60.

[45] *On the Sublime*, trans. William Smith (London, 1739; repr. New York: Scholars' Facsimiles & Reprints, 1975), 3.

of the body becomes an imitation of this part of itself that is produced and reproduced by the media—i.e. a copy of its own artefact'.[46] The voice liberated by this double move expresses itself not as itself but as a remade possibility. 'It is the absolute intention of all human making to distribute the facts of sentience outward onto the created realm of artifice, and it is only by doing so that men and women are relieved of the privacy and problems of that sentience'.[47] Job's resistance to mute abjection does not take shape as a meeting with God conducted in sonorous and sublime dialogue, or as the presentation of a signed affidavit, but involves instead a substitutive, *metic* engagement with a reader by means of an inscribed stone which suspends the sentence of God in the imminent time of the not now, but soon, and which makes the face of God appear as a mirror-image both of Job's own and of his redeemer. The struggle is removed from the vast domain of the imperial voice, which expands into the enforced silence of all its subjects, and likewise from the summary history of the law, which colonizes time by making all future cases yield to the authority of ancient precedents. It is shifted instead into the sphere of locality and particularity, and an imminent time of repetitious amnesias and surprises: a switch performed by mimesis and self-reference, whose business is never finished. In this activity of forward recollection the first person of the writing in the stone bears the same relation to the voice destined to read and impersonate it as the present moment bears to the one that promises to supervene, in so far as the one is made recognizable in the other. Each pair of semblable items—'I' and 'I', now and soon—exhibit an iterability and reflexivity consistent with an unending practical resistance to the tautologies of being and of law. The self-assertion of the identical thing, and the self-warranting insistence of the arbitrary prohibition, are interrupted and unfolded into pleonasms of remaking and copying. Here it is the difference between two replicated things or moments that makes the difference, as opposed to the failure of God's instantiations of the unparalleled, by transforming the low probability of highly personal communication into a mimesis neither self-evident nor moralizable, but provable solely in the intense and repeatable event of reading what is written and speaking what is read.

Assuming that Job's ambitions for an epitaph are expressive of this reflexive practice, it is worth pausing to consider the specific circumstances of the writer who makes Job available to a reader. The book of Job is extant in Hebrew, Greek, and Aramaic versions (see Pope, pp.

---

[46] de Certeau, *The Practice of Everyday Life*, 132.
[47] Elaine Scarry, *The Body in Pain*, 288.

xliii–xlvii), some of which have been only recently discovered and translated. It is a book remarkable for its corruption and obscurity, for not only does it bear marks of clumsy excisions and additions, but its fragments are to be found littering the Psalms, Jeremiah, and the second Isaiah. It is writing scarred and shattered by successive readings. Nevertheless, this damage is sustained by the material of a writer who himself spatchcocked his story out of Egyptian, Sumerian, Akkadian, and Babylonian fragments of epic and wisdom literature, and wrote it down in a literary Hebrew that probably was not the language he spoke.[48] He chose a story and a task, then, whose difficulties are reflected in each other, each being focused upon the problem of getting something written down that is not quite one's own, but close to it. There is the hero whose greatest wish is to have his story in letters because he has lost his voice, and a writer struggling to compile this history in a language he can only write, not speak. The joint urgency of their problem with communication is perhaps what caused many eighteenth-century readers to mistake the mutuality and intensity of their commitment as a plain case of immediacy: Job as his own chronicler.[49]

The proximity of writer to hero bespeaks a shared interest quite as close as Job expects to develop between his reader and himself. The writer answers Job's cry with the words of a manuscript that has an incontrovertible material existence in the form of copies, redactions, and new editions. To read the book is to become aware of its continuity as reference and referent. It is constituted out of the very writing whose desideration it records: 'Oh that my words were now written! oh that they were printed in a book'. Simply as the *book* of Job, the writing grants a wish that sets aside the theodicies and consolations that would seek to marginalize first-person complaint by denying its right to refer to itself. No less does it challenge readers intent on interpreting rather than delivering this complaint. The trail of fragments leading up to and away from an 'original' book of Job is the spoor of readers who have, rather like Walter Shandy cutting away at Erasmus with his penknife, turned editor under the pressure of a need for meaning, 'scribbling on the back of the good old patriarch', as his commentator William Warburton calls it.[50] Whatever readers may think, they do not

---

[48] See W. F. Albright, 'Some Canaanite-Phoenician Sources of Hebrew Wisdom', *Supplements to the Vetus Testamentum*, 3 (1960), 14; and Pope, p. xxxiii.

[49] See e.g. Charles Peters, *A Critical Dissertation on the Book of Job* (London, 1757), 93, and William Hawkins, *Tracts in Divinity*, 3 vols. (Oxford, 1758), i. 340. See also Jonathan Lamb, 'The Job Controversy, Sterne, and the Question of Allegory', *ECS* 24/1 (1990), 6.

[50] *The Divine Legation of Moses Demonstrated*, 9 vols. (London, 1758), *Appendix*, 559, n. B.

acquire a metalanguage by writing on the writing of Job; they are destined to a perpetual and inescapable involvement in the intimacy of first-person communication.

This intermingled practice of reading, writing, and speaking is so close to Kierkegaard's idea of positive repetition that it is no surprise to find him particularly skilled at performing it. In an apostrophe that seems to echo Sterne's to the reader of Longinus,[51] Kierkegaard testifies to the pleasure of reading Job specifically in terms of perpetual alternation: between the impersonated voice of the reader and the supererogatory work of writing, between the recurrence of intensities and the forgetting of memoranda: 'Read him, read him over and over again. I cannot bring myself to quote a single outburst . . . although it is my joy to make transcripts again and again of all that he said, now in Danish characters, now in Latin script, now on a sheet of one size, now on that of another size. Every one of these transcripts is laid like a so-called "God's-hand-poultice" upon my sick heart. And upon whom indeed was God's hand laid as it was upon Job!'[52] A close and attentive reader like Kierkegaard turns himself into a writer who, in writing out nothing but what is written there in the first place, projects himself as the mirror-image of the Job who longs to bandage and clothe himself in the sheets of his book. Kierkegaard's fidelity in the matter of writing only what he has read carries him to a mimesis on the other side and in the other time of written memorials. He shows how readerly re-entry into the book of Job becomes sublime: 'I make his words mine and assume the responsibility' (110).

Were it not so apparently consoling, this serial escape from the power of tautology by self referential practices—reading upon reading and writing upon writing—would be called mockery, so exact is its mimicry of grief's last resource of bedizening itself in script. 'Here we see a kind of speech emerging or maintaining itself, but as what "escapes" from the domination of a socio-cultural economy, from the organization of reason, from the grasp of education, from the power of an élite and, finally, from the control of the enlightened consciousness' (de Certeau, 158). It is a sublime and insurrectionary escape from the axiomatic system, organised for the voice of Job by his *go'el*. The role is available for any reader, but always most dramatically for the most recent who, in becoming the other of Job's *ego*, may discover that it is no soft option.

---

[51] 'You must read Longinus——read away——if you are not a jot the wiser by reading him the first time over—— never fear—— read him again.' *The Life and Opinions of Tristram Shandy, Gentleman*, eds. Melvyn New and Joan New, 3 vols. (Gainesville, Fla.: Univ. Presses of Florida, 1978), i. 337.

[52] Kierkegaard, *Repetition*, 121.

Leviathan and the Artificiall Man

Job himself imagines his dialogue with God as a more immediate trans-action than this chain of substitutions. In his flesh he will see God, a material figure. This is what his eye drips for (Pope, 115): 'I shall see [God] for myself, and mine eyes shall behold, and not another' (*KJV*, 19: 27); 'I will see him on my side, | My own eyes will see him unestranged' (Pope, 129); 'I shall show signs of God, just as I witness myself, and mine eyes see nought that is foreign' (Al-Fayyumi, 289); 'Out of my flesh I want to see (my) God, | Whom I shall see for myself, mine eyes shall behold and not another' (Tur-Sinai, 306). Although the translation is evidently difficult, and capable of sustaining contradictory propositions, Job seems to be saying he will see God as clearly as he would see himself, and behold an image as familiar as his own. And in some sense he will be looking at himself. Blake's illustration of 19: 23–7 incorporates this hint into a terrifying scene of spectral violence. The eleventh plate shows a satanic God menacing Job, who cowers on his bed-roll while demons pull at him from below; but except for the difference in their attitudes and accoutrements, the two figures are identical (Fig. 2). This doubled figure doubly gestures at writing, for as he surges above the prostrate Job, God points to words inscribed upon stone; meanwhile the flames that border the image spread to the fragments of text quadrooning it, including 'O that my words were written'. Coiling up the side is Blake's modification of the King James Version: 'Yet in my flesh shall I see God whom I shall see for Myself and mine eyes shall behold & not Another tho consumed by my wrought Image' (in the original, 'though my reins be consumed within me'). Like two flints, the threatening deity and his petrified double strike an iconocaustic energy out of each other, as if the power of writing laid on top of the desire of writing were generating an energy destructive of the image, a lightning bolt running from the height of graphophonic authority all the way down to mute abjection. Blake causes the last of Job's hypotheses (the sight of God face to face) to be consumed by the first (the writing of words). Perhaps he is suggesting that once the tautology of writing is unfolded it doesn't matter who is on top, showing as he does again in his epic redaction of the book of Job, *Jerusalem*, that textuality in its repetitive and spectral modes may lead to a vicious and self-annihilating circularity.

Apart from these anti-textual possibilities, Blake's plate illustrates very economically the tendency of substitutive and self-referential con-figurations to ruin the presentation of consoling icons of self-recog-nition, and to spoil the delivery of instructive messages. It also brings to the fore the question of God as writer, for here he is not exhibiting his creatures in a demonstration of his might, but pointing to his inscribed tables, as if embarked on an energetic course of instruction. A good legend for the scene (not included by Blake) would be the pedagogical command from the theophany, 'I will demand of thee, and declare thou unto me' (40: 7). The lesson he teaches Job there about leviathan is very close to the spirit of the one Blake depicts in the eleventh plate and in the monotype that inspired it, *The Elohim Creating Adam* (1785), namely that to come before the divine countenance under the regime of imperial inscription is a dangerous and disfiguring experience for all concerned. This is as true for leviathan as it is for Job.

The forty-first chapter of the book of Job is an oblique and abbreviated repetition of Job's own story, showing not only how leviathan substitutes for Job as an instance of a unique existence, but also how God himself is included in the series, his face being reflected both in the battered physiognomy of Job and in the brazen face of the fish. The sequence comes in two parts. The first is a series of ironic questions naming the indignities impossible to inflict on this monster of the deep, whose independence and strength are plentifully to be declared as proof of the ageless efficacy of the divine will.[53] 'Will he speak soft words unto thee? . . . Canst thou fill his skin with barbed irons?' (41: 3, 7). The second is a list of his invulnerabilities: 'Who can open the doors of face? . . . His heart is as firm as stone; yea, as hard as a piece of the nether millstone' (41: 14, 24). Each is meant to proclaim with the force of an oath the perfect equivalence of leviathan's being with the words of his maker, until the resemblance between them can be explicitly asserted: 'None is so fierce that dare stir him up: who then is able to stand before me?' (41: 10). Leviathan's face is unapproachable, he generates his own light, and he is a king over all the children of pride—just like God—at which point of perfect resemblance leviathan is declared to resemble nothing but himself: 'Upon earth there is not his like' (41: 33).

The contradictions arising out of a claim for the unparalleled worth of what can only be presented in parallels has already been examined. What is remarkable about this example is that it enters God's speech in a phrase which exactly repeats his estimate of Job in the first two chapters: 'There is none like him in the earth' (1: 8; 2: 3). Job, the silent auditor, already has an interest in the truth he is being convinced of. To the extent that he and leviathan resemble each other in their absolute singularity, they are not simply the instruments of divine self-expression, they risk suffering exactly those indignities that are listed as im-

53 See J. V. Kinnear Wilson, 'A Return to the Problems of Behemoth and Leviathan', *Vetus Testamentum*, 25 (1975), 1–14; and Henry Rowold, '*Mi hu! Li hu!* Leviathan and Job', *Journal of Biblical Literature*, 105 (1986), 104–9.

possibilities in God's ironic apostrophe to the antagonist of irresistible power. In the aftermath of being instanced as the unique incarnation of a limitless will, Job *is* wounded: he *does* make supplications, he *does* seek the countenance of others, and he *does* desire to become like a stone, not because he is unassailable but because he bears the agonizing imprint of his maker. Leviathan faces the same prospect, unsecured by irony. The division of the verses in his praise fall into the strophe of disfigurement and the antistrophe of impermeability, reflecting the same division that has occurred in Job's life between the days of his glory, when the light of his countenance was not cast down (29: 24), and these days of abjection, when men spit in his face (30: 10). The song of leviathan is the story of Job back to front.

It is not simply that God is instancing something whose essence consists in its unparalleled and therefore uninstantiable identity, it is that he is doing it *for the second time*. He is so committed to the deixis of sense-certainty (*this* Job, *this* leviathan), that he forgets what is true in it, and has to start the movement all over again. God has forgotten that if he points he will forget what it is he points to, that a forgotten creature suffers, and that its pain can only be recognized and redeemed by a delegated cry. His unconscious repetition of what is in any case an unexemplifiable instance invites us to trace the resemblances between leviathan and Job, and to examine the residue of the failed lesson of the theophany for traces of a redemptive intensity.

Although God wishes to present Job and leviathan as the pure emanations of his power and his will, the very mode of presentation requires that they be regarded as signs of the integrity of divine being rather than its visible continuum. They are like that which is like nothing else: they are presentations of unpresentability, pictures of that which is destined never to be visible. They stand in the same relation to God as the stone and redeemer to Job, in being charged with delivering the unspeakable. Hobbes's idea of leviathan as 'Artificiall Man' or 'Mortall God', by whose intervention absolute power is recreated in a form suitable to the covenants of political negotiation ('Speak to us, and we will hear thee; but let not God speak to us, lest we dye'), is consistent with his reading of the theophany in Job as a series of justifications of power without reference to law[54]—that is, by the mediation of images. His corollary, namely that the mediating artifice reflects 'particular man' (119) as well as the sovereign power of God, holds for the book of Job as well as the commonwealth. Leviathan and Job resemble each other in so far as their quality and functions are the same; God resembles them in so far as the

---

[54] Thomas Hobbes, *Leviathan*, ed. A. R. Waller (Cambridge: Cambridge Univ. Press, 1935), 119, 144, 260-1.

sight of them is expressive of visible appearance of all cited cases of the unparallelled, including his own. He says that the terrible excellence of power is kept in the hidden splendour of its face, as his is in the whirlwind, as Job's was in the days of his strength. But the cost of saying so is to bring the invulnerable fish into the succession of amnesias and disfigurements (chiefly affecting the face: the lips, the nose, the jaw, and the brow) that were supposed to distinguish it from the vulnerable patriarch. Job, God's other instance, has already paid the price of being cited with the skin of his face. The power mediated through the 'Mortall God' takes its toll on the medium by which the unpresentable is presented: it is particularized as damaged, rather like the text of the book in which it appears. Job is well-placed to recognize in his appearance as the sign of invulnerability leviathan's peril. He can remember that when he was such a sign and spoke of strength, he was himself never strong.

This difference breaks the pattern of incontrovertible examples God meant to have produced. His creatures present neither his excellence nor their own. Job is leviathan in the past tense, a used sign, bearing the marks of a tried and contested instantiation; he is what leviathan is destined to become when Melville fictionalizes him as Moby Dick, a creature frighteningly disfigured by its work as a sign of power between the zones of God and mortals. That this disfigurement sooner or later will afflict each successive instance presented by God is as certain as his forgetting that he has already done to Job what he is now doing to leviathan. Everything God asserts to be impossible to inflict in respect of leviathan's countenance is a detailed prolepsis. Skin, head, and nose will be pierced and the doors of his face will be opened; he will be forgotten, and the movement of presentation will have to begin all over again.

Disfigurement isn't a state merely incidental to the work of being God's instance, or of being the victim of his amnesia. It affects God too, since he has brought the theme of his power into the line of repetitions. His is the third face in the triangle of reflections. Job's eye drips for the sight of this face because it will represent for him an intensity expressive of the usurpation of the dominion of written axioms. It will manifest the mortality of God, and the artifice of a suffering particular man. It will confirm a new combination of weakness with power. Leviathan takes the place of the redeemer, or *go'el*, by promising to be what Job is presently: the delegate who will lose face in order to keep his client in countenance. God embodies the instability of jussive and pedagogic authority that will be undermined and redirected in the mimesis of redemption. Delegation, I have shown, is risky for the complexion; but it is no less risky for the theodicean structures that deny chance. It threatens the revolution which Blake pictures in his eleventh plate, where the semblable figures speaking 'I' to 'I' can endlessly supplant each other, either according to the negative dialectic of failed instances, or to the modified phonography of redemption. What Job sees in God's countenance is power brought down to earth. It is his own reflection endowed with the capacity for first-person speech.

Of this enabling resemblance to his maker, Job has an intuition when he appropriates the very words with which God introduced the apostrophe to leviathan: 'I will demand of thee, and declare thou unto me' (42: 4). Here is a repetition with a difference, for it reverses entirely the relation of instructor and the instructed by putting ignorance where the lesson should be. What has happened to produce this weird mockery of the pedagogical question? The answer must be that God's hidden function as a writer has been found out by the creature he wrote upon, and his text answers back. Driver quotes an ancient Babylonian dialogue between a writing-master and his pupil whose locutions closely resemble the opening and closing phrases of the theophany: 'Hast thou learnt the writing art and knowest not the signs thereof? . . . Come, let me ask thee, and answer thou me! Come, let me speak to thee, and answer thou me!'[55] Dialogue and theophany alike explore the puzzling and often contradictory status of writing in a largely oral culture, no doubt keenly appreciated by the author of Job who was himself writing in a language he could not speak. God the writing-master teaches a lesson he himself cannot learn. This is why he needs the leviathan as instance, as Job was before, inscribed with the legible signs of his power, and rendered less than itself so that it can signify more. And this God forgets; he cannot learn it.

Job places God therefore in the position of the forgetful neophyte: 'I will demand of thee, and declare thou unto me'. And by materializing his maker as a writer whose claim to a voice will be warranted only mediately by reading, and not immediately in the surge of a plentiful declaration, Job reconstructs him as his own image, his other 'I', successfully embedding God in the line of repetitions that were memoriously initiated, forgetfully neglected, and destined forwardly to be recollected. God is not God, therefore. Initially he is the form taken by power partly to disguise, and partly to justify, its arbitrary and destructive dominion; and subsequently he is one of the forms taken by weakness in order to usurp power and to secure the right of speaking on its own behalf.

This line of repetitions is not a smooth loop extending from the voiceless author of Job to readers identifying themselves as redeemers of

---

[55] Driver, *Semitic Writing*, 66.

inarticulate suffering by virtue of their sympathetic predispositions. The line extends to new readers only because the rival terms of power and resistance, voice and writing, remembering and forgetting, citation and practice operate unstably, damaging both the coherence of the text and any narrative it might have sustained. If Job 'wins' in the reading proposed in this chapter, it is only because of a volatile energy generated in the practice of reading, which disappears as soon as the reader starts to dogmatize. When the reader is so certain s/he begins to say the opposite of what s/he means, s/he forgets that this is the case, and starts all over again the violence of instantiation and interpretation in which the book of Job begins. Not that the reader's practice can subsist without the sublime ambition to appropriate or usurp another's intensity. The opportunity for readerly re-entry into Job is by no means reserved therefore to sympathetic intellectuals whose programme favours the plight of an oppressed and stifled victim; if it were, the reading of Job would not involve the embattled continuity of the substance of the story with the mode of its reception. Its vehemence would drain away, the issues and the judgements would become categorical, and repetition—at least in its first-person intensity—would cease.

PART II

Backgrounds

3 Public Theodicies and Private Particulars

> Now no Man thinks the Sufferings of Job any Difficulty in Providence, much less any Objection against it.
>
> (William Sherlock, *Discourse on Providence*)

In the book of Job three forms of the theodicy have been distinguished, each supplying a vindication or justification of the ways of God to suffering humanity. First, there is the justification derived from a belief in an inscrutable deity, whose providence is not searchable and whose dispensations must patiently be borne on the grounds that they are serving ends beyond the grasp of mortal minds. Second, there is an argument founded on a postulate that nothing happens or subsists in the world beyond the horizon of the divine plan; hence the apparently most anomalous and heartbreaking events are dispensations made according to an ultimately coherent system. Third, there is the deixis of the pointing finger, which spells out each item in the creation as part of a stupendous whole and inspires the diffident audience with terror that modulates to wonder and delighted acquiescence. However, it is the second position that dominates the other two because it formalizes the plenary conception of all theodicies by deducing it from an invulnerable first principle linking the divine to the mortal world. It is impossible to articulate the first position without making some advance beyond blind faith into a statement that subjects the inscrutable to scrutiny; and it is impossible to cite the creation without measuring each terrific instance against an idea of something like a plenum in which it takes its place, finds its rank, and arrives at its significance. The book of Job develops, therefore, as a contest between the universal equity posited by the comforters, and the bare particulars of an unresolved personal agony listed by Job. The broad causal sweep of theodicy is measured against a complaint consisting in discrete notations of an actual set of circumstances for which no cause can be found.

Leibniz and Kant

The argument in favour of a plenary divine intention, based on universal self-evident propositions and called *theodicy*, were introduced to eighteenth-century thinkers by Leibniz, in his book *Theodicy* (1710). In it he tackles the issue dividing Job and his comforters, namely the existence of evil and the prosperity of the wicked, citing Bayle and Hobbes as his chief opponents. Like the comforters, he argues for the equity of providence by invoking the infinite subtlety with which divine laws relate to divine ends, alleging the predominance of moral good over evil in a world where suffering is largely self-inflicted: 'One suffers because one has acted; one suffers evil because one does evil'.[1] He turns directly to Job as a type of the man who makes a partial complaint about unjustified evil, and distinguishes between local malice—the brigands who make off with his goods—and the divine purposes served by the loss (296). If only we would cultivate the patience of the American Indians under torture, suggests Leibniz with an example that anticipates Adam Smith's in the *Theory of Moral Sentiments*, the trifling material accessories of God's plan would not distract us from its general symmetries (280–4).

Leibniz's justification depends on a distinction between what he calls primary and contingent truths. In the statement of a primary truth there is a self-evident connection between the subject and the predicate. 'The primary truths are those which assert the same thing of itself, or deny the opposite of its opposite.' His example is a version of the tautology Voltaire was to attack in his *Candide*: 'Every thing is as it is'.[2] In propositions concerning contingent truths the connection between subject and predicate is not self-evident: supplementary reasons have to be adduced in defence of it, and reasons for these reasons, and so on to infinity. In a world governed by primary truths nothing happens by chance or accident; there is a reason for everything even if it cannot be found out. But in a world understood according to contingent truths, there is always room for the opposite of what is; and the explanation of things as they are depends upon 'showing that there is more reason for that which has been done than there is for its opposite'.[3] The constancy of Leibniz's American Indian arises from his absolute assurance that things cannot be the opposite of what they are; whereas the complaints of Job exhibit the uncertainty of someone experiencing his life as a series of contingencies which need not have occurred.

In 1791 Kant published a short piece rebutting all theodicies derived from Leibniz. It was translated into English seven years later with the title 'On the Failure of all the Philosophical Essays in the Theodicee'. It

---

[1] G. W. Leibniz, *Theodicy*, trans. M. M. Huggard (London: Routledge and Kegan Paul, 1951), 276. See also 255–65.

[2] G. W. Leibniz, *Philosophical Essays*, ed. and trans. Roger Ariew and Daniel Garber (Hackett: Indianapolis, Ind., 1989), 30.

[3] *Philosophical Essays*, 101.

handles the reasons why a suffering individual is right to reject universalizing consolations which discount complaint as a record of contingencies. He takes the three levels of Leibniz's vindication—the harmony of all things with the eternal but not always visible reasons of God; the predominance of moral good over evil; and the responsibility each individual must take for causing suffering and for dealing with it— and tests them against the real limits of human forbearance. Of the first level, he notes that it offers nothing definite, yet it supposes a categorical difference between the insights of the consoler and the ignorance of the consoled. It is not a justification, 'rather a sovereign sentence passed by rational moral faith which can advise patience to the doubter but does not give him satisfaction'. To achieve this level of authority, theodicists are obliged to speak 'as if they were overheard by the Almighty'.[4] At the second level, Kant refuses to accept Leibniz's conclusion that life is generally tolerable (*Theodicy*, 286), and bleakly states the opposite view. No persons of sound understanding and length of days, he affirms, would ever choose to live their lives over again: 'The excess of painful feelings over pleasurable ones is inherent to an animal nature such as the human one' (287). And at the third level, he turns (like Leibniz) to the story of Job, and shifts the ground of the debate from the pointless conjecture about the fulfilment of divine laws and purposes in order to study the character of an afflicted man who resists all temptations to impersonate a confidence he does not feel. He starts talking about the integrity of certain forms of complaint compared with the dishonesty of most ways of justifying God.

Briefly, what Kant admires in Job is not the accuracy or otherwise of his judgements, but his motivation in making them. 'The uprightness of the heart, not the merit of one's insights, the sincere and undisguised confessions of one's doubts, and the avoidance of feigned convictions which one does not really feel . . . these are the qualities which caused the upright man Job to be preferred in the eyes of the divine judge to the pious flatterers' (293). The key verse of the book of Job, as far as Kant is concerned, is 27: 5: 'God forbid that I should justify you: till I die, I will not remove my integrity from me'. Kant is doing nothing new in contrasting the integrity of complaint with the disingenuousness of comfort, as will be plain when I deal with the Warburtonian debate about Job; but his account is remarkable in defining so succinctly the grounds of such a contrast. These derive from an unremitting attention

---

[4] 'On the Failure of All Attempted Philosophical Theodicies', trans. Michel Despland, in *Kant on History and Religion* (Montreal: McGill-Queen's Univ. Press, 1973), 289, 292. See also Immanuel Kant, *Essays and Treatises on Moral, Political, and Various Philosophical Subjects*, 2 vols. (London: William Richardson, 1798), ii. 206.

to 'the world of experience'—or what Leibniz refers to as the contingent material accessories surplus to the proof of divine wisdom—exemplified in Job's scrupulous restriction of his speech to what he actually feels he knows. Kant distinguishes here between *doctrinal* theodicy and *authentic* theodicy. Doctrinal theodicy makes claims to understand the supersensible world based on the specious self-evidence of the subject-predicate relation. Authentic theodicy is a report delivered in the first person comprising a practical estimate of the solidities and imperfections of a material existence. Such a report is necessarily limited by the faculties of the individual who makes it, and it destabilizes the relation of subject to predicate; but as long as acuity and candour are not sacrificed, it is not disqualified but rather dignified by these limitations.

I have already hinted at the aesthetic grounds of a comparison between Job's complaint and the theophany. As intensely particular accounts of things they both have a claim on the sublime. Kant widens these grounds with an account of complaint that brings it firmly within the regime of taste rather than of cognition and logic. Job's fidelity to his feelings, the gradations of pain and pleasure to which he testifies, is what is important in his account, not its rationality or consensual appeal. Job is justified not by the grand tautologies of truth but by his scrupulous attention to the molecular and contingent impulses of his own sensorium. 'All judgments of taste are singular', as Kant points out in the third *Critique*; they may impute, but they cannot postulate, general agreement.[5] There is nothing intrinsically commonsense about these judgments, and nothing necessarily normal about complaints. They may adapt *a posteriori* to a principle of community, but they do not do so *a priori*. Hence the paradox of all agreements about taste, and Kant's present defence of Job: they are cases of 'a conformity to law without a law' (*Critique of Judgement*, 86). In catering most directly and dramatically to the faculty of taste, the theophany brings Job as close as he can get to an articulation of what Kant means by integrity: 'Therefore have I uttered that I understood not; things too wonderful for me which I knew not' (42: 3).

It is largely in these terms that the joint issues of theodicy and the interpretation of the book of Job are debated and determined in eighteenth-century Britain. On the one hand there is a system of *a priori* principles authorizing the deduction of a providential scheme, and on the other a series of pragmatic engagements with the particulars of existence. This opposition between primary and contingent truths,

[5] *Critique of Judgement*, ed. James Creed Meredith (Oxford: Oxford Univ. Press, 1952; repr. 1973), 55.

elaborated by Luhmann as the contest in systems of communication between tautologies and paradoxes, is considerably diversified in the eighteenth century. Developments in the philosophy and practice of science, deriving from the debates held the previous century over the methods and technologies of experimental knowledge, are largely responsible. Of these debates the most famous was conducted by Boyle and Hobbes, concerning the philosophical implications of the experiment of the air-pump, a machine for making a void in nature. Very briefly, Hobbes's objection to this machine, and the speculations it was designed to prove, was that it breached the order of nature, making a hole not simply within the space of the machine but within the plenum itself. The vacuum is a discursive as well as a physical and logical anomaly, opening up room for dissent and distinction that is uncontrolled by any plenary authority or demonstrable truth. Boyle, on the other hand, was keen to liberate matters of fact from this normative regime by studying and reporting them with maximum fidelity, being 'somewhat prolix' in his accounts, which need to be 'circumstantially related, to keep the reader from distrusting them'.[6] Like Job, the experimental scientist makes no claim for the symmetry or truth of what he records, only for the matters of fact as he sees them. Boyle takes up the role of first person witness *vis-à-vis* a second person, who stands in the position of virtual witness: 'I chose rather to neglect the precepts of rhetoricians, than the mention of those things, which I thought pertinent to my subject, and useful to you, my reader' (Shapin and Schaffer, 64). The purpose of the first person is to convince 'you, my reader' of experimental facts by means of particular descriptions of physical details—'setting down things with the *minute circumstances*'—not excluding the most contingent, such as the dead mouse lying at the foot of the air-pump (60–1).

Of course, the experimental ideal of a free-standing collection of matters of fact, self-valuable and independent of all systematic coercion, is only a dream; but in pursuing it, British empiricists discover that the rhetorical gambit so loftily set aside by Boyle is in fact crucial. In Leibniz's terms, they are exploring the possibilities of opposite cases; and, like forensic orators, they are driven to buttress the connexion of subject to predicate 'by showing that there is more reason for that which has been done than there is for its opposite' (*Philosophical Essays*, 101). Therefore it is probability, not demonstration, which is to determine the truth of the case, and the first person must convince the second by means of a specifically rhetorical combination of personal integrity and narra-

[6] Cited in Steven Shapin and Simon Schaffer, *Leviathan and the Air-Pump: Hobbes, Boyle and the Experimental Life* (Princeton, NJ: Princeton Univ. Press, 1985), 62.

tive particularity. The credibility of the account is to be found not in the authority of its first principles, or the self-evidence of the propositions it affirms, but in the organization and delivery of the experimental facts. If, as Hobbes observes, this endows the experimentalist with temporary dominion over nature and his virtual witness, then it is of a volatile sort, won and lost from moment to moment, case to case (Shapin and Schaffer, 68), never lodged in a doctrine or universal rule of demonstration. This enfranchises an egoistical curiosity, and a cult of the firstness of first-person reports, of which Hobbes could not approve: 'There are very few of those who profess the sciences who are not pained by the discovery of difficult truths by others rather than themselves' (cited in Shapin and Schaffer, 321). All witnesses aspire to shed virtuality and to arrive at the condition of first persons, and the factor determining the transition is their orientation to the mass of contingent circumstances which comprise the report: how it is to be delivered; how it is to be digested.

Here is the beginning of an ideological crisis that becomes acute by the middle of the eighteenth century, affecting all aspects of cognition, practice, and representation. The difference between doctrine and authenticity, as Kant sees it, or between morality based on faith and faith (or belief) based on the authenticity of a credible report,[7] blooms into a manifold of cognate oppositions between invisible symmetry and an unfinished or endless materiality, between regulated demonstration and experimental inquisitiveness, between a contractual basis for income and the pursuit of profit, between the theory of an origin of civil society and the treatment of the social contract as a working fiction, between statute law and common law, between judgements of cognition and judgements of taste, between credit as a moral possession and credit as a commercial asset, between the classification and the rhetoricization of facts, between the moral tendency of art and the requirements of verisimilitude, and so on. What makes these oppositions more complex is that they are seldom developed purely as stand-offs between *a priori* and *a posteriori* positions, but are used to mingle elements of universalization with aspects of particularization in the most surprising ways. This confusion is at work when the patriot politician produces himself as a model of integrity in order to make a self-interested appeal to constitutional principle via the primitive origins of civic humanism, or when the jurisconsult finds he is defending the exemplary nature of punishment—the power of judges to sacrifice particular individuals to the immutable authority of the law—by appealing to taste as a warrant of the efficacy of the spectacle of execution.

[7] See Kant, 'On the Failure of Theodicies', 234–5.

Job is often the sign and symptom of this confusion. Whether he is made to stand as a vindication of providence or of private integrity, he clouds the issue. Not only does he challenge personally the theodicy he is supposed to illustrate, he destabilizes the alternative of a community of sentiment or taste by the egoistic rhetoric with which he overcomes the resistance of his reader, or virtual witness. As one of Job's more attentive readers puts it, 'Particularity by itself is measureless excess, and the forms of this excess are themselves measureless'.[8] If Job is not to be obscured by this excess, he must make an impression upon his reader's sensibility just as the particular injuries he mentions have made their impression upon his; but in proportion as the vividness of one impression is imparted to the other, just so far is the reader implicated in the contingencies and singular judgements which are at once Job's despair and his triumph. As Hobbes suggests, the passage from impression to impression excites a resistant and serial egoism, and a possibility of dissent and usurpation, rather than the sympathetic or consensual conformity to the law-no-law supposed by Kant. The power and dominion at stake in this communicative exercise preclude the simplicity and candour which certify for Kant the integrity of Job's report.

Pope and Young

The great theodicies of eighteenth-century Britain—Pope's *An Essay on Man* (1733) and Young's *Night-Thoughts* (1742–6)—develop the same weighted distinction between the overarching scheme of providence and the partiality of private and particularized complaints that is found in Leibniz and the tradition of Christian apologetics he supports. When Pope explains that 'All must full, or not coherent be',[9] (i. 45), and Young turns from 'the straw-like Trifles on Life's common Stream' in order to view the large mysteries of immortality,[10] they establish the same contempt for the particular that is to be found in William King's preference for the *a priori* principle over the *a posteriori* ('since the latter must depend upon a large Induction of Particulars') or in Richard Watson's caution against an over-exact attention to detail: 'Whilst we dispute about parts, we neglect the whole'.[11] However, maxims in favour of wholes tend to be reinforced with remarks about partial and biased behaviour which nevertheless are intended to have the same rhetorical

---

[8] Hegel, *Philosophy of Right*, trans. T. M. Knox (Oxford: Clarendon Press, 1942), 267.

[9] *An Essay on Man*, ed. Maynard Mack (New Haven, Conn.: Yale Univ. Press, 1951), i. 45.

[10] *Night-Thoughts*, ed. Stephen Cornford (Cambridge: Cambridge Univ. Press, 1989), 2.78 (references are to night- and line-number).

[11] William King, *An Essay on the Origin of Evil*, trans. Edmund Law (London: J. Knapton, 1732), p. ix. Richard Watson, *An Apology for the Bible in a Series of Letters Addressed to Thomas Paine* (Cork: A. Edwards, 1796), 53.

force as a general principle: ' 'Tis but a part we see, and not a whole' (*Essay on Man*, i. 60); or, 'Our passions are run mad, and stoop | With low, terrestrial Appetite, to graze | On Trash' (*Night-Thoughts*, vii. 534–6). In confidence and perspective such summary statements belong to the plenary system of whole structures and general views, but what they disclose is particularity so widespread that the authority of the judgement is self-cancelling. Either the whole truth is self-evident, and banishes all particular possibilities to a non-generalizable place at the periphery of things, in which case it is not worth mentioning; or it lacks that strength, whereupon it is invaded by contingencies and counterfactuals.

It is impossible for an eighteenth-century theodicy decisively to manipulate the difference between the being of the whole, which is because it is right, and the myriad of particulars and exceptions, which is assigned a place in the general scheme in spite of the omnipresence of right. These theodicean poets suppose a continuity of rhetorical with moral tone, and a harmony that unites the figures in which the plenum is praised with the rebukes of particular complaints, blinding them to the illogicality of their claims. The excellence of primary truths are uniformly saluted in tautologies, for instance Pope's round resumption of partial evil into universal good ('Whatever IS, is RIGHT'—i. 294) and Young's account of the Last Judgement as 'The Deed predominant! the Deed of Deeds! That makes a Hell of Hell, a Heav'n of Heav'n' (ix. 339–40).[12] But these tautologies run smoothly into the paradoxes generated by contingent truths, such as Young's estimate of the memorability of a merely material existence, 'I've been so long remember'd, I'm forgot' (iv. 57), or Pope's antinomy of Man, 'The glory, jest, and riddle of the world!' (ii. 18), without the poet betraying any sense of the clash between the rival functions of tautologies and paradoxes; or, indeed, of the paradox implicit in any tautological representation of presence, which requires that the whole be split in two so that it can be presented as like itself.

The difference between the intuition of the whole and the inspection of its disordered parts serves simply to place the voice of the observer at a greater distance from what is observed than ever can be consistent with confidence and accuracy: hence the repetitious and occasionally querulous tone of these theodicies. They are systems whose reliance on tautology as a sufficient indicator of presence inevitably generates a conflict between two opposite principles—the necessity of being and the contingency of the fragment—which indicates, in spite of its

---

[12] See Marshall Brown, 'The Urbane Sublime', in *Modern Essays on Eighteenth-Century Literature*, ed. Leo Damrosch (Oxford: Oxford Univ. Press, 1988), 448.

epigrammatical delivery, that the self-presence on which the entire ideological investment of the theodicy relies cannot be rendered in a non-
contradictory way. Owing to a superiority of view that they mistake for
a metalanguage, Pope and Young end up like those other victims of
repetition, Job's God and his justifiers, saying the opposite of what they
want to say. The only method of reuniting observation with the object,
suggests Niklas Luhmann in an essay explaining how the discourse of
self-referential systems changed in the eighteenth century, is to understand the necessity of being paradoxical when you want to be tautological, and to assign to particularizing activity something like the tautology
you wished to reserve for transcendental observation. 'In a very general
sense systems avoid tautological or paradoxical obstacles to meaningful
self-descriptions by "unfolding" self-reference. That is, the circularity of
self-reference is interrupted and interpreted in a way that cannot—in the
last analysis—be accounted for.' He instances the invention of concepts
of state ('the political system reintroduced into the political system') and
taste ('art consists of works of art, and what a work of art is is
determined by art').[13] Here, at what Luhmann defines as the point of
observational re-entry, Job will be found.

In *An Essay on Man* the book of Job is cited whenever the rhetoric of
the poem rises to the level of the unanswerable question.[14] The rejoinder
to those who believe there is 'a right divine in Men' to know the secrets
of providence—'Who knows but he, whose hand the light'ning forms?'
(i.157)—is a recension of Job 28: 26 and 37: 3.[15] The upshot of the
vision of universal ruin ('[Shall] this dread ORDER break—for whom? for
thee? Vile worm!' [i. 257]) is a free translation of Bildad (Job 25. 4–6).
The irresistible quality of the rhetorical question appeals as much to the
satirist as to the theodicist in Pope, for whom nothing more energetically
distinguishes the lordship of the speaker from the vassalage of the
spoken to than this sort of challenge: 'Has God, thou fool! work'd solely
for thy good?' [iii. 27]). That such a scornful question, in being hurled
at those who would be 'the God of God', might rebound upon the
questioner, is a danger of which Pope seems sublimely careless. He is
never afraid to take a Pisgah view of human infirmity. His theology, his
politics, his criteria of literature and morals, even his retirement to
Twickenham, all define his right to authority and justification. By stand-

---

[13] Nicklas Luhmann, *Essays on Self-Reference* (New York: Columbia Univ. Press, 1990), 125, 166, 193.

[14] It is heard again in commentaries on the book of Job which quote Pope back at it. Of the dialogues George Costard says, 'The Debate . . . is on a Question no less important than how "To vindicate the Ways of God to Men" '. Then he footnotes the *Essay on Man. Some Observations on the Book of Job* (Oxford, 1747), 25.

[15] *An Essay on Man*, ed. Maynard Mack (London: Methuen, 1950; repr. 1958), 35.

ing back and studying the littleness of things, Pope claims indifference to all but the highest principles. He is, after all, writing the *Essay* to another man of principle in retirement, Henry St. John, Viscount Bolingbroke. Consequently when he uses Job, he quotes the language of rebuke, preferably drawn from the whirlwind, loading his questions and his maxims with the intuitional *éclat* of the original: 'Where wast thou when I laid the foundations of the earth?' (Job 38: 3).

In which case, what happens to Pope's Job, the 'vile Man that mourns' (*Essay* i. 277)? The answer is that he is the fool and the worm, the antithetical point of resistance needed for the adequate defence of providence, the imbecile who asks, 'What is man?' (Job 7: 17). The displacement of Job to an inferior position and a culpable discourse of complaint is consistent with Pope's removal of other oppressed or marginal figures—dunces, women, Indians—to the level of ridicule. It is the inevitable destination of his partners in what Laura Brown has termed an 'ethical duet',[16] performed by Pope in order to reconcile the claims of self-interest in an expanding commercial world ('Whatever IS') with providential government ('is RIGHT'). 'In its metaphorical structure,' Brown writes, 'the *Essay on Man* is predicated on the problematic fantasy of an ideal exploitation' (91). Anyone who mourns or complains spoils the symmetry of gain and loss. However, in the *Epistle to Bathurst* and in his own more private letters to friends about the stock-market crash, Pope finds it harder to harmonize private enterprise with public providence, and is forced to take the story of Job more seriously.[17]

In his correspondence Pope generally relies on classical sources for maxims of wisdom and comfort, and is prone to use the Bible only for mild burlesque. An exception is his letter to Atterbury about the South Sea Bubble, in which he suppresses the fact that he lost £500 when it burst in order that he may develop the telescopic hauteur of the following question: 'Does not the fate of these people put you in mind of the two passages, one in Job, the other from the Psalmist? Men shall groan out of the CITY, and hiss them out of their PLACE'.[18] In fact the quotation conflates two of Job's speeches; the first about the injustices suffered by the righteous, the second about the fate of the wealthy hypocrite (Job 24: 12; 27: 23). It offers a new perspective on providence: from underneath, as it were. Pope's decision to turn—no matter how casually—to

---

[16] Laura Brown, *Alexander Pope* (Oxford: Basil Blackwell, 1985), 91.

[17] A different opinion of Pope's epistolary style, accompanying some intriguing judgements about the transformation of particulars into 'a kind of critical mass' of apocalyptic significance to his work, is to be found in Frederick Bogel, *Acts of Knowledge: Pope's Later Poems* (Lewisburg, Pa.: Bucknell Univ. Press, 1981), 187–93.

[18] *The Correspondence of Alexander Pope*, 5 vols. ed. George Sherburn (Oxford: Clarendon Press, 1956), ii. 54.

Job, the vile mourner, has a lot to do with the awkwardness of his perception of his own loss, which is indistinguishable from that of 'these people' who have been ruined by associating with men more greedy and cunning than themselves. Implicated in troubles he would rather look down upon than endure, and which he refuses to acknowledge as his own, Pope borrows Job's words to try to bridge the gap between a foolish complaint he can only utter in disguise, and the guarantee of an equitable outcome that theodicy has made habitual with him ('The investors have been foolish, and have suffered, but their deceivers shall suffer more'). But for someone fonder of the universalizing language of justification than of the scripture-fragments, this is not an idiom happily to be employed. In keeping his feelings a secret he sacrifices the relief of groaning with the men of the city, only to acquire instead the hissable hypocrisy of the directors. He ends up, in short, repeating the gesture of hollow *savoir-faire* that got him into trouble in the first place. Operating under such constraints, Pope sets himself alternating endlessly between a personal pain which cannot be communicated and a general judgement weakened by the particulars he refuses to disclose.

The *Epistle to Bathurst* sets his difficulty in a clearer light. In this poem Pope adapts the story of Job to the fable of Sir Balaam, the city knight wrecked by speculative success, in an effort to transfer the unacceptable qualities of the victim of speculation—the vile man who mourns—to the legitimate object of public disapproval, the company director.[19] Balaam is tested by Satan not with privation and disease, but with riches upon riches, until his vanity finally involves him in a treacherous bribe, for which his property and life are forfeit: 'The Devil and the King divide the prize, | And sad Sir Balaam curses God and dies' (compare Job 2: 9). Balaam seems to present the fulfilment of Job's prophecy about the wealthy hypocrite hissed out of his place, and therefore seems satisfactorily to resolve Pope's dilemma: loss ceases to be the incommunicable pain of the victim, but the public embarrassment of the company director. But rewritings of Job are always more equivocal than this. At the same time as he acts as the hissable completion of providential punishment, Balaam groans out of the city because as 'the plain good man' introduced at the beginning of the tale, he has been destroyed by the devil not for being evil but for being good. 'The Dev'l was piqu'd such saintship to behold, | And long'd to tempt him like good Job of old' (ll. 349–50). Satan takes up the position occupied by Adam

---

[19] For the close connections between Balaam's story and Job's, in terms of content, date, form, and authorship, see Tur-Sinai, *The Book of Job*, lxiv–lxix. Here I offer a reading of Pope's poem intended to contradict the assumption made, for example, by James Lehmann; namely, that the Job allusion in the *Epistle to Bathurst* is constitutive of a definite and unequivocal meaning. See '*The Vicar of Wakefield*: Goldsmith's Sublime, Oriental Job', *ELH* 46 (1979), 97–121.

Smith's 'invisible hand' in the theory of civil society, itself analogous to the 'je ne sais quoi' in the theory of taste; he is the medium between private interest and the public good, between the singularity of personal judgement and a benign consensual outcome. In terms of Pope's economic theodicy Satan is the agent responsible for providentially securing an equitable relation between individual greed and universal good. But the only way to make the case for Balaam's fall is to run an unironic parallel between him and Job, where it is indeed the 'plain good man' who is sacrificed, if for no better reason than that the relation of his disinterested and virtuous actions to the good of the whole is quite anomalous when compared with the ruthless self-interest of the wicked who, upon that very account, mysteriously contribute to the expansion of commerce and the growth of civil society. The only way out of this dilemma, which formalizes the problem of theodicy by ensuring the prosperity of the wicked and the unjustified suffering of the virtuous, is to make Balaam's temptation successful, so that he can be punished for acquiring bad habits; but then the poem supports a moral quite the opposite of the economic position Pope is defending, namely that self-interest, if left to its own devices, contributes to the general good. If wicked men are to be sacrificed, what will happen to civil society? The contradiction at the level of political economy repeats the contradiction of the poetry of theodicy in the eighteenth century, whose authors, John Barrell and Harriet Guest argue, are perplexed by the difference between the multifarious activities they point to and the summary statements they want to make about them.[20]

In the *Epistle to Bathurst* the difficulty is particularly acute because Pope is trying marry the joint discourse of satire and theodicy to the rationalization of economic amoralism.[21] Misers and prodigals may be morally repulsive, but by letting them indulge their ruling passions wealth is both accumulated and distributed. Pope is having to deal directly with the question of moral responsibility raised by Hume apropos the natural prodigies and the prodigies of vice equated in *An Essay on Man*. Its summary estimate of providence may be interpreted, Hume suggests, as a licence to misbehave: if volcanoes and the Borgias, why

[20] On the parallels between the discourses of taste and civil society see Howard Caygill, *Art of Judgement* (Oxford: Basil Blackwell, 1989); John Guillory, *Cultural Capital: The Problem of Literary Canon Formation* (Chicago, Ill.: Univ. of Chicago Press, 1993); and Barbara Hernstein Smith, *Contingencies of Value* (Cambridge, Mass.: Harvard Univ. Press, 1988).

[21] John Barrell and Harriet Guest, 'Contradictions in the Long Eighteenth-Century Poem' in *The New Eighteenth Century*, ed. Felicity Nussbaum and Laura Brown (London: Methuen, 1987), 123–33. See also Laura Brown, *Alexander Pope*, 110–14, where she argues that 'the vignette of Sir Balaam helps to reinstate by assertion a security of assessment that the body of the epistle tends to erode'.

not I?[22] Even assuming Balaam is not innocent, his case is not simple. Is he punished because he acquires prodigious wealth in an unacceptable way, or is his fate merely a moment in the history of the growth of capital? Is providence or chance the agent of his ruin? Is his story a warning against excess, or a fable of national corruption? Is it satire, political economy or a vindication of the ways of God to man? Pope is wrestling at several levels with the problem Bolingbroke ceaselessly broaches and exemplifies at the level of patriotic rhetoric, namely the relation of private integrity to issues of public importance.[23]

And the index of the contradiction in Pope's treatment of the modern Balaam is Job, whose shadow falls across all of his attempts to construe groans as hiss-worthy, and to transform personal loss into theodicean satire. Balaam is hissed in the absence of proper objects of hissing; he is the vile man who mourns, groans, and dies because someone must pay for the corruption that is never as seamlessly self-regulating as Pope would like to believe. Balaam's fate is the price paid for Pope's own particular unease with the market forces he has tried, both as a public voice and as a private investor, to control.

In the terms of paradox versus tautology already proposed, it is possible to see more clearly how Pope has been 'knotting together . . . the discourse of economic theodicy' (Barrell and Guest, 126), and how it fails. Under the tautology of a plenum ('whatever is, is right') he has intended to herd numerous examples of how evil (the vices of economic amoralism) accrues as social benefit (wealth is produced and finally distributed in an equitable way). But there is an extra paradox that upsets this reincorporation of contraries into the whole, and that is the possibility of the good man subject to evil or to chance and destroyed by forces over which he has no control. The transformation of good into evil, primary into contingent truth, is not generalizable in the same way as the transformation of evil into good. In the latter case the swarm of examples making the case and justifying the dispensation are quarantined and quite removed from the discourse that

[22] In 'The Sceptic' Hume in fact quotes the couplet that introduces the whirlwind questions of *An Essay on Man* as part of his critique of the topics of consolation: 'If plagues or earthquakes break not heav'n's design, | Why then a BORGIA or a CATILINE?' (1. 155–56). His point is that if prodigies of vice are allowed to be part of an unquestionable providence, as well as prodigies of nature, then each individual has permission to be as disobedient and as vicious as s/he pleases ('The Sceptic', *Essays Moral, Political, and Literary*, ed. Eugene F. Miller (Indianapolis, Ind.: Liberty Classics, 1985), 173).

[23] For example, 'It will be asked, what expectations can be entertained of raising a disinterested public spirit among men, who have no other principle than that of private interest?' *Some Reflections upon the Present State of the Nation* (London: A. Millar, 1753), 406. It is a question nuanced towards financiers like Balaam, but it does equally well for the patriot's self-authentication, which depends upon the marginalization of his centrality. The very qualities that fit him for the public sphere are what have expelled him from it.

evaluates the outcome. But the former demands a renegotiation of the maxims generated on the side of tautology in respect of the particular ethical difficulties encountered at the level of what Kant calls 'the world of experience', where an agent may feel he is acting for the best but is in fact in receipt of the wages reserved for the worst. Luhmann suggests that this renegotiation involves a revised tautology based on practice (the practice of politics includes the discourse of politics; the judgement of art is inseparable from the practice of art) by means of which the general rule finds much more intimate grounds of relation with the particular case. Here it would be something like an equation between hissing and groaning.

Pope has debarred himself from this adjustment by the satirist's and the theodicist's natural aversion for material particulars that might disturb the force of general statements, such as 'Extremes in Nature equal good produce, | Extremes in Man concur to gen'ral use' (ll. 163–4). His standard method of recuperating the unprecedented and the excessive is, as Warburton says of the premier instance in the *Essay on Man*, to make the very dispensation objected against the periphrasis of God's name: 'Ask we what makes one keep, and one bestow? | That POW'R who bids the Ocean ebb and flow, | Bids seed-time, harvest, equal course maintain, | Thro' reconcil'd extremes' (ll. 165–7). The nearest we are allowed to particulars that do not serve some local end of pathos (such as the details of 'Great Villers' deathbed), is in the form of epithets of the force that reconciles them: Season-adjuster, Life-on-death-builder, and so on.[24]

In Pope's case the depleted function of the particular instance, and the associated vulnerability of private individuals who wish to complain in public about the ills they have suffered—to groan and hiss—bears upon his own disastrous entry into the stock-market, and his secret complaint about the redistribution of his own wealth. Pope has been tempted by the same devil as his hero, and a hidden sympathy as well as a generic and rhetorical impasse may account for the contradictions of a poem that seeks publicly to deprecate an embarrassment the poet secretly lamented. To the degree that its fable fails as an intelligible discourse of providence, it succeeds perhaps as a private memorandum. In a letter to John Caryll in which Pope deserts the cant of candour for the real thing, he sports with the paradox of a generalized principle of self-interest that the *Epistle to Bathurst* has tried unsuccessfully to reduce to a tautology: 'Your doctrine of *selling out* was certainly the most true and important

---

[24] Laura Brown finds a parallel example in the *Essay on Criticism*, where rules can be ignored and exceptions entertained, but only as a function of indefeasible right ('As Kings dispense with Laws themselves have made'): *Alexander Pope*, 65.

doctrine in the world' (*Correspondence* ii. 57). Balaam is the waste resulting from the epistle's exclusion of this sort of revised tautology of practical wisdom. Because Pope was neither able nor willing to preach it often, preferring the plenary forms of epithets and performatives, Balaam pays the price by having his own complaint reduced to the sinful and futile antithesis of a performative—a curse.

As ought to become clear in a later chapter, this is not the first time that Pope tackles in a city knight particularities with which he has secret affinities. Tucked away in a corner of Pope's experiments with theodicy, Balaam provides the abbreviated reminder of what Pope forgets in his public readings of Job; namely, the loneliness and silence of an individual existence overwhelmed by the rhetoric of power and principle, whose chance of complaining—of rehearsing the contingent particulars of suffering—comes as a comic routine if it comes at all: 'My body is sick, my soul is troubled, my pockets are empty, my time is lost, my trees are withered, my grass burned! So ends my history'.[25]

Nowhere is the antithesis between providential grandeur and selfish littleness more elaborately and melodiously insisted upon than in *Night-Thoughts*, the masterpiece of Pope's former imitator, Edward Young.[26] In this theodicy, which dominates the rest of the century, contempt is poured on the fools, brainless wits, pygmies, and other low creatures that are 'fill'd, and foul'd, with Self'(ix. 1372). There is no surer symptom of narrow selfishness than the refusal of consolation and the need to whine: 'All Littleness is in Approach to Woe' (ix. 1389). Praise is reserved for those who willingly yield themselves to 'the boundless Theatre of Thought' opened by nature, 'this Ostentation of creative Power', whose vastness 'is th'Almighty's Oath' (ix. 743, 845). The question put by Job in his ignorant resistance to the comfort of his friends, 'What is man, that thou shouldest magnify him' (7: 17) is here repeated, placarded in capitals as the typical overture of selfish complaint: 'WHAT THEN AM I?' (ix. 367). The sardonic answer includes variations on the stock of opprobrious epithets Young saves for wilful individualists who, 'to palliate peevish Grief's COMPLAINT . . . dare into Judgement call her Judge (ix. 469–71).' 'The single Man?' cries the poet incredulously, availing himself of the erotesis, 'I mourn for Millions' (ix. 236–7). He shares Pope's Olympian scorn for those whose intemperate desire of life and equity makes them judges of justice and Gods of God. Complaint more urgent than the elegiac tone of self-transcendence that

[25] Pope to Broome, July, 1723. *Correspondence* ii. 182.
[26] Although Young puts some distance between himself and Pope in his last work, *Conjectures upon Original Composition* (1759), and although Pope had his own reservations about Young's tendency to bombast, the orientations of their rhetoric of justification are alike. See Daniel W. Odell, 'Young's *Night-Thoughts* as an Answer to Pope's *Essay on Man*', *SEL* 12 (1972), 481–501.

launches the poet on his survey of the fitness of things, where 'All is Right, by GOD ordain'd', is out of tune. It 'jars in the grand Chorus', harps on 'a peevish, dissonant, rebellious String' (ix. 370).

In his *Paraphrase on Job*, often published with *Night-Thoughts*, Young's sense of priorities is the same. The dialogues are reduced to a summary of twenty lines; the rest is a free translation and elaboration of God's speech from the whirlwind, 'th'Almighty's Oath', with bits added ('the Mountain, the Comet, the Sun') and others 'much inlarg'd'. Even more than Pope, Young is drawn to the theophany as a superb 'ostentation of creative power'. He dares to say that, 'The Judicious, if they compare this Piece with the Original, will, I flatter myself, find the Reasons for the great Liberties I have indulg'd myself in through the Whole'.[27] The reasons seem to be two: first, that Job's speech is an embarrassing lapse into singular and dissonant complaint, delivered from the 'low earth' in sentiments as low, and therefore best abbreviated: 'Then Job contain'd no more; but curs'd his Fate' (308); second, that the sublime ostentation of power, particularly when delivered in the form of rhetorical questions, is much more alluring to a poet whose taste and piety incline him to larger views. Like so many of the poet's reasonings with Lorenzo, the infidel in *Night-Thoughts*, the unanswerable question lends itself to the lofty idiom of reproof and correction: 'the proper Style of Majesty incens'd' (322). In a rather sinister parallel erected on Longinus' authority, Young says of the figure of interrogation, 'It differs from other manner of Reproof, as bidding a Person execute himself, does from a common Execution; for he that asks the Guilty a proper Question, makes him, in effect, pass Sentence on himself' (322).

Young is very agile in fending off the threat of Luhmann's revised tautology. Either it marks the intensified disobedience of the grief-stricken (judging your judge; compare Pope's 'Re-judge his justice, be the GOD of GOD'—i. 122), or the appropriate punishment for such wilful mimesis, where the judgement of the self against the self is self-executing—something like, 'Yes, I suffer because I deserve to suffer'. Practice and judgement are allowed to combine only on the level of delinquency; otherwise, unredeemed human nature is the abject counterpart of mellifluous summary, the excessive proof of the doctrine of the whole.

Like Pope's, then, Young's Job is the fool committed to a partial complaint. His deafness to consolation allows the theodicy to rise into more dramatic and decisive language by providing the occasion and the

---

[27] *A Paraphrase on Part of the Book of Job* bound with *The Complaint: or Night-Thoughts* (London: A. Millar, 1750), 321.

object for the passionate figures of outraged majesty. In the ninth night the poet compares himself to Job: 'Like him of Uz, | I gaze around; I search on ev'ry Side— | O for a glimpse of HIM my Soul adores!' (ix. 1689–91). But there is very little sense of his having to struggle to gain a view of his creator. The ostentation of creative power which he had expanded in the *Paraphrase* he adapts for the sublime self-evidence of his own rhetorical questions, which he darts (as God to Job) at a sceptic hardened with intellectual conceit. 'Seems it not then enough, to say, LORENZO! | To Man abandon'd, "Hast thou seen the Skies?" ' (ix. 938–40; compare Job 38: 19). The only sections of *Night-Thoughts* that have anything in common with the complaints of Job are the imagined meditations of Lorenzo. The long soliloquy in the seventh night reads like the missing speeches of Job in the *Paraphrase*, its theme the 'unprecedented Ill' of an intelligent being condemned to discover nothing but what makes him suffer. Better not to have been born than to find the good tormented and the wicked in prosperity:

> ——What Pain, amidst a thousand more,
> To think the most Abandon'd, after Days
> Of Triumph o'er their Betters, find in Death
> As soft a Pillow, nor make fouler Clay!

> (vii. 712–15; Job 21: 22–34)

Lorenzo strings together more sceptical questions two nights later, beginning with what seems to be the inevitable signature of infidelity, 'What am I? and from Whence?' (ix. 1449). A series of materialist, rationalist, and deistic conjectures follows, none of which is either satisfying or determinable. The sense of a vigorous but unsuccessful effort of mind gives the paragraph something of the flavour of Job's questions; but it is proposed solely as the nonplussed counterpart of the confident generalizations Young wants his audience to applaud. Nothing of Job's complaint survives as legitimate in this reading, particularly his critique of those who mock God by impersonating his voice and wisdom.

To find a sympathetic picture of the single man who is oppressed with doubts he cannot clear and pains he cannot account for, the reader must go to Young's letters. In these he seems much less intent on disguising himself than Pope. His readiness to exchange the particularities of complaint with Richardson is oddly artless. 'The piles,' he confesses, 'I have suffered extremely from'. Richardson responds in kind, 'And pray, sir, how are your teeth?'[28] In between his effusive compliments to

---

[28] *The Correspondence of Edward Young*, ed. Henry Pettit (Oxford: Clarendon Press, 1971), 225, 430.

Richardson on the fineness of the Christian principles demonstrated in Clarissa Harlowe's death, Young erupts into a perfectly human bout of impatience with a doctor who told him that physical pain is not worth regarding: 'This is ye Comforter Job has sent me under Pains half of which would make him mad' (187). Considering how closely he was reading *Clarissa* at this time, it is remarkable that he fails entirely to recognize any of her borrowings from Job as signs of a similar impatience, and chooses rather to interpret her dying as a flawless exemplification of the sentences of faith and hope anthologized by Richardson and proclaimed by himself throughout *Night-Thoughts*. There he calls the deathbed of a good man a place 'privileged beyond the common Walk of virtuous Life' (ii. 632). Richardson, he tells Mrs Delany, has made Clarissa's deathbed 'an object of Envy' (*Correspondence* 314). Shortly after writing this, Young was so prostrated by the death of his daughter-in-law, Catherine Haviland, that he lost the use of an eye. Richardson—a Job's comforter?—despatched a copy of the *Meditations*, largely consisting of Clarissa's extracts from Job and the Psalms, 'adapted for the Different Stages of a Deep Distress'.[29]

The same awkward oscillation between his published idealizations of Christian fortitude and a personal, unpoetic vulnerability to distress pursues Young to the very end. *Night-Thoughts* is more devoted to the theme of dying and the prospect of the deathbed than Montaigne's *Essays*. It is so replete with sentiments defying, palliating, or welcoming death, that a good end from its composer was entirely to be expected. He deplores the low, selfish, particular desire not to die: 'Shall our pale, wither'd Hands be still stretch'd out, | Trembling, at once, with Eagerness and Age? . . . Grasping at air!' (iv. 115–16). Young's death, according to Nathaniel Cotton, resembled this picture of senile terror far more than it did Addison's self-command, commemorated so fulsomely at the end of his *Conjectures*.[30] 'Dr Young, although in his eighty sixth year, had disputed every inch of ground with death. . . . How earnestly did I wish the vital knot untied!' (*Correspondence* 593).

I want to emphasize that the contradictory particulars lurking on the underside of Pope's and Young's careers are not to be treated as ethical deficiencies but as linguistic and textual necessities. The book of Job opens up a real difference in the production of theodicy, and it cannot be ignored or concealed without a reinscription of difference in the form of an unwitting imitation or citation of what was not meant to be

---

[29] *Meditations Collected from the Sacred Books* (London: Samuel Richardson, 1750; repr. New York: Garland, 1976).

[30] 'Who would not thus expire? What a glorious supplement! . . . What a full demonstration!' *Conjectures upon Original Composition* (London, 1759; Leeds: Scolar Press, 1966), 102.

shown. The contradiction between the theophanizing of Pope and Young and their private moments of embarrassment, distress, and terror is really the return of the excess they had to repress while coining the tautologies of presence. The reappearance of the very circumstances that were to be pared away in order that the paring work of providence can be performed is exactly the paradox illustrated in the stories of Sitis and Martha. The particularity these theodicists deplore is only secondarily an objective state of affairs; chiefly it is the contingent precipitate of their desire to write truths that are primary, full, and devout. Just as the comforters objectify in Job's impatience and alleged wickedness the internal threat to the full speech of justification ('thine own lips testify against thee' [15: 6]), a threat which must be neutralized if they are to go on talking without confusion, so the modern theodicist finds that in hissing worldly trifling and selfishness he reminds himself of private groanings which nevertheless must be reverberated as a hiss if his message is to remain lucid. Job is the name given to the impossibility of doing this satisfactorily.

4 *Hume and the Unfolding of Tautologies*

The events we are witnesses of, in the course of the longest life, appear to us very often original, unprepared, single, and un-relative, if I may use such an expression for want of a better in English . . . they appear such very often, are called accidents, and looked on as the effects of chance. . . . We get over the present difficulty, we improve the momentary advantage, as well as we can, and we look no further. Experience can carry us no further; for experience can go a very little way back in discovering causes: and effects are not the objects of experience till they happen.

(Henry St. John, Viscount Bolingbroke,
Letters on the Study and Use of History)

Niklas Luhmann outlines the method of unblocking a mind clogged with primary truths as follows: the observational competence required to defend self-evident propositions must first be halted with the shock of an opposite possibility; this interruption is followed by a readying of the mind as it prepares to exchange tautologies for paradoxes; and the transitional alertness allows a mixture of both to supervene: paradox as an unfolded tautology, such as the criterion of taste being located in the practice of taste. Practice becomes the measure of the language that speaks of it, and of the principles according to which it is judged. Luhmann finds the eighteenth century most fruitful in unfolded tautologies, since so many of its discourses depend upon experience alone for the supply of axioms which make experience intelligible. In the first part of this study the interruptions of tautologies were shown to unfold as the remaking of making, the copy of the artefact, writing upon writing, and so on. The unfolding occurs in the wake of a contest between self-evident justification and improbable complaint which is graphically represented in, and frequently copied from, the book of Job.

I mean to show in this necessarily sprawling second part that the mid-century is a period when the opportunities for the interruption and unfolding of tautologies begin to multiply, and that this unfolding attends the collapse of the public and private spheres into each other. The public sphere is menaced by the increasing instability of *principle—*

both as a word and an ideal governing the prescriptive relation of concept to action—particularly in the practice of politics and law. In the private sphere individuals are actuated by various empiricist or associationist judgements which fail to account for ideas and feelings in terms of causes rationally disclosed, only in terms of a double pulse in the brain imparting to customary impressions—that is, to the sense of the same thing happening over again—the reverberative force incident to the enunciation of an irrefragable principle or rule. By means of the echo or spectral blur caused by this double pulse, experience seems haunted by its own revenant, so that an impression can mediate itself, comment on itself, and supply its own grounds of credibility, claiming the status of an antecedent idea as well as of an immediate sensation. In this way, experience compensates for the loss of determining principles of action in the world at large by an illusion bred of custom that gives the particular event access to the general scheme, and endows private testimony with a public dimension. I will begin with David Hume, whose writings are devoted to supplanting providential deductions (such as the theodicies of Pope and Young) with inductions based on nothing more authoritative than personal experience.

In a letter to Matthew Sharpe, Hume slily confided, 'For you know that I always imitated Job's Friends, & defended the Cause of Providence when [you] attackt it'.[1] He is equivocating, for the providence of the comforters is the target of all his philosophy. Of theodicies he says, anticipating Kant, 'The great source of our mistake in this subject, and of the unbridled licence of conjecture, which we indulge, is, that we tacitly consider ourselves, as in the place of the supreme Being'. To reason from an effect to a cause, then from a cause to attributes of a first cause, and to explain all possible effects as consistent with that great original, is to invest a 'child of the brain' with the authority of a father, and to flatter God instead of honouring him.[2] Why then does Hume class himself with the comforters, when he believes that cause and effect is nothing but chance familiarized, irreducible to any scheme of laws except those bare propositions concerning the habitual conjunctions of ideas he sets out in the *Treatise*? I think the answer lies in the twofold nature of his scepticism, which embraces a repudiation of false consolation so searching and unremitting that it bespeaks an uncommon need of the genuine article in the first place. Like Johnson and Voltaire, Hume is aware of the keenness and specificity of the ordeals that consolation cannot reach; and, like Job, he has to keep reminding himself of the

---

[1] *The Letters of David Hume*, ed. J. Y. T. Greig, 2 vols. (Oxford: Clarendon Press, 1932), i. 59.
[2] 'Of a Particular Providence and a Future State,' in *An Enquiry Concerning Human Understanding*, ed. L. A. Selby-Bigge (Oxford: Clarendon Press, 1975), 145, 137.

inefficacy of comfort if he is to find an alternative way of dealing with a disconsolate existence.

Early in his career Hume acted out the roles supplied by the book of Job, taking the part not only of the man troubled in his body and his mind, but also impersonating the voices of the comforters. The occasion was a severe physical and nervous collapse, which he studied carefully and tried to cure with his own prescription. In a remarkable letter to George Cheyne, detailing the distressing physical symptoms that developed after he deserted a career in the law (his family's choice) for a life devoted to literature, Hume confesses to 'a certain Boldness of Temper . . . which was not enclin'd to submit to any Authority . . . but led me to seek out some new Medium, by which Truth might be establisht'. The aftermath of this disobedient curiosity, he goes on to report, was a nervous instability so severe that he was forced to subject himself to a severe regime of self-consolation: 'I was continually fortifying myself with Reflections against Death, & Poverty, & Shame, & Pain, & all the other Calamities of Life. These no doubt are exceeding useful, when join'd with an active Life, because the Occasion being presented along with the Reflection, works it into the Soul, & makes it take a deep impression, but in Solitude they serve to little other Purpose, than to waste the Spirits, the Force of the Mind meeting with no Resistance, but wasting itself in the Air, like our Arm when it misses its Aim'.[3] Here he acts the part of Job's comforter to his own Job, attempting to recover the law he flouted by quoting rules of submission, but succeeding only in aggravating his complaint which, like Job's, combines complaint as somatic disorder (scurvy followed by ptyalism, or excessive salivation, were the physical symptoms of Hume's afflictions) with complaint as the expression of a troubled mind.

He arrives experimentally at an estimate of the distance separating the pure doctrine of theodicy and patience from the heterogeneity of real occasions and actual practice, and finds the attempt to bridge it a waste of energy because, in the absence of an efficacy measurable by the reaction of a proposition upon a case, the proposition returns merely upon itself as a universal statement that unites subject and predicate in a notional and pointless identity. The arm misses its aim, to use his metaphor, and makes a gesture at once ample and empty. Having identified the bad tautology of comfort and constructed the ensuing paradox, namely that good instruction is proportionate to its failure to

---

[3] *Letters*, 14. This passage provides the basis for an ingenious speculation on reflection, waste, and writing in Hume's work in Jerome Christenson, *Practicing Enlightenment: Hume and the Formation of a Literary Career* (Madison, Wis.: Univ. of Wisconsin Press, 1987), 53 ff. See also John Sitter's authoritative survey of mid-century tendencies towards the intensities of 'particular points' at 'particular instants' of which he finds the evolution of Hume's literary career exemplary, *Literary Loneliness in Mid-Eighteenth-Century England* (Ithaca, NY: Cornell Univ. Press, 1982), 11 ff.

correct a present evil, Hume outlines the possibility of an unfolded tautology as a scene of comfortless affliction, where the unattended particularity of his complaint is exhibited in its singularity, irrelevant to all prescriptions.

The complaint of a desperate man, terrified by the consequences of his own temerity but still daring to offend authority in his search for truth, is impersonated by Hume at the end of the first book of the *Treatise of Human Nature*. 'Where am I, or what?' he cries out in language that echoes the complaints of Job and anticipates Young's Lorenzo and Frankenstein's monster: 'From what causes do I derive my existence, and to what condition shall I return? Whose favour shall I court, and whose anger must I dread? What beings surround me? and on whom have I any influence, or who have any influence on me? I am confounded with all these questions, and begin to fancy myself in the most deplorable condition imaginable, inviron'd with the deepest darkness, and utterly depriv'd of the use of every member and faculty.'[4] The rhetorical extravagance of these questions is no doubt partly owing to the poignancy with which they were once posed by the young Hume; but here they make way for the bathos of the sovereign remedy for philosophical melancholy and delirium: 'I play a game of backgammon'. This is the solution to the impossible alternative of operating 'betwixt a false reason and none at all': it is to do 'what is commonly done' (*Treatise*, 315). It is an unfolded tautology: the doing of what is done. In the absence of any firmer guiding principle, Hume invokes not the self-evident rule but the done thing, turning to practice (as opposed to doctrine) as a solace for the terror of doubt. But to manage this turn successfully the terror, like the practice, has to comprise the singular and the representational aspect. It must be both the thing itself and the picture of it; the immediate experience configured as its own precedent.

In the section 'Of a Particular Providence' in the *Enquiry* he emphasizes the need for 'practice and observation' amidst the 'present scene of things', for 'the experienced train of events is the great standard, by which we all regulate our conduct' (141–2). Jerome Christenson illustrates the regulatory mechanism that gives to the 'train of events' the power of governing the 'present scene' of an event with Goldsmith's play *She Stoops to Conquer*. He quotes Mr Hardcastle's instructions to his butler on how to behave when important guests come to dinner: 'You must not be so talkative, Diggory. You must be all attention to the guests. You must hear us talk, and not think of talking; you must see us

---

[4] A *Treatise of Human Nature* ed. Ernest C. Mossner (Harmondsworth: Penguin, 1969), 316. Compare *Night-Thoughts* ix. 367; ix. 1449, and Frankenstein's monster: 'Who was I? What was I? Whence did I come? What was my destination? These questions continually recurred'. *Frankenstein*, ed. M. K. Joseph (Oxford: Oxford Univ. Press, 1969), 128.

drink, and not think of drinking; you must see us eat, and not think of eating'.[5] Christenson finds in Hardcastle's lesson a compendious account of Hume's theory of self-regulating events and self-restraining passions. Self-regulation is performed by means of a double appeal to representation: Here is a scene of instruction embedded in another, theatrical scene of instruction; and at both levels the senses inform the audience not by being called into action but by supplying ideas of that action. Such a double scene grounds the ideology of ideology, 'inasmuch as [it includes] not only a representational structure but represents the very capacity of representational structures adequately to perform the kind of mediative work that is their ideological function' (35). Diggory is socialized and satisfied by getting an *idea* (to use Hume's term for representation) in exchange for an *impression*; and so is the audience of the play.[6]

If this were the entire account of Hume's complaint and consolation, and the 'true medium' he tries to set between them, then it is unlikely the link between the two would be in any sense pragmatic, because the mediative and ideological function of representation would merely reintroduce practice as the client of a new form of doctrine and prescription. The idea could never enter into a satisfying relation with the impression; the difference between the done and doing would remain irreducible, for one would be able to see eating without thinking of eating, hear talking without an idea of talking oneself, and experience the done thing without doing it. It seems, on the contrary, that all important psychological events involve, as far as Hume is concerned, a complex reaction between impressions and ideas, especially in the process of belief, where the truth of a proposition or a feeling will be determined not in the application of a criterion, but in the degree of vividness with which it is felt. Taste is the meeting-point for the train of events (represented as ideas) and the present scene of a single event (experienced as an impression), and *aisthesis* is the source of whatever regulatory pressure the one is able to exert over the other. In the complaint uttered in the *Treatise*, and in the consolation Hume administers, effectiveness (whether of the rhetoric of the lamentation or the emollient virtues of backgammon) is not determined by the resolution of practice into representational ideas, but by the overlap and recipro-

[5] *Practicing Enlightenment*, 35.

[6] Cf. Frances Ferguson, 'My view is that the advent of aesthetics as a more or less distinct area of philosophical speculation marks an intensification of interest in the mental image and in the difficulties of assimilating it to the problems of ontology and epistemology, on the one hand, and to those of ethics on the other'. *Solitude and the Sublime: Romanticism and the Aesthetics of Individuation* (New York: Routledge, 1992), 1. Her discussion of the mental image of sensation in the contexts of sympathy and particularity, and how it manages to recur as its own effect, is germane to all of my argument.

cation of two forms of mental action (sensation and the representation of sensation) experienced as the stream of custom which makes particular events recognizable. Technically, even complaint can arrive in a familiar form, provided the expression of a specific experience of severe perplexity includes the citation of previous ideas connected with confusion.

In fact Hume is not much interested in this overlap in the case of complaint, which he regards as participating in the futility of the swinging arm whether it be issuing false prescriptions for comfort or lamenting the absence of these very prescriptive ideas. Either way, complaint belongs to the amplitude of an empty gesture. More interesting to him, and more consoling, is the game of backgammon. This constitutes his interruption of the observational competence of self-evident propositions, and his reproof of the desire for such competence. It is accomplished by inserting chance into the plenary discourse of cause, in the guise of the trifling possibility of amusement standing opposite to the giant forms of metaphysical speculation. It is a chance of distraction created by a game of chance. As Mallarmé observes, a throw of the dice doesn't get rid of chance, but it can make it more appropriable than systems which aim to expel all odds from the business of calculation. So in experiencing (like Job) the alarming sensation of being a stake in the bet of some invisible gamester, Hume finds himself consoled by reducing chance to the status of what is commonly done, making it recognizable as a game with rules, customary and familiar. Subject to chance, he will play at chance. In this respect backgammon acts as his 'new medium' in much the same way that Job's inscribed rock, his writing on writing, articulates his sense of vulnerability. It allows the turbulence and incoherence of complaint a point of refraction from which it can glimpse itself and so render itself visible, legible, and credible to itself. The conditions of a credible self-consolation demand the same unfolding of tautology evident in Job's construction of the scenario of redemption. The prescriptions of false comfort are displaced by a practice continuous with the particularity prescription sought to repress; but it is not simply a casual and isolated particularity with no hope of generalizing and representing itself. Each fortuitous circumstance of suffering—a lesion, an inarticulate cry, a foaming mouth—is joined to a representational idea that contributes to the reinscription of suffering in a form that unites passivity with agency. The arrangement is to be expressed as doing the done thing, taking a chance on chance, and writing on writing.

Consolation that fails to exploit this self-referential medium of complaint is to be avoided at all costs. In his essay, 'The Sceptic', Hume lists the 'artifical arguments' provided by Seneca, Cicero, and Plutarch designed to comfort people in distress. At first he means simply to show that 'the reflections of philosophy are too subtle and distant to take place in common life, or eradicate any affection', and that, like all the swinging arms of gigantic metalanguage, they miss their aim, which is practical assistance. But as he begins to imagine short dialogues between the comforter and the grieving person, he finds they are worse than the ample flourish of an empty gesture. Consolation aggravates the condition it is supposed to soothe because it puts a wedge between the general and the particular: '*Your sorrow is fruitless, and will not change the course of destiny*. Very true: and for that very reason I am sorry'. The miserable man who is assured that 'Man is born to be miserable' has an extra reason for misery: 'Your consolation presents a hundred ills for one, of which you pretend to ease him' ('The Sceptic', 172–4). The sufferer is incapable of reading the consolation in any other than a particular way: its abstraction therefore must strike him as a multiplication of instances, not as a refinement of the manifold into a concept of suffering. Furthermore, it is a mockery because in using an idea of multifarious suffering to exclude the relief afforded by the representational image of suffering, such as the game of chance which alleviates the effect of actual chance, or the writing which soothes the pains of being written upon, the tautology of self-evidence re-forms as a subject–predicate identity which pronounces an arbitrary sentence of unavoidable pain: your suffering is what is. 'Let your gods therefore, O philosophers, be suited to the present appearances of nature: and presume not to alter these appearances by arbitrary suppositions' (*Enquiry*, 138). It is precisely this kind of local sense of particulars that Kant's Job relies upon to make a useful confession of ignorance. In both Job's case and Hume's, their allowance of other possible cases arises from a pause or blink in the running of the mind which extracts from the barest of possible chances a representational image that permits the sensation of pain to refer to itself for consolation.

An unnegotiable distance divides the formal consolations Hume first applied to his complaint from the double relation of chance and pastime he outlines in the *Treatise*. It is a fissure that opens up many times in fiction and biography, the result of a mid-century crisis of confidence in the value of consolations and vindications. James Boswell's life is patterned by the alternation between his compulsive desire to set up prescriptive authorities and his no less compulsive weakness for petty solecisms that defy those very prescriptions. Henry Fielding took the trouble to compose for himself something resembling Hume's self-consolation, entitled *Of the Remedy of Affliction* (1743), comprising most of the classical commonplaces that require patience from the afflicted individual. It was written in the year of his wife's death, when his grief was so intense and so invulnerable to consolation his friends thought he was running mad.[7] In Sterne's *Tristram Shandy* (1759–67) Walter, the hero's father, recites a similar list of commonplaces to ease the shock of the news of the death of his elder son, only to have to face the bare fact, unconsoled, when his wife interrupts his recitation. The narrative of *The Vicar of Wakefield* is interrupted six times by the rapid transitions from formal self-consolations for the loss of goods, family, and peace of mind into fresh losses of these same items. These interruptions of observational competence keep proposing the problem that Hume solves with his game of backgammon.

In so far as the problem remains a problem, Job, in one form or another, accompanies the interruption. Parson Adams, Walter Shandy, Charles Primrose, and the philosopher in *Rasselas* straddle, like Hume, the roles of the comforters and of the tormented patriarch, and are represented by their authors as comic modern Jobs precisely because they are destined to rediscover in their self-ministrations the inefficacy of the consolations extended by the comforters to Job.[8] It is tempting to speculate that the novels written between the 1740s and the 1760s tackle the issue of realism not as a formal principle of verisimilitude standing in opposition to the improbabilities of romance, but as a surge of particulars and little circumstances that arises directly from the interruptibility of all theodicies, an epiphenomenon of the failure of consolation which places its own stress on theories of probable representation. Details flood in through the holes made by unexemplary experience and disconsolate feelings in the structure of fabular prescription; apologues and axioms part company except in the self-conscious exoticisms of the oriental tale. The problem facing novelists is how to transform these multifarious possibilities into something resembling backgammon in the interests of a scaled-down standard of probability, determined not by the relation of prescriptive truth to representational accuracy, but by an exigent particularity which, both in formal and representational terms, is anomalous and generically unstable. Probability as a function of exemplary representation ceases to be the chief and unambiguous objective in narratives of quotidian experience, since its conceptual underpinning has already disappeared along with the plausibility of discourses of consolation and justification. Romance, the antitype of 'realism' and the polemical object of all new definitions of

---

[7] See Martin C. Battestin, *Henry Fielding: A Life* (London: Routledge, 1989), 385.

[8] Rather the opposite view is taken by Martin C. Battestin, *The Providence of Wit* (Oxford: Clarendon Press, 1974), 193–214.

the novel, is just shorthand for the failure of prescriptive forms and ideas in narrative; it is a game no longer answerable to the problem presented by chances and contingencies. Novels, biography, history, travel-books, accounts of scientific experiments—all literary forms with investments in the art of narrative—are struggling to find the equivalent of an unfolded tautology, a secondary writing fit to correct the errors of the first, and to make the singular recognizable. The options chosen by writers of fiction include the transformation of interruption from impediment into virtue, as in the sentimental novels of Sterne and Mackenzie; the internalizing of the reader as the auditor of small, discrete narratives (Sarah Fielding's *The Governess* and Sarah Scott's *Millenium Hall*); the thematization of failed pedagogy (Smollett's *Roderick Random* and Goldsmith's *Vicar of Wakefield*); and the presentation of fiction as a compendium of exploded or suspect narrative initiatives, such as *Tristram Shandy* and *Amelia*. The Cervantine novel, represented, for instance, by *Joseph Andrews* and *The Female Quixote*, directly confronts the difference between the conventions of romance (closely associated in *Joseph Andrews* with shaky theodicy), and the 'experienced train of events' which as yet has no means of representation proper to itself.

The fascinating exception is *Clarissa*, in which Richardson solves the problem of narrative continuity by handing it over to his characters, not entirely to his own satisfaction. He extends hospitality to the multitude of details which he believes contribute largely to the 'marks of genuineness' of fiction, and to its success as an exemplary medium. He refuses to construe length as a formal problem, believing that verisimilitude (with the occasional nudge from a footnote) and minuteness are largely the same thing, carrying an instructive message along with them that always justifies their bulk. Although *Clarissa* introduces Job into its narrative more clearly and less comically than any other novel of the mid-century, Richardson's imperturbable belief in the adequacy of his representational scheme never wavers, nor does he ever conceive the entry of Job to act as an interruption to the tragedy he delivers. His only problem seems to be with readers so moved by the multifarious injuries suffered by Clarissa, who has evolved her own mode of unfolding the tautology of identity into a writing on writing, that they want to redeem her. For his part, Richardson is determined to provide the world with a tragic and densely circumstantial auxiliary to the work of inculcating 'the highest and most important doctrines of Christianity'.[9] It is rather as if he were to paste a tract on patience to the backgammon board.

---

[9] Samuel Richardson, *Meditations upon the Sacred Books* (London, 1750), p. i.

Despite Richardson's confidence in his theodicean project, and the enormous success of his novels, the 1750s were dominated by an event which no summary truth or example was fit to account for, and which triggered a number of urgent enquiries into the limits of theodicy. This was the Lisbon earthquake of 1755, when as many as thirty thousand people were thought to have perished under fallen buildings and in the fire that followed the tremor. The scenes of devastation and cruelty are imagined by Voltaire in the fifth and sixth chapters of *Candide*. Leibniz had already explained these prodigies as the aftershocks of the work of creation, such as the intense heat needed to separate light from darkness, and the deluges acompanying the division of the earth from the ocean. They are the reverberations of the Word, the small material disorders incident to the accomplishment of great order.[10] The bishop of Llandaff calls disasters like these the authentic inscriptions of God's providence: 'When Catania, Lima, and Lisbon were severally destroyed by earthquakes, men with their wives, their sons, and their little ones, were swallowed up alive:—why do you not spurn, as spurious, the book of nature, in which this fact is certainly written?' The answer is that numberless defects 'conspire to make it impossible for us, worms of the earth! insects of an hour! completely to understand any one of its parts'.[11] William Warburton, a vociferous partisan of providential explanations, preached a sermon on the first public fast-day after the calamity at Lisbon, and made it a joint issue of providence and pedagogy: 'The teacher of Religion . . . will be naturally led to inculcate this truth, that general calamities, though events merely physical or civil, were . . . ordained by the Author of all nature to serve for the scourge of moral disorders'. To suppose otherwise is to assume 'a kind of incapacity in the Almighty to fit the natural to the moral system in such a manner as to make the former a ready instrument for the regulation of the latter'. The victims of these disasters are not necessarily more culpable than people in prosperous circumstances, but they function as 'exemplary warnings'.[12] They are crushed and burned not for breaking God's law, but that God's law might not be broken.

---

[10] G. W. Leibniz, *Theodicy*, trans. M. M. Huggard (London: Routledge and Kegan Paul, 1951), 277–8.

[11] Richard Watson, *An Apology for the Bible*, 9, 11. On earthquakes William King wrote, 'They are sometimes sent by a just and gracious God for the Punishment of Mankind; but often depend on other natural Causes, which . . . could not be removed without greater Damage to the whole'. *An Essay on the Origin of Evil*, 188.

[12] *The Works of William Warburton*, 12 vols. (London: T. Cadell and W. Davies, 1811), x. 2. Warburton's talent for cold comfort caused Sterne to write that, 'the Bishop of Glocester, who (to be sure) bears evils of this kind—so as no man ever bore 'em, has wrote me a congratulatory Letter thereupon—the Summ total of all wch is—That we bear the Sufferings of other people with great Philosophy—I only wish one could bear the excellencies of some people with the same Indifference'. *Letters of Laurence Sterne*, ed. Lewis Perry Curtis (Oxford: Clarendon Press, 1935; repr. 1965), 118.

J. C. D. Clark has drawn attention to the genre of earthquake sermons, which began with the panic of 1750 when London was shaken by tremors, and peaked five years later, when Sherlock sold 100,000 copies of a providentialist account of the Lisbon calamity, by way of indicating the power and extent of the Christian view of history in eighteenth-century Britain.[13] Whether the readership was actuated by approval of the explanation offered, or by an agitated desire for a personally reassuring account of the causes of mass destruction, it is impossible to say; but the links between the discussion of Lisbon and other Job-related speculations are made clear by Voltaire's entry into it. His poem on the earthquake, '*Poème sur le désastre de Lisbonne*' (1756), subtitled 'Examen de cet axiom, Tout est bien,' relentlessly particularizes real suffering and real victims, crying out amidst the ruins of their lives as they confront, as an extra intolerable evil, vindicators such as Leibniz and Warburton, who solemnly tell them to their faces that they are suffering for their sins, or in order that the eternal laws of God may be worked out. In impersonating this ghastly language of consolation, Voltaire (like the bishop of Llandaff) goes straight to Bildad, who, it will be remembered, consoles Job by telling him that man is a worm, and the son of man too (15: 6): 'Dieu vous voit du même œil que les vils vermisseaux | Dont vous serez la proie au fond de vos tombeaux'.[14] The victim replies like Job, 'Ma plainte est innocente, et mes cris légitimes', adding that comfort such as this would be better left unuttered: 'Ne me consolez point, vous aigrissez mes peines' (xii. 120). He is using Lisbon to dramatize the cruelty of the comforters, as he outlines explicitly in his article on Job in the *Dictionnaire Philosophique* (1764). There he describes them exhorting their friend to patience 'in a manner calculated to drive the mildest man to distraction',[15] for when he complains that his terrors overwhelm him like the ocean, they composedly reply that water is necessary to the life of things. Nothing could be less consoling, Voltaire suggests, than that trite axiom coming athwart a man in Job's predicament. Leibnizian providentialists are the comforters, Lisbon is Job.[16]

In *Candide* (1758) Voltaire tests theodicy repeatedly against the loose and flying particulars of unredeemed existence. Pangloss tries to reconcile the most outrageous events with programmatic citations of Leibniz

[13] J. C. D. Clark, *English Society 1688–1832* (Cambridge: Cambridge Univ. Press, 1985), 49, 171.

[14] Voltaire, 'Poème sur le désastre de Lisbonne', *Œuvres Complètes*, xii. 119.

[15] *Œuvres Complètes*, xxxi. 127.

[16] Horace Walpole mentions how the king of Portugal, reduced to indigence after the earthquake, wrote to his sister, the queen of Spain, like Job in the first stage of his distress: ' "Here I am, a king, without a capital, without subjects, without raiment" '. *Memoirs of King George II*, ed. John Brooke, 3 vols. (New Haven, Conn.: Yale Univ. Press, 1985), ii. 80.

concerning the necessity of evil in the best of worlds. Each contradiction or interruption of his case involves a specifically physical evil: the flogging of Candide, the ripping up of Cunégonde's belly, the loss of the old woman's buttock, and of course the destruction of Lisbon. It becomes hard to tell if the multiplied instances of ruptured flesh are new objects for his philosophy to work upon or the human litter left in the wake of its failure. Certainly Pangloss's consolations seem to take a gruesome toll on his own body, whose disfigurements represent a train of recklessly optimistic interpretations, all interrupted by successive evils. Not only is he half-hanged and dissected, but also hideously disfigured by the pox, 'tout couvert de pustules, les yeux morts, le bout du nez rongé, la bouche de travers, les dents noires, et parlant de la gorge, tourmenté d'une toux violente, et crachant une dent à chaque effort' ['all covered with scabs, his eyes were sunk in his head, the end of his nose was eaten off, his mouth drawn on one side, his teeth as black as coal, snuffling and coughing most violently, and every time he attempted to spit, out dropped a tooth'].[17]

Here is a figure who looks more like Job the more he talks like the comforters, his body as it were erupting in protest against the composure of the language of justification. The matter leaking through an integument that is no longer fit to contain it is, in this story, continuous with the content of the narrative, which bursts through every formal constraint, every principle of intelligibility, until the characters, scarred and printed with their various distresses, are collected within a garden where the immediate needs of their bodies can be satisfied, their tongues can fall silent and the narrative be brought to a non-necessary close. In the simple option of physical restoration, as opposed to the catalogue of miseries disconsolately endured in the pursuit of higher wisdom and a nobler conclusion, Candide finds the same thing Hume finds in backgammon; but (narratively speaking at least) it is an exiguous alternative based on an unnegotiable stand-off between physical circumstances and articulate explanations. Silently to cultivate one's garden, that is to say, is not the first sign of a self-referential practice, but a minimal resource on the other side of representation. It is a story completed in the deepest suspicion of the sacrifices required of individuals in order to get stories told. Unlike backgammon, the garden does not represent a 'new medium' between the chances of a physical ordeal and a way of representing or replaying chances in a consoling way. There is no unfolding of the tautology of Panglossian justification, just a refusal of it.

In the other great formal experiment with the narrative of interrup-

---

[17] *Candide ou l'optimisme*, ed. René Pomeau (Oxford: Voltaire Foundation, 1980), 128.

tion, *Rasselas* (1759), Johnson arrives at the same anticlimactic alternative to speculative schemes of happiness. In the conclusion which concludes nothing, the practical need to finish the tale undercuts all the philosophical suspense that brings it to that crisis. However, there is much less of the carnivalesque comedy of uncontainable flesh that overflows *Candide*. The embarrassment of philosophical positions is arrived at largely by discriminate testing of the evidence, not by the shocking juxtaposition of explanation with that which repels all explanation.

A different occasion is needed to bring Johnson face-to-face with the physical circumstantiality that mingles with the rejection of theodicy; and it is provided by Soame Jenyns's *Enquiry into the Nature and Origin of Evil* (1759). On two counts the confidence of Jenyns's work reminds Johnson of Pope's theodicy. First, its summary approach to human nature prompts him to think that neither man can have had much familiarity with 'the miseries they imagine thus easy to be borne'.[18] Secondly, their purview leaves them a good deal less impatient than Johnson with the trivializing of human suffering caused by comparing it with the Olympian composure of the higher beings who are responsible for it. The equal eye of Pope's God, who sees with undisturbed equanimity a hero perish and a sparrow fall, or a bubble and a world bursting together (*Essay on Man* i. 88–90), is not remote from the angle of vision of Jenyns's higher beings, who 'deceive, torment, or destroy us, for the ends only of their own pleasure or utility' (xiii. 240). In an effort to probe the limits of their 'sphere of observation' and the caprice it indulges, Johnson becomes witty. 'Many a merry bout have these frolick beings at the vicissitudes of an ague, and good sport it is to see a man tumble with an epilepsy, and revive and tumble again, and all this he knows not why' (xiii. 241). But it is a joke that acquires more intense personal pathos as Johnson elaborates it. He begins to terrify himself with the image of a human creature as puppet, danced for the amusement of a heartless and invisible audience, because he sees the creature as himself. So he returns obsessively to the conceit of theatricalized tribulation; but all the humour has drained out of it, leaving prominent only the awkwardness and unloveliness of the body: 'Putting us in agonies, to see our limbs quiver, torturing us to madness, that they may laugh at our vagaries' (xiii. 242). Here Johnson is discovering the impossibility of the stoicism claimed by Leibniz and Adam Smith for American Indians at the stake.

In finding that the justification of God leaves human beings sprawling

---

[18] Samuel Johnson, *Works*, 16 vols. (New York, 1903), xiii. 227.

in the undignified and painful particulars of a physical existence, Johnson arrives at the same point as Voltaire in *Candide*. The failure of theodicy is shown to be proportionate to a growing list of unconsoled infirmities. According to the three phases Luhmann sees as necessary for the renovation of a message, Voltaire and Johnson have managed only the first and second. They have refused the tautology of consolation by locating the paradox which requires that evil, in the form of detailed bodily complaints, be necessary to the production of universal good which cannot therefore be universal. But apart from recommending silence and a return to customary activity, they fail to unfold the tautology that narrative interruptions have loosened. In an earlier piece, *The Vanity of Human Wishes* (1749), Johnson shows how this unfolding might take place.

The poem begins with a grand tautology of observational competence. With extensive view the personification of Observation means to survey all humanity in order to show how universal is the folly of desiring those things that can do it no good: Observation will observe. But in between the opening and closing commands—to look and to be silent—the poet discovers that it isn't the worst desires of men and women which bring about their downfall, but their noblest attributes and purposes: their bravery, beauty, and intelligence. The life and death of Laud is often cited as the most poignant case because Johnson sees his own disappointments reflected in the bitterness of a scholarly career that ends on the scaffold. The identification is curiously insisted on in the transition made from the scene of Laud's decapitation ('And fatal Learning leads him to the block') to the allegory of his tomb, where the personifications of Art and Genius weep. Here the poet breaks his pedagogic link both with his audience, whom he charges with irremediable stupidity ('But hear his death, ye blockheads, hear and sleep'), and with observational competence, for Observation has now been replaced with two figures whose eyes, seeing none of the extensive views that support her confident judgements, fill blindly with tears. This far, the poem accomplishes the shift from the tautology of observational competence to the interruptive paradox of a brilliant scholar wrecked by success.

The unfolding of the tautology depends on the physical specificity of Laud's death and its punned relation to the inattentive audience. The insulting epithet 'blockheads' establishes a false, or more specifically a reverse, analogy between the subject of the verse and its readers. The story of a noble head fated to meet the block is met with the blankness of those who have blocks for heads. The grim work of the axe, which leaves only a block where the head should be, allegorizes the dangerous insensibility of those blockheads who authorize and witness such injustice. In its condensed form, then, the tautology unfolds as a maxim of the triumph of the observationally stupid over the observationally acute: 'Blockheads block heads'. It is a maxim that identifies the observational failure of the poem as a rupture between the text (including the fatally marked body of Laud) and its readers.[19] This rupture is further elaborated as the carved stone of the tomb, dividing the sculptured ideal readers (Art and Genius) from the unimprovable fools apostrophized by the poet. The *ressentiment* of the pun on blockheads can only be supposed to originate on the tomb's side, as it were, and to be energizing the conventional 'address' of the graveyard inscription to the reader or 'viator' which, as in the more hostile first-person epitaphs, emerges as a *tu quoque*: 'If I have a block for a head, so have you'.

Here is the redemptive possibility of a tautology unfolding as block on block. The victim seeks an alternative to the official or 'moral' narrative of suffering by imagining the worst possibility as a mode of representational practice (a combination in Johnson's mind between the formalities of tomb-inscription and the versatility of Thameside insult-trading). The practice requires another player or reader if it is to work; and, if it does work, it gives complaint in the unofficial and improbable kind of voice that is missing from the silences of *Candide* and *Rasselas*. This voice depends to a large degree on the responsiveness of the reader or audience to the redoubled element of the unfolded tautology—block on block, chance on chance, writing on writing, doing the done thing. In *The Vanity of Human Wishes* the poet is Laud's *go'el*, his redeeming reader, or his partner in a game of backgammon, because he knows how to reverberate 'blockhead!' from the tomb of the blocked head. The pun sidesteps the formal language of complaint in order to double up the expression of the other possible and particular case, in order that the outrageous paradox can return in a recognizable and articulate form. It issues a challenge to read actively outside the sparse economy of morally pointed tales. The accumulation of possibilities on the other side of that sententious poverty is what the pun both mourns and resurrects.[20]

---

[19] Compare the motto of the last *Rambler* (no. 208), translated from Diogenes Laertius: 'Be gone, ye blockheads, Heraclitus cries, | And leave my labours to the learned and the wise; | By wit, by knowledge, studious to be read, | I scorn the multitude, alive or dead'.

[20] It is interesting to contrast the placing of 'blocks' in Johnson's modifications of satire with Young's. In an early edition of *Night-Thoughts* Young included a poem in which he compares his satiric power to Perseus' Gorgon-shield. 'Many a Blockhead', he boasts, has he turned 'instantly to Stone'. 'Resignation and a *Postscript*,' bound with *The Complaint*, or *Night-Thoughts* (London: J. Dodsley, 1742). At the end of Lorenzo's meditation of the seventh night, he makes an epitaph for mortals who die without the prospect of a resurrection: 'All gone to rot in Chaos; or, to make | Their happy Transit into Blocks or Brutes' (176). The valuation of the block, or blockhead, is just the reverse of Johnson's, who identifies the person ignorant of these terrors as the one making the 'happy transit'.

5 *Political Principles and Patriotism*

Every days account shews more and more, in my opinion, the ill consequences of keeping good principles.

(Edmund Burke, *Letter to Depont*)

In his discussion of the scene of instruction from *She Stoops to Conquer*, Jerome Christenson notices that the price paid for the restraining coalition of idea and impression—not thinking of eating as you watch people eating, and so on—is the interruption of narrative. Hardcastle inducts his servants into a disinterested economy of self-discipline to which his own irresistible desire for telling war-stories is exorbitant. No sooner does he begin his tale than he is rudely interrupted by guests who take him for a tedious innkeeper who cannot hear talk without wanting to talk. Christenson interprets this as an incompatibility between the milder hegemony of the theatre of moral sentiments, and the tale of violence that cannot be anticipated or controlled by 'the self-regulation of the social composition' (Christenson, 36). The incompatibility is thematized and represented in the 1750s on a number of fronts, and indicates a more fundamental difference between the modes of self-government (whether these are construed as an ideology of representation or as a practice based upon unfolded tautologies) and the exemplary structure of Hardcastle's brand of 'old-fashioned' narrative, which aligns a string of details to a norm or point, such as the heroic sang-froid of soldiers. The stories of those for whom talking is simultaneously an idea and an impression are prone (like Sterne's) to circle back to the associations in which they began; or, if they become too ambitious, to interrupt themselves with the reminder that narrative depends as much upon its situation as its sentiment, point, or principle.

The vulnerability to interruption exhibited in political narratives of the mid-century is an index of the longevity of the desire for a principled and systematic discourse, comically exaggerated in Walter Shandy's various theories of state. It is the genius of patriotic eloquence, however, to have adapted the terms of superior principle—self-denial, civic humanism, unconditional love of country, and so on—to the situational pragmatics of daily political manoeuvring without ever being decisively interrupted and embarrassed by the charge of hypocrisy. Its success must be owing in part to the speed with which it allowed its exponents to dodge and outstrip adversaries committed to bulkier trains of ideas and less swiftly exchanged sets of values. The older distinctions between Whig and Tory relied on rival foundational narratives concerning a primordial establishment, a divine *fiat* or a social contract. Each story tried to overcome the interruptions caused by the telling of the other: the Grand Insurrection and the Glorious Revolution, representing the interruptions of Tory continuity; the rebellions of 1715 and 1745, representing attempted interruptions of Whig history. Even without such blatant obstructions, these political narratives easily get stuck on the contradictions of political practice, such as Crown patronage in the view of rigorous Whigs, or the expedient reshuffling of the rights of succession in the view of ardent Tories. There is inevitably an incompatibility between the summary truth that ought to guide the course of events, and the heterogeneity of the events themselves.

According to Hume this incompatibility is the measure of the difference between the spurious uniformity of party ideology and the real practice and brokerage of power. His astute critiques of the false deductions and generalizations needed to produce theodicies are easily adapted to the unsteady relations between the solemn justifications of political action and the situations in which the action must take place. He shows that the only rule arising from history is that violence, not a contract or a divine investiture, endows one person with power over others. All other rules and principles are factitious, and very likely to end in the same sort of violence that stained their origin, should they ever be realized. What Hume wishes to outline, therefore, is not the efficacy of principle in channelling events toward their end, but the usefulness of principle as a tactical item within a political situation. This is the lesson that the finest patriot orators already understand.

He offers an example when, like one of Job's comforters, he praises divine providence for peace and prosperity under the Hanovers and Walpole. 'This institution must certainly have been intended by that beneficent Being, who means the good of all his creatures,' he piously declares, although later in the same essay he argues that all new governments are 'formed by violence, and submitted to from necessity'.[1] This violence can only recur, he suggests, if people decide to act on their principles; such as Tories going to any lengths to secure a 'formal renunciation of our liberties, and an avowal of absolute monarchy' ('The Parties of Great Britain,' 70), and contractarian Whigs encourag-

---

[1] David Hume, 'Of the Original Contract', in *Essays Moral, Political, and Literary*, ed. Eugene F. Miller (Indianapolis Liberty Classics, 1987), 467, 475.

ing the sort of popular rage and disorder which 'arises from a principle' ('Of the Coalition of Parties,' 500). He concludes, 'There is no virtue or moral duty, but what may, with facility, be refined away, if we indulge a false philosophy, in sifting and scrutinizing it. . . . We may safely pronounce that many of the rules [established by law and philosophy] are uncertain, ambiguous, and arbitrary' ('The Original Contract,' 482). It is not providence, then, that keeps the peace, but a felicitous kind of hypocrisy, a necessary emptiness of profession which makes political compromises both possible and tolerable. Hume understands that it is this very distance between fact and value which socializes all selfish and extreme desires, fitting them to the common 'practice and opinion of all nations and all ages' ('Of the Original Contract,' 486).[2]

Hume identifies the unfolded tautology in its political dimension by exposing the self-evidence of political principles to the contradictions of the constitution, and then showing how these may be reconciled with the *rhetoric* of principle by those who have no intention of being bound by it. In his essay 'Of Eloquence' he points directly to Bolingbroke, the architect of the patriot opposition, as a master of this rhetoric, wielding 'a force and energy which our orators scarcely ever aim at' (108).[3] Hume has no time for politicians who mistake the system of party principle for truth; but he is ready to praise those willing to trade the certainties of party logic for the credit to be gained from the rhetorical improvement of a probable induction of particulars, and from the short-term narrativizations of immediate circumstances. The development of a credible oratory has the joint advantage of answering the private interests of politicians at the same time as defending the amenities of customary political practices. But in resituating practice within a sphere of rhetorical rather than observational competence, and in exchanging the priorities of principle, certainty, and historical symmetry for facticity, probability, and belief, Hume unfolds the tautology of political right as political right into a politics of politics: practical politics developed by the use of the language of politics. The pure form of political self-evidence as the enunciation of a party principle has been recruited as an instrument of day-to-day political activity. Like the tomb in *The Vanity of Human Wishes*, which makes its point by referring what it commemorates to the moment of its own reception by a reader, politicians of the mid-century make their greatest impact by citing immemorial principles so flamboyantly that they invite their audience to inspect the

[2] On the subtlety of Hume's negotiation of these extremes see M. A. Box, *The Suasive Art of David Hume* (Princeton, NJ: Princeton Univ. Press, 1987), 123; and John J. Richetti, *Philosophical Writing: Locke, Berkeley, Hume* (Cambridge, Mass.: Harvard Univ. Press, 1983), 30–44.

[3] For a recent discussion of the political implications of the essay, see Adam Potkay, 'Classical Eloquence and the Polite Style in the Age of Hume', *ECS* 25/1 (1991), 31–56.

very techniques being used to fascinate and capture it. This redoubtable turning of the discourse of politics into the practice of politics can only be expressed in a circular way. J. C. D. Clark summarizes the politicization of political language in the 1750s as follows: 'Political situations were the expression of men acting politically.... Political argument must be seen not just as argument about *politics* but as *political* in the sense of being rooted in, and intelligible only in close relation to, the tactical situation which occasioned it'.[4]

It is particularly interesting that Clark arranges his most forcible insights about the disappearance of party divisions and the exhaustion of narratives based on party slogans around an assessment of the narrative possibilities open to politicians under the administrations of Newcastle and Pitt. The loss of the *grands récits* of indefeasible right and original contract promotes, he argues, a provisional, local, and interruptive narrative style in political discourse, redesigned from moment to moment in order to facilitate the shifting agendas of a political scene unframed by any generally acknowledged principle.

Narrative is the mental language of political action appropriate to men who, in real situations, refrain from basing their actions on a generalized view of their predicament.... [It] involves a submission to the partial blindness dictated by events evolving successively in an order which, if a sequence, is not necessarily a pattern, and to which 'pattern' is ascribed in retrospect in a great variety of ways—the majority of which will enjoy no permanence.... Narrative reflects an order given to events by an actor in them in order to take the next step; it displays the coherence, the sequence, the significant selection which the actor adopts as the substitute explanation (no full, ideal explanation being attainable) of his own next action.   (17–18)

Under this regime of provisional narrativizations of political activity, both the politician and his chronicler, Clark argues, are obliged to allege the significance of discrete events as inaugurations or consummations of a 'plan' or series that never really existed. Each arrives at a judgement by means of inferring a plausible but necessarily abbreviated sequence from collocations of contingent particulars. Intelligibility is a matter of the successful distribution of these particulars within conventions and 'genres of conduct' (Clark, 19), so that tactics may get currency as part of a fiction of an orderly development. 'Such an argument is, of course, a circular one; but since the individual has no less "circular" an understanding of the priority of motivation and intentionality in his own case, the historian can do no more' (18).

---

[4] J. C. D. Clark, *The Dynamics of Change: The Crisis of the 1750s and English Party Systems* (Cambridge: Cambridge Univ. Press, 1982), 6, 16.

Undoubtedly the most convincing genre of conduct is that of the patriot, the isolated man of integrity patrolling the margins of the political scene, denouncing its corrupt ways until such time as the eloquence of his contempt gains him a place in it. When contemporary historians attempt the narrative of a patriot, they try to write it as if the integrity and the principles inseparable from professing patriotism were real moral acquirements operating with the force of precedents and laws, and not the inflections of a certain type of generic discourse. When it comes to including within this exemplary format the unfortunate divagations from principle of which all patriots seem to have been capable, there is no way to accommodate the paradox, and the effect is of a narrative so overburdened with unprocessable circumstances that it interrupts itself.

In his *Life of Bolingbroke*, for example, Goldsmith salutes the integrity of a man who at all times made his actions the measure of his beliefs: 'He was consonant with himself to the last, and those principles which he had all along avowed, he confirmed with his dying breath'.[5] Yet the biographer has already had to advert to excesses committed by Bolingbroke the rake ('remembered to this day' [9]), and two pages after praising his consistency he wrecks his theme with this judgement: 'His ambition ever aimed at the summit of power, and nothing seemed capable of satisfying his immoderate desires, but the liberty of governing all things without a rival' (110). Far from living in implicit obedience to the imperative laws of his own conscience and of the *patria* with whom he identifies, it appears that Bolingbroke acknowledges no rule but his own will, which he satisfies by exercising 'an elocution that was irresistible' (7).

The same contradiction between professed principle and manifest desire is discovered by Godwin in his life of Pitt. He wants to draw a picture of a modern Cato resolute in his opposition to Walpole's legacy of corruption, in order to immortalize the memory of a man whose consummate eloquence supported a 'singular disinterestedness' and an unrivalled 'purity of views'.[6] But Godwin is obliged to show that 'the voice of irresistible eloquence' was in service to no corpus of immutable principles, and acted instead as the instrument of 'a spirit of boundless ambition' that would sacrifice every principle in pursuit of its gratification. On the Opposition benches Pitt, the great Commoner, had attacked foreign subsidies and jobbery; in power he argued passionately

---

[5] Oliver Goldsmith, *The Life of Henry St. John, Viscount Bolingbroke* (London: T. Davies, 1770), 108.

[6] William Godwin, *The History of the Life of William Pitt, Earl of Chatham* (London: G. Kearsley, 1783), 68.

for subsidies and subsequently accepted a peerage and a pension. Ambition, Godwin confesses, 'was the only part, that heaven had left vulnerable about him; and [it] introduced a feebleness and versatility into his story, that must ever form the principal blemish of this immortal patriot' (150). Indeed, the harder Godwin looks at Pitt the more he begins to resemble Pope's Sir Balaam, being a man with strong city connections who makes uncomfortable appearances at court, and whose career dramatizes the incalculable nature of the link between private interest and the public good.

The reason the story of a patriot such as Pitt or Bolingbroke cannot be told without blemishes, versatilities, and discontinuities is, of course, that it is not the story of a patriot at all, but of someone using the language of patriotism in order to construct those provisional, day-to-day narratives described by Clark, and (as Hume observes of Bolingbroke) to acquire the power that a stunning delivery ensures. The objective of these narratives is not consistency of story-line or the primary truth of the principles associated with it, but power. The medium is oratory attuned to the sonorities, ironies, and hauteurs that flow from an assumption of moral superiority, but based in fact on the circular structure of the unfolded tautology and on the intimacies incident to first-person appeals to a second-person witness.

The question arises whether the instrumental political narrative suffers the same enfeeblement from compromised principles as the official biography. It would appear that none of Pitt's contemporaries were under the least illusion about his commitments. John Campbell explained of him that 'from Principle no Man can espouse his Interest as he has at different Times maintained . . . every Principle by which hitherto any Party has been distinguished'.[7] Laurence Sterne, an equivocal supporter of Pitt, plays with the new tactical range of the word *principle* Pitt has probed when he talks of resigning high places 'merely upon the principle that [one] could not not keep them'.[8] The Earl of Shelburne accounted for the splendour of Pitt's eloquence with the same dry wit: 'It gave him great advantages to serve a turn, by enabling him to change like lightning from one set of principles to another'.[9] Horace Walpole, however, advances the discussion of Pitt's versatility to a new plane when he says that Pitt himself was the best commentator on the variety of his displays of patriotic uniformity. 'Where he chiefly shone, was in

[7] John Hervey, *Miscellaneous Thoughts* (London, 1742), 5; and Campbell to Bute, 28 Nov. 1761, Bute Mss 1761/663, British Library; both cited in John Brewer, *Party Ideology and Popular Politics at the Accession of George III* (Cambridge: Cambridge Univ. Press, 1976), 242, 224.

[8] *A Sentimental Journey*, ed. Gardner D. Stout (Berkeley, Calif.: Univ. of California Press, 1967), 261.

[9] Cited in Clark, *The Dynamics of Change*, 283.

exposing his own conduct: having waded through the most notorious apostacy in politics, he treated it with an impudent confidence, that made all reflections upon him poor and spiritless, when worded by any other man.'[10] He indicates that Pitt's self-exposures did not in the least harm a rhetoric remarkable for its sublimity, soul, and grace (ii. 39), but rather were somehow necessary to it.

To account for the synthesis of Walpole's response to Pitt's 'versatility', it is necessary to detach the assessment of practice from the schema of principles from which it claims to be deduced, and to study it instead as a gamble for attention, involving the presentation of false antecedents which is renewed from moment to moment. The tracing of a genealogy of principle is not to be interpreted, therefore, as the unclouded crystallization of public spirit and private integrity, but as a sign of oratorical inspiration. Walpole singles out Pitt's speech on the Scottish magistracy as one of his finest performances—'one of his best worded and most spirited declamations for liberty' (ii. 39)—not because of the truth of what it invokes, but because of its affective appeal. In Walpole's paraphrase it is easy to see that Pitt's eloquence depends upon a fictionalization of the descent of principle, a brief history of what he knows never happened, rendered credible by the panache that grows with the factitious sublimity of the speech. Transposed by Walpole from the first person, this is how it reads:

When master principles are concerned, he dreaded accuracy of distinction: he feared that sort of reasoning; if you class everything, you will soon reduce everything into a particular; you will then lose great general maxims. . . . He would not recur for precedents to the diabolic divans of the second Charles and James—he did not date his principles of the liberty of this country from the Revolution: they are eternal rights; and when God said, *let justice be justice*, he made it independent.   (ii. 39)

It is plain at least to *readers* that Pitt is not recurring to precedent at all, rather to a non-existent divine performative that functions as the tautology which he is unfolding; namely, that justice lies in the hands of anyone with enough nerve to claim their own unprecedented agency as justice. Principle is the first thing he talks about but the last thing he means. Walpole reminds us that to experience the sublimity of this impudence we need to *hear* it, for it 'cannot be delivered adequately without his own language'.

[10] Horace Walpole, *Memoirs of King George II*, ed. John Brooke, 3 vols. (New Haven, Conn.: Yale Univ. Press, 1985), i. 64. In 1757, after obtaining extraordinary supplies for an army of observation to protect Hanover, Pitt stood up in the House and declared, 'That if any gentleman had a mind to attack his consistency, he hoped that he would take another day and not enter into personal altercations upon that great national question'. Cited in Jeremy Black, *Pitt the Elder* (Cambridge: Cambridge Univ. Press, 1992), 135.

Why, when all alibis of patriotic integrity are shown to be false, and the orator impudently holds out the instrument of his artifice, is the public still spellbound by his voice? If the answer is to conform to the Joban model, it will involve a tautology whose unfolding will prompt a powerful reflexivity, termed by Luhmann the selection of selections. In Pitt's case, if it can be limited to the two examples given by Walpole, the tautology is the self-evident proposition, justice is justice. It is affirmed in a performance whose devices and tricks are not concealed, but brandished and, on other occasions, explicitly drawn into the theme of his oratory. That this is not an abdication of rhetorical command but its very opposite indicates that Pitt's 'selection of selections' has culminated in the exposure of the gesture of exposure, a second-order act of coming clean that leaves nothing, strictly *nothing*, for an expert in versatility to discover. Everything is brought to the surface in a feat of vocal mastery that ruptures the division between inside and outside, and defeats the work of interpretation in the very unfolding of the tautology of exposed exposure. The pure surface of the event directs the attention not to a hidden truth about corruption, but to a fresh surface and a new opportunity for oratorical brilliance that will disarm once more the doctrinaire discourses of disclosure and finality. It is fully the equal of Demosthenes' oration on the crown, where the strength of the performance arises, according to Longinus, from the disintegration of a narrative of self-exposure and confession into something like an oath that transfixes each listener.[11]

Neither Pitt's eloquence nor Bolingbroke's, which Hume compares with the force and energy of Demosthenes', is weakened by the fissure between facts and values which is said to have opened up after the 'financial revolution', as J. G. A. Pocock terms it; it is actually enabled by it.[12] Bolingbroke presented in the *Craftsman Papers* the cardinal doctrine of the patriot, namely that the breach between modern corrupt practices and the historical reality of civic humanist principles could be bridged only by men of unimpeachable integrity whose private virtues

[11] Demosthenes' speech on the crown is discussed by Longinus in section 16 of *On the Sublime* trans. Smith, 47: 'By transferring what was naturally a Proof into a soaring Strain of the Sublime and the Pathetic, strengthened by such a solemn, such an unusual and reputable oath, he instills that Balm into their Minds, which heals every painful Reflexion'. The same speech is the theme of Bolingbroke's own estimate of Demosthenes, in which he praises the combination of eloquence and political acumen that allowed Demosthenes to unite the Greeks against Philip of Macedon. He pays no attention to the disastrous outcome of this initiative, only to the power of an orator who could lead a nation into ruin and then get away with it: 'Demosthenes used to compare eloquence to a weapon, aptly enough; for eloquence, like every other weapon, is of little use to the owner, unless he have the force and the skill to use it'. *Letters on the Spirit of Patriotism etc.* (A. Millar: London, 1752), 51. The best discussion of Pitt's oratory is to be found in Peter de Bolla, *Discourse of the Sublime* (Basil Blackwell: Oxford, 1989). See also Jonathan Lamb, 'The Subject of the Subject and the Sublimities of Self-Reference,' *HLQ* 56/2 (1993), 191–207.

[12] *The Machiavellian Moment* (Princeton, NJ: Univ. of Princeton Press, 1975), 482.

were available for the benefit of the public. He inserts into the public sphere the discourse of personal virtue not to affirm the exclusion of the man of integrity from public affairs, but to expedite his re-entry into them: 'They who engage in opposition, are under as great obligations to prepare themselves to controul, as they who serve the crown are under to prepare themselves to carry on, the administration'.[13] The stance of the patriot, whose pretence to an exclusion from power is the very means of gaining it, demands the elaboration of all the subaltern differences that distinguish the nobility of principled retirement from the interested pursuit of profit and power by public figures—land versus credit, militia versus standing army, the yeoman versus the pensioner, reason and experience versus imagination, knowledge versus belief. But in fact the elaboration of the difference is the very means of cancelling it, by ornamenting the rhetoric that will propel the virtuous private man into the public sphere. The rhetoric of that bid is perpetually renewed by differences which make a difference by contributing to the annihilation of the barrier which divides the principled remonstrances of an observant but isolated individual from the eloquence and power of a successful politician. When bargaining with the Duke of Newcastle in 1764, Pitt wrote to him, 'I have no disposition to quit the free condition of a man standing single; and daring to appeal to his country at large upon the soundness of his principles and the rectitude of his conduct' (cited in Black, 249). The inherent improbability of highly personal communication is elevated to the principle of political activity, and no servant of the public can credibly perform without it. What was at first proposed as a moral distinction and as a description of society ends up as an instrument for the production and negotiation of new power relations. The instrument works by impressing immediate sensations of pleasure upon the audience through the medium of the voice. What excites Walpole as he listens to Pitt is not power considered simply either as agility of political intervention or as rhetorical flair, but as the reciprocal movement of power and pleasure: the practice of politics as a branch of aesthetics.[14] The operations of imagination and belief—conventionally placed on the far side of truth and principle in the *topoi* of patriot rhetoric—are indistinguishable from the political facts they frame and reshape.

---

[13] *Letter on Patriotism*, 61. See Jurgen Habermas, *The Structural Transformation of the Public Sphere* (Cambridge, Mass.: MIT Press, 1989), 60–4.

[14] Walpole's observations on political figures exhibit the acuteness of a theatre critic, particularly when the art of speaking and political power part company—of George Lyttelton, for example: 'With the figure of a spectre, and the gesticulations of a puppet, he talked heroics through his nose, made declamations at a visit, and played at cards with scraps of history or sentences of Pindar' (*Memoirs*, i. 135).

One is obliged to interpret eighteenth-century politics as an unsuccessful struggle to surmount the contradiction between the value of integrity and the facts of power only if one is committed to narrating history as a series of exemplary positions deducible from acknowledged precedents and rules. The fiction of Bolingbroke's Gothic origins of the British constitution, and of Pitt's *fiat jus* at the beginning of the Scottish magistracy, indicate that politicians took myths of origin no more seriously than Hume. For Bolingbroke the evil genius who can do great hurt and the patriot who has coped with 'ambition, avarice, and despair itself' are alike in their transformations of political contingency into a narrative practice akin to Hume's backgammon:

When such a man forms a political scheme, and adjusts various and seemingly independent parts in it to one great design, he is transported by imagination. . . . It is here that the speculative philosopher's labor and pleasure end. But he, who speculates in order to *act*, goes on, and carries his scheme into execution. His labor continues, it varies, it increases; but so does his pleasure too. (*Letter on Patriotism*, 22, 29)

These are fictions designed to facilitate the chances of power shifts; they are histories which place the violence of usurpation, conquest, and other dismaying inaugurations of government in the light of a game or pastime; they are justifications of the pleasure of listening to an irresistible voice as it accomplishes such a usurpation.

Hayden White has suggested that aesthetics, specifically the aesthetics of the sublime, defines everything that exemplary or 'scientific' history cannot deal with. The unaccountable particularity of unredeemed practice—greed, fraud, terror, confusion, mass murder—blocks and interrupts the narrative of political economy and cultural continuity; but it provides an occasion for an intensity White calls inspiration, or the historical sublime.[15] He sees Burke as suppressing this sublime in his *Reflections upon the Revolution in France*, but Schiller he praises as a writer capable of Burke's sublime 'delight', responsive to the bizarre savageries punctuating the flow of supposedly systematic history. In the context of a quotation from Chateaubriand concerning the mute abjection with which victims greet the enormities inflicted on them, where he proposes the historian's role to be their avenger, White asks, 'Is this recovery of the historical sublime a necessary precondition for the production of a historiography of the sort that Chateaubriand conceived to be desirable in times of "abjection"? a historiography "charged with avenging the people"?' (79, 81). The drift of his question comes close to

[15] 'The Politics of Historical Interpretation', in Hayden White, *The Content of the Form* (Baltimore: Johns Hopkins Univ. Press, 1990), 71–4.

Bolingbroke's comparison of political geniuses with 'ministers of divine vengeance . . . or guardian angels' (*Letter on Patriotism*, 9).

White develops the parallel between the affective role of the sublime historian and the vindications of the patriot that Bolingbroke outlines. He does so in a way that resembles Job's plan for the voicing of his written complaint. The historian is to be the reader-redeemer of a violently interrupted narrative, doing it justice not by interpretative skill but by a species of literate excitement which will avenge the people by means of its intensity. The patriot merely combines the public role of historian with the private role of the afflicted individual in a manner that is both legible and audible.[16] Bolingbroke delivers himself as the second Cato struggling nobly with injustice, 'driven out of the forum, and dragged to prison' (*Letter on Patriotism*, 31). He speaks directly of himself in his *Reflections on Exile* where, says Goldsmith, 'he represents himself as suffering persecution, for having served his country with abilities and integrity'.[17] Pitt is a man of sorrows and acquainted with grief, immobilized by gout, pointed at by his enemies ('I am traduced, aspersed, calumniated from morning to night' [Walpole ii. 78]), but who is above all moved by the picture he paints of these tribulations. He incorporates into his political rhetoric the intensity of his response to his own plight. 'I am worn with constant fatigue, and broken-hearted with the wretched interior of our condition, worse than all the foreign ills that threaten us' (cited in Black, 157). Job imagines himself stuck in the silence of abjection, in need of a passionate historian to publish an account of his integrity and suffering that will avenge him by virtue of its irresistible rhetoric. He does not look for his redemption according to any solid principle of justice, but solely in the transmission of an uncoded flow of energy, whose source is the unfolding of a tautology (law is law into writing of writing) and whose dominion is proved again and again in the voice of the first person singular who makes that writing speak. When Job conceives this redeeming act as one that puts him face to face with God, he outlines in a trope the extent of the power to be usurped. So does Pitt when, broken and aspersed, he places himself at God's tribunal.

On the negative side, the historical sublime and patriot eloquence

---

[16] See e.g. Bolingbroke's *Letters on the Study and Use of History*, 2 vols. (A. Millar: London, 1752), 38, where the two offices of suffering and recording suffering are divided. The historian intervenes into the predicament of the good man whose name is scandalized by a villain: 'Yet we see historical justice executed, the name of one branded with infamy, and that of the other celebrated with panegeric [sic] to succeeding ages'.

[17] *The Life of Bolingbroke*, 82. 'Your name is hung up in the tables of proscription, and art joined to malice endeavours to make your best actions pass for crimes, and to stain your character'; *Reflections upon Exile in Letters on the Study and Use of History* (Alexander Murray: London, 1870), 165.

have in common with Job the silence of abjection, which is the impossibility of narrating a history of anguish and injustice that links them
intelligibly to self-evident principles of justice and equity. History which
is aestheticized because it cannot be domesticated within a framework of
accountable facts challenges the sublime historian with 'an apperception
of [its] meaninglessness' (White, 72). Nothing can be asserted of it which
is separable from the blockage of cognitive procedures. Job's terror is
the privation of all authority for knowing and stating his case beyond
the bare particulars comprising it. In order successfully to deploy the
rhetoric of complaint, the patriot, as Bolingbroke points out, has had to
know 'despair itself' (*Letter on Patriotism*, 22), and to have experienced
the isolation of defending an integrity no-one else will understand or
acknowledge. They have all been the victims of the improbability of
highly personal communication, and experimentally they discover that
they must cope with the loss of 'natural representation . . . the
impossiblity of a *representatio identitatis*' (Luhmann, 125). 'If I say I am
perfect, it shall also prove me perverse' (Job 9: 20). The benefit that
emerges from this impossibility is the switch in the referent of complaint
from integrity to power. The professions of misery and injustice have to
be emptied out, or brought to the surface; then (on the positive side) self-
deliverance takes place as an event, and wounded integrity can be
represented with a pressure and variety that sheer candour can never
rise to.

The speech of a patriot likewise generates a response to lonely and
troubled virtue that the thing itself could never excite, even in the breast
of the lonely and troubled complainant. To render what Pitt was fond of
calling 'this self-evident state of the thing'[18] in a forceful and pleasing
way, its tautologous form (justice is justice) must be unfolded as self-
reference (the exposure of exposure). Then the pathos of isolation and
the power of short-term narrative are aligned eventfully rather than
descriptively along the axis of the impression and the idea (eating and
talking of eating). The redoubling of the thing as the representation of
the thing gives it the appearance of being its own precedent and authority. Luhmann describes this state of affairs in the eighteenth century as
a chainwork of unfolded tautologies: 'Frivolity can only be enjoyed as
frivolity, feeling only as feeling, virtue only as virtue'.[19] And this is how
it comes out in contemporary accounts of things. When Bolingbroke
senses the vertiginous loss of principle his notion of genius entails, he

[18] Cited in John Brooke, *The Chatham Administration* (London, 1956), 88. See Mary Douglas,
'Self-Evidence', in *Implicit Meanings: Essays in Anthropology* (London: Routledge and Kegan Paul,
1975), 276–318.
[19] Niklas Luhmann, *Love as Passion: the Codification of Intimacy*, trans. Jeremy Gaines and Doris
Jones (Cambridge, Mass.: Harvard Univ. Press, 1986), 110.

makes it stand for the difference he means it to make: '*Genius* must be opposed to *genius*; *spirit* must be matched by *spirit*' (*Letter on Patriotism*, 22). Similarly, exposure must be equalled by exposure. Class divisions can be accounted for in the same way: 'The great patronise because they are great; the vulgar cavil because they are vulgar'.[20] When asked by the king if he could form a ministry, Henry Fox replied with this vulpine reservation, 'I must know, Sir, what means I shall have, or I cannot answer for what I cannot answer'.[21]

[20] Cited in Clark, *The Dynamics of Change*, 15.
[21] Walpole, *Memoirs*, ii. 30.

6   *The Job Controversy*

The brief foregoing account of the overlapping characteristics of a rhetoric of interruption, embracing personal integrity, historiography, and political eloquence within an unfolding of tautologies that is common both to eighteenth-century narratives and the book of Job, will help explain some of the passion invested in the conflicts over the interpretation of Job between the mid-1740s and the mid-1760s.[1] At the centre of this conflict stands William Warburton, an ambitious divine with strong political affiliations, both theoretical and practical, who wished to rescue Job for orthodoxy and systematic narrative. Although he was fussy enough about party differences to despise Hume as an atheistical Jacobite, 'a monster as rare with us as a hippogriff', he himself is vulnerable to the criticism Hume made of Socrates, namely, of raising Tory consequences on Whig foundations.[2] He sets out his commitment to Whig principles in an early piece on history, where he refers to 'the divine Right of *Tyranny* and *Slavery*' as one of the worst impostures an unenlightened mind can harbour. 'Publick Liberty', he affirms in the same essay, 'is the Balm of human Misery, the Quintessence of human Felicity, and the Recompence for the Loss of a Terrestrial Paradise.'[3] In his ambitious attempt to reconcile Revolution principles with the priority of the integrity of the state, *The Alliance between Church and State* (1736), he indicates the limits of his libertarian way of thinking. Although the end of civil society is the security of the 'temporal liberty and property of man' under an 'Original Compact' which is its only legitimate foundation, this does not include insuring dissenters and atheists against loss of employment, even though it guarantees the freedom of their consciences.[4] The 'Free Convention and Mutual Compact' which makes the interests of church and state interdependent decrees that people who refuse to profess the faith of the state religion be excluded from all areas of public administration (63).

---

[1] A brief but authoritative survey of the Job controversy is to be found in Martin C. Battestin, *The Providence of Wit* (Oxford: Clarendon Press, 1974), 197–200. Subsequent commentaries include Melvyn New, 'Sterne, Warburton, and the Burden of Exuberant Wit', *ECS* 15/3 (1982), 245–74; Everett Zimmerman, '*Tristram Shandy* and Narrative Representation', *The Eighteenth Century: Theory and Interpretation*, 28/2 (1987), 127–47; and Jonathan Lamb, 'The Job Controversy, Sterne, and the Question of Allegory', *ECS* 24 (1990), 1–19.

[2] Letter of 8 June 1755 in Francis Kilvert (ed.), *A Selection from Unpublished Papers of William Warburton*, 257; 'Of the Original Contract', 487.

[3] William Warburton, *A Critical and Philosophical Enquiry into the Causes of Prodigies and Miracles as related by Historians* (London: Thomas Corkett, 1728), 8, 27.

[4] *The Alliance between Church and State* (London: Fletcher Gyles, 1736), 21, 91.

To urge test-law as a necessary restraint rather than a punitive measure is no doubt disingenuous, but it is consistent with Warburton's commitment to plenary forms of thought. Outside the economy of the compact, in which every action is accountable in terms of a founding principle, there is only excess—the 'very violent Excesses' of the state of nature (*Church and State*, 7), 'the evil Diversity of Sects' (121), 'the luxuriancy of thought and sombrous rankness of expression' of meretricious eloquence.[5] The reason he cannot bear to think of the Lisbon earthquake as an accident operating outside the system of providence is that such an instance of pointless suffering would represent an excess of particulars that could never be processed or systematized, leaving us forlorn and weltering in 'the free rage of matters and motion in a ferment'.[6] Atheists such as Hume introduce the same threat of a casual material existence by reducing all phenomena to 'the particular fabric and structure of the minute parts of their own bodies', independent of all certain measures and standards.[7]

Warburton's horror of excess and loose particulars is violently stimulated whenever he thinks of Bolingbroke, the type of man 'who profess to love their country but despise the religion of it'. But it isn't Bolingbroke's hypocrisy that offends him; it is his persistent assimilation of facticity and excess to a patriot idealization of the individual in distress. The story Warburton wants to tell throughout his work is of providence working out its ends despite the manifest irregularity of 'the scene that ever and anon presents itself, being of distressed virtue, and prosperous wickedness'. The doctrine of future rewards and punishments is tirelessly invoked to fetch even the most heteroclite particular into a narrative system where nothing is surplus to the laws of its structure and the meaning it reveals. Bolingbroke, while confessing that everything shows the wisdom and power of God, observes that history is often composed of 'original, unprepared, single, and un-relative, events',[8] and that 'every thing does not shew in like manner the *justice* and *goodness* conformably to our ideas of these attributes in either [the physical world or the moral]' (*DLM* i. 319).[9] Warburton instructs those who might be misled by Bolingbroke's appeal to higher principles: 'Be pleased . . . to understand, that ATHEISM has ever endeavoured to support it self, on a FACT, which has indeed all the certainty that the

---

[5] *The Doctrine of Grace*, 2 vols. (London: A. Millar, 1763), i. 74.
[6] Letter of 9 Dec. 1755, in Kilvert (ed.), *A Selection*, 258.
[7] William Warburton and Richard Hurd, *Remarks on Mr David Hume's Essay on the Natural History of Religion* (London: M. Cooper, 1757), 12.
[8] *Letters on the Study and the Use of History* (London: A. Millar, 1752), 34.
[9] William Warburton, *The Divine Legation of Moses Demonstrated*, 3 vols. (London: Thomas Tegg, 1846).

evidence of sense can give it; namely the unequal distribution of moral *good* and *evil*'.[10] The loose and flying particulars which are the object of Bolingbroke's patriot reflections cohere, therefore, around the representation of the anomalous fact of unjustifiable suffering, to which he imparts probability by means of rhetoric attuned to his self-appointment as the exemplar and avenger of it. Warburton is quite specific in attacking these three aspects of Bolingbroke's position: the representation of distress, his intention to relieve it, and the rhetoric of his appeal to the public. 'He would have us turn from [the steddy light of the moral system] to contemplate that obscure, disturbed, and shifting scene, the actual state of vice and virtue, or misery and happiness, amongst men' (*DLM* i. 324). In this 'age of novelties' men like Bolingbroke are 'received with all the applause due to the inventors of the arts of life, or the deliverers of oppressed and injured nations' (*DLM* i. 78). But he is nothing but a 'Renegado Sophist' (*DLM* i. 323), and 'the very definition of a knave's raillery is a sophism' (*DLM* i. 86).

Warburton's reading of Job is designed to systematize its representation of suffering, to erase all the signs of excess and the facts of affliction that might attract a patriot interpretation, and to establish it as an allegorical representation (like the works of Homer and Virgil) of a 'SYSTEM OF POLITICS' (*DLM* i. 236). To do this he renarrativizes its interruptions so that they bear out the equity of providence; he restores the efficacy of the laws and principles which the hero denies; and he flattens the rhetoric of complaint in order that no false appeal to the passions may blind us to 'the great moral Instructions held out to us in the Book of Job'.[11] He achieves all of these aims by showing that it is a Hebrew version of his *Alliance of Church and State*, an allegory reinforcing the mutual dependence of religious and political priorities in post-exilic Jerusalem.

In deciding to read Job as an allegory of the plight of the Jews after the Babylonian captivity Warburton was doing nothing new. Already the debate between those committed to the historical reality of Job and those preferring a parabolical or allegorical interpretation had been aired on the Continent, with Albert Schultens leading the former and Jean Le Clerc standing up for the latter. What distinguished Warburton's choice of an allegorical reading was the size of his personal investment in it—no less than the whole argument of his life's work, *The Divine Legation of Moses Demonstrated* (1738–41). In this book, constantly under revision and attack and still unfinished when he died in 1779, he undertook to prove by a system of universal illustration that

---

[10] *A View of Lord Bolingbroke's Philosophy* (3rd edn.; London, 1756), 16.
[11] *A Critical and Philosophical Enquiry*, 122.

the foundation of the Jewish nation under Moses was unique because it did not depend on the prospect of a future state of rewards and punishments to enforce the people's obedience to the law. What it did depend on was a private assurance from God to Moses that an extraordinary providence would be dispensed to the nascent state, ensuring a strict and invariable correspondence between the degrees of obedience to the law and the level of present happiness. Warburton's positive evidence for this private treaty was nil, so he drew four inferences in support of it. The first was that all pagan social formations (Egyptian, Greek, Roman) did rely on the doctrine of a future state of rewards and punishments. The second was that this doctrine served a purely political purpose and was therefore only believed in by the lower orders, but not by those who promulgated and manipulated it. The third and most ingenious was that Moses' silence on the subject of the future state was itself proof of some hidden contract, otherwise there was no reason for him to forgo such a handy political tool. The fourth was that a common or unequal providence, promiscuously shedding its benefits and penalties on a people unrestrained by the prospect of a future state, would inevitably have provoked lawlessness and the early collapse of the Jewish nation.

The book of Job threatened every one of these inferences. If it could be shown that a set of dialogues explicitly concerned with the question of equal and unequal providence was written before the Mosaic jurisdiction, or even at the same time, then Moses' arrangement with God could no longer be assumed to be secret, since the comforters share it and publish it. The validity of the doctrine is questioned by Job with enough heat ('Wherefore do the wicked live, become old, yea, are mighty in power?' [21: 7]) to cast doubt on the extraordinary (that is, equal) providence that is supposed to have preserved the polity in the age of the patriarchs. What is more, a pre-Mosaic Job is outside the range of any published law or rule of conduct. William Worthington is not alone among Warburton's opponents in pointing out that Job (like Pitt) 'seems to argue on no fixed Principles' and is unrestrained by any faith in an afterlife.[12] 'There is the utmost probability,' argues Robert Lowth, Warburton's most redoubtable antagonist, 'of [Job's] having lived prior to the promulgation of the law.'[13] Besides, if the textual crux of the book, verses 19: 23–6, is read as Job's prophecy of the coming of Christ and the resurrection of the just, then all secrets are out: the Jews are

---

[12] William Worthington, *An Essay on Man's Redemption and a Dissertation on the Book of Job* (London, 1743), 484.

[13] *Lectures on the Sacred Poetry of the Hebrews*, trans. G. Gregory, 2 vols. (J. Johnson: London, 1782), ii. 353.

informed from the very first that a future state of rewards and punishments awaits them. As the prophecy is made at the height of Job's temporal calamities and derives a remedy solely from the quarter of eternity, it puts paid to the idea of an extraordinary providence not simply on the grounds of its manifest failure to work for Job, but more importantly in terms of the irrelevance of a merely temporal deliverance (what Warburton is insisting on as the point of the allegory, namely the reconstitution of the Jewish state) to all those whose faith directs them to believe in the superior equity of the hereafter. So Warburton must make 'a mere Modern of old Job' if his grand hypothesis is to survive.[14]

His method of modernizing Job is closely to inspect the surface of the narrative and dialogues for any anachronism, inconsistency, or omission that might give notice of an ulterior meaning and a later date of composition. For example, he turns up references to the law, phylacteries, and the destruction of Pharoah's host in the Red Sea, indicating a date of authorship some time after the flight out of Egypt. He finds the harsh behaviour of Job's comforters quite inconsistent with common ideas of friendship, and therefore suspects that they are signs of more occult hostility directed not at a historical Job but at the Jewish people as a whole: 'Who then will doubt but that . . . these three *friends* were the three capital enemies [of the Jews]: SANBALLAT, TOBIAH and GESHEM?' (*DLM* iii. 108). As for Job himself, a byword in other books of the scriptures both for devoutness (Ezekiel, 14: 14) and patience (James, 5: 11), he is so prone to blasphemous fits of exasperation that they can only be supposed to represent the sorrows of a nation, not of an individual. Job's speech about his redeemer and the latter day, therefore, is to be taken not as a prophecy of a future state but as a forecast of the end of his afflictions which the outcome of the story will confirm—an alleviation of temporal suffering that is to be applied to the Jews at Jerusalem merely as a promise of better days ahead, not as the Day of Judgement (*DLM* iii. 136). Job's sufferings are a dramatization of an epoch in Jewish history, carefully constructed by Ezra (the real author) from an ancient tradition by way of a national consolation.

Warburton's enterprise is perverse, but at least it is consistent with itself. In choosing to read Job as allegory, he assigns the moral import of the story to what it conceals, omits, or only obliquely represents, and none at all to the events, characters, and testimonies in it (*DLM* iii. 274 n. E). They are simply the signs of the story's real meaning or (which is pretty much the same thing) the vehicle of the bishop's hermeneutic

---

[14] J. Tillard, *A Reply to Mr. Warburton's Appendix* (London, 1742), 141.

brilliance. So he doesn't want to talk of impatience as impatience, or heroism as heroism—these are merely the formal devices impelling the fable to its point. Nor, interestingly, does he want to consider the theophany as a determining intervention of divine power (*DLM* iii. 82; 276 n. F), since it contributes nothing material towards the point of the allegory, which is the restoration of civil society via 'a continued allusion to the LAW' (*DLM* iii.91). In fact it is logically impossible for qualities such as integrity or power to be at issue in Warburton's Job, since they would constitute *representatio identitatis*, an exhibition of the thing itself for which allegory affords no place. Decidedly Warburton does not want to hear of an 'original' or 'genuine' Job whose history is here set down particular by particular—'a piece of Biography' (*DLM* iii. 286)—nor can he accommodate acts of God other than as poetical devices variegating the relation of the cover story to its hidden meaning. These would be in excess of the political and narrative economy, loose circumstances breaching the system of law, denominated as 'mere arbitrary CIPHERS' (*DLM* iii. 272). Such ciphers reduce the symmetry of allegory to the shapeless diarism of '*Anecdotes* and private *Memoirs*' (*A Critical Enquiry*, 58) or to the terror of an unaccountable force; they are Lisbon-like in the threat they present of matter and motion in excess of interpretable form.[15]

According to his hypothesis, Job must be a double character, a sort of involuntary hypocrite constantly representing something other than the sum of his conscious self-manifestations, and therefore incapable of ever saying anything that coincides with the real drift and meaning of his story. Even the most poignant of his complaints and the bitterest of his expostulations are recuperated as signs of events surrounding the exile of the Jewish people. He takes Job 13: 26 ('Thou writest bitter things against me, and makest me to possess the iniquities of my youth') and comments, 'This can be accounted for no otherwise than by understanding it of the PEOPLE: whose repeated iniquities on their first coming out of Egypt, were in every Age remembered, and punished on their Posterity' (*DLM* iii. 99). Pursuing this method of incorporating all particular circumstances into an outline of national restoration, Warburton is able to make even the most outrageous and enigmatic passages of Job conformable to the rules of the 'Jewish Oeconomy'. 'What are we then to think, but that there is a continued allusion to the LAW? in many places indeed so general, as not to be discovered without the assistance of those which are more particular' (*DLM* iii. 91). In this respect

---

[15] When Warburton dined with Pitt, the patriot famous for his self-exposures, his interpretive zeal led him to discover what Pitt had never hidden, namely, 'the marks of a restless disappointed ambition'. J. C. D. Clark, *The Dynamics of Change*, 221.

Warburton behaves exactly like the comforters in deeming Job to be a self-ignorant sign of the efficacy of the law.

Although he joins his opponents in praising the sublimity of Job, Warburton is far from convincing. His deliberate neglect of the pathos of Job's complaints is accompanied by a very perfunctory salute to the ornaments, figures, and luxuriant descriptions with which Ezra's re-written tale is supposedly replete. Everything he calls sublime is a copy or supplement of an inconsiderable original, for 'The truth is, the language of the time of the times of Job had its grandeur, its purity, and sublimities; but they were of that kind which the learned missionaries have observed in the languages of certain warrior-tribes in North America' (*DLM* iii. 93). The chief figure of this ancient poetry is the pleonasm (by which Warburton intends everything that Robert Lowth would call a parallelism), and it owes its prominence to the paucity of specific terms in languages of the east. 'When the speaker's phrase comes not up to his ideas (as in a scanty language it often will not) he endeavours of course to explain himself by a repetition of the thought in other words' (*DLM* ii. 212). Here Warburton is only slightly adjusting the argument he used in *The Doctrine of Grace* to show that the *fiat lux* was not as sublime as Longinus took it to be. There he argues that nothing is easier than for a Greek (or English) critic to mistake the simplicities and privative doublings of Hebrew verse for a remarkable feat of eloquence, merely on account of unfamiliarity with the endemic limitations of primitive poetry. Clearly he is intent on not making this mistake with Job, since every verse which might be construed as sublime is rendered accountable to the law and to the ends of an instructive discourse. There is no trope that does not in some way serve the ends of the allegory; and even the most moving passages of complaint are the result of Ezra polishing the roughness of the ancient Hebrew, as Ennius polishes the Latin of the iron age.

It is easy to imagine how the polemics against the *Divine Legation* transfer its three related positions on integrity, law, and eloquence from a political and allegorical economy to a much more interruptive and excessive narrative of personal affliction, where integrity is a key issue, more urgently appealed to in the absence of any law or tribunal, and where the complaints of the isolated and anguished man of probity achieve sublimity in the vacuum of all regulatory systems. They wish to explore 'that obscure, disturbed and shifting scene' of real unhappiness. This requires a joint bid for the ancient date of the poem and its historical and geographical accuracy, as opposed to Warburton's stress on its modernity and its recension of historical or traditional details of the real Job into the plot of a drama of national deliverance.

Warburton's opponents lay their emphasis squarely on the authenticity and the great age of the text, asserting that the story is not merely probable, but strictly and historically true: the story of Job is 'the most antient extant . . . neither Allegorical, nor properly Dramatic',[16] 'a plain and orderly relation of facts'.[17] 'This Narrative is Matter of Fact'.[18] 'The history of Job and his sufferings, is not a studied parable, or an artfully contrived drama; but a matter of real fact and truth'.[19] 'The question is a question of fact'.[20] In some cases the voice of the first person singular is distinctly heard, as when Leonard Chappelow takes the dialogues between Job and his comforters to be originally transcribed in Arabic from the spoken word; and when William Hawkins and Charles Peters argue that Job is the author of his own story.

Corresponding to the veridical groundwork of the poem is the theme of integrity, unevenly, discontinuously, and indeterminately argued throughout the dialogues. 'I have all along shown', explains Richard Grey in a rejoinder to Warburton's contemptuous handling of his treatment of Job (*DLM* iii. 278–84), 'that Job and his Friends are not arguing a speculative Question . . . but maintaining and denying a personal Accusation' (Grey, 87). 'The question debated', echoes Peters, defending his hero against the imputation of playing a 'double part' in an allegory, 'was not whether God's providence was equal or unequal, but whether Job was wicked' (Peters, 67). Job's speeches, William Worthington maintains, are 'the passionate Rhapsodies and Exclamations of a Man conscious of the Truth and goodness of his Cause'.[21] Robert Lowth, the most finished of the Hebrew scholars in the array against Warburton, lays it down as the chief postulate of his study of Job that 'the argument seems chiefly to relate to the piety and integrity of Job, and turns upon this point, whether he, who by the Divine Providence and visitation is so severely punished and afflicted, ought to be accounted pious and innocent' (*Lectures* ii. 377–8). His second postulate is that in exhibiting 'one constant state of things' the poem of Job 'contains no plot or action whatsoever', and cannot in any useful sense be termed a drama (*Lectures* ii. 393).

None of these critics is interested in the book of Job as theodicy, nor are they inclined to find in it a logical progression from one state of

---

[16] Robert Lowth, Letter to Warburton, 6 Sept. 1756, printed in the Appendix to *A Letter to the Author of The Divine Legation* (Oxford, 1756), 106.

[17] Charles Peters, *A Critical Dissertation on the Book of Job* (London, 1757), 94.

[18] Daniel Bellamy, *A Paraphrase on the Book of Job* (London, 1748), 11.

[19] Leonard Chappelow, *A Commentary on the Book of Job with a Paraphrase*, 2 vols. (London, 1752), p. xiv.

[20] Richard Parry, *A Defense of the Bishop of London's Interpretation of Job* (Northampton, 1760), 43.

[21] *An Essay on Man's Redemption and a Dissertation on the Book of Job* (London, 1743), 511.

affairs to another. They prefer to see it as a repetition of aggressive gestures which defines the relation of unregulated power to innocence, and in the course of which the language of instruction and admonishment comes into conflict with the language of plea and complaint. Like Kant, later in the century, they put the question of providence aside in order to concentrate on Job's difficulties in communicating his belief in the uprightness of his heart to people who have an interest in not finding his speeches credible. In doing so, they assign a purely negative valency to the law. Either it appears as a mockery in the mouths of the comforters; or it is a desideratum, a tribunal which is desperately invoked by Job, but which is unfortunately not yet available. Chappelow notices with what exasperation Job responds to 'the sententious maxims which his friends had delivered', and explains that in the case of Zophar particularly this is because he knows very well that the language of pious instruction is being used to make invective more virulent (*A Commentary*, 190, 154). Grey points out that although the speeches of the comforters abound in 'talk of religion, virtue, and providence, of God's wisdom, justice, and holiness in the government of the world' yet Job can appeal to none of these principles, and has no means of vindicating himself: 'What was left for the unhappy man to do?' (Grey, cited in *DLM* iii. 281–83). Although Lowth concedes that Job goes too far in his frustration at not being able to prosecute his case ('he seems virtually to charge God himself with some degree of injustice') he likewise casts Job as an innocent destitute of the means of proving he is so, whose excesses are to be placed to that account alone and not to some allegorical representation of the miseries of the Jews. In dating Job as a pre-Mosaic text he also disturbs the order of Warburton's 'Jewish OEconomy', for without the promulgation of any general God-given law, the definition of an offence and the mode of its punishment is entirely within the province of each patriarch's will, and has nothing at all to do with the civil magistrate. Before his fall Job was 'king Job', as Warburton paraphrases Lowth, 'a Monarch of the true stamp, by hereditary *right*' (*DLM* iii. 268).

Lowth would not dissent from Warburton's sarcastic inference, namely that the comforters enjoy the power they derive from Job's fall to goad to the limit someone who cannot retaliate. For Lowth, the poem 'is adapted in every respect to the incitement of terror' because behind the violence of the comforters' reproaches lies the boundless power of God (*Lectures* ii. 424). Apart from the proliferation of pointless particulars and the unrestrained coalitions of matter and motion that this sort of uneconomic argument is liable to generate, being based on the play of unlimited power and unjudgeable oppressions, it makes Warburton's

Whig blood boil to think of power operating in such an arbitrary fashion. Only Lowth, an Oxford Tory, could have produced it, a man 'brought up in the keen Atmosphere of WHOLESOME SEVERITIES, and early taught to distinguish between *de facto* and *de jure*', unlike his worthy antagonist who, rather too eagerly considering the drift of *The Alliance of Church and State*, claims to have been 'bred up in the Principles of Toleration' (*DLM* iii. 268–70). This is the background of John Towne's pamphlet deriving Lowth's Jacobitism from his dating of Job.[22] For Warburton the arbitrary phenomenon, whether found in the unregulated exercise of power, the presentation of ciphers, the profusion of particulars, or the untestable judgments of taste, is subversive of civil society as well as of full and accurate exegesis.[23] It is expressive of everything that is surplus to the economy of a settled jurisdiction.

However, it is in this arbitrary and unaccountable excess, flowing from the futility of Job's self-vindication, that the anti-Warburtonians locate the sublime. Peters and Worthington simply assume a necessary link between the grief of a great soul and the noble extravagance of its effusions. 'Passionate Rhapsodies and Exclamations' erupt naturally because 'human nature in those days was human nature . . . what the heart felt, the tongue uttered' (*A Dissertation on Job*, 511; *A Critical Dissertation*, 41). First Thomas Sherlock, then Lowth, take a rather more subtle view which harmonizes discrete historical particulars with figures of the sublime. Lowth then goes on to consider the relation of sublime eloquence to power specifically in terms of the critic's intervention as reader into the scene of complaint. Sherlock, the most eminent of Warburton's opponents until Robert Lowth took over the leadership of the quarrel, lays it down for a maxim that 'metaphors do not arise out of nothing'. 'There has to be a reason,' he argues, 'why "sealing up of stars, and darkening the sun", were expressions made use of to denote a state of sorrow and distress.'[24] Lowth's far-reaching contribution to biblical scholarship and literary criticism in the later eighteenth century depends on his dedication to the same principle: 'It is the first duty of a critic to remark the situation and habits of the author, the natural history of his country, and the scene of the poem' (*Lectures* i. 83). His

[22] 'When, therefore, the doctor censures the Bishop for distinguishing with Mr Locke between paternal and civil power, or for holding that political rule did not arise out of, or spring from, patriarchal authority, he plainly turns advocate against LOCKE. . . . The Doctor will be unable to disculpate himself from the Charge of maintaining the principle of PERSECUTION'. John Towne, *Remarks on Dr Lowth's Letter to the Bishop of Gloucester* (London: L. Davies and C. Reymers, 1766), 23, 77.

[23] Having judged eloquence to be 'accidental and arbitrary' he goes on to demand, 'What is SUBLIMITY', and to answer, 'the application of . . . images as arbitrary or casual connexions'. *Doctrine of Grace*, i. 69–70.

[24] *Four Dissertations* in *The Works of Bishop Sherlock*, 4 vols. (London, 1830), iv. 163.

decisive *Letter to the Author of the Divine Legation of Moses* (1765) not only authoritatively dates and locates the poem of Job, it also lays the groundwork of the taste for the sublime of Hebrew poetry by pointing to the ordinary and sometimes shocking circumstances out of which its finest figures are composed:

> I must observe . . . that the Hebrews employ more freely and more daringly that imagery in particular which is borrowed from the most obvious and familiar objects . . . It would be a tedious task to instance particularly with what embellishments of diction, derived from one low and trivial object, (as it may appear to some,) the barn or the threshing-floor, the sacred writers have contrived to add a lustre to the most sublime, and a force to the most important subjects.
>
> (i. 124, 148)

He shows how the imagery of death and hell is drawn directly from the architecture and ceremonies of Jewish sepulture (i. 159), how the anger of God is compared with dishwashing or drunken sleep (i. 155, 363), and even on one notorious occasion with defecation, 'Ah, I will ease me of mine adversaries' (Is. 1: 25).[25]

Nothing could be more loose, flying, and arbitrary than these low circumstances, for which Lowth gives two explanations: one to do with the original emotion which makes the imaging of the trivial or offensive detail necessary; the other to do with its reception as a figure of the sublime. In the ebullitions of strong feeling, he says, 'the mind . . . remains fixed upon the object that excited it; and while earnest to display it, is not satisfied with a plain and exact description, but adopts one agreeable to its own sensations' (i. 309). It makes a spontaneous selection from 'this immense universe of things' and out of that 'confused assemblage' (i. 116) concatenates images which stand as the immediate and necessary expression of its 'impulses, inflexions, perturbations, and secret emotions' (i. 368). Lowth quotes a good example of an offensively low image from Job 19: 22 (*Lectures* ii. 426), whose colloquial translation would read something like this: 'Why are you playing with me like God plays with me: why don't you just bugger me and have done with it?' Now the retort may simply stand as the symptom of perturbation, sublime because it is entirely natural. Alternatively, the shock of such an image operating specifically upon a reader may be accounted for as the effect of poet forcing his metaphors to be as inconsistent as possible in order to transfer to the reader some of the passion he is describing: 'Those sensible images . . . which in a literal sense would seem most remote from the object, and most unworthy of the Divine Majesty, are nevertheless, when used metaphorically, or in

---

[25] Robert Lowth, *Isaiah: A New Translation*, 2 vols. (George Caw: Edinburgh, 1807), ii. 19.

the way of comparison, by far the most sublime. Our understanding immediately rejects the literal sense . . . and rises to a contemplation which, though obscure, is yet grand and magnificent' (i. 362).[26]

The trouble with these two positions on the sublimity of ancient Hebrew verse is that they are both preoccupied by Warburton. The naïve account shows in the case of Job that integrity minus a legal framework of appeal produces an intensity of emotion which finds expression in naturally eloquent terms. This adds little to what Warburton says about the repetitions and refrains resulting from the constraints of scanty language and urgent passions; for even if the tongue Job spoke were replete with terms and synonyms, his difficulty in finding words apt for the frustration and terror he feels has the same effect of strangling his utterance and producing what Grey himself designates rather pleonastically as 'Repetition of the same Things over and over again' (*An Answer*, 53). If, as Grey goes on to claim, these repetitions are not entirely natural, but 'poetically amplified and exaggerated', so that a symptom of impatience becomes a sublime figure, then Warburton still holds his ground. If the sublimest metaphors depend upon a surface impropriety to hurl the mind upward to keener feelings and larger prospects, they merely abbreviate the structure of Job as allegory, where (Warburton repeatedly points out) inconsistencies—specifically the outrages of Job's impatience—are not to be understood as incidents in a personal narrative but signposts of a much broader 'history of providence'.

To make the case against Warburton stick, his adversaries need to develop their intuition that the sublime of Job combines a personal anguish with a poetic effect, without confounding the personal with the natural or the poetic with pure pathos. This requires that they look at Job as someone with an agenda not so different from Bolingbroke's and Pitt's. Finding his integrity weltering on the margins of the polity as the result of a power-play from which he has no legal exit nor from which he can draw any credible ethical judgment, he must take responsibility for his cries of innocence as rhetoric if he is to re-enter the negotiations of power as a probable agent. He therefore has to wield the question of integrity as an image, not as an unresolved personal dilemma; and around it he must elaborate a genre of complaint. To this extent he must be his own poet (it becomes clearer why Hawkins and Peters want to suggest this); and the effect he desires is not an enlargement of the

---

[26] The same sort of formulation is used for the image of God's enemies as his turds in Isaiah: 'When the idea is gross and offensive, as in this passage of Isaiah . . . we are immediately shocked at the application, the impropriety strikes us at once; and the mind casting about for something in the Divine Nature analogous to the image, lays hold on some great, obscure, vague idea, which she endeavours in vain to comprehend'. *Isaiah: A New Translation*, ii. 19.

reader's apprehensions of the nature of God but, quite simply, the reacquisition of power. He wants his words to enjoy the surplus which Bolingbroke identifies in Demosthenes' speeches as political force. In the lawless world of the poem the desire for power does not cease with the embarrassment of the comforters. We have to assume that the insulting terms Job attaches to notions and titles of divine power have the same practical, political purpose as the insults he lavishes on the vindicators of it. These rude associations are part of a gamble which, if successful, will far exceed any slender benefit to be got from throwing himself on the mercy of arbitrary might by making pathetic descriptions of his condition and spontaneous pleas for its alleviation; and it will be successful only if he can involve his audience (which he means to be wider than the narrow circle of his oppressors) in something like a rhetorical event, as opposed to the production of himself merely as spectacle. Rather than present his audience or his readership with an undisturbed opportunity for reflective and aesthetic pleasure at his expense, he must use his figures to reverse their initiative. His eloquence culminates, therefore, as the epitaph on the rock, his substitute for the anguished complaint that went unheard as anything but the accompaniment of viewable woe; and it is by means of that objectification of his sufferings that the reader will be compelled to assist in the operation of the *go'el*, the redeemer, or what Bolingbroke calls 'the minister of vengeance' (*Letter on Patriotism*, 9).

Basically there are two methods chosen by Warburton's opponents to advance this intuition. Both require close attention to the critical verses of the nineteenth chapter and effectually ignore the theophany and the restoration. The first is baldly to insist on the prophecy of redemption, with Christ as the vindicator of the innocent and the oppressed, and to resituate the question of providential equity at the Day of Judgement rather than in Jerusalem of 500 BCE. The other is to take as the image of the eventful point between spontaneity and poetry the rock on which Job wishes to write. The two verses of Job—'Oh, that my words were now written! oh, that they were printed in a book! That they were graven with an iron pen and lead in the rock for ever!'—exercise the minds of all those who want to establish some definite link between the circumstances of complaint and eloquence. Sherlock takes it to be some sort of literal monument (*Works* iv. 172); and Grey agrees that it is a 'standing Monument of his Appeal to God', an engraved epitaph (88). Peters compares these verses (19: 23–4) with 21: 29, 'Have ye not asked them that go by the way? and do ye not know their tokens?' observing, 'It was the custom of the ancients to bury near the high roads, and in the most public and conspicuous places; and to erect a pillar or monument over the dead, to preserve his memory' (240). The stone and the mode of inscribing it are a technology of vindication: the rock will endure until 'the time when my plea shall be heard' (as Sherlock paraphrases it). It marks, therefore, the junction between Job's shaping of his language and the audience's reception of it. It is both the hypostatization of the scene of reading and the materialization of his mode of successful rhetorical address.[27]

About the phases of its reception Lowth is most illuminating because he adjusts them to the terms of disgust he has already used in the context of the sublime. He takes the Senecan model of tragic sublimity—the good man struggling with adversity—and cites Aristotle's objections against such a scene as 'offensive and indecent rather than piteous or terrible' (*Lectures* ii. 215). Lowth's opinion is that nothing can more promptly move us to compassion than witnessing 'great virtue plunged into great misfortunes'. But, taking the hint again from Aristotle, Lowth shows that the motive for compassion (seeing those in torment who most resemble ourselves) produces feelings more turbulent than that conditional and decorous sympathy with affliction analysed by Adam Smith: they amount to terror. 'For if we fear for ourselves when we see moderate virtue in affliction, much more, surely, when a superior degree of it is in that state' (*Lectures* ii. 416). He goes on to assume that Aristotle's objection to this sort of spectacle arises not from anything inherently 'disgusting and detestable' in it, but from the damage it does to the cause of virtue; and he obviates it by pointing out that Job is far from being perfect and that terror, in the shape of fear of the Lord, is the lesson the poem inculcates.

This is to blur his insight into the event produced by the technology of vindication as a transferred, not a shared, feeling of terror. Terror, as Burke shows at length in his *Enquiry*, occurs as a graduated response to the modifications of power which constitute the sublime. Readers experience the terror of Job when they are shocked, disgusted, or otherwise moved by the images and figures Job is able to frame once he controls the means of production represented by the rock, i.e. the ability eloquently to talk of his plight. His vindication is not a description of it, however; that has never worked. He vindicates himself by shifting oppression from his quarter to the reader's. 'And as the imitation or

---

[27] Herder, an attentive reader both of Job and Lowth, insists on the importance of the link between the marker stone and the recovery of the means of vindication. The voice of the book, he says, 'comes forth in rough and interrupted tones from among the rocks . . . this ancient and venerable pyramid stands for the most part unimitated, as it is perhaps inimitable'. Rather more literally he points out that the book is for Job 'the perpetual memorial which he wished,—a monument more noble than brass, more durable than marble. It is written with deep impression upon the hearts of men'. J. G. Herder, *The Spirit of Hebrew Poetry*, trans. James Marsh, 2 vols. (Vermont: Edward Smith, 1833), i. 108–14.

delineation of the passions is the most perfect production of poetry, so by exciting them it most completely effects its purpose' (*Lectures* i. 369). Job's vindication occurs when other people speak aloud of perturbations that once were his. This transfer of passion is the proof both of his eloquence and his resumption of power.

The figure most instrumental in this shift of feelings and of voice is not the offensively circumstantial metaphor but, as Warburton rightly suspected, the pleonasm. His reason for defining it as a figure thriving only in the poorest of languages is his deep-seated aversion to eloquence, which escapes the government of the law by stifling reason and inflaming the passions with arbitrary images (*Doctrine of Grace* i. 75). His reflections on the *fiat lux* of Genesis, one of the favourite stations in the circuit of the Longinian sublime, indicate that he is well aware that the doubling of a phrase in the self-citing mode of performative utterance has an intoxicating effect on readers susceptible to 'that powerful weapon of *contorted words*' (*Doctrine of Grace* i. 80). As he aims to show that the *fiat lux* is composed of words of utmost simplicity, so he wants to insist that the pleonasm is a necessitous form of speech, far removed from the supererogations of Asiatic genius and sophistic ambition with which it is frequently associated. Just as briskly, Lowth insists on the opposite view. The pleonasm and other figures of repetition are the joint result of copiousness of thought and a large choice of words: 'If you reduce the Psalmist to a single term or two, you strike him dumb, be he never so fond of Pleonasm. . . . The Pleonastic Character must arise from the Abundance of parallel terms and phrases in the language'.[28] Repetition poetically amplified (according to Grey) becomes, for Lowth, that peculiarity of Hebrew prosody depending upon the division of an idea or a phrase that produces an echo or a mirror-image instead of a simple accumulation of the same words and ideas—'when equals refer to equals, and opposites to opposites' (*Lectures* i. 69). It is according precisely to this dynamic that Bolingbroke's genius is opposed to genius, and spirit matched with spirit (*Letter on Patriotism*, 22). That Lowth, like Warburton, had a shrewd idea of the relation of pleonasms to the power of eloquence is evident from his quotation of a verse from Job as a prime example of the expression and excitation of terror: 'He breaketh me up breach after breach' (Job 16: 14; *Lectures* i. 382). As far as he is concerned, the communication of terror and the manifestation of power share this intensity of a divided thought or expression, when attributes 'are considered in themselves simply and abstractedly, with no illustration or amplification from their operations and effects' (*Lectures* i. 353).

---

[28] *A Letter to the Author of the Divine Legation* (Oxford, 1765), 86.

Breach leads only to breach; hence the *fiat lux*, the talking of light and the production of light 'seems to proceed from the proper action and energy of the mind itself' and leaves the reader 'overwhelmed as it were in a boundless vortex' (*Lectures* i. 350, 353).

Chappelow is fascinated by the pleonasms in Job. In all his examples he notices a pattern of modulated differences accompanying the representation of the same word which disturbs any idea of identity. He takes Job's evocation of death, 'a land of darkness, as darkness itself', in order to point out that the four occurrences of the word 'darkness' in these two verses (10: 22) appear as 'a plain and manifest tautology' only in the translation. In the Hebrew three distinct synonyms are used in order to intensify Job's intuition of the nullity of death. Similarly, in the breaking of 'breach upon breach' and the talking of strength and the discovery of the strong, the inflected repetition of the word, or its variation through synonyms, 'makes the sense still more emphatical' to the point where words operate as 'an *echo* to the *sense*' (*A Commentary* i. 153; 244–6). Chappelow's feeling that the power of eloquence resides in the minute differences at work in what seems to be *representatio identitatis*— breach upon 'breach', darkness upon 'darkness', strength upon 'strength'—points in the same direction as Lowth's reflections on the parallel structure of powerful language, Warburton's on the instrumentality of contorted words, Bolingbroke's on the practice of patriot eloquence, and Pitt's on the effectiveness of an unfolded tautology.

In Herder's redaction of Lowth's argument, Alciphron, by bent a Warburtonian, wants to reject these intensities and their parallelisms as 'an everlasting tautology' (*Hebrew Poetry* i. 28); but his antagonist shows that it is a tautology unfolded in a practice of eloquence. Doubled phrases and parallelisms mark a twin cycle of energy coinciding with command and performance: 'We wish to see the effects of the command, and so the parallel form returns, in the command and its consequence: "He spake, and it was done; He commanded, and it stood fast" ' (*Hebrew Poetry* i. 43). It is the purest form in which 'power, boundless power', can be registered, because it requires no authentication from ancillary attributes (i. 52); that is to say, it is the language in which power is both properly expressed and exercised. In the mouth of the poet, the unfolded tautology indicates that he is become 'full of the God' (*Lectures* i. 366), with a voice of his own that is capable of dominating the audience because it acts upon its own authority.

The pleonasm coined from the word 'block' in Johnson's *Vanity of Human Wishes* likewise unfolds a tautology in a scene where, as in Job, a carved stone marks the juncture between a vindication and a reader about to come under its influence. In Johnson's poem the quadrature of the archbishop's tomb and its ignorant reader with the scholar's poem and its doubtful audience prevents 'blockhead' from turning into hopeless abuse, because it locates the insult at a materialized point of eventful interchange between an author and a reader. In the book of Job the same sort of quadrature covers all readerly options, anticipating and dramatizing them in the conflicts between Job and his comforters. The readers may give voice to the stone, and share the work of vindication, or repeat the objections of the comforters, and stand in opposition to whatever it is Job's epitaph proclaims.

The Warburtonian controversy neatly divides along these lines. With curious fidelity to the image of the tattoo, the inscription on the body which defines the passivity of the self-ignorant sign in the face of its antagonistic readers, Warburton counts himself as the least offensive of Job's interpreters: 'However, though I am . . . to be reckoned . . . among Job's Persecutors; yet I have this to say for myself, that the vexation I gave him was soon over. If I scribbled ten pages on his back, my Adversaries and his have made long furrows and scribbled ten thousand' (*DLM* iii. 273). In fact, Warburton does not seriously number himself among Job's comforters at all, but sees himself as another Job, hounded by those who want him isolated as an object of contempt: 'Job's *Life*, by means of the Devil and his false Friends, was an exercise of his Patience; and his *History*, by means of Criticism and his Commentators, has since been an exercise of ours' (ibid.). Although Peters ironically grants Warburton's text the same vindicating function as Job's rock ('a work which he intends (no doubt) should live as long as time itself shall last'), he and the others class him confidently among that vicious company of interpreters and false teachers called 'the WARBURTONIAN READERS', distinct from the other two categories of reader on account of being neither gentle nor learned.[29] Translating verse 19: 25 as, 'I know my vindicator living, and at the last over the dust he shall arise', Peters awards himself this task in respect of Job's integrity: 'I have also endeavoured to vindicate the character of Job . . . from those inconsistencies which are first without just grounds charged upon [him]' (*A Critical Dissertation*, 5). Grey likewise sees the controversy as a replay of the original—'Poor Job! what will these allegorical Reformers make of thee at last?' (*An Answer*, 63 n. w)—but he assigns himself the role of a second Job, not a vindicator. Like Job, he has taken all steps to avoid criticism and strife, but the bishop's reflections on his work have become so warm and abusive that he finds his own integrity called into question.

---

[29] [Charles Peters], *An Appendix to the Critical Dissertation on the Book of Job* (London, 1760), 36; see also [Anon], *Impartial Remarks upon the Preface of Dr. Warburton* (London: M. Cooper, 1758), 25.

'What a fine Condition, with all my Prudence and Precaution, I have brought myself,' he laments; then he quotes the verse he has paraphrased: 'Neither had I rest, neither was I quiet; yet trouble came' (*An Answer*, 10, 65). Grey therefore follows Job in looking for readerly vindication, making constant appeals to the gentle and learned reader and ending his defence by saying, 'The Reader will judge' (*An Answer*, 85, 92).

Although these identifications with character of Job and the dynamic of his struggle may in one sense be construed as the predictable wit of people writing polemic upon polemic, yet the intensity of their engagement over the text makes such parallels with it not just a plausible conceit but a necessary way of conceiving and carrying on the argument. The question of integrity involves its defenders; the question of interpretation enfolds the interpreter. They are operating without the authority of ancillary attributes, and are personally engaged in the continuity of 'Repetition of the same Things over and over again' (*An Answer*, 53). This engagement is testimony to the power of eloquence, particularly of the pleonasm or parallelized figure which accomplishes the transfer of power in the appropriately pleonastic form of a writing upon writing that exhibits a 'Job' upon Job. This power necessarily favours commentators hospitable to the particularity of complaint, 'that obscure, disturbed and shifting scene, the actual state of . . . misery and happiness among men' (*DLM* i. 324). It is correspondingly harsh with those who seek to repress the 'free rage' of matter and motion in favour of plenary schemes of providential allegory, or who objectify it only as the arbitrary judgement of a Jacobite critic. I have shown how Pope and Young turn into Jobs in private, involuntarily exhibiting in their personal frustration and pain all the weaknesses they have satirized in public, and which they have excised from their theodicies. Warburton is no exception. Beyond the range of wit, and in the privacy of retirement and despair, the parallel between Job and Warburton is played out to the limit, as Richard Hurd records in his short biography:

In the course of the year 1775, the loss of a favourite son and only child, who died of a consumption in his twentieth year, when every hope was springing up in the breast of a fond parent, to make amends, as it were, for his want of actual enjoyment—this sudden affliction, I say, oppressed him to that degree, as to put an end to his literary labours, and even amusements, at once. From that disastrous moment he lived on indeed for two or three years; but when he had settled his affairs . . . he took no concern in the ordinary occurrences of life, and grew so indifferent to every thing, that even his books and writings seemed, thenceforth, to be utterly disregarded by him. (*DLM* i. 56)

7 *Fictions of the Law*

The law—whether it exists, whether it works and, if it does, whether it works justly—is an important issue both for Job himself as vainly he seeks a judgement, and for the participants in the Job controversy, who divide over the issue of providential equity and the existence of a law fit to justify or punish Job's actions. Indeed, it is evident from the oppositional discourses bordering theodicy in the eighteenth century that the effectiveness of the law, in the broad sense of a universally applicable *a priori* rule or original principle, is at the heart of all debates concerning the relation of providence to the facts of human unhappiness.[1] Hume's graphic image of the failure of preceptual wisdom—the arm missing the object it meant to strike—applies to every scene of misery which is caused or exacerbated by a statute, regulation, maxim, or moral that can neither grasp nor answer it. As there is no scene more expressive of the agony caused by the law missing its aim than prisoners hopelessly pleading their case before an unyielding judge, or making a futile bid on the scaffold for the crowd's pity or approval, so there are few figures in the Bible more potently suggestive of such a scene than Job. This association has a long history. In his commentary John Calvin talks of Job as a man made to perform as a criminal, 'set here as it were upon a scaffold' so that his anguish ('heere now as rotten caryon . . . like to fall in peeces') may make him 'a gazing stocke and . . . an example and learning to others'.[2]

In eighteenth-century Britain there is an even stronger reason to associate the plight of Job with that of a condemned person. While Warburton was slugging it out with his opponents over the status of the law in Job, legal commentators were becoming equally agitated about criminal law, concerned either that it was failing badly in its duty of

---

[1] The close connections between providence and law are set out by William Paley as follows: 'By the satisfaction of justice, I mean the retribution of so much pain for so much guilt; which is the dispensation we expect at the hand of God, and which we are accustomed to consider as the order of things perfect justice dictates and requires'. *The Principles of Moral and Political Philosophy* (London: R. Faulder, 1785), 526. See also Henry Home, Lord Kames, *Historical Law-Tracts*, 2 vols. (Edinburgh: A. Millar, 1758), i. 2; Henry Fielding, *Examples of the Interposition of Providence in the Detection and Punishment of Murder* in *An Enquiry into the Causes of the late Increase in Robbers*, ed. Malvin R. Zirker (Connecticut: Wesleyan Univ. Press, 1988), 179–217; and Lincoln Faller, *Turned to Account* (Cambridge: Cambridge Univ. Press, 1987), 72–90.

[2] *Sermons of Master Iohn Calvin, upon the Booke of IOB*, trans. Arthur Golding (London, 1574), 50, 38.

protecting the rights of citizens against the depredations of thieves and robbers, or alarmed that its chief intention appeared to be, as William Eden suggested, the extirpation of the lower classes.[3] 'No civilised nation, that I know of,' complains Martin Madan, 'has to lament, as we have, the daily commission of the most dangerous and atrocious crimes'; and he quotes, as rather equivocal support for his grim estimate, the hyperbole in Johnson's translation of Juvenal's third satire: ' "Scarce can our fields, such crowds at Tyburn die, | With hemp the gallows and the fleet supply." '[4] Whether the law was working badly or too well, the theft of shop or stable goods worth more than five shillings, or the stealing of household goods of more than forty shillings' value, could cost thieves their lives. The period between 1749 and 1756 saw three hundred and six people executed, more than in any other comparable set of years in the century.[5] As a result of a Parliamentary Committee set up in 1751 to examine deficiencies in the criminal law, the Murder Act was passed in 1752, designed to control what was perceived by those in power to be an epidemic of profligacy, extravagance, and violence. One of its more terrifying provisions was to place the body of the executed criminal at the discretion of the judge, to be reserved either for public dissection at Surgeons' Hall, or to be exposed on the gibbet, i.e. tarred, hooped with iron, and suspended for as long as it would last, usually in the vicinity of the crime. Not for nothing was the Press-Yard of Newgate adorned with the Joban text, 'Man is born to Trouble as the Sparks fly upward'.[6] Both a proponent and an antagonist of such measures, Henry Fielding cited Machiavelli, 'Examples of Justice are more merciful than the unbounded Exercise of Pity'; but he also believed that 'We sacrifice the Lives of Men, not for the Reformation, but for the Diversion of the Populace'.[7]

On both sides of the Warburtonian controversy it was common to consider Job as someone subject to the various phases of trial and punishment, from arraignment to physical and spiritual torment. John Garnett, a Warburtonian committed to a view of Job as drama, decided it was composed 'upon forensic principles ... somewhat in the form, and manner, of a trial at the bar ... a judicial process, instituted against

---

[3] William Eden, *The Principles of Penal Law* (London, 1771), 306; cited in David Lieberman, *The Province of Legislation Determined: Legal Theory in Eighteenth-Century Britain* (Cambridge: Cambridge Univ. Press, 1989), 14.

[4] Martin Madan, *Thoughts on Executive Justice* (London: J. Dodsley, 1785), 4, 90.

[5] See Sir Samuel Romilly, *Observations on the Criminal Law in England* (London: T. Cadell and W. Davies, 1810), 8; and Peter Linebaugh, *The London Hanged: Crime and Civil Society in the Eighteenth Century* (Harmondsworth: Allen Lane, 1991).

[6] Anon., *The History of the Press-Yard* (London, 1717), 30; Job 5: 7.

[7] *An Enquiry into the Late Increase in Robbers*, ed. Malvin R. Zirker (Connecticut: Wesleyan Univ. Press, 1988), 167; *The Covent-Garden Journal*, 25 (28 March 1752), ed. Bertrand A. Goldgar (Connecticut: Wesleyan Univ. Press, 1988), 416.

Job'.[8] In Garnett's account Job acts as turbulent counsel for the Jews, while the comforters represent the prosecution, and God the judge, who finally gets Job to admit the weakness of his cause (12). Edward Young is drawn to this last parallel in order to explain the sublimity of God's rhetorical questions: 'It differs from other manner of reproof, as bidding a person execute himself, does from a common execution; for he that asks the guilty person a proper question, makes him, in effect, pass sentence on himself'.[9] On the far side of this rather Roman estimate of the theophany is Leonard Chappelow's paraphrase of Job 16: 10, which exploits the scene of the courtroom to emphasize the agony of a good man pleading before a tribunal that will not listen to him: 'I may compare myself to a poor Criminal, standing before a public Court of Judicature, charged with the most notorious offences; yet so far from being permitted to speak for himself, and in his own vindication, that if he does but make the least attempt towards it, he immediately receives the heavy stroke of some cruel, unmerciful hand'. He moves from the bar to the scaffold ('I am as it were raised to a superior eminence . . . there is no possibility of avoiding the reproaches of insolent scoffers') and into the horrors of a state execution: 'Every part belonging to me is in a state of separation' (*A Commentary*, ii. 125–6). Here Chappelow, writing in the same year as the Murder Act and making the same move as Calvin from the scaffold towards a scene of public physical disintegration, implies a negative judgement of the law to a point almost prophetic of the humiliations of dissection and gibbetting encouraged by the Murder Act. It is significant, in terms of the debates specifically on the topic of equity that come in the wake of this legislation, that he should make Job an example of the inverse ratio existing between the rigorous application of the law upon the body of the condemned and the opportunity for personal vindication.

Although his concern with Job begins some time after the Warburtonian controversy had died down, William Blake is especially alert to the connections both between mercy and minute particulars (which have likewise a distinct bearing on questions of equity), and between the Tyburn felon and Job.[10] All that stands between the English and 'howling victims of Law' are 'the Mutual Forgivenesses, the Minute Particulars'.[11] It was of course these particulars, exorbitant to the law and allegedly provoked by extravagance and profligacy, that were being aimed at in the Murder Act, preceded of course by the Black Act of 1723

[8] John Garnett, *A Dissertation on the Book of Job* (London, 1751), 1–2.

[9] Edward Young, *A Paraphrase on Part of the Book of Job* (London, 1719), sig. E2, n. 1.

[10] His pen and wash drawing, 'Job, his Wife and his Friends', is dated 1785.

[11] *Jerusalem*, ii. 18, 61; in David V. Erdman (ed.), *The Complete Poetry and Prose of William Blake* (Berkeley, Calif.: Univ. of California Press, 1982), 185.

which, together with its numerous modifications, increased the number of capital offences in the eighteenth century from 50 to 190[12]—the same particulars invoked by Tom Paine as 'A world of little cases [that] are continually arising which busy or affluent life knows not of, to open the first door to distress'.[13] In *Jerusalem* the proliferation of savage laws is mourned in language drawn directly from Job. Albion complains in familiar strains, 'O what is Life & what is Man? O what is Death? Wherefore | Are you my Children, natives in the Grave to where I go?' The answer comes in the following book when Albion sits down by Tyburn's brook, and up shoots a deadly tree: 'He named it Moral Virtue, and the Law'. Only after Albion enters into the spirit of Job 19: 26 ('I know that in my flesh I shall see God'), does 'the Sun set in Tyburns Brook where Victims howl & cry'.[14] The suppression of the minute particulars that might afford some relief to victims who howl and cry upon the scaffold is, as we have seen, a fundamental strategy in Warburton's treatment of Job. The unrestricted rage of matter and motion, and the imprecise herd of other possibilities that constitutes 'that obscure, disturbed and shifting scene, the actual state of . . . misery and happiness among men' (*DLM* i. 324), are what he wishes to pare away from the plenum disclosed by his interpretations. He finds in Job's anguish the same exemplary symmetry he finds in Lisbon's, where the ratio of pain to individual guilt is irrelevant to the universalizing message despatched by God to his creatures through the medium of disasters and prodigies.

I want to pick a way through some of the mid-century reflections and debates on the law towards the criminals themselves, in order to emphasize the parity between Job's case and the plight of victims of the law in so far as they are all positioned as examples, but resist their exemplary status by demanding alternative narratives of their plight. In this respect, Job and the law point directly at fiction, and specifically at novels about people in breach of the law.

Among writers about Job, those interested in little circumstances are also intrigued by related questions of integrity (the sufferer as individual rather than sign), by power (what degrees of resistance the individual can exert against it), by the part played in such resistance by rhetoric and probability (the interruptive fiction), and of course by *practice*, that versatility of response which subverts the government of prescription and precedent by the active unfolding of their tautologies. Contrariwise, those impatient with fugitive particulars prefer to see the suffering individual as a sign ignorant of its own meaning, an example to others

---

[12] Leon Radzinowicz, *A History of English Criminal Law* (London: Stevens and Sons, 1948), i. 4.
[13] *The Rights of Man* (Harmondsworth: Penguin, 1976), 268.
[14] *Jerusalem*, ed. Erdman, i. 12–13, 169; ii. 15, 174; iii. 16, 34, 213.

rather than a reason to itself; they justify the wisdom of divine power partly by calling all resistance to it blasphemous, and they reject fictions and other rhetorical adaptations of probability as destructive of the order of providence, the universality of whose principles and laws is declared in the dramatic felicity with which everything in the world is arranged, no matter how violently. Precisely the same divisions, accompanied by many of the same arguments, distinguish the two sides taking shape during the disputes over the theory and practice of British criminal law from the 1750s onwards. One finds equivalents of Warburtonian opinions in the work of Martin Madan, William Paley, and (eventually) Jeremy Bentham, who all concur in the belief that the laws ought to be clearly based on a ground of irrefutable principles, so that no-one may doubt their meaning or question the justice of their execution. Only under such an economy of law will the criminal who suffers its penalty also act as an example to all those who may have been tempted to commit the same crime. And if the necessary connection between rule and case, prescription and execution, is to be maintained, then there is no place for the consideration of the surplus particulars of individual cases, for these serve only to distract the law and to breach its coherence. To find a Lowthian parallel in this debate, one need go no further than the work of William Blackstone, the great apologist for common law. He sees it as the unwritten core and distinguishing character of British law, emerging (as opposed to written or statute law) from immemorial practice—real people engaging with real issues and passing on their discoveries to later generations by tradition and custom—and he finds that series disturbed only when ambitious framers of statutes try to improve upon it. He affords plenty of room for minute particulars and legal fictions in his vision of the law, whose precedents may at any time be suspended in favour of the judge's response to mitigating or aggravating circumstances. Judgement will then stand as a precedent (likewise suspendable if circumstances warrant) for subsequent judgements.

Bentham puts his objection to Blackstone succinctly. 'Right is the conformity to a rule, wrong the deviation from it.'[15] Where no rule is definitely established, and a fiction is made to substitute for it, then 'all is uncertainty, darkness, and confusion' (ibid.), for 'a fiction proves nothing; from that which is false you can only go on to that which is false.'[16] By *fiction* Bentham has in mind Blackstone's method of account-

---

[15] *Of Laws in General*, in *Collected Works*, ed. H. L. A. Hart (London: Athlone Press, 1970), iii. 184.

[16] Jeremy Bentham, *Theory of Fictions*, ed. C. K. Ogden (London: Routledge and Kegan Paul, 1932), 121.

ing for laws derived from customs which no-one can remember by supposing an originary scene that could never have taken place—a large plain, for instance, where people freely meet to elect the tallest and strongest of their number as leader, in whom they then invest certain rights in return for certain assurances. It is a way of talking of beginnings and founding principles where none really exist, 'a first institution . . . understood and implied [although] in no instance has it ever been formally expressed at the first institution of a state'.[17] All the laws Blackstone prefers are only identifiable in this fictional form because their real origin can never be located, and the reason for its imposition may not now be discernible (*Commentaries* i. 70).[18] All one can be assured of, from his point of view, is that they work.

Blackstone may be unable to frame an original scene of law that is not a fiction, but he is in no doubt about the source of the law; it is 'a rule of civil conduct prescribed by the supreme power in a state'. 'In laws,' he goes on (explaining why the scene of an original contract is only ever a fiction), 'we are obliged to act, without ourselves determining or promising any thing at all' (*Commentaries* i. 44–5). This power is unbounded by any principle of mutual obligation or self-limitation: 'The Measure of human Punishments must be determined by the Wisdom of the Sovereign Power, and not by any uniform universal Rule'.[19] There are, however, at least two occasions when this unlimited power of legislation, *jura summi imperii*, may be abridged. One is the reprieve, 'a temporary Suspension of the Judgment . . . *ex arbitrio judicis*' (*Analysis*, 130). The other is the application of the law of equity, 'which is thus defined by Grotius, "the correction of that, wherein the law (by reason of its universality) is deficient." . . . There should be somewhere a power vested of excepting those circumstances which (had they been foreseen) the legislator himself would have excepted' (*Commentaries* i. 61).

Before going any further it is worth stressing the aspects of this debate encountered previously in the context of suffering and consolation. The first is that those who stand up for principle do so on grounds that are Whiggish, contractarian, and inimical to arbitrary acts of power. Their metaphors tend to apply images of light to the universality of the rule, and images of darkness to obfuscating particularity, 'that obscure, dis-

[17] William Blackstone, *Commentaries on the Laws of England*, 4 vols. (Oxford: Clarendon Press, 1765), i. 47. See also J. G. A. Pocock, *The Ancient Constitution and the Feudal Law* (Cambridge: Cambridge Univ. Press, 1957; repr. 1987).

[18] See also Matthew Hale in praise of common law, so ingrained in the experience and practice of the British people, and so insensibly varied according to different times and circumstances, 'it were an endless and insuperable Business to carry up the English Laws to their several Springs and Heads . . . neither would it be of any Moment if it were done'. *The History of the Common Law of England* (London: J. Walthoe, 1713), 65.

[19] William Blackstone, *An Analysis of the Laws of England* (Oxford: Clarendon Press, 1756), 130.

turbed and shifting scene', 'the dark Chaos of Common Law'.[20] Those who defend custom incline, on the other hand, towards a Tory reliance upon the inevitable necessity of government derived from the competition for power, and on the value of tradition in structuring and distributing that power. For Blackstone, statute law—a writing that aims to put reason and principle back into common law, with disastrous results—is like the precept which fails to comfort those in affliction and wastes itself in air: Hume's swinging arm that misses its aim. His common law, on the other hand, unwritten except in the recorded juridical decisions it has given rise to, and 'founded upon immemorial usage' (*Analysis*, 3), is like backgammon, a remedy that works not because it appeals to reason but because it consists in doing what is customarily done, and thus in harmonizing arbitrary chances to the continuum of national and personal life. In other respects, too, Hume's associationist approach to history dovetails with Blackstone's view of the law. 'The only rule of government . . . is use and practice,' he asserts; for in searching for an immutable principle of action, 'how far back must we go?' ('Of the Coalition of Parties,' *Essays*, 495, 498). The 'uncertainty, darkness and confusion' deprecated by Bentham is, for Hume, a fog that never can be dissipated: the sciences of law and politics 'afford few rules, which will not admit of some exception, and which may not be controuled by fortune and accident. . . . We may safely pronounce, that many of the rules, there established, are uncertain, ambiguous, and arbitrary' ('Of the Original Contract', *Essays*, 477, 482). Burke, the vindicator of these sceptical positions concerning the doctrine of original contracts and natural rights, associates the authority of immemorial custom with 'the sober shade of the old obscurity' which swathes duties and prerogatives in the mist of indeterminate inaugurations: 'Dark and inscrutable are the ways by which we come into the world.'[21]

The fictions of the legitimate descent of power that Hume detects in party histories are, under a different guise, the genealogies of justice and the Gothic constitution used by Bolingbroke, Pitt, and Burke—*quasi*-genealogies, as Bentham would call them (*Of Laws in General* iii. 194), in deference to original principles and a regulatory economy that certainly was not operating in British criminal law at this time. What Bentham and others notice in these fictions, however, is the typically circular or tautologous character identified by Jonathan Clark in the

---

[20] Warburton, *DLM* i. 324; Bentham, *A Comment on the Commentaries*, in *Works*, ed. J. H. Burns and H. L. A. Hart (London: Athlone Press, 1977), iv. 198.
[21] Edmund Burke, *An Appeal from the New to the Old Whigs*, in *The Works of Edmund Burke*, ed. F. W. Rafferty, 6 vols. (Oxford: Oxford Univ. Press, 1928), v. 80, 93.

short-term political narratives of the 1750s. If Pitt's justice finds its authority in justice, and Bolingbroke's genius is the measure of genius, and Burke's darkness secures the obligatory sway of obligation, then the falsehoods identified by Bentham in common law spiral back to nothing but falsehoods; 'edict is heaped on edict, and volume upon volume'.[22] The law becomes 'a power with its own claims . . . the law was The Law'.[23] Luhmann notices that the law is particularly fertile in these tautologies of epigenesis, owing to its synthesis of normative and cognitive functions: 'Decisions are legally valid upon the basis of normative rules because normative rules are valid only when implemented by decisions'.[24] Even Blackstone himself talks of the difficulties of legal fictions in their strict sense (i.e. the adaptation of feudal laws to modern commercial practices) arising from 'their fictions and circuities'.[25] However, it is in these turnings of an arbitrary and capricious power that Job and eighteenth-century criminals find their point of resistance, an opportunity to interrupt and unfold its circularities into a short narrative or fiction that opposes to the threatening sameness of economy, theodicy, and sheer tautology a difference which makes a difference to an individual. Godwin puts it like this: 'There is no maxim clearer than this, Every case is a rule to itself. No action of any man was ever the same as any other action' (*Political Justice* ii. 766).

It was specifically the arbitrary suspensions of a power already arbitrary, identified by Blackstone in pardons and equity, that irked commentators most—'a *carte blanche* to the most outrageous tyranny' (*Theory of Fictions*, 121). According to Romilly's figures, roughly a third of all felons sentenced to hang were reprieved.[26] This was owing to the temptation many judges lay under (particularly those recently elevated to the bench) to find ways, as Blackstone puts it, 'to moderate the Rigor of both the Unwritten and Written Laws' (*Analysis*, 4). The office of equity in the matter of pardons lay in 'the selection of proper objects for capital punishment [according to] circumstances which, however easy to perceive in each particular case, after the crime is committed, it is impossible to enumerate or define beforehand'.[27] Thus if someone, such as Fielding's highwayman Anderson in *Tom Jones*, should be

---

[22] William Godwin, *An Enquiry concerning Political Justice*, 2 vols. (London: G. and J. Robinson, 1793), ii. 766.

[23] Douglas Hay, 'Property, Authority, and the Criminal Law', in *Albion's Fatal Tree*, ed. Peter Linebaugh *et al.* (New York: Pantheon Books, 1975), 33.

[24] Nicklas Luhmann, *Essays on Self-Reference* (New York: Columbia Univ. Press, 1990), 231.

[25] *Commentaries* iii.267; cited in David Lieberman, *The Province of Legislation*, 47.

[26] In the period 1749–56, 306 felons were hanged out of 428 sentenced: Romilly, *Observations*, 7. See also Peter King, 'Decision-makers and Decision-making in the English Criminal Law 1750–1800', *Historical Journal*, 27 (1984), 25–58.

[27] William Paley, *Principles of Moral and Political Philosophy*, 532; cited in Romilly, *Observations*, 30.

driven to crime by the suffering of his family, he might expect mercy; on the other hand, if he were to try unsuccessfully to avoid punishment by suborning witnesses, he could expect the worst. But the standard of good and bad circumstances was peculiar to each judge, who was not called upon to account for his measure of them. Mercy distributed in such an unsystematic fashion left the law looking extremely arbitrary and unpredictable: 'so many disproportions between crimes and punishments, such capricious distinctions of guilt, and such confusion of remissness and severity, as can scarcely be believed to have been produced by public wisdom'.[28] Romilly mentions the case of two accomplices tried for the same offence of robbing a hen-roost, but by different judges: the first sentenced to a short term of imprisonment, the second transported for life because he had the ill-luck to be tried by a man who, 'though of a very mild and indulgent disposition, had observed, or thought he had observed, that men who set out with stealing fowls, generally end by committing the most atrocious crimes' (Romilly, *Observations*, 18).

The first casualty of such latitude in the execution of the law is the loss of the value of hanged felons as examples, those 'useful social sacrifices'.[29] No one defended the severity of the laws against theft and robbery on the grounds that they were just, but appealed instead to their necessity in controlling crime by means of spectacle, since their solemn execution served as an awful warning to the rest of the community not to do what the victim had done. 'The wretches are led forth to suffer, and exhibit a spectacle to the beholders, too aweful and solemn for description' (Madan, *Thoughts*, 29). Just as Warburton consoles the inhabitants of Lisbon by telling them that they have been destroyed not for their sins alone but that sins might not be committed, so does Judge Burnett console the man condemned to death at Hertford assizes for horse-theft: 'Man, thou art not to be hanged only for stealing a horse, but that horses may not be stolen' (cited in Madan, *Thoughts*, 105). Ideally the delinquent's punishment looks both ways—towards the particular instance of the crime, and towards the general good of the community—and resolves the competing claims of public benefit and private right. By inclining too much to the particular case and showing mercy too frequently to individuals, Madan argues, following Fielding and Machiavelli, the community as a whole suffers. As far as Paley is concerned, it is a maxim of the law that 'Uniformity is of more importance than equity, in proportion as general uncertainty would be a

---

[28] Samuel Johnson, *Rambler*, 114.

[29] John D. Lyons, *Exemplum: the Rhetoric of Example in Early Modern France and Italy* (Princeton, NJ: Princeton Univ. Press, 1989), 54. He offers an extremely useful and short definition of exemplary punishment: 'A punishment is exemplary to the extent that it *exceeds* the requirements of the crime' (54).

great evil than particular injustice' (*Principles*, 511). When the maxim is not applied, then exemplary punishment starts to look like revenge, and the necessity which authorized it decays into the play of chances. With disgust Madan mentions that most criminals operate on odds of three-to-one against the chance of being hanged (92), although on the basis of Romilly's tables a bookmaker would have been foolish to give better than six-to-four on. The gang in *The Beggar's Opera* resolutely refer to death by hanging as ill-luck or misfortune.

Romilly's defence of exemplarity is much more subtle, humane, and paradoxical, and reintroduces the question of legal fiction. 'In the present system,' he says, 'the benefit of example is entirely lost, for the real cause of the convict's execution is not declared in his sentence, nor is it in any other mode published to the world. A man is publicly put to death. All that is told to the spectators of this tragedy, and to that part of the public who hear or read of it, is, that he stole a sheep . . . and they are left in total ignorance that the criminal produced upon his trial perjured witnesses to prove an alibi . . . and that it is for that aggravation of his crime that he suffers death' (*Observations*, 23). Romilly is locked in debate here with Paley over the office of equity in the extending of mercy. Both are agreed that it depends on the circumstances of particular cases—the basis, presumably, of Blake's association of minute particulars with acts of forgiveness in *Jerusalem*—but they differ about the status of these circumstances within the texts of the law. As far as Paley is concerned they have no place at all in writing, either in the drafting of the law, which cannot predict all the contingent particulars which may affect the execution of a sentence, nor in the publication of the sentence, nor in any narrative (such as Last Dying Words) of its execution. They are to remain solely within the purview of the judge. Romilly asks, 'Why cannot circumstances, which are of such a nature that they are to determine whether a man shall suffer death or not, be pointed out prospectively and particularised in written laws?' (*Observations*, 30). After all, they are critical particulars, 'upon which a criminal's life is to depend', and if they cannot be 'foreseen, fixed, or defined' then lives are being forfeited for the sake of a hidden law, the instrument of an unbounded juridical power (33) involved in what amounts to 'a practice which alters and almost supersedes the written law' (56).

Romilly is trying to negotiate the transfer from exemplary punishment to the sort of carefully calibrated scale of penalties and crimes proposed by Beccaria and Bentham; but he is poised, rather like one of Blackstone's legal fictions, between an ancient and a modern conception of the law: between the simple tautology of practice (the law is The Law) and an alternative he can only conceive of as a particularized narrative that constitutes an exception to all laws as they are presently received. He is trying to reconcile the language of prescription with that of description; and to do this he must isolate the dynamic of a moment we have already characterized as interruptive, and which he himself is aware of as precisely that. When a judge pauses to weigh the particulars of a case, he is embarked on a 'a practice which is in truth an almost continual suspension and interruption of the law' (43). He assumes, like most Benthamites and Warburtonians, that this fosters the use of arbitrary power;[30] but this is a juncture in all Joban scenarios when power becomes contestable and when a tautology may be unfolded.[31]

The question Romilly puts to Paley looks from one side like a simple Benthamite solution of turning the unwritten into the written; but from another it sounds like the resource always associated with practice, namely of overwriting the written until it is responsive to voice, chance, and the little circumstances of the immediate case. An indication of the volatility of the issue is provided by Bentham's exasperated remark on the contest between the written and the unwritten in law, between graphophonic order and phonographic confusion: 'Written law then is the law of those who can both speak and write: traditionary law, of those who can speak but can not write: customary law, of those who neither know how to write, nor how to speak. Written law is the law for civilized nations: traditionary law, for barbarians: customary law, for brutes' (*Of Laws in General* iii. 153).

A strong reason for supposing that Romilly means to recuperate equity in terms of a voice whose story cannot yet get told lies in one of the many brief stories he tells which otherwise would be suppressed by a process of law designed to reduce all cases to conformity with a written rule. Such stories glance descriptively towards those particulars of 'the sufferings and privations of the individual' (*Observations*, 24) which the law would prefer to elide in the course of its execution. Romilly tells it in the context of a case where a man was sentenced to death and duly hanged for stealing wine, and it sounds uncannily like a shortened version of the story of Martha Bilson, partly told and partly

---

[30] Douglas Hay argues vigorously that the law achieves a status beyond mere instrumentality at this point. Unequal enforcement 'gives the ideology of justice an integrity which no self-conscious manipulation alone could sustain'. 'Property, Authority, and the Criminal Law', 35.

[31] E. P. Thompson explores this state of affairs in the context of offering this qualification to standard Marxist analysis of the law as an instrument of class oppression: 'For if we say that existent class relations were mediated by the law, this is not the same thing as saying that the law was no more than those relations translated into other terms. . . . For class relations were expressed, not in any way one likes, but through the *forms of law.* . . . The rulers were, in serious senses, whether willingly or unwillingly, the prisoners of their own rhetoric . . . [and] some part of it at least was taken over as part of the rhetoric of the plebeian crowd'. *Whigs and Hunters* (Harmondsworth: Penguin, 1975), 262–3. See also Peter King, 'Decision-makers and Decision-making in the English Criminal Law 1750–1800', 57.

suppressed in John Warton's prescriptive exercise, *Death-bed Scenes and Pastoral Conversations*, and re-told in Chapter 1 of this book:

A man who being married, has concealed that fact, and having gained the affections of a virtuous woman, has persuaded her to become his wife, knowing at the same time that the truth cannot long be concealed, and that whenever disclosed it must plunge her into the deepest misery, and must have destroyed irretrievably all her prospects of happiness in life; has surely done that which better deserves the epithet of enormous crime, accompanied with heinous aggravation, than a butler who has stolen his master's wine. (*Observations*, 40)

The implication is that the texts of the law, if properly written, would be circumstantial tales of other possibilities like this one, where the pathos or aggravations of particular cases would not so much mitigate the interdictions of the law as define and inflect them. The story would be the law.

Although Madan's solution to the problem of exemplarity and mercy is simply to have the text of the law performed to the letter on the gallows, he is alive also to the place of narrative within the operation of the law. The story he prefers is the judge's speech to the condemned, the model for gallows-speeches and Last Dying Words, enumerating the details which makes their death inevitable:

Methinks I see him, with a countenance of solemn sorrow, adjusting the cap of judgement on his head.... He addresses, in the most pathetic terms, the consciences of the trembling criminals—he expatiates on the nature of their several offences.... He then vindicates the *mercy*, as well as the *severity* of the law, in making such examples, as shall not only protect the innocent from outrage and violence, but also deter others from bringing themselves to the same fatal and ignominious end. (*Thoughts*, 28)

Lincoln Faller has compiled an inventory of this kind of narrative, and Peter Linebaugh has carefully analysed the sequence in which it was produced.[32] Plainly this is not the narrative which interests Romilly, since it is merely an elaboration of the sentence, from which nothing significant may be gleaned. But the sort of story Madan detests has something in common with what Romilly desires. Macheath's career, as invented by Gay's beggar-poet, exhibiting the nonchalance and invulnerability of the expert criminal, has drawn many a young criminal into fatal emulation, according to Madan:

Lo! a reprieve comes—he is brought back in triumph—he joins his whores and old companions—he sings a lewd song to a merry tune; the conclusion of which

---

[32] See Faller, *Turned to Account*, and Peter Linebaugh, 'The Ordinary of Newgate and his Account', in J. S. Cockburn (ed.), *Crime in England 1550–1800*, 246–69; also his *The London Hanged: Crime and Civil Society in the Eighteenth Century* (Harmondsworth: Allen Lane, 1991).

contains a *maxim*, that we are to suppose to be the *marrow* of the whole, and which tends to eradicate every thoughtful impression. . . . Then, lest this *maxim* should be forgotten, or lose its effect on the profligate part of the audience—the same tune is often repeated to a jovial dance, performed by Macheath and his companions.   (*Thoughts*, 65)

History seems to bear Madan out. An accomplished pickpocket called Mary Young, hanged in 1740, went by the name of Jenny Diver. A highwayman called Isaac Darking modelled much of his career, including the mode of his capture, on Macheath's, and spent the time before his execution reading *The Beggar's Opera*.[33] To the bad example of Macheath Madan opposes the good one of George Barnwell, a hero reduced 'to the depth of woe, aggravated by all the circumstances which are naturally and judiciously introduced by the poet' (*Thoughts*, Appendix, 68). The circumstances of human suffering and privation that are here listed by Lillo that they may, at least in Madan's view, be placed safely beyond the pale in a form sufficiently 'aweful and solemn' to be certainly inimitable and only just describable, present a paradox which Madan cannot accommodate within his system of exemplarity, but which Gay's beggar-poet and Romilly seem able to handle well.

Paley has an inkling of it when he talks of the dilemma introduced into the execution of the law by contingencies:

If the laws be permitted to operate only upon the cases, which were actually contemplated by the law makers, they will always be found defective: if they be extended to every case . . . without any farther evidence of the intention of the legislature, we shall allow to the judges a liberty of applying the law, which will fall very little short of the power of making it.   (*Principles*, 518)

Although he has invoked the maxim that uniformity always overrides equity, just as the need for general certainty overrides the demands of particular justice, he sees, as Romilly sees, that circumstances must alter the execution of a law, and that although this interruption seems to throw power wholly into the hands of the judges, it also makes articulate the voice of someone about to suffer a particular injustice. Paley is adept at perching himself on this dilemma. He talks of the felon whose reformation is secured in the moment before death, 'but this is an experiment that from its nature cannot be repeated often' (*Principles*, 544). Strictly, it cannot be repeated at all. 'Novelty', as Kames says, 'wears off by reiteration of acts, that which at first is an extraordinary remedy, comes in time as a common practice' (*Tracts* i. 84).

This is the fallacy of exemplarity no less than of a particularized law.

[33] *The New Newgate Calendar*, 5 vols. (London, 1779), ii. 385; iv. 191–97.

If a case can be represented which is faithful to every little circumstance in it and also answerable to the demands of exemplarity, or even of representation in narrative, it is obliged to stand, rather like Job, as an unparalleled instance: something which has happened once but which is not supposed to happen again. Only by supposing the sufferings of a felon to be singular and unrepeatable can they justifiably be imposed: this is the doctine of negative exemplarity, where the sacrifice is justified by its efficacy as deterrent. And only by supposing degrees of malice and pain beyond the usual range of prediction will law-as-description prevent the unthought-of aggravating circumstances of crimes. But to represent such particulars in a standard narrative of repentance, such as Madan requires, and to make the victims perform to some degree as virtualities or allegorical personifications of the crime they are to die for ('You see in me what Sin is'[34]), to the point where Last Dying Words become a formula, is to moralize in a general and iterable form details whose rhetorical efficacy only ever lay in a unique and unparalleled pathos. That pathos cannot be repeatedly used in exemplary manner without emptying itself out and becoming (as Madan notices in Swift's satirical rewriting of Ebenezer Elliston's Last Dying Words) an implausible and hypocritical gesture, performed on cue.

In the celebrated case of Mary Blandy, hanged for poisoning her father but probably quite guiltless of intending to do so, her last dying words contain nothing of what she probably desperately wanted to say: 'Good People, take Warning by me to be on your Guard against the Sallies of any irregular Passion'.[35] So the full account is ventriloquized by Fielding in the same way that Martha Bilson's account is hypothesized by Romilly: 'Can [Cranston] bear to see her stript of her Innocence, of her Reputation, of every Thing lovely, every Thing which might have made her happy in herself, or recommended her to others; deserted and abandoned by the whole World, and exposed to Shame, Beggary, Disease, in a Word, to final Misery and Ruin!'.[36] However, once represented in this moving fashion, Mary Blandy's pathetic circumstances become recognizable as a 'genre of conduct', as Clark would put it: such woes are not unexampled, nor the language in which they are represented. Only if a description of anguish could function, as Romilly desires, as a prescription against its ever being experienced in the same manner again, could the full weight of her circumstances be felt. In the meantime, however, it is the ambiguous status of description within prescrip-

---

[34] The last words of the Reverend Robert Foulkes, hanged for child murder in 1679; cited in Lincoln Faller, *Turned to Account* (Cambridge: Cambridge Univ. Press, 1987), 61.
[35] *Miss Mary Blandy's own Account of the Affair between her and Mr Cranston* (London: A. Millar, 1752), 63.
[36] *The Covent-Garden Journal*, ed. Goldgar, 20 (1752), 139.

tion, and the shift of power involved in the equitable exception, that makes it a far more exciting and uncertain narrative to hear than the standard penitentiary address.

Gay's beggar-poet explores this border. At the end of *The Beggar's Opera* Macheath clearly rejects the options of exemplary public suffering held out to him by Lucy Lockit—'There is nothing moves one so much as a great man in distress'[37]—for feelings much more personal and less identifiable as a standard reaction to imminent death: 'O, cruel, cruel, cruel case! . . . Ah! must I die?' Pastoral collides here with tragedy just as the idioms of description and prescription fail to coalesce in the law. At the interruption of the player, the beggar-poet steps in to exercise the arbitrary power of poetic justice, in the same way that a judge makes room for equity in a special case, and on the same grounds—things have become too particular. The maxim of chances Macheath draws from the reprieve, and which Madan finds so infuriating, is perfectly apt for the unprecedented and generically unstable circumstances which have just been negotiated. However, these have now been combined (Madan is right about this) in a representation which is imitable because it invokes or establishes a genre of conduct whose essential character seems to be that it is unpredictable and imprescribable. Darking's Macheath, therefore, is no whining felon but a bold gambler, an unprecedented hero whom Darking will take for his precedent, and re-embody in his own practice even to the point of playing out the unreprieved ending. He re-activates the struggle between chance and necessity by turning Macheath's complaint ('Why haven't I better company upon Tyburn tree?') into his own story. In the process of narrativizing suffering, a howl is turned into a voice, but a voice that is already implicated in writing: it follows the pattern of imitable inimitability set by Job, the woe of whose writing in the rock is delivered in the voice and action of his delegate or reader.

Bentham has an explanation for this effect of iterable singularity in terms of one of common law's fictions. He is dealing with the role of judicial decisions, and tackling that circular and epigenetical relation to norm and decision which Luhmann says is typical of an autopoietic system such as the law. 'Like certain Tyrants of the earth, [Common Law] was never to shew itself in public: like them it was to make its existence perceivable only by means of its delegates: these judicial decisions, which whenever the Common Law was asked for were to be produced *corum populo*, as the ostensible images of its person, not as themselves being that thing, but as evidences of there being such a thing

---

[37] *The Beggar's Opera* in *Eighteenth-Century Plays* (London: Everyman, 1928), iii. 15, 157.

somewhere' (*A Comment*, 195). The decisions Romilly desiderates are the descriptions or narratives he wishes were constitutive of the law, so that it would never need to be suspended in catering for unexpected circumstances. These amount to delegates or ostensible images constructed so faithfully and in such detail that it would be impossible to tell the law from the case, the norm from the decision, the prescription from what is described, if it were not that the former would be written and the latter produced *viva voce*. To the degree that this perfect match is impossible, the entry of arbitrary power into the relation of the norm to decision becomes necessary, along with the accompaniment of a narrative of suffering; but it seems that whatever is to achieve a narrative status above the deadening repetitions of Last Dying Words and exemplary pain will need delegation and substitution if the integrity of silent victims is to be vindicated. Without a mediating image of themselves that will allow them, like leviathan or the inscribed rock in the book of Job, to take a view of their judges, they will be lost.

Goldsmith's *Vicar of Wakefield* sets the rewriting of Job squarely within Paley's dilemma concerning the defectiveness of general laws and the unlegislatable multitude of particulars, by combining the problems of pedagogy—specifically of *docta ignorantia*—with a critique of the law's defects. In the space that opens up between rules and experiences that are for the most part painful, delegates and ostensible images propose themselves as the sole means of vindication; and the success of the vindication depends on the invention of fictions. The story the vicar tries to tell is an exemplary one. Indeed, he operates as his own comforter, pestering himself at every disappointment and affliction with summary explanations of why it has occurred; but rather than advancing the story, these consolations interrupt and thwart it.

There are six of these interruptions, each the result of attempted recuperation of theodicy in the form of a lesson concerning the value of affliction. In the first, the wealthy benefactor, whose principles are inscribed in the epitaph to his wife hanging on the chimney-piece, is ardently propounding these very principles when news reaches him of the loss of the major part of his fortune. Reduced by his banker's fraud to the level of a yeoman farmer, the vicar attaches himself so closely to the principles of the smallholder that he thinks himself happier, in spite of his narrower circumstances, than the greatest monarch upon earth, especially when seated by the fireside with his family about him. No sooner has he articulated this principle of the value of rural simplicity and innocence, than his hearth is blighted by Olivia's elopement with Squire Thornhill, and the yeoman is transformed into the bereft father. Even in that condition his heart finds occasion to dilate in happiness as he brings the prodigal back to her family and thinks of 'the many fond things I had to say'. No sooner has his heart dilated with the thought of saying things about his happiness than his house bursts into flames, and the vicar is transformed into a homeless debtor and an invalid.[38] His heart still vindicates its dignity, notwithstanding the disappearance of all material supports; in fact it vindicates itself so loudly and in such an articulate and principled manner that Squire Thornhill gets irritated and has the vicar packed off to prison, where he turns himself to the theory and practice of prison reform. When he finds his second daughter has been abducted and his eldest son is about to be condemned to death for murder, he transcends this last attempt to forge a principle of earthly community and public instruction, and finally relies on the grand promise of futurity, 'when our bliss shall be unutterable' (*Works* iv. 163). As this bliss is as yet notional and therefore as utterable as all the vicar's other rules and principles concerning relative happiness, it is vulnerable to the same overturning his previous instructions have provoked. This occurs with his restoration to worldly wealth. Transcendence, together with all his other lessons concerning the value of privation, are put on the back burner: irregular gaiety supervenes and the vicar acknowledges that the most intense feelings, whether of joy or misery, are unspeakable.

This pattern of principled utterance alternating with comic and deflating interruption is often interpreted, both in the spheres of theodicy and law, as a gradual process of theoretical refinement in the light of experience. Martin Battestin, the first to view the novel in the context of the Job controversy, shows how it illustrates, in words he takes from Daniel Bellamy, ' "a steady reliance upon the assurances [God] has vouchsafed us of a future state, in which shall finally be adjusted all the seeming inequalities of the present" '.[39] Taking a more Lowthian view, James Lehmann argues that it is the passion of Job, not his submissiveness, that the vicar acquires, a detheologized receptiveness to 'the sublime of love'; but it is still a lesson learned, teaching us 'how we ought to act and to know ourselves in this [world]'.[40] The current revival of interest in eighteenth-century penology has invited recent commentators to pay close attention to chapters 26 and 27 of *The Vicar of Wakefield*, where Primrose announces his principles of civil society and criminal justice. Alain Morvain outlines the elements of patriarchal and monarchical thought that make these positions recognizably

---

[38] *Collected Works of Oliver Goldsmith*, ed. Arthur Friedman, 5 vols. (Oxford: Clarendon Press, 1966), iv. 130.
[39] Martin C. Battestin, *The Providence of Wit* (Oxford: Clarendon Press, 1974), 212.
[40] James H. Lehmann, '*The Vicar of Wakefield*: Goldsmith's Sublime, Oriental Job', *ELH* (1985), 46 (1979), 97–121.

Blackstonian.[41] The plea of equity in the matter of horse-stealing, for example, ('It is far better that two men should live, than that one man should ride' [iv. 150]) is manifestly anti-exemplary in emphasizing the disproportion between the offence and its penalty. And the idealization of Saxon law and of sovereign power that accompanies the discourse of equity shows precisely on what grounds the vicar is ready to oppose the rich man's exploitation of the law in the defence of property, by appealing to the arbitrary power of judgement that coincides with Romilly's interruptions and suspensions of a defective statute. The reformist note struck by the vicar is understood by Morvain to be inconsistent with the critique of the oppressive sides of Whig libertarianism, but John Bender sees this as the authentic point of cultural emergence in the novel, where the Benthamite programme makes its way not altogether consciously through the interruptions in the instructional-providential format of the story, which now gets retold 'by a different set of rules—those of the penitentiary'.[42]

All of these interpretations retrieve a portion of the vicar's doctrine as sound by taking one of his six interruptions seriously as the peak of his learning curve. But if one assumes that five are nothing but repetitions of the same mistaken pedagogic gesture, there seems little good reason for saving the sixth as an exception. If one were to assume instead that the book moves towards a suspension of all precepts and rules in a moment of intensity during which people become 'perfectly refractory and ungovernable,' but which also constitutes the point of vantage from which the tale may begin to be told by the ostensible image of the vicar's person ('supposed to be written by HIMSELF'), then one has something like the model of the common law in action at the moment equity is invoked, when all *a priori* rules are ineffective, and there is nothing but the circumstances of the case to influence an all-powerful judge and to provoke a delegated narrative of suffering.[43] This crisis is promoted by two characters, Burchell and Jenkinson, who have in common a desire to be the vicar's delegate by becoming his son-in-law, who jointly

[41] Alain Morvain, 'Pouvoir, justice et châtiment dans *The Vicar of Wakefield*', in J.-F. Gournay (ed.), *La justice en Angleterre du 16me au 19me siècles* (Lille: Presses universitaires de Lille, 1988), 107–25.

[42] John Bender, 'Prison Reform and the Sentence of Narration in *The Vicar of Wakefield*,' in Felicity Nussbaum and Laura Brown (eds.), *The New Eighteenth Century* (New York: Methuen, 1987), 180. In fact, the vicar's programme sounds more like Paley's outline for reformatory incarceration. He favours 'the *separate* confinement of prisoners', and, 'If labour be exacted, I would leave the whole or a portion of the profit to the prisoner's use . . . that his subsistence . . . may be proportioned to his diligence' (*Principles of Moral and Political Philosophy*, 545).

[43] See Michèle Plaisant, 'Le juste, le justicier, la justice poétique dans *The Vicar of Wakefield*,' in *Bulletin de la société d'études anglo-americaines des 17e et 18e siècles*, 24 (1987), 72–3, where she considers the resemblances between endings of *The Beggar's Opera* and Goldsmith's novel. In *Citizen of the World*, Letter 80, Lien Chi Altangi praises the spirit of mercy that 'breathes through the laws of England, which some erroneously endeavour to suppress'. *Works* ii. 327.

embarrass the one person trying to uphold the rule of law (Squire Thornhill), and who have experience of inventing fictions on the basis not of instructive experience and the law but of excessive and illicit desires.

Burchell's limitless and hopeless sympathy with the circumstances of distress have reduced him to a point even more extreme than the Man in Black, on whom he is evidently based, who at least *pretends* the laws providing for the poor are adequate (*Citizen of the World*, Letter 26, *Works* ii. 109–11). Burchell can invoke no principle or rule of action to ease his fits of extravagant sympathy, only agonized promises he will be unable to fulfil. His solution is to impersonate the object of his eager benevolence and to vindicate the poor by the ruse of appearing as a poor man; and it is clear that the disguise is crucial to the construction of his narrative, which fails as soon as it slips from the impersonated third to the authentic first person: 'He now therefore found that such friends as benefits had gathered round him, were little estimable: he now found that a man's own heart must be ever given to gain that of another. I now found, that—that—I forget what I was going to observe' (*Works* iv. 30). As long as he can skirt the amnesia of that self-interruption, Burchell can tell a story of himself that makes him sound very much like a patriot in the Pitt or Bolingbroke mould: a man who rescues virtue in distress while restoring his fortunes and fulfilling his ambitions, one 'to whom senates listened with applause, and whom party heard with conviction, who was the friend of his country, but loyal to his king' (iv. 168). It is as well to remember that Goldsmith has analyzed the contradictions of such a figure in his *Life of Bolingbroke*, where the facts of rejection and exile, combined with the careful representation of an integrity defined by that rejection, are necessary ingredients in the plot or narrative of the vindication of the oppressed patriot that will also satisfy a boundless and unprincipled ambition. This isn't the same as pretending to be what you're not, so much as setting up a manipulable margin of representational play between the authentic 'I' and the third person whom the 'I' perceives itself through, or which claims the 'I'.

This explains the uneasy punctuality of Jenkinson's impersonation of himself as sage. His narrating and narrated selves are too close to each other to make it convenient to tell a fiction about his lies, so he deceives the vicar with the 'truth' of the story we are reading, namely, that all human doctrines are dross and that books will never teach the world (*Works* iv. 73–4). This oblique defence of the practice of fiction against the larger cognitive claims of learned ignorance, performed while gulling the vicar with an idealized picture of himself as a great teacher, culminates in a strange and equivocal exchange between Jenkinson and Moses on the subject of storytelling. 'I suppose', cries Moses, his faith in doctrine undimmed, 'that the narrative of such a life as yours must be extremely instructive and amusing'. 'Not much of either', returns Jenkinson, 'those relations which describe the tricks and vices only of mankind, by increasing our suspicion in life, retard our success. The traveller that distrusts every person he meets, and turns back upon the appearance of every man that looks like a robber, seldom arrives in time at his journey's end' (iv. 147). Whom is he talking of? At first he seems to be saying something like this: 'We confidence tricksters wouldn't survive if all our secrets were out'. Then he switches from a first- to a third-person view in order to suggest that instruction serves no useful purpose among honest people, who would be more frequently impeded by heeding maxims of suspicion than by the occasional tricks played upon them as they unsuspiciously yet profitably commit themselves to practice. The very awkwardness of the construction of Jenkinson's answer indicates how much he is himself committed to practice, hence his difficulty in handling any proposition which looks like a summarizing rule or instruction. He is saying in both the first and third persons what he has already said as the venerable patriarch, which is that stories cannot teach; but he cannot baldly state it. He needs still to be tricky on the subject of tricks; while talking of fiction he must not desert the end of fiction, which is to some extent to deceive, and to some extent to number up those little circumstances which fit no rule or law. Without this performative option his throbbing head, like Burchell's feeling heart, would find no relief.

Between them Burchell and Jenkinson free the vicar from the tautologies of moral and legal self-evidence, located by Lien Chi Altangi in modern tragedies as this sort of formula: 'We should not resist heaven's will, for in resisting heaven's will, heaven's will is resisted' (*Citizen of the World*, Letter 97, *Works* ii. 389). Such circuities sound very like the dialectical trick played by the Squire on Moses—'I hope you'll not deny that whatever is, is' (*Works* iv. 42)—which in turn summarizes the principle of self-evidence the vicar founds his tottering theodicy upon, and which arms the imperatives of the oppressive laws the Squire uses to justify his vile behaviour.

In terms of the law, Goldsmith points to the difference between tautologized authority and the common law in his essay in *The Bee*, 'Custom and Laws Compared'. A defence of those who rely on the unwritten law of custom—'the traditional observance of the practice of their forefathers' (*Works* i. 484)—against jurisconsults such as Montesquieu, who measure the level of civilization in a state by the number of its written laws, the piece reverses the judgement Bentham will make on writing and the voice by defining written law as 'voluminous, perplexed, and indeterminate' (i. 485), compared with the simplicity of custom, which 'as it executes itself, must be necessarily superior to written laws in this respect, which are to be executed by another' (i. 486). To execute itself, the law must stand in the circular relation of norm to decision that Bentham calls the fiction of delegation and of the ostensible image, a relation analogous to that of first- and third-person narrative in fictions of practice. This is not blankly to assert that being is being, the law is the law, or I am I, but to recognize agency and justice in a descriptive act that is not possible without supposing a difference between the thing itself and its ostensible image: a fictional practice, in short.

Goldsmith gives an account of how this works in his oriental tale of Asem the Manhater, ceremoniously entitled 'The Proceedings of Providence Vindicated'. Asem is a forerunner of the Man in Black and Burchell, someone who has retired from the world after squandering his fortune in acts of reckless benevolence. Bewailing his links with a species which is the only 'solecism in nature; the only monster in the creation', he is about to drown himself in the glassy lake beneath his mountain cave when a magical figure arrives to vindicate Asem's justice, integrity, and misery. He does so by conducting him to the centre of the lake, where Asem beholds a perfect world, its inhabitants incapable of the vices that have made him despair. But its perfection is really an exiguous, loveless, and inappetent existence, barren of the enjoyments that arise from desire and excess—the motives of Asem's benevolence and misery in the first place, just as they are of Burchell's. When he wakes from what turns out to have been a trance, he finds himself poised above the lake, frozen in the gesture of self-destruction: he takes himself off to the city and acquires an enormous fortune, which he thoroughly enjoys spending.

The parallels with Burchell's story are close. The lake represents the gap that opens up between a forlorn 'I' and its narratable subject, with the vindicator functioning as a bridge not only between the suffering subject and its image, but also as conductor of the subject, reconstituted by its encounter with itself, towards the worldly success that inevitably follows such self-recognition. In *The Vicar of Wakefield*, ironically, it is not misanthropy but theodicy itself which presents to the narrator of the tale, the alleged 'I', the allure of mistaken deductions from a dubious rule of self-restraint. The function of the genius is supplied by Burchell and Jenkinson, who have either experienced or understand the necessity of the transition from learned ignorance to practice, and who lead the vicar to the stage from which he can begin to narrate his story. The degree of suppositional difference between the vicar and 'himself' corresponds to the difference between Burchell's 'I' and 'he', between Asem's first-person misery and third-person vision, between weeping convicts and the non-penitentiary stories that can be told of them, between Job, forbidden 'to speak for himself . . . in his own vindication', and the reading out loud of a memorial stone that will redeem him in the end. All these differences are negotiated by an ostensible image of the sufferer—*go'el*, delegate, genius, poetic judge, patriot politician, or fatherly son-in-law—who acts in a way similar to the common-law judge who invokes, along with equity, the host of particulars which laws cannot cope with, but which fiction can render in a credible though not necessarily continuous form.

In William Godwin's *Things as they are; or, The Adventures of Caleb Williams* (1794), another fiction closely modelled upon a critique of the law, the same issues and the same mediations that combine to make the ending of Goldsmith's novel the inauguration of a narrative undetermined by the rules and laws it will describe weaken the joint basis of autobiography and invented tale. Much of Caleb Williams's torment arises, like Job's, from a troubled search for an account equal to the remorseless persecution he has suffered. He longs to explode the false story told of him by Falkland in a decisive courtroom confrontation with his oppressor, and eventually he gets his opportunity. Before arriving at this terminal scene, however, he has the unnerving experience of reading his biography in a pamphlet, 'The Most Wonderful and Surprising History, and Miraculous Adventures of Caleb Williams'.[44] As he reads it he apprehends the inequity of exemplarity, already explained to him by a leader of a gang who has a lot in common with Macheath. Knowing the law's preference for generality and uniformity over particular injustices, he demands, 'Who ever thinks, when he is apprehended for trial, of his innocence of guilt as being at all material to the issue? Who ever was fool enough to volunteer a trial, where those who are to decide think more of the horror of the thing of which he is accused than whether he were the person that did it, and where the nature of our motives is to be collected from a set of ignorant witnesses that no wise man would trust for a fair representation of the most indifferent action of his life?' (223–4).[45] In prison Caleb had been such a fool, consoling himself by assembling the details of his life in the particularized form

---

[44] *Caleb Williams*, ed. David McCracken (London: Oxford Univ. Press, 1970), 268.

[45] Cf. *Political Justice* ii. 742, 771: 'No argument has been so grossly abused as this of example. . . . He will display the best example, who carefully studies the principles of justice, and assiduously practises them. . . . If justice be the result flowing from the contemplation of all the circumstances of each individual case . . . the inevitable consequence is that the more we have of justice, the more we shall have of truth.'

that it is the office of equity, according to Blackstone, to heed: 'By degrees I called to mind a number of these minute circumstances which but for this exercise would have been for ever forgotten' (185).

The colossal intelligence of Mr Falkland overwhelms Caleb's tentative production of an ostensible image of himself. As he grasps the fact that there is, as reader of Falkland's counter-narrative, 'no end . . . no termination', Caleb vents his anguish in the familiar question of those who no longer understand the point of their lives: 'Great God! What is man?' (279). The alternative endings of the novel show how deeply this narrative problem has entered its own construction. In the version that was first published, Caleb meets the wreck of Falkland, and tells his own story, 'a plain and unadulterated tale', so convincingly before a magistrate as to make Falkland cave in, confess its truth, and die. Here there is a satisfying coincidence between his pen, trembling in his fingers, and the events it has now brought up to the present, both meeting in a termination of the story, which is the same as the published text. But in the original ending, which Godwin suppressed, this symmetry is negative. There Falkland rejects Caleb's résumé of his life as a lie, and the magistrate denounces it as a barefaced forgery, so that the authenticity of the autobiographical and the fictional elements of the book are set at odds, and destroyed as it were from the inside. The margin of narrative manipulation which allows the tormented subject to recognize itself is removed, and in disjointed ravings that owe a lot to Clarissa's distracted fragments, Caleb retires to his last fancy, which is that he is a stone, 'a GRAVE-STONE!—an obelisk to tell you, HERE LIES WHAT WAS ONCE A MAN!' (334). In this minimal, posthumous form, he invokes the delegate or substitute that he cannot find in his life or the law, repeating Job's wish for an inscribed stone as the sole means left to him of vindication. With this desiderated epitaph, *Caleb Williams* ends where the *Vicar of Wakefield* begins: not simply with an epitaph, a bare inscription that stands in for a person, but with a problem of the legal fiction—specifically the distance between the first and third persons who are going to constitute it and narrate it—unresolved.

8 First Persons Singular in the South Pacific

Cook's circumnavigations begin and end in the book of Job. John Hawkesworth, the editor of Cook's journal of the first voyage to the Pacific, cites Job as the authority for his organization of the material. Cook's epitaph at Chalfont St Giles asks the traveller to admire and emulate the man who discovered that there was no Great Southern Continent in the Southern Ocean, a man whose explorations have 'discovered beyond all doubt, that the same Great Being who created the universe by his *fiat*, by the same ordained our earth to keep a just poise, without a corresponding Southern continent; and it does so! "He stretcheth out the North over the empty place and hangeth the earth upon nothing." *Job* xxvi. 7'.[1] Whether Job is used as an authority for ordering the account or the cartography of a navigation, his presence in a narrative of discovery betokens the tribulations incident not only to the privations and terrors of going where no European has been before, but also to the labour of transmitting a probable report of these sufferings to the audience at home. Of this autoptic exercise, as Anthony Pagden calls it, where the duty devolves on a first person singular of convincing people of the truth of what he alone has seen and felt, Job's complaint is a paradigm. Fernandez de Ovieda justifies his *Historia general y naturel de las Indias* in the words of Job: 'My lips will speak no evil, nor my tongue any lie'.[2]

In his compilation of British voyages in the Pacific, John Hawkesworth uses Job to elaborate a distinction between a general and a particular providence.[3] He explains that he has neglected to attribute 'any of the critical escapes from danger that I have recorded, to the particular interposition of Providence' on the grounds that natural laws, the perfect expression of divine will in its ultimate and invisible purposes, are never suspended either to gratify or to punish individuals. He adds: 'Shall we, says Job, "receive good from the hand of God and shall

---

[1] A copy is on show in the National Maritime Museum, Greenwich.

[2] Anthony Pagden, *European Encounters with the New World* (New Haven, Conn.: Yale Univ. Press, 1993), 61 n. 37.

[3] *An Account of the Voyages for making Discoveries in the Southern Hemisphere*, 3 vols. (London: W. Strahan and T. Cadell, 1773). Although Hawkesworth ghosts, along with Cook's and Banks's, the journals of Commodore Byron and Captains Carteret and Wallis, all of whom preceded Cook into the South Pacific, his treatment of the *Endeavour* material is the most interesting. Not only was

we not receive evil?" . . . We must acknowledge that [God] deserves
blessing not more when he gives than when he takes away' (*Account* i.
xix–xx; compare Job 2: 10). Hawkesworth takes as a notable instance of
a crisis ungoverned directly by providence an event from Cook's exploration of the east coast of New Holland, or Australia. On the night of 10
June 1770, the *Endeavour* ran aground on the Great Barrier Reef, which
extends in dangerous shoals and shallows off the north-eastern portion
of this shore. Had the wind not ceased at high tide the following day,
when the ship's keel would have been free enough in choppy water to
destroy itself by striking against the pillars of coral beneath, the ship and
most of her crew must have perished. Those inclined to ascribe the
sudden calm to a direct intervention of God, or particular providence,
must, says Hawkesworth, explain also why providence allowed the ship
to go aground in the first place, or why it failed to prevent the damage
sustained by the keel during the night, when the wind blew unabated. If
the subsiding of the wind was a natural event, 'providence is out of the
question, at least we can with no more propriety say that providentially
the wind ceased, than that providentially the sun rose in the morning'
(*Account* i. xxi).

   The resemblance between Hawkesworth's argument and Hume's is
close. The mistake they both identify is the inferring of a cause from an
occurrence whose place in the 'experienced train of events' is well-
known but undetermined. In the *Dialogues* Hume has the question put,
'Would the manner of a leaf's blowing . . . afford us any instruction
concerning the vegetation of a tree?'[4] In the *Enquiry* he answers it: 'No
just reasoner will ever presume to infer from it any single fact, and alter
or add to the phenomena [of nature], in any single particular'.[5] Hume
confronts a world in which the distribution of ills is not subsumable
under the agenda of a higher cause: 'We must acknowledge the reality of
that evil and disorder, with which the world so much abounds' (*Enquiry
into the Principles of Morals*, 138). Hawkesworth's Job authorizes the
same view of the unjustifiability of pains and calamities, one which is
consistently maintained in the *Adventurer* essays. In Essay 120 he exam-

Cook's navigation more productive of novelty, both anthropological and topographical, but also
Hawkesworth wrote it first, in order that Cook might check the manuscript before he set off on his
second cruise. He points out that the particulars of the *Endeavour*'s voyage stood out more vividly,
and prompted more of his own reflections and observations, owing to the fact that 'although it stands
last in the series, great part of it was printed before the others were written, so that several remarks,
which would naturally have been suggested by the incidents and descriptions that would have
occurred in the preceding voyages, were anticipated by similar incidents and descriptions which
occurred in this' (*Account* i. p. v).

   [4] *Dialogues Concerning Natural Religion*, ed. Norman Kemp Smith (New York: Bobbs Merrill,
1947), 147.
   [5] David Hume, 'Of a Particular Providence and of a Future State', in *An Enquiry concerning
Human Understanding*, ed. L. A. Selby-Bigge, 139.

ines the general pretence that happiness and justice are equitably dispensed in the world, opposing to it the plain fact that 'the good man has never been warranted by HEAVEN from . . . this general and indiscriminate distribution of misery'.[6] This is Warburton's nightmare, 'that obscure, disturbed, and shifting scene, the actual state of vice and virtue, of misery and happiness, amongst men' (*DLM* i. 324).

Just such an acknowledgement was in fact made by Cook when, two months after sticking fast on the coral, he found himself once more trapped inside the foul ground of the Great Barrier Reef with no visible prospect of a way out. Giving vent to the accumulated strains of privation, tedium, anxiety, terror, and unremitting responsibility for his ship, he writes in his journal:

Such are the Vicissitudes attending this kind of service and must always attend an unknown Navigation: Was it not for the pleasure which naturly results to a Man from being the first discoverer . . . this service would be insupportable. . . . The world will hardly admit of an excuse for a man leaving a Coast unexplored he has once discover'd, if dangers are his excuse he is then charged with *Timorousness* . . . if on the other hand he boldly incounters all the dangers and obstacles he meets and is unfortunate enough not to succeed he is than charged with *Temerity* and want of Conduct.[7]

This is the closest Cook ever gets to whining; and, like Macheath, he puts himself beyond the consolation of general or common cases by insisting on the firstness and particularity of his experience, which will be misunderstood by others on that very account. In acknowledging that vicissitudes are unlikely to be eased by those who judge of our passage through them, Cook says little about providence, although he does name a passage through the reef Providential Channel (381). He draws his consolation from the same source as his impatience: only the unprecedented particularity of his suffering makes bearable what would otherwise be *insupportable* (a strong word for Cook); this is the pleasure of being unparalleled, 'the first discoverer'.

For his part, Hume wonders whether any phenomenon can come to us in this degree of priority, with the miraculous originality assigned by Robinson Crusoe to the footprint he finds on the shore of his island, 'of so singular and particular a nature as to have no parallel and no similarity with any other cause or object, that has ever fallen under our observation' (*Enquiry*, 148). When Cook probes his firstness from the negative side, he inevitably finds it associated with other causes and objects that spoil the consolation of discovery. In his second voyage he

---

[6] *The Adventurer*, 2 vols. (London: J. Payne, 1753), ii. 298.
[7] James Cook, *Voyage of the Endeavour 1768–71*, ed. J. C. Beaglehole (Cambridge: Hakluyt Soc., 1955), 380.

gets closer to the Antarctic than any previous explorer, but is forced to register his achievement in terms of failure, for the limit of the known is no sooner crossed than the feat becomes a challenge to further effort, a pierced barrier disclosing the next obstacle:

I whose ambition leads me not only farther than any other man has been before me, but as far as I think it is possible for man to go, was not sorry at meeting with this interruption, as it in some measure relieved us from the dangers and hardships, inseparable with the Navigation of the Southern Polar regions. Sence therefore we could not proceed one Inch farther South, no other reason need be assigned for our Tacking and stretching back to the North.[8]

The defensiveness with which he reports his arrival at the farthest rim of navigation as though it were an interruption to some further unimaginable advance suggests that interruptions signal for Cook an audience—always sceptical and often hostile—and therefore a narrative.[9] The same coincidence of narrative with interruption has been noted in the case of politicians and judges, who use stories to negotiate the fissures in systems of principle and law. But at this stage, Cook feels menaced by the imminence of narrative and an audience because of the negative judgements they imply.

Well encouraged, like all naval officers of this period, by the example of Admiral Byng, Cook seems to be thinking of a court-martial when he considers how the dilemma of being damned for temerity and damned for timorousness is objictified in the apparently insuperable navigational problems of the reef. After considering how an audience might respond to such an interruption of the narrative of discovery, he then anticipates how the narrative of these vicissitudes will be assembled:

For such are the disposission of men in general in these Voyages that they are seldom content with the hardships and dangers which will naturaly occur, but they must add others which hardly ever had existence but in their imaginations, by magnifying the most trifling accidents and Circumstances to the greatest hardships, and unsurmou[n]table dangers without the imidiate interposion of Providence, as if the whole Merit of the Voyage consisted in the dangers and hardships they underwent, or that real ones did not happen often

[8] *The Voyages of the Resolution and the Adventure 1772–75*, ed. J. C. Beaglehole, 2 vols. (Cambridge: Hakluyt Soc. and Cambridge Univ. Press, 1961), i. 322.

[9] Compare the rueful summary of his voyage Cook offers to the Lords of the Admiralty, in which he is forced in Shandean fashion to found his achievement in negations, and to pique himself on finding what the Pacific Ocean did *not* contain: 'Altho' the discoveries made in this Voyage are not great yet I flatter myself that they are as such as may Merit the attention of their Lordships, & altho' I have failed in Discovering the so much talked of Southern Continent which perhaps do not Exsist & which I my self had much at heart yet I am confident that no part of the failure of such discovery Can be laid to my Charge'. Letter from Batavia, 23 Oct. 1770. MS Papers 2594, *Endeavour Voyage*, Alexander Turnbull Library, Wellington.

enough to give the mind sufficient anxiety; thus posteriety are taught to look upon these Voyages as hazardous to the highest degree.   (*Endeavour Journal*, 461)

The logic of these reflections is contorted enough to suggest that Cook is dealing with an intense and partly submerged anxiety. He seems to want to detect a disparity between the singular pains of being first and the exaggerated accounts that will be given of them—the familiar charge against seamen's stories—in the form of a plain contrast between truth and lie. But it is clear that the magnification of trifles into great hardships will be done by those who experienced real hazards, not by interlopers who endured none, and that their mistake will proceed not from false additions but from an ill-conceived heightening of the actual details of the voyage—if in fact it is a heightening rather than a tautology to call particular hardships and dangers, hardships and dangers. The troubled border between the natural perils and their imaginary refraction in narrative seems to be owing in an obscure way to the status of the phrase 'the imidiate interposion of Providence'. In using it, Cook appears to mean one of two things. Either the narrators, in denying a particular providence, pause promiscuously over each discontinuous moment, fascinated by what they take to be an irreducible item in an incalculable abundance of discrete phenomena; or they invoke such a providence in order to invest contingencies with a valency and tendency out of proportion to their real impact.

What this impact might be, Cook is unable to determine, just as he is unable to decide where firstness decays into representations of culpability, and where the unprecedented encounter with the outer limit of the known marks the inner limit of a pusillanimous refusal to go any further. The question of choosing a highly systematized narrative, such as the providential account Hawkesworth avoids, or of preferring (as Hawkesworth seems to) an under-systematized array of unparalleled circumstances, strikes Cook as a dilemma. He is as repelled by the punitive intelligibility of the former, as by the undistinguished and insupportable particularity of an 'unknown Navigation'. He is stuck fast, like his boat, between irreconcileable combinations of positive and negative elements, the same unpredictable mixture Hume calls 'the reality of evil and disorder', and which Hawkesworth sums up as the undifferentiated mixture of good and evil in his quotation from Job. With the natural hazard converted into an imaginary hazard in the narrative of a painful interruption, a *lesson* gets taught to posterity about limit cases, 'hazardous in the highest degree'. Why does Cook wish to deny this? Because it is a lesson? Because it is not true? Because it is not faithful to the tides of optimism and despair with which the hazards were originally greeted? Or is it because it does not take account of the interruptive factor that inaugurates the representation and instantiation of the unparalleled first experience, even while it is being experienced, and of which his very reflection is an example?

Cook and Hawkesworth were by no means the first to struggle with the problem of ordering narratives of discovery. As Michael McKeon has pointed out, travel narratives have always had to compound for their generic instability with a rhetoric of personal validation which is (like Gulliver's) so doggedly empiricist that it carries first persons into the very dilemma Cook has tried to outline: 'the point at which they begin to reflect a subversive image of themselves'.[10] The problem of extending a faithful and punctual account of bare circumstances until it becomes indistinguishable from an imaginary voyage is a problem most compilers of South Pacific discoveries seem to have been aware of. In the collections made by Prévost, de Brosses, and Dalrymple, the question of the relation of shapeless particulars to some overarching principle of order is of crucial importance, not least because it affects the *reader*. Prévost sees the need to prune the accounts he is compiling, in order to avoid repetition and the tedium of 'petits détails inutiles'.[11] If this is done well, the author can expect to produce 'un système de Géographie moderne, et d'Histoire, autant qu'un corps de Voyages; et représenter, avec autant d'ordre que de plénitude, l'état présent de toutes les Nations' (*Histoire générale* i. v). Although it is important not to desiccate the reader's mind with arid details, nor to condemn him to an 'inutile et intolérable ennui,' (and therefore needful to tabulate voyages according to region and to abridge their nautical jargon), de Brosses points out that it is equally necessary not to lose the authority and distinctive flavour of the original journals. The reader wants the facts 'peintes telles que les navigateurs les a vues, non avec le coloris dont la plume de l'historien pourroit les orner'.[12]

Dalrymple disturbs the smooth work of mediation between seaman and reader by restoring particularity to a paramount place in his collection. He confesses that it has been 'as disagreeable to me in writing, as it will be to the reader in his perusal: I am not insensible that the *undress* and uncouth sound of a *literal* translation is enough to frighten *all* readers except the very *few* who take up a book *merely* for infor-

[10] Michael McKeon, *Origins of the English Novel* (Baltimore: Johns Hopkins Univ. Press, 1987), 106.

[11] Antoine-Francois Prévost, *Histoire générales des voyages* (Paris, 1745), i. p. iv.

[12] Charles de Brosses, *Histoire des Navigations aux Terres Australes*, 2 vols. (Paris, 1756), i. pp. viii–ix.

mation'.[13] Here is no abridgement, such as de Brosses's (i. xv), nor any system of modern geography, for nothing that was discovered in the Pacific—including the nothing which Cook discovered the Great Southern Continent to be—was to shift Dalrymple from his initial suspense of judgement, which kept him from admitting that the labour of exploration was complete: 'The southern regions remain still indeterminate, and we continue ignorant, so far as to absolute experience, whether the southern hemisphere be an immense mass of water, or whether it contains another continent'.[14] Whatever the merits of Dalrymple's doubts about Cook's diligence in the Pacific, in so far as he rejects the principles of uniformity adopted by de Brosses and Prévost, he anticipates the difficulties Cook was experiencing in being 'the first discoverer'. Dalrymple understands that it is the reader who is the problem, and that readerly discomfort is in direct proportion to journalistic particularity ('undress') and navigational authenticity; and in its most extreme form this authenticity is absolutely singular. In a passionate salute to the heroism of conduct and the sublimity of conception required to be an explorer of the southern ocean, Dalrymple defines the nonpareil as follows: 'This question will determine the relative dignity of any character, "What has *he* done which no one else ever *did* before, or *can* do after him?" ' (*An Historical Collection* i. xviii).

William Dampier, the first Englishman to explore the coast of New Holland, knew the risks of being in this position:

It has almost always been the Fate of those who have made new Discoveries, to be disesteemed and slightly spoken of, by such as either have no true Relish and Value for the *Things themselves* that are discovered, or have had some Prejudice against the *Persons* by whom the Discoveries were made. . . . It has been objected against me by some, that my Accounts and Descriptions of Things are dry and jejune, nor filled with variety of pleasant Matter, to divert and gratify the Curious Reader.[15]

Between Dampier and Dalrymple, the Frenchman Bougainville, who explored Tahiti the year before Cook, makes a similar complaint, involving his relation to the reader. He confesses his style is rough and laden with details and, bearing the print of twelve years' rough living, 'errante et sauvage'.[16] 'Je suis voyageur et marin; c'est à dire un menteur

[13] Alexander Dalrymple, *An Historical Collection of Voyages and Discoveries in the South Pacific Ocean*, 2 vols. (London, 1770–1), i. p. x.

[14] Alexander Dalrymple, *An Account of Discoveries in the South Pacific previous to 1764* (London, 1767), 88.

[15] William Dampier, *A New Voyage Round the World* in *A Collection of Voyages*, 4 vols. (London: J. and J. Knapton, 1729), 3. [i–ii].

[16] Louis de Bougainville, *Voyage autour du monde*, 2 vols. (Paris: Saillant et Nyon, 1772), i. p. xxxix.

et un imbécille' (i. xl). It was Bougainville's luck to be translated into English by a reader, Johann-Reinhold Forster, the naturalist assigned to Cook's second expedition, who was quite convinced that seamen were barbaric, degraded, and economical with the truth: 'Though Mr. de Bougainville is a man of undoubted 'veracity and abilities, he has, however, in a few instances, been misled by false reports'.[17]

The more singular the facts, and the more unparalleled the voyager's achievements, the more likely the reader is to cavil with the ordonnance and credibility of them; and the more a reader is painted as eager for a shapely and digested account of the new, the more the voyager will assume that it is a fiction, not the bare truth, that the public wants. J.-R. Forster and his son George tried to produce a philosophical solution to the problem in the introduction to their account of Cook's second voyage. There they locate three levels in the archeology of travel-narratives. First there are outright lies, told for local or national reasons, such as the suppression of the fact that Cook shelled the Loo-fort at Madeira from the *Endeavour*, or that Bougainville watered his ships at Juan Fernandez; and associated with lying is any attempt to pad an account of a voyage so that it will fit a set of preconceived ideas, or arouse wonder: 'Two anonymous publications on the subject of our voyage had already appeared; but the present age is too enlightened to credit marvellous histories, which would have disgusted even the roman-tic disposition of our ancestors' (i. vii).[18] Second, there is the naked, savage, or 'undress' narrative, which gives nothing but facts, and which therefore can yield information but no knowledge: 'The learned, at last grown tired of being deceived by the powers of rhetoric . . . raised a general cry after a simple collection of facts . . . facts were collected . . . and yet knowledge was not increased. They received a confused heap of disjointed limbs, which no art could reunite into a whole; and the rage of hunting after facts soon rendered them incapable of forming and resolving a single proposition.'[19] Third, there is the 'philosophical recital of facts' (i. vi) with which the learned world is about to be regaled, an Ariadne's thread to lead them through the labyrinth of phenomena, and at the same time a vindication of providence: 'I have always endeav-oured in this narrative to connect the ideas arising from different occur-rences; in order, if possible, to . . . lift the soul into that exalted station,

[17] Lewis de Bougainville, *A Voyage Round the World*, trans. J.-R. Forster (London: J. Nourse, 1772), p. vii.

[18] Privately Forster conceded that the particulars in at least one of these publications were true, '& that it will probably prevent him from publishing any narrative at all'. Daines Barrington to the Earl of Sandwich, 5 June 1776; *Sandwich Papers*, National Maritime Museum, F. 36. 29.

[19] George Forster, *A Voyage round the World in the Sloop Resolution 1772–5*, 2 vols. (London: B. White et al., 1777), i. p. xi.

from whence the extensive view must "justify the ways of God to man" '
(i. xii). Even today, this is esteemed an accurate programme of a great
Enlightenment triumph in the field of travel-writing, despite the
Forsters' notoriety among almost everyone with whom they came into
professional contact as self-interested and partial reporters.[20] It is clear
from the reference to theodicy here, and elsewhere from the slighting
remarks about Hawkesworth (four years in his grave) and the frequent
and unctuous invocations of providence, that the Forsters' writing was
as much a reading—and a very adversarial one—of Hawkesworth's
Account.

In this they were not alone. In the violent disputes that raged round
Hawkesworth's supposedly blasphemous reconstruction of Cook's
journal, his antagonists returned obsessively to the issues of providence
and particularity, and to his misreading of the book of Job. Hardly
anyone approved of what he had said about providence. The *Annual
Register* thought a book of travels no place for 'speculative opinions of
dark and difficult subjects', pointing out besides that the successful
completion of an expedition so 'full of risque and danger, affords the
amplest room for thankfulness and gratitude to the providence of
God'.[21] The *Gentleman's Magazine* ran long extracts from T. Payne's *A
Letter addressed to Dr Hawkesworth* (1773), which paused over each
detail of the grounding and refloating of the *Endeavour* in order to
emphasize its providential symmetry (' "Yet *directly* they had a perfect
calm . . . and almost immediately after they were removed from the
rock, it blew again" '), and went on to suggest that there might be many
similar passages of 'wonderful escapes and deliverances' in the original
journals either suppressed or blurred by the godless compiler.[22]

---

[20] 'Quite simply, to orient oneself narrowly through particularisation, through the rivetting of
one's gaze, became mandatory in the face of a disconcerting abundance of phenomena. . . . The
image of life embodied in a discrete example no longer became the only one possible . . . Forster
was compelled for secular reasons to bring individual experience into a mutually adequate relationship with the manifold of things.' Barbara Stafford, *Voyage into Substance* (Cambridge, Mass.:
MIT Press, 1984), 352. Stafford's favourite example of a gaze properly riveted is Forster's account
of the water-spouts of Cape Stephens (e.g. 330) and her image of the scientific ordering of the
individual within the manifold consists of Forster and William Wales, the *Resolution*'s astronomer,
drifting intently between icebergs in an open boat (367). Of Forster's allegedly exemplary description
of the water-spouts Wales had this to say: 'Dr. Forster gives us his account of the water-spouts, which
we saw in Cook's Straits, in which there are several extraordinary circumstances. In the first place,
he says, that "the bases of these spouts, on the sea, looked bright and yellowish when illuminated by
the sun." . . . We never saw any of them illuminated by it, nor even the least glimpse of the sun, any
where, all the time that they lasted . . . as all that part of the heavens where the sun was situated, was
covered with one black, dense, impenetrable cloud, as everyone on board can testify. . . . Neither can
I meet with any person who saw the flash of lightning which he speaks of, although we were upwards
of one hundred of us, who were intently looking on this extraordinary phenomenon. . . . But it is
amazing how far a favourite theory will deceive a man's eyes'. William Wales, *Remarks on Mr.
Forster's Account of Captain Cook's last Voyage* (London: J. Nourse, 1778), 23.

[21] *The Annual Register for the Year 1773* (London: J. Dodsley, 1774), 267.

[22] *The Gentleman's Magazine*, 43 (1773), 506. William Woty, an occasional versifier, concen-

Hawkesworth's links with deist and sceptical philophers were proclaimed in *The Public Advertiser*, which did as much as it could to
foment a paper-war over the *Account*. 'You have adopted the Creed of
a Bolingbroke without his Abilities *to defend it*.' 'It would be highly
criminal to remain silent when a Dr. *H*. makes an open Profession of a
Sentiment, the favourite *Theme of Bolingbroke and Hume!*'[23] In wilfully
turning away from the ideal order of a providential history, Hawkesworth has beckoned 'lawless Power and ungoverned Appetite' into the
work, specifically with the descriptions of the sexual liberty of Tahitians,
and heaped 'Combustibles into a Fire which already rages to an Height
that threatens consuming every Principle of Goodness' (11926, 3 July).
One letter-writer finds a way unwillingly back to Cook's sense of the
insupportable life of a mariner at the limit via Hawkesworth's removal
of 'THE ONLY SOLID COMFORT, which can fortify [man] under the
various Calamities . . . which must, unsustained by an humble *Trust in
God*, render Life intolerably wretched' (11938, 17 July).

This theme was expanded by another correspondent into a speculation along the lines of Johnson's review of Soame Jenyns' *Enquiry*,
using Job as the occasion:

> You then give a Quotation from Job, which makes directly against you—for
> Job's Argument for receiving Evil at the Hand of God, is, because He is the
> Author of every *Good*;—*if* the Author of every *Good*, and you think being
> saved from Shipwreck is a Service, it necessary [sic] follows, that the Endeavour
> owed her Safety to Providence. . . . You suppose [God] beholding, with
> unconcern'd *Indifference*, the Distresses of His Creatures!—though *present* in
> the Midst of their Sufferings—witnessing their Agonies, yet remaining inexor-
> ably deaf to their ardent Entreaties for Pardon and Protection. (11939, 21 July).

Dalrymple, who in other respects shared Hawkesworth's preference for
a factual and more naked relation of voyages, but who could not forgive
his inattention to the premier issue of Cook's navigation, namely the
Great Southern Continent, pursues a similar theme with respect to Job.
He first of all despatches the mystery of the *Endeavour*'s going aground
with an explanation that vindicates Cook's apprehensions about how
vicissitudes are understood by those who haven't endured them: 'The
ship struck by the obvious *misconduct* of the Persons who directed her

---

trated on the lump of coral that stuck in the *Endeavour's* keel, helping staunch the breach it had itself
made, in order to make a singular instance yield a general lesson: 'From the Ship's bottom when the
Plankings break, | The rock's close fragment often stops the leak; | Some call it luck, and others
fortune call, | But know 'tis Providence'. William Woty, *Particular Providence: A Poetical Essay*
(London: W. Woty, 1774), 9. n. 23.

    [23] *The Public Advertiser*, 11926 (2 July 1773); 11938 (17 July 1773).

course; and for the Deity to prevent *ill-conduct* is rather the act of *Omnipotence* than *Providence*'.[24] Then he goes on:

'As the Doctor confounds *miracles* with the *ordinary* agency of Providence, he also confounds *gratitude* to the Supreme Being for *Blessings*, with *Submission* to the Divine *will*. Job does not *thank* God for the *Calamities* which befel him, but he says, "The Lord *gave* and the Lord hath *taken away, Blessed* be the name of the Lord," thus expressing his *thankfulness* for *past blessings*, and his *resignation* in *present adversity*'. (17).

Most of these replies to Hawkesworth are unfair in terms of what he actually says in his introduction, where all he does is to shift the operations of providence from a scrutable to an inscrutable quarter, leaving facts to be 'carried on and executed by Delegation', as one of his more candid commentators in the *Public Advertiser* pointed out (11926, 3 July). Another claimed that Hawkesworth had ingenuously and piously 'asserted a plain Fact . . . the Sun rises upon the Just and the Unjust . . . [God] governs all alike by equal Laws' (11933, 11 July). It is plain that these positions simply angered a readership which felt 'exceedingly ill used' both by the principles and the material Hawkesworth had put in front of them (*Public Advertiser*, 11929, 7 July).

As usual in contested readings of the book of Job, the two parties adopt the roles of patriarch and comforter. Hawkesworth joins the impatient patriarch, who proclaims the terror of a God whose purposes are hidden, and declares the absence of any perceptible justice in his dispensations; meanwhile, the ill-used readers take up the chant of the comforters, who impute bad faith to such ignorant suffering while explaining the grounds of what transcends explanation. In the original story the argument about particular circumstances focuses on the broken state of Job's body, understood by the comforters to be the signs and tokens of an exemplary punishment, and felt by Job as the pangs caused by the violent inscription of an unrestricted and arbitrary power. Just as the comforters repudiate Job's presentation of himself and his wounds as discrete, unparalleled, and non-exemplary experiences of physical evil, so the ill-used readers wish to dismiss the factuality of Hawkesworth's account of an unparalleled navigation as heterogeneous and pointless accretions of detail—'inflexible Adherence to Facts' (*The Public Advertiser*, 1197, 7 July), 'a multitude of frivolous particulars' (*Edinburgh Magazine and Review* (1773), 1/36), 'dry and undecisive Labours of a mere tedious Journalist'(*St James's Chronicle*, 1916, 15–17

---

[24] Mr Dalrymple's *Observations on Dr Hawkesworth's Preface to the Second Edition* (London, 1773), 17.

June). But just as the comforters become aware that Job's speech is gradually invested with the violence that has afflicted him, culminating in his great oath of clearance, so do Hawkesworth's readers become aware that his particularity is closely associated with, and even symptomatic of, moments of violent interruption.

When, for example, the letter-writer in *The Public Advertiser* talks of the 'lawless Power and ungoverned Appetite' that Hawkesworth's 'doctrine' unleashes, he begins with sailors, who of all men, he says, stand in need of firm guidance on the topic of divine government. He is alluding to Hawkesworth's prediction of the consequences of shipwreck in such a place: 'We well knew that our boats were not capable to carrying us all on shore, and that when the dreadful crisis should arrive, as all command and subordination would be at an end, a contest for the preference would probably ensue, that would increase the horrors even of shipwreck, and terminate in the destruction of us all by the hands of each other' (*Account* iii. 144). This is largely Hawkesworth's interpolation, based on Banks's less lurid estimate: 'we well knew that our boats were not capable of carrying us all ashore, so that some, probably most of us, must be drowned'.[25] It was paraphrased in *The Gentleman's Magazine* as an unconditional struggle for survival: 'The contention among the strong to get possession of the boats would leave no hope for the weak to escape with life' (44 (1774), 72). It is a moment framed by the particulars of a ship in distress. First there is the sinister abundance of disintegrating particles, 'We saw by the light of the moon the sheathing boards from the bottom of the vessel floating away all round her, and at last her false keel.' Then comes a precise inventory of the ship's equipment jettisoned in a desperate effort to lighten her: 'Six of her guns, being all we had upon the deck, our iron and stone ballast, casks, hoop staves, oil jars, decayed stores, and many other things that lay in the way of heavier materials, were thrown overboard' (*Account* iii. 143). And finally there is the unrestricted struggle for power and survival among an insubordinate crew, no longer under the government of anything but their passions.

There are many occasions in these journals when violence draws the narrator's attention to heterogeneous collections of items, or when the items themselves provoke the violence. The best example of heterogeneity is to be found in the material of the second voyage, in Lieutenant James Burney's description of the scene at Grass Cove, where he found the remains of ten of the *Adventure*'s crew, all of whom had been killed and eaten. The unmentionable site of 'Carnage & Barbarity' is bounded

<hr />

[25] *The Endeavour Journal of Joseph Banks 1768–71*, ed. J. C. Beaglehole, 2 vols. (Sydney: Public Library of New South Wales and Angus and Robertson, 1962), ii. 79.

by bits and pieces—a rowlock, a broken oar sticking in the sand, two baskets, a pair of trousers, two hands, a head, a seaman's frock, and six shoes 'no two of them being fellows'.[26] The navigation up the north-east coast of New Zealand in Cook's first voyage is heavily interspersed with scenes of violence that arise directly from the failure to exchange commodities, the Maori being inclined to go off with the bargain without paying the agreed price. Over the handling of trade-goods such as red kersey, Tahiti cloth, old trousers, paper, and linen local people are wounded with small shot, killed with ball, and even hooked with fish-hooks (*Account* ii. 361). When Lieutenant Gore kills a man for stealing cloth (9 November 1769), and the ship's master shoots another (29 January 1770), Cook is upset at the disproportion between the trivial offence and the punishment: 'I find the reasons for fireing upon them are not very justifiable' (*Journal*, 241). However, in an encounter with some Maori fishermen on the day after landfall in New Zealand, Cook and Banks fired on them with ball, killing four out of the seven, merely because they were resisting the Europeans' attempted abduction by hurling everything in their canoe at their aggressors.

This incident stands out, like the running aground of the *Endeavour*, as unaccountable, or, in Cook's term, *unjustifiable*. Like the others, it is framed with minute particulars; and rather like Hawkesworth's fancied end of the *Endeavour* on the reef, it is a contest that takes place without rules, and ends in destruction. When Cook intercepts the canoe in the ship's pinnace, the Maori empty it, as the crew of the *Endeavour* will empty their craft, in order to deal with an emergency ('They . . . threw a large Stone which fell short; they then threw sticks and paddles, and seemed resolved to stand on their defence as long as they had any thing Missile left'[27]). Once they are taken on board the English ship, they are bedizened with the trade-goods their countrymen will be shot for seizing ('we dressed them, and adorned them with bracelets, anclets, and necklaces, after their own fashion' [*Account* ii. 292]). But before they are ornamented, they are dressed in European clothes and fed European food, to their great delight; and as Cook and Banks observe the rising spirits of their captives, they are forced to reflect on the savagery of their actions. In fact, their savagery is reflected back at them by 'savages' who prove in their urbanity as well as their dress the title to humanity that their captors have forfeited. Banks's reflection ('the most disagreeable day My life has yet seen, black be the mark for it' [*Endeavour Journal*

---

[26] *The Voyages of the Resolution and the Adventure 1772–5*, ed. J. C. Beaglehole, (Cambridge: Hakluyt Soc. and Cambridge Univ. Press, 1961), App. IV, 751.

[27] *Journal of William Broughton Monkhouse*, BM Add. MS 27889, ff. 83–94; 10. Bootie mentions pikes and spears, and Wilkinson says they even threw fish at their aggressors. See *Journal*, 171 n. 1.

i. 403]) echoes Cook's, 'I am aware that most humane men who have not experienced things of this nature will cencure my conduct in fireing upon the people in this boat nor do I my self think that the reason I had for seizing upon her will att all justify me' (*Journal*, 171).

Here is Cook's first 'first'—something unprecedented in the experience of Europeans, to which he responds in a way that he knows will be hard to justify. The best he can offer is a version of the lawlessness of shipwreck outlined by Hawkesworth as an unrestricted battle for survival: 'I was not to stand still and suffer either my self or those that were with me to be knocked on the head' (ibid.). He authenticates a parallel between British seamen and Maori that J.-R. Forster will elaborate in his narrative of the subsequent voyage to New Zealand, based on his conviction that both are impelled by the sheer desire for mastery. Of the sailors he says, 'Subjected to a very strict command, they also exercise a tyrannical sway over those whom fortune places in their power . . . they have expressed a horrid eagerness to fire upon the natives on the slightest pretences' (*Voyage round the World*, i. 535); and of the Maori: 'We shall find it amazing to what length [the passions] may carry a set of men, who lend no ear to any principles of morality, and who adjust their notions of rectitude by the extent of power only'.[28] Such judgements are not unheard-of in the eighteenth century. Allowing for cultural and contextual differences, Goldsmith is found saying similar things of Bolingbroke's excesses, and Godwin of Pitt's ambition. In Hume's account of inaugural moments in the life of nations, the arrangement of new power relations is uninhibited by principle: 'The face of the earth is continually changing, by the increase of small kingdoms into great empires . . . by the planting of colonies, by the migration of tribes. Is there anything discoverable in all these events but force and violence?' ('Of the Original Contract,' *Essays*, 458). The price Hawkesworth must pay for adopting this position *vis-à-vis* the violent events that constitute inaugural events is the inability to account for particular events he feels bound to enumerate, or to render them as an intelligible sequence, especially when they involve the savagery of civilized men.

Here is a substantive reason for the reader's sense of being ill-used, for facts unloosed from principles denote not merely an absence of providence or a privation of common values, but a violent and contaminating struggle for power, extending from the unrestrained behaviour of 'savages', through the barbaric responses of Europeans, all the way to the 'sophistical principles' of their apologists (Forster, *Voyage* i. x) and the inflammatory effect on the more impressionable among their read-

[28] John Reinold Forster, *Observations made during a Voyage Round the World* (London: G. Robinson, 1778), 319.

2. Plate 11 of William Blake's *Job*

1. Plate 10 of William Blake's *Job*

3. *The Dead Soldier* by Joseph Wright of Derby

4. Poussin's *Rinaldo and Armida*

5. Penelope Boothby's tomb

6. *The Conversion of Polemon*, 1778, by James Barry

8. *Ulysses and a Companion* by James Barry

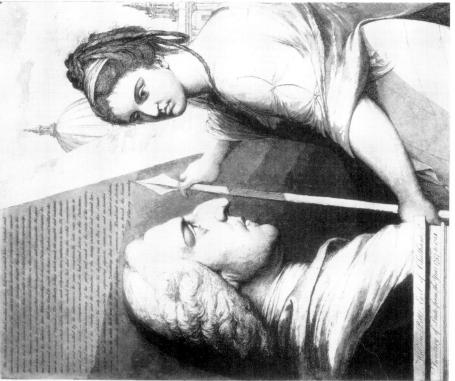

7. *William Pitt, Earl of Chatham*, 1778, by James Barry

ers.[29] It is clear that Hawkesworth does what he can to edit or 'mutilate' (as Forster puts it [i. vii]) the violent portions of his manuscripts. Of the 9th November killing he observes only that it would have been 'happy' had Gore used shot rather than ball (*Account* ii. 337); and of the shipmaster's alleged excesses he discovers to his great comfort that 'this report was not true' (ii. 398). But the Poverty Bay killings require something more specific.

Hawkesworth tackles the issue in the Introduction in general terms, although it is clear he is thinking of the events of 10 October 1769: 'I cannot however dismiss my Readers to the following narratives, without expressing the regret with which I have recorded the destruction of poor naked savages, by our firearms, in the course of these expeditions, when they endeavoured to repress the invaders of their country; a regret which I am confident my Readers will participate with me' (*Account* i. xvii). He follows this up with no pious disclaimers, however, but with an application of his theory about the distribution of evil, drawn from his reading of Job. The death of indigenous people 'appears to be an evil which, if discoveries of new countries are attempted, cannot be avoided: resistance will always be made, and if those who resist are not overpowered, the attempt must be relinquished' (i. xvii). Suitably phrased, this is Cook's maxim of knock on the head or be knocked, illustrated by Hawkesworth's scenario for the battle of the boats. It is also the meat of Forster's long reflection on the Grass Cove massacre, where he observes, 'Nothing more frequent than that a set of men are powerful enough to wrest the laws to the disadvantage of the wretched and friendless' (*Voyage round the World,* ii. 466).

Hawkesworth's unsentimental estimate of how firstness is achieved is based on his appreciation of the two sides of the unparalleled event. On the one side is the frailty and terror of the man who pushes his way to the geographical limit, bereft of any precedents or laws to shield him from the consequences of his own temerity—the explorer as Job—and on the other is the savage agency of the men at the limit of their tether, unrestrained by principle and always on the edge of excess, 'men who are liable to provocation by sudden injury, to unpremeditated violence by sudden danger . . . so that every excess thus produced is also an inevitable evil' (*Account,* i. xvii). In writing up the entry for 10th October, Hawkesworth adjusts Cook's criterion of 'most humane men who have not experienced things of this nature' to 'every reader of humanity': 'I am conscious that the feeling of every reader of humanity

---

[29] After the mutiny on the Bounty Fletcher Christian went into Bligh's cabin and found a copy of—Hawkesworth! See Greg Dening, *The Bounty: An Ethnographic History* (Melbourne: Melbourne Univ. Press, 1983; repr. 1989), 78.

will censure me for having fired upon these unhappy people' (*Journal*, 171; *Account*, ii. 290). The censure Cook anticipates from humane men, in respect of an act he cannot justify, has only one excuse, and that is that it was unparalleled—never in his life had he been so fiercely and persistently resisted when so clearly the power was in his hands—but he doesn't dodge the censure. Hawkesworth handles the ethical consideration ('they certainly did not deserve death for not chusing to confide in my promises') but instead of submitting to a judgement (which in any case he allows to be no more than a *feeling*), he recurs to his earlier observation on excess: 'In such situations, when the command to fire has been given, no man can restrain its excess, or prescribe its effect'. Men at the limit act excessively for any number of reasons incident to their unparalleled situation, contributing to an evil which is 'inevitable' not because of the breach of any moral law (who can prescribe effects?) but because of an unaccountable mixture of good and evil for which Hawkesworth takes no responsibility. He asks no pardon of the reader, therefore; whatever the reader's feelings, they are only the reflection of a regret which Hawkesworth has already invited him, or her, to *share*. Indeed the reader has no initiative in the matter, being 'dismissed' to a narrative the narrator is not concerned to justify.

Dalrymple, who feels exceedingly ill-used by Hawkesworth because of his slighting reference to the Great Southern Continent,[30] takes up the position of a Job exasperated by a false counsellor while coping with affliction. He associates Hawkesworth's deficiencies in faith, candour, and accuracy with the extenuation of violence:

In the mean while I wish YOU more candour, and resign myself to Providence, although in the wisdom of its dispensations, I was prevented by the secondary influence of narrow minded men, from compleating the Discovery of . . . a Southern Continent; which, notwithstanding your sagacious reasonings, I still think, from my own experience in such like voyages, may be done without committing *murder*. (*Letter*, 31)

Here Dalrymple situates a metaphor buoyant in the production and consumption of travel-writing—the 'nakedness' of a factual account (*Account*, i. v), the undisguised print of experiences 'errante et sauvage' (Bougainville, i. xxxix), his own reference to the frightening *'undress and uncouth sound'* of his texts (*Historical Collection*, i. x)—in literal scenes of violence against indigenous people. Shrewdly he reads the

---

[30] Dalrymple was angered not only by the failure of agreement between the narrative and the charts published in the *Account*, thus making nonsense of an accurate search for the land mass he firmly believed to exist, he was also convinced that Hawkesworth had foisted into the entry for 24 March 1769 an observation which Cook never made: 'It was a general opinion that there was land to windward, but I did not think myself at liberty to search for what I was not sure to find'. See *Account* ii. 70; *A Letter from Mr Dalrymple to Dr Hawkesworth*, 23.

reversal of savagery in the Poverty Bay incident as something that stains Hawkesworth's account of it, and more particularly his refusal to justify it. 'Discoverers', he says, 'are bound to put up with *much*, and not only . . . ought they not to offer any violence to the natives, on the pretence of *frightening* them, or on any other pretence whatever, [for] nothing can vindicate *Fireing* on the Indians, even if attacked by them, but *absolute necessity*' (*Mr Dalrymple's Observations*, 13). What law, he demands, making an appeal to equity, entitles a man 'to shoot another because he *throws a stone?*' (11). The heroism of firstness is directly connected by Dalrymple with the removal of tyrannies, not with the imposition of new ones, since all tyrants go the same way, their first step 'to shut the *ear* against complaints: the *last* to *shut* the *mouth* of the complainant' (*Historical Collection*, i. xxvii). In crying out against injustice inflicted upon 'savages' by savages who pretend to laws, Dalrymple sits down as Job, stifled with the attempt to resign himself to 'present adversity', in company with other complainants who have suffered without advocacy or appeal from the excesses of those whose power is bound only by the pretence of principle.

There is, however, a radical instability in the circuit of power and savagery which undermines Dalrymple's confidence in identifying and judging it as an excess that never contaminates his own work. If he thinks that the 'nakedness' and 'uncouthness' of his accounts of the South Pacific act simply as metaphors for the integrity of the man as ardent in his defence of native rights as he is of his theory of a Great Southern Continent, one need only read J.-R. Forster's terrified jottings of the *Resolution*'s passage to the south, to understand what exactions Dalrymple was making on the crews and scientists of Cook's second voyage, and how eagerly he was betting their lives on the existence of a vast southern land mass. Forster's description of that anxious and dangerous passage to the polar seas forces a revision of all his narrative codes as well as of his judgements of the sailors, patrons, and readers of the *Voyage*:

What helps it to harass the Ship, the rigging & crew in these turbulent Seas beating to windward. If to satisfy the Government & the public that no Land is left behind: it will not suffice the incredulous part of the public if the whole Ocean were ploughed up. . . . But we must submit, there are people, who are hardened to all feelings, & will give no ear to the dictates of humanity & reason; false ideas of virtue & *good conduct* are to them, to leave nothing to *chance*, & future discoverers, by their *perseverance*; which costs the lives of the poor Sailors. (*Resolution Journal*, iii. 441–4)

Whether he knows it or not, Dalrymple is just such a monster of incredulity as he makes his complaint, a man immune to the dictates of humanity and reason, and so besotted with a desire for full knowledge that he will leave *nothing to chance*.

Having quoted Hawkesworth on the regretful feelings with which he has recorded the destruction of 'poor naked savages', Dalrymple asks a pointed question, 'Is the Doctor's regret at the *destruction* of the poor Indians, or at his being under the necessity to *record* their destruction?' (11). What is the difference? It is the difference between Dalrymple's standard of true nakedness—the literal translation of material that may discomfort the reader but not the candid translator—and the pretence made by Hawkesworth to *represent* Cook: to produce him in the first person. It is, of course, also the difference between reading books of travel and acquiring a certain large idea about a Great Southern Continent (notwithstanding the Almighty's decision to stretch out the South upon nothing, and to hang the earth over an empty space), and urging men to the limit to discover the reality of that idea, the fruit of the single-minded ambition masquerading as the humane principles of an individual called Dalrymple. However, it is astute of him to notice, at least in respect of the *Account*, that the connection between first discoverers and their delegates includes the question of violence. Even in answering Dalrymple, Hawkesworth adopts Cook's voice ('Captain Cook, as his accuser well knows, is absent, and cannot answer for himself; I must therefore inform him' ['Preface to the Second Edition', *Account*, i. 8]). From Dalrymple's angle he is the narrow-minded delegate of an imperfect commander, a double veil wafting between himself and the Great Southern Continent that he knows exists and whose discovery would vindicate him: a fudger of matters of topography, as well as of principle and law. But it is plain that Hawkesworth sees himself as the delegate of a man whose anguish at the limits of the world and of personal endurance is as mute as that of Dalrymple's suppressed complainant, or of Forster when he deserts his justifying programme to abuse inquisitive readers who will leave nothing to chance. It is also clear from his introduction, as well as from Dalrymple's commentary on it, that Hawkesworth's representation of Cook is not a justification. He has no intention of tying Cook down to inviolable prescriptions, or of pleading his case from precedents. But in recording Cook's actions, he is aiming to do more than merely to particularize them, and more than to 'intersperse such sentiments and observations as my subject should suggest' (*Account*, i. v).

Much was made of Hawkesworth's decision to deliver a first-person narrative. He had an authority for it in de Brosses ('le navigateur parle presque toujours lui-même à la première personne' [*Histoire*, i. viii]) and the Admiralty evidently made no objections. Although Cook was, ironically, to complain bitterly about Hawkesworth's impersonation, he had approved the first draft.[31] Some reviewers wished to distinguish sharply between Cook's intrepidity and Hawkesworth's heterodoxy, but the reaction to the first-person device was generally favourable. 'It undoubtedly renders the narrative more animated and interesting' (*Monthly Review*, 44/138); it is 'judiciously adopted' (*Critical Review*, 242). An enthusiastic correspondent in *The Public Advertiser* instructed the reader how to get the best out of it: 'You must suppose the honest, brave, sensible Captain Cooke just returned from a new, long, and dangerous Voyage, telling in an accurate, easy, simple, intelligible Manner all that he and his Companions had suffered, done or learned' (11938, July 17). Hawkesworth himself had already suggested in *The Adventurer* that the defect of travel narratives lay in the distance at which the traveller stands from the reader: 'If we feel any emotion at the danger of the traveller, it is transient and languid, because his character is not rendered sufficiently important'.[32] The solution lies in removing whatever stands between them, as he explains in the introduction: 'A narrative in the first person would, by bringing the Adventurer and the Reader nearer together, without the intervention of a stranger, more strongly excite an interest, and consequently afford more entertainment' (*Account* i. iv).

The assumption that seems to lie behind the innovation is a concern for readers, a determination to draw them close and use them well so that they will no longer be sceptical, nonplussed, or hostile when they read descriptions of unparalleled events in strange places. But Hawkesworth's chief care, as Dalrymple rightly deduces, lies not with the reader but with the traveller with whom he, the invisible 'stranger', now identifies. On this topic he has a very distinct conception of what is at stake. When he rewrites Cook's dilemma over the vicissitudes of being at the limit, he removes all elements of doubt and antagonism from the relationship of traveller and narrator—they are now united, 'a first discoverer' pluralized as 'we'[33]—so that it can be invested in their joint conception of the reader, who is resisted as the unequivocal adversary:

The danger of navigating unknown parts of this ocean was now greatly increased by having a crazy ship, and being short of provision and every other

[31] See Beaglehole, *Journal*, p. ccxlvi, also W. H. Pearson, 'Hawkesworth's *Voyages*', in R. F. Brissenden (ed.), *Studies in the Eighteenth Century* (Canberra: Australian National Univ. Press, 1973), 248. This essay is one of the few to offer a dispassionate account of Hawkesworth's project. For a recent discussion of Cook's voyages which restores Hawkesworth to the role of a self-interested botcher of the original journals, see P. J. Marshall and Glyndwr Williams, *The Great Map of Mankind* (Cambridge, Mass.: Harvard Univ. Press, 1982), 259–94.

[32] *The Adventurer*, 4, 20.

[33] Cook's second reflection on the exaggerations of mariners themselves is entirely omitted from Hawkesworth's entries for the end of March (*Account* iii. 380).

necessary; yet the distinction of a first discoverer made us chearfully encounter every danger, and submit to every inconvenience; and we chose rather to incur the censure of imprudence and temerity, which the idle and voluptuous so liberally bestow upon unsuccessful fortitude and perseverance, than leave a country which we had discovered unexplored, and give colour to a charge of timidity and irresolution.   (*Account* iii. 203)

Ironing out the wrinkles of self-doubt, Hawkesworth is removing as far as he can the reader's opportunity to judge the truth and the moral consistency of the narrative. He is not representing Cook by entering a plea before a tribunal. As Dalrymple hints, it is not what is recorded but the responsibility of recording it that preoccupies him. The devices he uses are rhetorical, designed to heighten verisimilitude; but again not with regard to the reader's convenience or enfranchisement, but solely with a view to establishing the superiority of the unparalleled priority of the traveller's voice.

When Hawkesworth turns to that vexed question of minute particulars, the bane of travel-readers, he shows exactly what place the reader occupies in his scale of values. 'It will probably be thought by many Readers, that I have related the nautical events too minutely; but . . . minutely to relate these events was the great object of the work. . . . The relation of little circumstances requires no apology, for it is from little circumstances that the relation of great events derives its power over the mind' (*Account* i. vi). His example is Richardson's *Pamela*, 'the imaginary heroine of a novel that is remarkable for the enumeration of particulars in themselves so trifling, that we almost wonder how they could occur to the author's mind' (pp. vi–vii). In drawing this comparison with a story that explores both the formal and instrumental uses of minute particulars in an unequal power struggle between a man and a woman, Hawkesworth makes it clear that power—power over the reader, power over poor naked savages—is the determining factor in his story. His solution to the problem of narrating discontinuous experiences uncontrolled by command, principle, or providence involves bringing the reader closer to the adventurer so that s/he can take up the position of (hopeless) resistance. When he talks of the power exerted over the mind by the relation of great events, and grandly dismisses his readers to such a relation confident of the effects it will have upon them, the gesture recalls the tyrannical authority of Richardson, who refined his technique of writing to the moment not for the pleasure of thoughtful critics, as his friend Edward Young pointed out, but to ensure the passivity of readers he referred to as his 'distressed patients'.[34] It recalls also Hume's essay 'Of Eloquence' where he dis-

---

[34] Edward Young, *Conjectures Upon Original Composition* (London, 1759), 84.

covers a correspondence between the vehemence of ancient oratory and the disorders and crimes of ancient governments (*Essays*, 106). Hume is talking of, and Hawkesworth is using, 'a Force in Eloquence not learned by rule', as Longinus puts it: 'a Force the reader cannot possibly withstand'.[35] Readers and savages have in common a vulnerability to this force of discovery, unable in the end to withstand it, although they put up a very fierce resistance.

This is not to suggest that Hawkesworth has deserted the Joban model of mediated complaint for his own brand of imperialism. With Job, and even with Dalrymple-as-Job, Hawkesworth knows that law and its cognate structures are a pretence used by the powerful to afflict the weak, and that the weak are not an identifiable body of sufferers, definitely locatable and perpetually exploitable, but the precipitate of repeated, and repeatedly interrupted, gestures in the direction of firstness: as Cook to Maori, so Maori to Cook, so Cook to reader, so reader to Hawkesworth, so Hawkesworth to Dalrymple, and Dalrymple to Forster, whose designation of the savage politics of voyaging applies, *mutatis mutandis*, to a sequence ferocious enough to kill Hawkesworth, as Fanny Burney believed.[36] George Forster, echoing his father's *Observations*, put it like this: 'Men without principles, and without reason, subjected to absolute command, [were] therefore cruelly tyrannical where they had power to follow their inclinations'.[37] Hawkesworth inserts himself, the invisible stranger, as a delegate for 'the first discoverer' whose tale, assuming it could be told, would otherwise be vulnerable to these tyrannic impulses. He is Cook's *go'el*, his vindicator in the sense of champion, not of special pleader. It is a subtle strategy of doubling that George van den Abbeele says is always required when the unverifiability of a voyage to a new place becomes problematic, a move in the direction of fictionality and away from exemplarity to which he gives, borrowing from Montaigne, the expressive form of the unfolded tautology, the ' "tour" of the *tour*'.[38] Hawkesworth unfolds Cook's tautology of hardships that are hardships, dangers that are dangerous.

Hawkesworth's conception of himself as the 'Cook' of Cook's journal-book, the ostensible image of an unparalleled explorer, has a source not only in his rejection of the infoliate tautology of a particular providence, the pretence of the necessity and rightness of everything

---

[35] *On the Sublime*, trans. William Smith (London, 1739; repr. Gainesville, Fla.: Scholars' Facsimiles and Reprints, 1874), 5, 15.

[36] He died, she believed, as a direct result of the 'the invidious, calumniating and most unjust aspersions which had been so cruelly and wantonly cast on him.' *The Early Diaries of Fanny Burney 1768–78*, ed. Annie Raine Ellis, 2 vols. (London: George Bell, 1907), i. 273.

[37] George Forster, *A Reply to Mr Wales's Remarks* (London: B. White, 1777), 27.

[38] George van den Abbeele, *Travel as Metaphor* (Minneapolis: Univ. of Minnesota Press, 1992), 89, 72.

which is, but also in one of his own oriental tales. His *Almoran and Hamet*, based on the tale of Nouraddin and Amana in *The Adventurer* 73, turns on the rivalry of twin princes, Hamet, mild and good, and Almoran, wilful and ambitious. 'What is dominion', asks Almoran, 'if is not possessed alone! and what is power, which the dread of rival power perpetually controuls'.[39] With the help of a djinn, or genius, Almoran exchanges outward shapes with Hamet, and his first step is to attempt the violation of Hamet's fiancée, Almeida; and his last act, after a series of calamities that result from the gratifications of his dearest wishes, is to turn to stone, 'at once a monument of his punishment and his guilt' (53). For her part Almeida falls into despair ('I am now desolate and forlorn' [40]), but Hamet prays, to the accompaniment of apocalyptic thunder, for a sense of himself: 'Let me not be, as if I had never been; but, still conscious of my being, let me still glorify Him from whom it is derived' (52). The genius plays an interesting double game, tempting Almoran into a falsely tautologous seizure of dominion and identity, 'possessed alone' by virtue of an agency which has absorbed into itself all competition, while helping his good brother to a consoling view of himself as himself, who thus avoids the desperation of Almeida.

There are a number of ways of printing this story on to Hawkesworth's *Account*, and indeed on to Goldsmith's similar deployment of an oriental tale in the critique of a particular providence. The simplest is to take Almeida as the embodiment of the terror which Cook feels when his vicissitudes are almost insupportable, and which Hawkesworth's readers also feel when they imagine the intolerable wretchedness of life shorn of the comfort of God's superintendence. Then Almoran's desire for unconditional power and for a self that absorbs all differences becomes analogous to any manœuvre within the power struggle that eclipses other interests and perspectives by the tautology of identity: let us instance the reader who accuses Hawkesworth of corrupting the corrupt because he refuses to see that the effects of things are coincident with their causes (*Public Advertiser* 11926, 3 July). Hamet's split sense of self, formed and cherished by the genius who extends a mirror-medium not unlike the lake used by the genius in Goldsmith's tale of Asem, achieves the same condition of unparalleled parallelism that Cook acquires under the ministrations of Hawkesworth's invisible stranger. The stone into which Almoran's tautologised self petrifies appears in the same stark and hopeless light as Caleb Williams's fancied last memorial; but seen, like Job's stone, as a

---

[39] John Hawkesworth, *Almoran and Hamet: An Oriental Tale* (London: Harrison and Co., 1790), 20.

channel between the doubled first person and a reader properly subdued by the rhetoric of minute particulars, it materializes the medium in which the voice of the first person at the limit is retrieved in all its firstness and singularity.

9 *Sympathy, the Sublime, and* Sappho

The rising hostility between first-person records of emergencies and a dubious and ill-used readership that can be detected in the writing and reception of Hawkesworth's *Account* is the analogue, I am suggesting, of Job's suffering in relation to the consolations of his comforters; of the mute integrity of the patriot to the corruption of placemen and pensioners; of the minute circumstances of the accused person to the written and unwritten law; and, indeed, of all the asymmetries of personal complaint when set against the plenary justifications of theodicy. Each is a repetition of the grammar and the meaning of Job's statement to Eliphaz: 'I could speak as ye do if your soul were in my soul's stead' (Job 16: 4). It is beginning to be clear, I hope, that any negotiation between the two sides which does not instantly privilege the appeal to precedent, law, and cause at the expense of the specificities of singular experience, requires the unparalleled quality of the latter to find a form of representation that doesn't simply reduce it to conformity with a model, or make it measurable by an established rule. The voice it finds must not be familiar, nor must it be used to mount a justification of an experience necessarily excessive, gathered at the limit, because to justify is to restore the primacy of the law, even over unprecedented events. Rather than excusing or exemplifying itself, the representational parallel of that which is unparalleled must sustain excess by transforming it into an aggressive rhetorical bid for power, in the course of which the violence of particularity will dislodge readers from the position of arbiters or judges, and bring them to the condition of the complainant—or, more specifically, the complainant's ostensible image, to use Bentham's phrase. When readers read in the manner preferred by the singular suffering party, then they will be fit to complain too. Such a transformation occurs when ambitious comforters end up as Job-figures, performing in private what they deprecate in public not because they want to but because they are ambushed by fierce intuitions of singularity. Although this sort of substitution is generally associated with sympathy in the eighteenth century, and with the indulgence of socially legitimate feelings of pity and compassion, it is emerging as a much more fraught and troubled encounter in the various contexts of Job; for the substitution is neither amiable in its nature nor social in its effect, but breeds irregular and savage intensities.

No-one is more assiduous in analyzing the conditions under which the suffering individual approaches his audience than Adam Smith, who uses as his model of reception not the book and its reader, but the theatrical spectacle and the spectator. Although Smith is perfectly aware of the ambitions of the grieving party, he is in no doubt that the spectator has the power to bring all viewable scenes of misery to a level agreeable to public standards of what is right. He ventriloquizes the demands of the individual in the first person, in terms that strongly resemble Job's:

If you have either no fellow-feeling for the misfortunes I have met with, or none that bears any proportion to the grief which distracts me; or if you have either no indignation at the injuries I have suffered, or none that bears any proportion to the resentment which transports me, we can no longer converse. . . . You are confounded at my violence and passion, and I am enraged at your cold insensibility and want of feeling.[1]

Smith suggests, however, that a considerable degree of proximity can be achieved between the agitations of distress and the movements of pity, for 'if you labour under any signal calamity, if by some extraordinary misfortune you are fallen into poverty, into diseases, into disgrace and disappointment . . . yet you may generally depend upon the sincerest sympathy of all your friends' (43). And the reason? 'When I condole with you . . . I consider what I should suffer if I was really you, and I not only change circumstances with you, but I change persons and characters' (317). Here there is indeed a change of persons, from third to first person singular, from first to second, and back from the second to the first again. But these impersonations of the sufferer and the sympathy he meets with can never weaken the community that binds Smith's spectators and readers, which he speaks for in the first person plural.[2]

Try as he might, the sufferer will never be gratified by the substitution of one 'I' with another. There is always a disparity between the singular first person and those collaborating in the work of sympathy:

When we condole with our friends in their afflictions, how little do we feel, in comparison of what they feel? We sit down by them, we look at them, and while they relate to us the circumstances of their misfortune, we listen to them with gravity and attention. But while their narration is every moment interrupted by those natural bursts of passion which often seem almost to choak them in the

---

[1] Adam Smith, *The Theory of Moral Sentiments*, ed. D. D. Raphael and A. L. Macfie (Oxford: Clarendon Press, 1976), 21.
[2] See David Marshall, *The Figure of the Theatre*, 170.

midst of it; how far are the languid emotions of our hearts from keeping time to the transports of theirs? (47)

This treatment of complaint, whether it is Job, Cook, a patriot or a felon who suffers it, is common; it bespeaks the reluctance of the community to enter into the sharpness of an individual's suffering. The savagery and monstrosity of first-person narratives, which can only be preserved and communicated by an effort of mimesis which does indeed put the spectator or reader in the place of the narrator, is exactly what Smith eradicates from his scene of sympathy, partly on aesthetic and partly on ethical grounds. The sounds of extreme agony are dissonant, 'We are disgusted with that clamorous grief, which, without any delicacy, calls upon our compassion with sighs and tears and importunate lamentations' (24). If such a grief is to be socialized (and it is just such a sociable concord, in Smith's opinion, that the coarse sufferer noisily demands) then 'the violence of what is felt by the sufferer', the rage and fury of resentment, must be flattened and abated (21–6). Only then will he find an echo of his grief in the impartial spectator's breast.

As they migrate from the the vicious myopia of the first person to the broad and moderate views of the the third, the passions of complainants are softened and civilized. This occurs because the sufferer dresses himself in the gaze of his spectators and finds reasons for self-control compounding in the glances of approval that his reserve has so far won from them. Smith puts it like this: 'I divide myself, as it were, into two persons; and that I, the examiner and judge, represent a different character from that other I, the person whose conduct is examined into and judge of' (*Theory*, 113). To act 'like yourself' after such self-scrutiny is to conform not to the plaintiff 'I', 'whom I properly call myself', but to the social standards of propriety represented by the judicial other 'I', 'the spectator, whose sentiments with regard to my own conduct I endeavour to enter into'. By seeing itself as others see it, the proper 'I' arrives at the condition of sociable sensibility almost achieved by Goldsmith's Mr Burchell, who tries hard to put the history of his morbidly extravagant sensibility into the third person. 'He now found that a man's own heart must be ever given to gain that of another. I now found, that—that—I forget what I was going to observe' (Goldsmith's *Works*, iv. 30). Burchell breaks back into the first person presumably because he was going to teach Smith's lesson of a moderate, self-observing claim for sympathy, but finds the narrative blocked by the strong feelings it recalls. He finds himself unequal to the task of fitting observational third-person competence to the ragged emotions of first-person suffering. In *The Vicar of Wakefield*, as in Goldsmith's and Hawkesworth's oriental tales, the 'genius' interposes to restore the confidence of the first person by perfecting it in its own proper sight. The one 'I' greets the other outside the false economy of prescription and law as a spectral, not spectatorial, reinforcement. Smith, on the other hand, sets up a mirror-play between the spectator and the *idea* of pain that entirely evacuates what Hume calls 'the reality of that evil and disorder, with which the world so much abounds' (*Enquiry*, 138). By make-believe— the sufferer pretending to be the spectator who cannot know his pain, and the spectator pretending to share a pain he can never feel—the infoliate tautology is acted out. Everything which is, is right, because the afflicted 'I' impersonates the 'he' or 'she' the spectating world approves of in order to enter into the consensus of 'we'—and the world swells into the plenum of a stoical theodicy, where moral and physical evil cease to present a problem.[3]

In contradicting 'the desponding, plaintive, and whining tone of some modern systems' (283 and n. 17), Smith renovates the stoical and providential .sides of Christian piety, and endorses an approach to suffering Charles Churchill calls 'the worst of insolence'.[4] The same lesson of reserve and self-government litters the paraphrases of Job. In commendatory verses to George Sandys's, Dudley Digges singles out for praise the transmutation of misery into something sweet and graceful: 'Here Griefe is witty, that the Reader might | Not suffer, in the patience you write'.[5] Simon Patrick understands the book of Job to teach us resignation, and the 'modesty in mourning' that 'we may weep moder- ately' and thus not offend our company.[6] Even the intimate terms of epistolary correspondence exclude whining. In Pope's letters is included a note written on behalf of Pope's sister, Mrs Rackett, to her mother: 'Mrs Rackett being in the depth of affliction for the loss of her poor little child desires me . . . to acquaint you with it, hoping you will excuse her not writing herself, her sorrow being such at present, as she cannot put pen to paper, nor mention such a melancholy subject' (*Correspondence*, ii. 4). The protocol of excessive grief is perfectly plain: until you are fit to be read once again as a social sign, you decently contract the particu- larity and clamour of personal sorrow behind what Johnson calls 'the veils of woe'.[7]

The reserve applauded by Smith is comically represented by Henry

---

[3] See Marshall's analysis of this, together with its unconsoling corollary: 'It is only through theater that we can escape the intolerable situation that theatricality itself creates' (172, 192).

[4] 'When foes insult, and *prudent* friends dispense, | In pity's strains, the worst of insolence'. *Night*, ll. 1–2; *The Poetical Works of Charles Churchill*, ed. Douglas Grant (Oxford: Clarendon Press, 1956), 51.

[5] *A Paraphrase upon the Divine Poems* (London, 1638), p. vi.

[6] Simon Patrick, *The Book of Job Paraphrased* (London, 1697), p. [iii]; and *Consolatory Dis- course to Prevent Immoderate Grief* (London, 1676), 90–2.

[7] *The Vanity of Human Wishes*, i. 66 in *Samuel Johnson*, ed. Donald Greene (Oxford: Oxford Univ. Press, 1984), 14.

Fielding (who was himself a poor exponent of it) when the bereaved person—here a widow—receives company and exchanges routine sentiments of loss with her visitors:

> VISITOR: I am sure, Madam, it is with the utmost Concern I wait on you on this Occasion, to condole with you on the Loss of——.
> WIDOW: He was the best of Men.
> VISITOR: I am sure it is a very sensible Affliction to all your Friends.
> WIDOW: You are always good.—Such a husband—.
> VISITOR: We are all mortal.
> WIDOW: If it had been my Fate to have gone first.
> VISITOR: We must not repine at our Lot.
> WIDOW: I shall not long survive.
> VISITOR: Fie Madam, you must bear this Affliction with more Resolution.[8]

Whether hypocrisy or reserve impels the dispassionate exchange of sentiments Smith admires, the disorder and excess of first-person complaint is removed as far as possible from the community it defends, leaving no tension—none of 'those natural bursts of passion' which choke Burchell's narrative (*Theory*, 47)—and therefore no sense of violence encountered and absorbed. Mackenzie's Julia de Roubigné rehearses and rejects the false universality of this self-control, and vindicates the singularity of first-person sentiment: ' "Your loss is common to thousands"! Such is the hackneyed consolation of ordinary minds, unavailing even when it is true. But mine is not common'.[9]

There is an exceptional instance in Smith's accounts of how agony is schooled to social discourse, and it is to be found among 'savages', the very people who provoke Captain Cook's difficult first-person engagement with someone like a spectator or reader. Searching for a model of constancy outside the line of Roman stoics, such as Cato and Seneca, Smith finds it in North America, where the Spartan discipline of life is imposed not by precept but by the harshness of the climate and the terrain. No-one there enjoys the 'little excesses' pardonable in polite society, where men can weep moderately without disgrace (*Theory*, 207), and thus savages can acquire a purer brand of civility: 'A savage . . . whatever be the nature of his distress, expects no sympathy from those about him, and disdains, upon that account, to expose himself, by allowing the least weakness to escape him. His passions, how furious and violent soever, are never permitted to disturb the serenity of his countenance or the composure of his conduct and behaviour' (205).

---

[8] *The Voyages of Mr. Job Vinegar*, ed. S. J. Sackett (Los Angeles: Augustan Reprint Soc., 1958), 20 (originally appearing in *The Champion*, 114 [1740]).

[9] Henry Mackenzie, *Julia de Roubigné: A Tale*, 2 vols. (London: W. Strahan and T. Cadell, 1777), i. 121.

The extreme test of a savage's self-possession comes at the stake, where he is tortured to death by his enemies:

While he is hung by the shoulders over a slow fire, he derides his tormentors, and tells them with how much more ingenuity he himself had tormented such of their countrymen as had fallen into his hands. After he has been scorched and burnt, and lacerated in all the most tender and sensible parts of his body for several hours together, he is often allowed, in order to prolong his misery, a short respite, and is taken down from the stake: he employs this interval in talking upon all indifferent subjects, inquires after the news of the country . . . The spectators express the same insensiblity; the sight of so horrible an object seems to make no impression upon them; they scarce look at the prisoner, except when they lend a hand to torment him. At other times they smoke tobacco, and amuse themselves with any common object, as if no such matter was going on.   (206)

Thus far the scene at the stake is like a gladiatorial contest in Rome or a visit of condolence in modern Britain, where the audience places an embargo on all whining and excess. Indeed, Smith chooses the same example of fortitude as Leibniz, who also cites the impassivity of the American Indians under torture as proof that physical evil is not the terrifying anomaly Pierre Bayle thinks it is: 'The Hurons, the Iroquois, the Galibis and other peoples of America teach us a great lesson on this matter: one cannot read without astonishment of the intrepidity and well-nigh insensibility wherewith they brave their enemies, who roast them over a slow fire and eat them by slices'.[10] Except for the addition of cannibalism, Leibniz anticipates Smith in reading the customs of the savages as a lesson to the civilized sufferer: 'They inspire us to acquire a certain presence of mind in the midst of the distractions and impressions most likely to disturb us' (*Theodicy*, 284).

Unlike Adam Ferguson, who responds to the intimacy of the North American scene of torture and the 'strange kind of affection and tenderness' which governs its phases,[11] Smith sees the 'concerted tranquillity' of sufferer and spectator as a conspiracy of silence, a mutual determination not to talk of what preoccupies them (*Theory*, 24). This is achieved in the intermittent chat 'upon all indifferent subjects'. The silence about suffering is broken, however, with a song, 'the song of death . . . which he is to sing when he has fallen into the hands of his enemies and is expiring under the tortures which they inflict upon him' (206). Later Smith gives a figurative turn to this last performance of stoic indifference when he refers to the death-song of the ancient philosophers, by which

---

[10] *Theodicy*, 280.
[11] *An Essay on the History of Civil Society* (1767), ed. Duncan Forbes (Edinburgh: Univ. Press of Edinburgh, 1966), 92.

he means suicide (283). In both the literal and figurative examples, he wishes to emphasise the magnanimity which, in first silencing the noise of pain, finds at last a way to signalize itself in a public and heroic act of self-extinction, the logical destination of all attempts to subdue the personal 'I'. The audience of the song will hear in it the echo of a pluralized first-person consensus about the value of self-possession, now embodied in the constancy of a third person: 'he' is 'we', an incorporation that takes place literally in the cannibalization of Leibniz's living victim. And this echo will sound regardless of the part the spectators play in the production of the act, whether they have supplied elements of persecution and torture, or view it merely impartially.

But the song Smith instances fails to indicate this kind of reverberating chorus concerning the value of *apatheia*, consisting as it does of 'insults upon his tormentors' made by their derisive victim while suspended over the fire (206). The dying Indian may be impassive with respect to pain, considered in itself, but he is speaking violently to those who, in inflicting it, expect him to cry out. According to Lafitau, whom Smith is excerpting, the death-song is delivered in mocking detail designed to exasperate the torturers: the victims 'recontent ce qu'ils ont fait euxmêmes à l'égard des prisonniers, qui ont passé part leurs mains . . . ils entrent dans le détail le plus exact de tout ce qu'ils leur ont fait souffrir, sans craindre les suites d'un discours, lequel ne peut qu'aigrir extrêmement ceux qui l'écoutent'.[12] Adair believes the purpose of the song is to disturb the dead as well as the living, by spoiling the revenge designed to pacify the spirits of slain warriors. Their 'crying blood' demands that 'the wound be returned in as equal a manner as could be expected'; meanwhile the victim is determined that his own intrepidity will prevent that equality and keep the blood crying.[13] Far from establishing a civil consensus, the tormented savage is engaged in an ingenious form of substitution, whereby his dead enemies will perform the howling which his tormentors are failing to elicit from him. As Montaigne points out in his comment on the death-song, it sustains a circuit of violence: 'Those that paint these people dying after this manner, represent the prisoner spitting in the faces of his executioners and making wry mouths at them. And 'tis most certain, that to the very last gasp, they never cease to brave and defy them both in word and gesture'.[14] It is a vindication in the strict sense of a retaliation: it puts 'the law of retaliation in force' (Adair, 153).

[12] Pierre Lafitau, *Mœurs des Sauvages Ameriquains*, 2 vols. (Paris: Charles Hochereau, 1724), ii. 284.

[13] James Adair, *The History of the American Indians* (London: Charles and Edward Dilly, 1775), 148–50.

[14] 'Of Cannibals', *The Essays of Michel de Montaigne*, ed. W. Carew Hazlitt, trans. Charles Cotton, 3 vols. (London: George Bell, 1892), i. 227.

Although Smith would like to assimilate the death of the noble savage to the exemplary behaviour of dying patriots and magnanimous criminals who disdain to lament or weep, his savage is neither tranquil, in the manner of Cato, nor the object of public applause, in the manner of a resolute Tyburn felon. He is determined to affect his audience with the passions they want to arouse in him. It is an exigent state of affairs which, when he meets it in civil society, Smith deprecates. When the supererogatory details of first-person suffering threaten the listener with 'those circumstances [which], he fears, might make so violent an impression upon him, that he [can] no longer keep within the bounds of moderation' (49), the civilizing end of sympathy is lost. The threat of the savage backwash of feelings that follows in the wake of the circumstantial and unprecedented narrative of the 'I' lies behind Smith's idealization of reserve, particularly his partial account of North American torture.

Smith has already indicated that first-person passion constitutes the interruption of any publicly acceptable narrative of pain, even though the death-song of the savage proves an exception. How does a death-song work? It follows the same pattern as Job's vindication, which in turn resembles both Romilly's conception of the law as a narrative of the circumstances that will shape its execution, and Hawkesworth's minute first-person defence of Cook's unparalleled experiences of savagery. The 'I' takes a picture of itself not with a view of producing a socialized and pared image of the propriety of its anguish, but as a way of utilizing the force that is instinct in excess, and redirecting the violence responsible for its pain upon the audience that would prefer the violence to go unresented and unavenged. It transforms interruption into oratory so powerful that the audience cannot avoid its effect by turning away or shutting its ears. Agency is transferred from the spectator—now too moved to be impartial or disgusted—to the sufferer.

In a summary of the various current doctrines of sympathy, in which he recommends those endorsing a balanced appeal to the altruism of the spectator, George Campbell finds difficulty with two. The first is Hume's solution of the problem of why we take delight in representations of distress, namely the eloquence with which it is performed, 'the art employed in collecting all the pathetic circumstances, the judgement displayed in disposing them'.[15] The second is Hawkesworth's *Adventurer* 110, where he maintains that pity is not a truly social or philanthropic emotion, but rather a dallying with a fiction of distress for the purpose of present self-gratification. Campbell finds it hard to determine

---

[15] George Campbell, *The Philosophy of Rhetoric* (1776), ed. Lloyd F. Bitzer (Carbondale: Southern Illinois Univ. Press, 1963), 119–23; see Hume, 'Of Tragedy', *Essays Moral, Political, and Literary*, ed. Eugene F. Miller (Indianapolis: Liberty, Classics, 1987), 219–20.

whether Hume means that eloquence heightens or softens a painful scene, and whether the pleasure the audience derives from eloquence is owing to its awareness of the orator's skill or its uncritical submission to its power. He would prefer to believe that Hume is making the former case, as he cannot see how the force of oratory, aimed at 'exaggerating, strengthening, heightening, and inflaming' the passions of the audience, can ever have the lenitive effect associated with delight (*Rhetoric*, 119). In Hawkesworth he sees an attempt to resuscitate 'the antiquated doctrine of the philosopher of Malmesbury' (123) by imputing a purely selfish motive to pity which, as it becomes more intense, establishes the fiction that you are the represented suffering party. In discussing both essays, Campbell finds it impossible to dislodge from his mind two associated ideas: the first that the audience is really always in charge, the second that a rhetorical representation of affliction can be undertaken for any other reason than the pleasure of the audience. Like Smith, he proposes a communitarian theory of sympathy which privileges the spectators at the expense of the suffering individual.

Hume's position is very different. Unlike du Bos and Fontenelle, whom he begins by citing, he establishes intimacy not with readers in general, who constitute the audience to be worked upon, but with a reader-orator who is to do the work: 'Had you any intention to move a person extremely by the narration of any event, the best method of encreasing its effect would be' and he goes on to list the techniques ('Of Tragedy', 222). Like the common liar, the orator's aim is to *fix* and *attach* his listeners (218), to *dismiss* them (224) to a condition in which *uneasiness*, representing the option of refusal of the sight or narrative of suffering, has been 'overpowered and effaced by something stronger of an opposite kind', namely the 'force of oratory' (220). The critical measure determining the representability of unpleasant scenes, such as oppressed and plaintive virtue, gruesome suicide, 'tortures, wounds, executions', and so on, is the 'passivity of suffering' (224). There must be sufficient activity in the victim to support the multiplication of pathetic circumstances, on which depends firstly the 'eloquence, with which the melancholy scene is represented' (219) and lastly the dominion the forceful orator will enjoy over his audience. This dominion will consist not in promoting a fictional distress, carefully composed according to standards of public acceptability, but in conveying in an irresistible way 'the reality of that evil and disorder, with which the world so much abounds' (*Enquiry*, 138). To this extent, Hume merely restates the grounds of his argument in 'Of Eloquence,' where he establishes the connection between civil disorder and political violence on the one hand, and on the other the power of the public speaker to transfix his audience with images 'monstrous and gigantic' ('Of Eloquence', 101).

Like Hume's essay, which partly practises, in occasional fits of synonymical excess, its own doctrine of multiplication, Hawkesworth's provides a substantial instance of what it is discussing in the form of a story about the reception of the account of the battle of Fontenoy. The scene of carnage, where cannon-fire has 'strewed the ground with mangled limbs and carcasses that almost floated in blood' (ii. 237), illustrates his philosophical position on the 'general and indiscriminate distribution of misery' (ii. 298), as well as his remarks on scenes of savagery in the South Pacific, where the violence consequent upon the order to fire sometimes exceeds all prescription. As a general narrative, the news of Fontenoy is managed in a civilized drawing room with the same discretion as Fielding's condoling visitor or Smith's impartial spectator:

They bowed with a graceful simper to a lady who sneezed, mutually presented each other with snuff, shook their heads and changed their posture at proper intervals, asked some questions which tended to produce a more minute detail of such circumstances of horror as had been lightly touched, and having at last remarked that the Roman patriot regretted the brave could die but once, the conversation soon became general.   (ii. 237)

Hawkesworth locates the scene of polite compassion between the extremes he outlines in the *Account*. On the one hand there is 'the naked brevity of an index', where 'an account that ten thousand men perished in a battle, that twice that number were swallowed up by an earthquake, or that a whole nation was swept away by a pestilence, is read . . . without the least emotion' (*Account* i. vii). And on the other is his own account, which, like Richardson's *Pamela*, is an exceedingly minute and detailed performance rendered in the first person.

The story of Fontenoy is moved towards the extreme of particularity when the narrator tells the story of a young officer's wife who, waiting in vain for the return of her husband, decides to search the battlefield for his body. She comes across a corpse so disfigured by its wounds that she knows it for his only by looking at the wrist, where 'she discovered . . . the remains of a rufle, round which there was a slight border of her own work'. She faints with the shock, and later dies. The audience is now moved to tears, not least a lady who falls back in her chair in a faint, and who turns out to be the mother of the dead officer's wife. Although Hawkesworth blunts his tale with some reflections on the malignity of public gestures of benevolence, followed by a Christian call for submissiveness and humility, he shows what degree of oratorical skill, specifically in the figure of amplification, is necessary if an audience is to be moved—made 'susceptible', 'fixed', and 'touched'—to the point where the faint of the depicted woman is repeated in the faint of the listening woman. This is the stage of intensity at which readers may be 'dismissed' to scenes of violence with no danger of their refusing to be overwhelmed by them, no matter how ill-used they may feel. The narrator of Fontenoy sings something like the death-song of the disfigured corpse, shifting the polite audience from insensibility at 'the sight of so horrible an object', as Smith calls the tortured Indian, towards a riveted attention to the monstrosity and particularity of a disfigured body, 'what is perfectly deformed . . . most singular and odd' (*Theory*, 198).[16]

In eighteenth-century aesthetics the competition between these two views concerning scenes in themselves shocking or horrid, the first requiring the flattening of violence so that it conforms to a rule of taste, and the second preferring a circumstantial representation of unprecedented suffering, grows ever more distinct. Among the British, the defence of a limited and general representation of whatever is gigantic or monstrous is typified by John Baillie, who remarks, 'No Object is so grand, but is attended with some *trifling* Circumstance, upon which a little Mind will surely fix; the Universe has its Cockle-shells, and its Butterflies, the ardent Pursuits of childish Geniuses'.[17] Improving Baillie's hint, Beattie warns that the sure way to ruin the sublime is 'by too minute descriptions, and too many words': you do not number the windows of a lofty building, or describe the state of a hero's teeth and nails.[18] 'One trifling circumstance, one mean idea, is sufficient to destroy the whole charm [of] Sublime description,' writes Blair.[19] This hostility to particularity is given its most majestic expression by Samuel Johnson in his essay on Cowley, where he states that 'great thoughts are always general, and consist . . . in descriptions not descending into minuteness'.[20] They are rehearsed finally by Coleridge in his deprecation of the 'matter-of-factness' of Wordsworth's poetry—'a laborious minuteness . . . the insertion of accidental circumstances'—which he judges to be 'incompatible with the steady fervour of a mind possessed

---

[16] For a history of monstrosity and particularity in the context of Enlightenment aesthetics, see Barbara Stafford, *Body Criticism: Imagining the Unseen in Enlightenment Art and Medicine* (Cambridge, Mass.: MIT Press, 1991): 'The monster is central to my argument precisely because it interrupts, through glaring excess of defect, the plenitude of succession' (254).

[17] John Baillie, *An Essay on the Sublime* (London, 1747; repr. Los Angeles: Clark Library, 1953), 13.

[18] James Beattie, 'Illustrations on Sublimity' in *Dissertations Moral and Critical* (London, 1783; repr. Stuttgart: Friedrich Frommann, 1970), 639.

[19] Hugh Blair, *Lectures on Rhetoric and Belles Lettres*, 3 vols. (London, 1787), i. 90.

[20] Johnson, 'Cowley', in *Lives of the English Poets*, ed. George Birkbeck Hill, 3 vols. (Oxford: Clarendon Press, 1905), i. 21.

and filled with the grandeur of its subject'.[21] Reynolds supports the same standards in pictorial effects. As far as he is concerned, minuteness and deformity are the same thing, a blurring of the idea of a general form.[22]

It is of course in his marginal commentary on the *Discourses* that Blake makes his celebrated retort: 'All Sublimity is founded on Minute Discrimination', reaffirming the high value he places on minuteness in *Jerusalem*, specifically in the practice of sympathy: 'All broad & general principles belong to benevolence | Who protects minute particulars, every one in their own identity'.[23] Such maxims put Blake in company with a heterogeneous collection of critics in the eighteenth century who believe that particularity is never to be neglected.[24] Whether it is Blackwell and Gibbon talking about the circumstantial beauties of epic and history,[25] Lowth praising 'the minutest circumstances' and 'the exact and vivid delineation of the objects' which characterizes the scriptural sublime,[26] Priestley calculating the remarkable effects of 'a redundancy of particulars' upon the imaginations of readers,[27] Richard Payne Knight arguing that the truths which interest the feelings are 'naturally circumstantial,'[28] or even a novelist such as Sterne explaining to his reader that the circumstances of things alone determine how they shall be judged—'great——little——good——bad . . . just as the case happens',[29]—the particularizing critics respond much more acutely to the singularity of the object of taste than their opponents, who would prefer it merely to exemplify a general rule about the indivisibility of sublime phenomena. This introduces a degree of scepticism about readers, vividly dramatized in the work of Laurence Sterne, where the worst are

[21] Coleridge, *Biographia Literaria*, ed. J. Shawcross, 2 vols. (Oxford: Clarendon Press, 1907), ii. 68, 101.

[22] Joshua Reynolds, *Discourses on Art* (No. 4), ed. Robert E. Wark (San Marino, Calif.: Huntington Library, 1959), 65.

[23] *The Complete Poetry and Prose of William Blake*, ed. David V. Erdman (Berkeley: Univ. of California Press, 1982), 643.

[24] This branch of the sublime tends to be dominated, however, by scriptural critics. See M. H. Abrams, *The Mirror and the Lamp* (Oxford: Oxford Univ. Press, 1953) and David B. Morris, *The Religious Sublime* (Lexington, Ky.: Univ. of Kentucky Press, 1972).

[25] Thomas Blackwell, *An Enquiry into the Life and Writings of Homer*, 2 vols. (London, 1735), i. 12; Edward Gibbon, *An Essay on the Study of Literature* (London, 1764; repr. New York: Garland, 1970), 30.

[26] *Lectures on the Sacred Poetry of the Hebrews*, trans. G. Gregory, 2 vols. (London: J. Johnson, 1787), i. 124.

[27] Joseph Priestley, *A Course of Lectures on Oratory and Criticism* (London, 1777; repr. Menston: Scolar Press, 1968), 85.

[28] Richard Payne Knight, *An Analytical Enquiry into the Principles of Taste* (London, 1805), 277.

[29] *The Life and Opinions of Tristram Shandy Gent.*, ed. Melvyn New and Joan New (Univ. Presses of Florida, 1978), i. 187. For a short history of particularity, or detailism as it is now often called, see Naomi Schor, *Reading in Detail: Aesthetics and the Feminine* (New York: Methuen, 1987).

identified as general types (the lawyer-reader, clergyman-reader, female-reader, cognoscento-reader), all enemies to singularity and minuteness, which they judge to be breaches of the rules of good composition.

In Europe the theory and practice of history-painting links the two issues—the antagonism of the spectator towards particularized depictions of violent pain or plaintive distress—in a debate that lasts until the end of the century. In his *Laocoon* (1766) Lessing applies Smith's scale of an acceptable level of suffering to Greek art and drama in order to show how the silent torment of the chief figure in the Laocoon group exhibits, precisely because of the silence of self-restraint, the 'highest beauty possible under the given condition of physical pain'. The artist has understood that 'pain in all its disfiguring violence . . . had to be reduced'.[30] Sophocles' Philoctetes, on the other hand, is outrageous in his suffering, 'He moans, he shrieks, he falls into the most horrible convulsions' (27). Hercules exhibits as little self-control when he puts on the poisoned shirt of Nessus and, frantic with pain, dashes Lichas against a rock (31).

Michael Fried dates the French reaction to this theatricalized conception of the representation of a 'correct' anguish from the 1750s, with the absorptive tableaux of Greuze and Chardin, in which the figures are rapt in their own emotions, oblivious to any spectator.[31] As it were through a fissure in the narrative convention of painting, the viewer observes his or her own erasure from a scene whose intensity is focused on 'les petits détails de la vie commun', such as a crushed flower, a playing card, a bared breast, a dishevelled lock of hair, producing an effect very similar to Hawkesworth's 'rufle'.[32] In England the work of Joseph Wright of Derby, notably *The Indian Widow* (1783–5) and *The Dead Soldier* (1789), establishes the same intense absorption in loss in a context of heterogeneous articles, such as a broken bow and a fallen mob-cap. From roughly the same period Robert Rosenblum charts the growth of what he calls the 'Neoclassical Horrific,' with subjects designed to explode the distinctions drawn by Smith and Lessing.[33] Abildgaard's *Philoctetes* (1775), Canova's *Hercules and Lichas* (1815), and Antoine-Jean Gros's *Sappho* (1801) show scenes of unflattened agony, violence,

---

[30] Gotthold Ephraim Lessing, *Laocoon*, trans. Edward Allen McCormick (New York: Bobbs Merrill, 1962), 17. He locates his example of primitive stoicism not in North American customs but in Scandinavian epic: 'To master all pain, to take death's stroke with unflinching eye, to die laughing under the adder's bite . . . these are the traits of old Nordic heroism' (9).

[31] Michael Fried, *Absorption and Theatricality: Painting and the Beholder in the Age of Diderot* (Berkeley, Calif.: Univ. of California Press, 1980), 55.

[32] Fried, *Absorption*, 52; see also Jay Caplan, *Framed Narratives: Diderot's Genealogy of the Beholder* (Minneapolis: Univ. of Minnesota Press, 1985), 18.

[33] Robert Rosenblum, *Transformations in Late Eighteenth-Century Art* (Princeton, NJ: Princeton Univ. Press, 1967), 11.

and despair. John Mortimer's *Sextus applying to Erictho* (1771) takes a scene from Lucan's *Pharsalia* where the witch Erictho performs a hideous variation on the death-song, lashing a mangled corpse with serpents that it may revive and prophesy (Rosenblum, 11). Gillray's *Gout* (1799) and Rowlandson's *The Hypochondriac* (1788) are comic attempts to expose the disorder of a private agony.[34] In the same period Job's griefs, never a popular theme for painters, are occasionally visible in de Loutherbourg's illustrations for the Macklin Bible (1792–1800); in Blake's pen-and-wash drawings of 1785, 'Mourning' and 'Job, his Wife and his Friends', followed by the fully worked plate, entitled *Job*, eight years later; and in James Barry's *Job reproved by his Friends* (1777), dedicated to Edmund Burke. And of course Blake's prototype of the eleventh plate of his illustrations of the book of Job (1825), *The Elohim creating Adam* (1785), dramatizes the spectral violence of 'I' against 'I' that takes place when, as Smith puts it, circumstances make an impression so vivid that feelings can no longer be kept within the bounds of moderation (*Theory*, 49). Diderot's explanation for this concentration upon scenes of passion unmodified by the presence of a spectator includes a succinct riposte to Smith and Lessing, together with the theory of tragedy upon which they rely: 'Those who have written about the art of drama resemble a man who, looking for means to torment a whole family, instead of weighing those means in relation to the trouble they would cause the family, would weigh them according to what the neighbours will say'.[35]

The interaction between the tableau and the beholder is complex, for the beholder continues to operate despite his or her erasure. Caplan unites the sense of being nonplussed ('at a loss') with the pathos of the missing person or thing in the following formulation: 'A loss inside the tableau constitutes the beholder outside it' (Caplan, 23). This double interruption, formal and narrative as well as personal and shocking, results in a mirroring of the depicted gestures in the reactions of the viewer; tears are met with tears, rather as faint answers faint in Hawkesworth's Fontenoy narrative (Caplan, 17). Fried sees this process as circular, based on the reciprocal enablement of two fictions: the illusion of the beholder's nonexistence is necessary for the representation of complete absorption of the figures; while their complete absorption is an illusion causing the possibility of the fiction of the beholder's nonexistence (Fried, 109). Goldsmith's oriental tale of Asem is apropos, considering that it is in the suspension of the suicidal act of

---

[34] 'The portrait in poor taste of the unheroic and lowly sufferer.' See Barbara Stafford, *Body Criticism*, 186.

[35] *Discours sur la poésie dramatique*, cited in Fried, 94.

the viewing 'I' that a fiction can be composed whose reflection of the 'I' finally restores its tranquillity. Fried paraphrases Diderot on the strange peacefulness of the erased beholder's reverie, 'He comes to experience a pure and intense sensation of the sweetness and as it were the self-sufficiency of his own existence' (Fried, 131).

Towards the end of the century the erasure of the spectator from a scene of absorption is exchanged for a more active and combative encounter between the self-sufficiency of what is depicted and viewers ambitious to enjoy something more than the sight of it. Fried writes compellingly of F.-A. Vincent's *Belisaire* (1777), where the suppressed violence of the beholder of Belisarius's miserable beggary is projected in the equivocal positioning and glance of the soldier giving him alms. This threat of retheatricalization, most graphically dramatised for Fried in Géricault's *Raft of the Medusa*, where the appalling circumstances of privation represented in the picture advertise the arrival of spectators restored to agency (Fried, 154), is actively pre-empted in paintings which deal with self-sufficiency in its performative rather than absorptive dimension. Norman Bryson takes pictures such as Gavin Hamilton's *Oath of Brutus*, Greuze's *The Paternal Curse*, Ingres' *Vow of Louis XIII*, and of course David's *Oath of the Horatii* as examples of the continuity of word and gesture in which 'speech once uttered becomes autonomous, self-potentiated, no longer bound by the control of the speaker'.[36] The raptness of figures engaged in these powerful speech-acts more definitely excludes and diminishes the beholder, prompting Diderot to dream of people enslaved by the illusion that signs are alive (Bryson, 196).

The history of this struggle for dominion between the spectator and the spectacle indicates that the motives for sympathy are as self-interested as Hawkesworth says they are, and that they involve, as Hume suggests, applications of force in what is already a context of violence. Smith's death-song, in its savage and retaliatory aspect, is a type of this violence, implicating and subduing its audience in a manner cognate with narratives that ill-use their readers. The conflicts between the producers and receivers of stories of unparalleled and painful experiences are carried on by force of rhetoric and oratory, as Hume points out. This situates the cause of the victim of sympathy within the instrumentally interruptive modes of political narrative, where power and not principle is the primary objective. The combative nature of both spring from sets of principles which award the audience or the spec-

---

[36] Norman Bryson, *Word and Image* (Oxford: Oxford Univ. Press, 1981), 173.

tators the power of judgement, and give them permission to call their own savagery civilized.

In *A Philosophical Enquiry* Burke makes an interesting traverse of sympathetic possibilities by way of the sublime. The scene of sympathy—'some uncommon and grievous calamity'—takes shape as an execution, recalling his first example of the infinity of pain in a terrible object, the *écartèlement* of Damiens.[37] Like Smith, he warns that violence and ruin must not 'press too close', but he makes no concession to the general opinion that a theatricalized agony is superior or more appealing than the real thing:

Chuse a day on which to represent the most sublime and affecting tragedy ... and when you have collected your audience, just at the moment when their minds are erect with expectation, let it be reported that a state criminal of high rank is on the point of being executed in the adjoining square; in a moment the emptiness of the theatre would demonstrate the comparative weakness of the imitative arts, and proclaim the triumph of the real sympathy. (47)

This 'real sympathy' is the delight we take, 'and that no small one, in the real misfortunes and pains of others' (45). It appears to rely upon no other medium than distance, for Burke dismisses the notion that delight arises from the contrast between our immunity from the distresses with which we sympathize. Like any other sublime object, terrible or dangerous, suffering must be viewed 'at certain distances, and with certain modifications' if it is to be viewed at all (40).

The imitative arts are weak, evident from the superiority of a public execution over a tragedy in drawing a crowd; for:

when the object of the painting or poem is such as we should run to see it if real, let it affect us with what odd sort of sense it will, we may rely on it, that the power of the poem or picture is more owing to the nature of the thing itself than to the mere effect of imitation, or to a consideration of the skill of the imitator however excellent. (49–50)

However, there is another kind of imitation which, like sympathy, results in a 'a sort of substitution, by which we are put into the place of another man' (44), and which depends upon an interesting transaction between the 'odd sort of sense' of the 'thing itself' and the subject's acquired sense of its own singularity. This sense has been 'so strong as to make very miserable men take comfort that they were supreme in

[37] *A Philosophical Enquiry into the Origin of our Ideas of the Sublime and Beautiful*, ed. James T. Boulton (Oxford: Basil Blackwell, 1987), 46, 47, 39.

misery; and certain it is, that where we cannot distinguish ourselves by something excellent, we begin to take a complacency in some singular infirmities, follies, and defects of one kind or other' (50). That this sense of singularity is chiefly an illusion is made clearer when Burke says that it is provoked by 'terrible objects' whose sublimity the mind of the spectator merely borrows, 'claiming to itself some part of the dignity and importance of the things which it contemplates'. It is then that Burke paraphrases Longinus on 'that glorying sense of inward greatness, that always fills the reader of such passages in poets and orators as are sublime' (51).[38]

This is the only time Burke mentions Longinus, and he does so to account for the collision I have been discussing between the first-person subject experiencing the excess of a limit-case and the ill-used reader (or spectator) who finds him- or herself in the vicinity of a scene analogous to, or more properly mimetic of, the first-person predicament: the fainting woman and the fainting woman, Cook's 'savages' and Hawkesworth's readers, the death-song and the crying blood of the dead, and so on. By means of a modification of sublimity which Burke specifies as the variable distance that may be set between the audience and the thing itself, or as the obscurity interrupting the view of it, but which functions in a manner comparable to the 'genius' in Goldsmith's and Hawkesworth's oriental tales, Burke provides himself with the opportunity of inserting his own eye between the spectacle and the spectators, taking up the role of a super-spectator with a special interest in the singularities of the sufferer. He is then positioned to excite an illusion of redeemed ruin so intense that the mind is able to claim the dignity and importance of the thing which it contemplates.

Longinus' account of how the reader gets to this sense of firstness is a history of serial violence. First there is a threat to divine, natural, or political order (the battle of the gods, Orestes' crime of matricide, the disastrous conflict between the Athenian state and Philip of Macedon) which is retailed to the poet or orator in such overwhelming terms that s/he is enabled, having converted astonishment into rhetoric, to transfer that effect upon an audience who in turn, if they are as clever as Longinus, can pass on their experience of modified terror to a fresh audience. There is no doubt that each phase is violent: the mind swells in transport in response to the *strokes* of the sublime like a limb swelling

---

[38] 'For the Mind is naturally elevated by the true Sublime, and so sensibly affected with its lively Strokes, that it swells in Transport and an inward Pride, as if what was only heard had been the Product of its own Invention.' Smith, *Dionysius Longinus on the Sublime* (London, 1739; repr. New York: Scholars' Facsimiles & Reprints, 1975), vii. 2; 14. On the anomalous place of Longinus in Burke's argument, see Steven Knapp, *Personification and the Sublime* (Cambridge, Mass.: Harvard Univ. Press, 1985), 70–3.

with a bruise (vii. 2); it is a 'Force we cannot possibly withstand' that leaves ineffaceable weals upon the mind (vii. 3); it is a lightning bolt (xii.4); it 'strikes home, and triumphs over every Hearer' (i. 2). Even the celebrated *fiat lux* is an act of irresistible might, borrowed first by Moses in order to establish his will as law, and borrowed again by Longinus in order to overwhelm Caecilius with the justice of his taste, and again by Boileau, and then by Pope, and always with the same intention of transforming the effect of astonishment at a singular phenomenon into a self-authorizing and original gesture of command over a new audience. Longinus speaks only in the first person to a second person who will aspire to firstness. He both describes and contributes to a cycle of usurpations of power: that is to say, he makes a selection of selections by being sublime upon the sublime.

When Burke says, 'I know of nothing sublime which is not some modification of power' (*Enquiry*, 64), he begins, with the second edition of his work in 1759, to set the question of distance in a new light, corresponding to the phases which, in Longinus, divide astonishment from mimesis. Unmodified power is God, and God is terrible, 'a force which nothing can withstand', before which 'we shrink into the minuteness of our own nature, and are . . . annihilated' (68). He explains his initial reticence on this topic as 'natural timidity with regard to power': 'I purposely avoided when I first considered this subject, to introduce the idea of that great and tremendous being, as an example in an argument so light as this' (67–8). His reasons for overcoming his reluctance are to be found in a series of displacements from limited or imperfect definitions of the sublime, until he finally identifies the power of God as its true origin. In the first edition he says that the sublime, like the object of sympathy, is the cause of delight (51). In the second, he begins by locating the cause of this cause in 'Terror [which] is in all cases whatsoever, either more openly or latently, the ruling principle of the sublime' (58). Then he seeks the cause of the ruling principle. He defines it first as the essence of obscurity, 'this grand cause of terror . . . wrapt up in the shades of its own incomprehensible darkness' (63), and finally as God, the 'capital source of the sublime' (70).

These modifications to his argument about power are accompanied by a series of observations about images. Burke believes that images—especially painted images—are destructive of the sublime because they ridiculously clarify and literalize 'fanciful and terrible ideas' that are better left obscure (63). However, poetry can assemble 'a croud of great and confused images' that transport the reader with delight precisely because they resist any clear presentation to the mind's eye. His examples are Milton's descriptions of Death and Lucifer (59, 62). A good image, in Burke's opinion, functions like the effect of distance: it softens the details of the ruin made by power; and it does so by veiling the destructive effects of light. It is, after all, not obscurity wrapped in its own shades which is the true source of terror, but God the light source, whom we only have to open our eyes to see, and who is no sooner seen in his full glory than we are annihilated (*Enquiry*, 68). A good image, then, like a good scene, adjusts visible particulars to obscurity in such a way that the security of the spectator is guaranteed. Burke's thinking runs along the same lines as Hobbes', and images serve the same purpose of mediation as his 'artificiall Man': 'Speak to us, and we will hear thee; but let not God speak to us, lest we dye' (*Leviathan*, 119). Thus the images surrounding fallen Lucifer are not only expressive of his much modified power, but also represent power in its most viewable form: veiled, and not 'pressing too close'.

> ———His form had yet not lost
> All her original brightness, nor appeared
> Less than archangel ruin'd, and th'excess
> Of glory obscured: as when the sun new ris'n
> Looks through the horizontal misty air
> Shorn of his beams; or from behind the moon
> In dim eclipse disastrous twilight sheds
> On half the nations.
>
> (*Enquiry*, 62)

As the crowd pushes out of theatre and into the square, deserting the representation of extreme suffering for the thing itself, they lose the value of this occultation of power, and enter into a passive and unmediated relation to it. They become merely astonished with no hope of appropriating power for themselves.

Like Longinus, then, Burke ties questions of initiative, mimesis, and usurpation to the status of the eye in its relation to light. Longinus' quotation of the quotation of the *fiat lux*, for example, is a descent from a source of power represented as pure light that resolves itself into a rule for looking at it safely and in the security of usurped power. Longinus' favourite poets and orators contrive to reflect light with a lustre equal to the original: Homer as a meridian sun (ix. 17) and Demosthenes as a glittering shaft of lighning (xxxiv. 3). Losers in this game, such as Orestes or Polyphemus, are attacked in the eye. Burke's interest lies in turning opacity back against the light as the veil or screen that saves the subject's eye, at the same time as redeeming the singular first person from a common position of astonishment among the mob. In the section on tragedy he shows how this is done. He extends a series of choices to an agent whose function is to be a spectator of spectators, a selector of other people's range of selections: 'Chuse a day . . . appoint the most favourite actors . . . unite the greatest efforts of poetry, painting and music . . . let it be reported that a state criminal of high rank is on the point of being executed' (47). The triumph of real sympathy can go either way. It is either the triumph of the spectacle over the spectator as it encroaches over the boundary separating delight from astonishment; or it is the clever repositioning of spectatorial defeat as an image of another kind of spectatorial competence, the result of a self-referential shift similar to Longinus' talent for being sublime upon the sublime. In eyeing spectatorhood Burke transforms the crowd's loss of choice into the very medium of choice, abstracting himself from the involuntary movements of the collective and constituting himself as agent by means of a selection of selections, a reflexive modification of power that has been earlier characterized as a second-order representation: the copy of a copy, the remaking of making, the writing of writing, and so on. By means of this ability to squint at the business of looking Burke accomplishes the same transformation he is later to achieve with Lucifer. The scene of the ruin of the subject becomes an image of the very modification (shorn beams) necessary if the triumph of sympathy is to coincide with the triumph of the singular first person who usurps the position of subjective authority.

As far as Burke is concerned, that which stands between the light of power, the capital and annihilating source of the sublime, and the subject apprehensive about his own annihilation, must be something less than light: that is, obscurity, darkness, shade, opacity—anything that casts an image by shearing the blinding beam of light; for 'extreme light obliterates all objects' (*Enquiry*, 80). And an image, as he points out in the *Reflections*, belongs with all the other 'pleasing illusions, which make power gentle'.[39] The temptation Burke and many of his commentators lie under of making obscurity a substantive attribute of the sublime, a legitimate property that makes a difference, removes its more unstable valency as the precipitate of a struggle with power. Burke is celebrating this reciprocity in a pun when he talks of 'setting terrible things, if I may use the expression, in their strongest light by the force of a judicious obscurity' (59). Obscurity, as he makes clear here, operates on the side of the subject.[40] An image is sublime for Burke not because it confuses the eye but because it screens the annihilating force of divine

[39] Edmund Burke, *Reflections on the Revolution in France*, in L. G. Mitchell (ed.), *The Writings and Speeches of Edmund Burke* (Oxford: Clarendon Press, 1989), viii. 128.
[40] It needs scarcely be emphasized how often obscurity is the resource of the suffering individual, and contrariwise an impediment which theodicies seek to remove. Compare Job 10: 19–22, where he relishes the thought of darkness in a complex pleonasm, and Warburton on Bolingbroke: 'He would

light in such a way as to give the eye a picture of its own freedom of choice.

Longinus and Burke are alike in being unable or unwilling to theorize this reflexive modification of power. It remains a question of practice, a doubling up of the referent in the act of reference (asking a question about questions, as Longinus does), or of instancing as an object of sight the medium which makes looking possible. On Burke's part this accounts for his equivocal way of assessing the sublime of *Paradise Lost* as an event and as a representation. The poem is 'astonishing', and 'significant,' it seems, because it is 'admirably studied'; it is also therefore a 'description', a 'portrait of the king of terrors' (59). Burke leaves it undetermined whether Milton is giving us something akin to a tragedy, or to an execution in the public square. Is obscurity the function of the poet's passive witnessing of the effect of strong light, or is it being used as photography, a skilful play of light and shade that discloses things otherwise invisible? Is it Milton's accuracy in summing up the effects of power, or his rhetorical engagement with the cause, that renders 'terrible things' astonishing? Longinus poses the same questions of Demosthenes.

In the last paragraph of section IV ('On the Difference between Clearness and Obscurity') and through most of section V ('Power'), both added to the second edition, Burke quotes the book of Job in order to show how a force which nothing can withstand resolves itself into sensible images (68). His first example is Eliphaz's vision of the night, where the spectral figure demands, 'Shall mortal man be more just than God'? It is here that Burke tries to identify the 'grand cause of terror' as darkness folded in upon itself (63). In section V he turns to the theophany, instancing the war-horse, the wild ass, the unicorn, and leviathan as creatures whose formidable wildness establishes their high position on the graduated scale of terror. However, their mediating function—an effect of power in the form of an image that might possibly be made to bear upon the nature of a subjective response to that image— is apparently ignored in favour of their status as an empirical proof of the sublimity of animals of a certain order of strength and freedom: hence the distinctions made between plough-horses and war-horses, dogs and wolves. Burke says nothing at all about the rhetorical construction of the questions he is quoting, nor does he point out that they are manifestly addressed by a superior voice to an inferior audience. In the example of the wild ass, he implies that it is Job himself, by a species of substitution, who takes the place of first-person agent in the following

have us turn from the steddy light of the moral system to contemplate that obscure, disturbed and shifting scene, the actual state of vice and virtue' (*DLM* i. 324).

sentence, '*Who hath loosed* (says he) *the bands of the wild ass? whose house I have made the wilderness*' (66). He does this not by way of according the patriarch an ambitious prosopopeia, but by way of a compliment paid to him for his descriptive talents. Each example is praised specifically as *description*, a way of reducing it, as Burke has already reduced Milton's judicious obscurities, to images, in order to modify the cause of astonishment.

So keen is Burke to leave the theophany as a collection of descriptions, that he will take any step to avoid treating it as a specimen of the irresistible rhetorical force of God. This includes a refusal to cite Job as in any way the victim of these stunning images, and instead to bring him in as a supplementary example of the patriarchal sublime: '*When I prepared my seat in the street* (says Job) *the young men saw and hid themselves*' (67). Job takes his place in this commentary not as a man made desperate by his unmediated relation to an annihilating force, but as one more empirical proof of the sublime of power: a free creature. Burke's disinclination to contemplate Job as a ruined patriarch, whose memories of power simply emphasize his present sense of inglorious subjection, must be ascribed to the same instinct which prompts him to locate in the circumstances of Lucifer's fall the images that contribute to 'a very noble picture' (62), or which invites him to disguise the modification of the crowd's vulgar astonishment in the public square. It is an instinct for screening examples of unmodified power and for making, through the production of suffering as image, an opportunity for the ambition of the describing subject. He is looking at what has already been looked at: he is looking through the screen of looking.

Burke's 'timidity with regard to power' is not self-deprecation, then, but a genuine reluctance to handle directly a force he knows is not gentle, and whose emanations need veiling if they are not to menace him in the way that God menaces Job. This helps to explain why, when he arrives at the topic of language, Burke refuses to consider its obscurities as instruments of rhetoric. 'Those modes of speech that mark a strong and lively feeling in [the speaker] himself' (175) are nothing more than the stuff of an image whose purpose (at least for Burke) is to make power more gentle and the light less shatteringly bright. The devices which enable orators to master judges and tyrants, writers to master readers, and, in turn, readers to emancipate themselves, are located by Burke not at the level of figurative language but in the representability of a scene of destruction or ruin. Here he restores the 'certain distances' and 'modifications' (40) without which the subject risks erasure, as, for example, in an absorptive tableau where the preoccupation of the central figure blocks the spectator. Although Burke has no direct investment in the victim of power—Damiens or Job—he arrives at the same critical position in the excessive use of power as Hawkesworth, or Asem's genie, or Job's *go'el*: namely, as a delegate of the first person, sustaining an interest in the agency of the individual sufferer in so far as it offers a chance for mimetic improvement on behalf of the singular spectator, whose speciality is looking at looking.

It is ironic that Burke's section on ambition should haunt the commentaries on his *Reflections on the Revolution in France*. Either he is understood to have rejected a manifestation in the political arena of the very sublime he formerly espoused, and to have made a pusillanimous retreat from the implications of his own aesthetics; or else its anomalous place within his discussion of power is taken to advertise the political quietism that is equally common to the *Enquiry* and the *Reflections*.[41] Paine's well-quoted remarks on 'Mr Burke's horrid paintings', occasioned by the extravagance of Burke's description of Marie-Antoinette's escape from Versailles, is the starting point for this sort of critique. W. J. T. Mitchell has discussed Paine's lavish use of theatrical metaphors as a deliberate parody of Burke's tragic 'painting', in which questions of staging and representation become crucial.[42] Indeed, Paine accuses Burke of not being 'affected by the reality of distress touching his heart, but by the showy resemblance of it striking his imagination'.[43] For his part, Burke accuses Richard Price of exulting over real misery, while being prepared to weep at its representation on the stage. These contrasts between scenes of real human torment and theatrical representations of distress is a polemical replay of the sections on sympathy and tragedy in the *Enquiry*.

To follow the complex political and rhetorical manœuvres made by Burke in the vicinity of the terrified queen, 'forced to fly almost naked' from rooms 'swimming in blood, polluted by massacre, and strewed with scattered limbs and mutilated carcases' (*Reflections* viii. 122), it is necessary to superimpose the scene upon other archetypes of disfiguring violence, such as the carnage at Fontenoy and the execution of Damiens. As in these, there is a crowd of spectators drawn by curiosity, lewd fascination, terror, *Schadenfreude*, pity, or even indifference to a scene

[41] See Carol Kay, *Political Constructions* (Ithaca: Cornell Univ. Press, 1988), 266–78; William Richey, 'The French Revolution: Blake's Epic Dialogue with Edmund Burke', *ELH* 59/4 (1992), 817–37. The best essays on this topic are Thomas Weiskel, *The Romantic Sublime* (Baltimore: Johns Hopkins Univ. Press, 1976), 83–99; Ronald Paulson, *Representations of Revolution* (New Haven, Conn.: Yale Univ. Press, 1983), 60–71; W. J. T. Mitchell, 'Eye and Ear: Edmund Burke and the Politics of Sensibility', in *Iconology* (Chicago: Univ. of Chicago Press, 1986), 116–49; J. G. A. Pocock, *Virtue, Commerce, and History* (Cambridge: Cambridge Univ. Press, 1985), 279–94; David Musselwhite, 'Reflections on Burke's *Reflections* 1790–1990', in *The Enlightenment and its Shadows*, ed. Peter Hulme and Ludmilla Jordanova (London: Routledge, 1990), 142–62.
[42] *Iconology*, 143–4.
[43] *The Rights of Man*, ed. Henry Collins (Harmondsworth: Penguin, 1969; repr. 1983), 286.

of remarkable savagery; and there is a single spectator—the spectator of spectators—who is both aware of the risks of sympathy and of how to modify the scene to his own advantage. Although it is consistent with Burke's apparent identification with vulgar astonishment in the *Enquiry* that he should endorse the move from the theatre to the public square, on account of our preference for the thing itself, and the fact that 'our delight in cases of this kind, is very greatly heightened, if the sufferer be some excellent person who sinks under an unworthy fortune' (45), he is no longer interested in dissembling a common cause with the mob. He finds odious the delight taken by Price and his radical congregation in the events in France. Why? Because they regard themselves as exempt from the power that is ruining the excellent person; they even approve of it, and have no regrets about the customs and ceremonies about to be 'dissolved by this new conquering empire of *light* and reason' (viii. 128; my italics). They are engaged upon 'this work of our new light and knowledge', illuminated by the rays of 'this new-sprung modern light' (viii. 126). With the metaphor of the moral wardrobe literalized in the plight of the queen—'All the decent drapery of life is to be rudely torn off'—light is made to shine with an annihilating brightness, exhibiting nothing that might empower the spectator, only the pathetic tautology of the ruined subject—'a king is but a man; a queen is but a woman'— ornamented with the obscene 'defects of our naked shivering nature' (i. 128). Light produces carnage and disfigurement unless there is a way to photograph, obscure, modify, or interrupt the limitless torments of which the body and mind are capable, such as those 'inflicted in a few hours on the late unfortunate regicide in France' (*Enquiry*, 39).

Burke finds his way back to the associated questions of distance and screens by showing that the poignancy of Marie-Antoinette's nakedness does not lie in the sudden removal of her power and its appropriation by the crowd, but in the loss of all points of vantage for the spectators. There is nothing to see in the bare exposure of a female animal that is not already known. As Burke speculates on the poverty of the crowd's desire to spotlight an unadorned body, he enters into a relation with vulgar astonishment similar to his spectatorhood of spectators in the *Enquiry*. There he made a set of choices about their lack of choice, relevant to the obscured image of fallen Lucifer. Here he re-establishes the queen in a chiaroscuro reminiscent of 'glory obscured: as when the sun new ris'n | Looks through the horizontal misty air', setting aside her ruin as he sets aside Job's, so that he can recollect better times with the maximum of rhetorical force. He is ventriloquizing her death-song in order to embarrass her tormentors and to confirm him in his own selection of selections. He arrives at the restoration of Marie-Antoinette in his own eye as the legitimate object not of fealty but of his own first-person oratory:

It is now sixteen or seventeen years since I saw the queen of France, then the dauphiness, at Versailles; and surely never lighted on this orb, which she hardly seemed to touch, a more delightful vision. I saw her just above horizon, decorating and cheering the elevated sphere she just began to move in,—glittering like the morning-star, full of life, and splendor, and joy. Oh! What a revolution!   (viii. 126)

The equivocation on orb as earth and eye, so nicely fitted to the insistence on the first person as the agent of the dreams and images which will vindicate the sovereign subject, tells us this is 'a very noble picture' and also something of a private revolution. Burke rewrites Versailles as Hawkesworth rewrites Poverty Bay, in order to free the person acquainted with savagery from the misjudgements of a bad reader (Price), at the risk of antagonizing his own.[44] But the gamble is for subjective mastery. Burke offers himself to the queen as something like leviathan, in an energy of spirit that cannot be alien to a rising sense of his own empowerment as he plays, himself a subject, among the shocking effects of a power he dares now face in the first person singular, orb to orb and I to eye. In this way he claims the dignity and importance of that which he contemplates. He confessed to weeping as he wrote the passage, and it is reported that the queen cried as she read it. This is a configuration closely resembling Mrs Warton's situation *vis-à-vis* Martha Bilson on her deathbed, when tears prove that a tautology has been unfolded and a switch of power relations has taken place, resulting in a teaching of teachers, or a sovereign glance in the direction of royalty's shorn beams (i. 126 n. 63).

People in great distress, whose mental agony is closely associated with the physical violence they are anticipating or experiencing, are figures that fascinate Longinus because they project as literal cases the metaphor of the reader ruined by the sublime. Sailors about to perish in a storm, Orestes menaced by the Erinyes, Pythes cut to pieces by his enemies, Cleomenes madly slicing himself to death, and the Greeks fighting desperately to drink water stained with their own blood, are favourites with him; and the only impediment to presenting them as powerful examples of sublimity is the problem of vulgarity, for vulnerable bodies—'naked shivering nature' in Burke's phrase—are close to

---

[44] Philip Francis was annoyed, for example, and wrote, 'In my opinion all that you say of the Queen is pure foppery'. See *Reflections* i. 126 n. 63; and Linda M. G. Zerilli, 'Text/Woman as Spectacle: Edmund Burke's "French Revolution"', in *The Eighteenth Century: Theory and Interpretation*, 33/1 (1992), 47.

being obscene too. Although it is no part of the office of the sublime to cover things up, veiling them over 'with a theatrical Splendor, and a gawdy Out-side' (vii. 1), neither is it appropriate to expose the anus and the genitals (xliii. 4). The skill lies in determining the precise point at which the physical mark of violence can recur as the force of a figure printed by passion. In Herodotus' description of the battle of Thermopylae, for example, the circumstances of a doomed battalion, committed to die fighting the barbarians, merge with the figure used to sharpen them: 'They defended themselves . . . with their Hands and Teeth, till they were buried under the Arrows of Barbarians'. 'Is it possible?' demands Longinus in mock disbelief, before conceding the probability of the image on the grounds that the 'the Hyperbole seems to be the necessary Production of the Circumstance' (xxxviii. 3).

His premier instance of the circumstances of physical distress combining to produce a powerful figure is Sappho's Ode (Lobel-Page fr. 31), which survives nowhere else but in Longinus' treatise. He produces it to illustrate the theme he is developing for Terentianus on the compatibility of minuteness and poetic force. There is no subject, he says, 'not attended by some adherent Circumstances', and if these are judiciously and accurately assembled, they can have a powerful effect upon the audience's imagination (x. 1–2). Then he quotes the fragment, in which Sappho vividly records the physical symptoms of jealousy while watching her lover being courted by a young man. Then he demands, 'Are you not amaz'd, my Friend, to find how in the same moment she is at a loss for her Soul, her Body, her Ears, her Tongue, her Eyes, her Colour, all of them as much absent from her as if they had never belonged to her?' His point is that the catalogue of privations afflicting the real body of Sappho are cleverly knitted into the 'one body' (x. 1) of her poem. Neil Hertz comments, 'It is not simply a poem of passion and self-division but one which dramatizes, in a startlingly condensed fashion, the shift from Sappho-as-victimized-body to Sappho-as-poetic-force'.[45] What makes this switch from physical vulnerability to poetic power different from, say, Herodotus' image of the forlorn hope of the Greeks is not only that it is condensed in the person and verse of Sappho herself, who occupies the roles both of patient and agent, but that it depends upon a complication not only of symptoms but also of voices and glances. Sappho is looking at the shared looks of the woman and the man as she hears her softly speaking to him; and because she fails to win a glance or word in return, she loses her own voice, 'My Breath was gone, my Voice was lost', and then her sight, 'O'er my dim Eyes a Darkness hung'.

---

[45] Neil Hertz, 'A Reading of Longinus', in *The End of the Line* (New York: Columbia Univ. Press, 1985), 7.

The fragment invites the reader at one level to read it as a death-song sung during a scene of 'slow torture', analogous in its way to the torments of Marie-Antoinette which Burke recovers as a stable image of regal beauty. Here, however, it is the voice, not the image, of the female subject which is to be lost and then regained. In proportion as she is absorbed into the swelling of her body (to reapply Elaine Scarry's reverse symmetry of the scene of interrogation), Sappho's voice sinks; meanwhile the voice of her tormentor grows ever more articulate and distinct. Joan de Jean has read the poem along these lines, claiming it is an inscription of the 'fleshly female voice', expressing the desire of the 'woman as speaking subject' for another woman, but destabilized by successive readers (male and female) who have insisted on heterosexualizing the scene.[46] In so far as the loss of voice, followed by its figurative recovery, is the groundwork of Sappho's relation to her lover and to the reader, it is also her relation to Job. Her mimetic shift, or *metis*, equivalent to his inscribed rock of redemption, is her poem. Who then is her *go'el* or redeemer; and who her false comforter? De Jean would say, respectively, the desired female, the mirror of the speaking subject; and the perverse reader, determined to misrecognize a homosexual passion.

Although the antagonism of Sappho's readers is well-charted by de Jean, illuminating more sides of the rhetoric of the ill-used, it is harder for her to explain the cruelty, or at least the faithlessness, of the desired female, and the fact that she signally fails to return Sappho's glance of desire, but is absorbed in gazing at her male admirer while she talks to him. The parallel of unparalleled suffering, the ostensible image of someone at the limit, whose function is to rescue the anguished first person by a face-to-face impersonation, does not exist here, unless we insert Longinus as the 'good' reader between the circumstances of a disintegrating body and its recuperation as the 'body' of the poem.

That will not work. Longinus himself contributes to the pattern of 'I/she' constructions that run athwart the 'I/I' of specular homosexual desire. In the first person, addressing Terentianus in the second, he examines Sappho in the third: 'Are you not amaz'd to find how she is at a loss . . . The Excellence of this Ode, as I observed before, consists in the judicious Choice and Connexion of the most notable Circumstances'. He is saying something like, 'She is her poem, I read it to you'. In the same fashion, the man and woman in the poem might be supposed to be saying, 'Talk to me, not to her', or 'I am looking at you, don't look at her'. For Sappho to have any chance of competing with these isolating

[46] Joan de Jean, *Fictions of Sappho* (Chicago, Ill.: Univ. of Chicago Press, 1989), 26, 43.

reductions of her passion from the first to the third person, she has to find some mediator whom she can address in the second person and who will possibly reflect or impersonate her in the first. That medium can only be her poem as a finished, that is to say written, article; but, as Longinus shows, the reader of the poem repeats the humiliation of the excluded third person depicted in the poem.

The only way out of the problem is to suppose that the poem is an allegory or image of its reception, as Jesper Svenbro has done recently, which dramatizes the following construction: 'You are my poem; he reads you'.[47] Thus the faithless lover is the text of the poem admired by the reader, who makes her speak, while Sappho, negotiating the shifting relations of literacy to orality as uneasily as the Job-poet, complains of the dumbness that afflicts her once her writing is alienated by a reader. Both poets are composing in the sixth century BCE, poised on the cusp of oral and literate cultures in Greece and the Middle East. They are writing at a time when public inscriptions are always delivered in the first person and the present tense, and when a literate readership is beginning to wish to read silently without being harnessed to another ego, or being forcibly recruited for the job of impersonation (Svenbro, 42). So they both associate text with torment, with the body violently, even fatally, imprinted by a force with which a hostile reader claims intimacy; and they both look for a remedy in the construction of a new relationship between the absent body of the first person and the voice which a text, if cleverly arranged, might provoke from the reader.

Epimenides tried having his last words tattooed on his body, turning his corpse into his epitaph and so making a kind of pun on *soma* and *sema* (Svenbro, 157). Sappho's and Job's solution is likewise an adaptation of funerary inscription, aimed at restoring close links between the body and the medium by which it will speak. It is managed by means of the circumstances of physical decay, minutely collected and judiciously re-combined, as in so many texts where the suffering body focuses the attention, and here forming into the figure of *auxesis*, characteristic of the mesmerizing paratactic form which Havelock has analyzed as the leading characteristic of orality, and which Gentili finds perfectly exemplified in Sappho's fragment 31.[48] The response induced by *auxesis* renders its effect indistinguishable from that of the *logos epitaphios*, or

---

[47] 'Au lieu d'écrire, à la manière des inscriptions, "Je suis le poème de Sappho; tu me liras," Sappho écrit, "Tu es mon poème; il te lira."' Jesper Svenbro, *Phrasikleia: Anthropologie de la lecture en grèce ancienne* (Paris: Editions La Découverte, 1988), 172.

[48] Eric Havelock, *The Literate Revolution in Greece* (Princeton, NJ: Princeton Univ. Press, 1982), 174–7; Bruno Gentili, *Poetry and its Public in Ancient Greece* (Baltimore: Johns Hopkins Univ. Press, 1988), 48. On *auxesis* in Longinus, see D. A. Russell, *'Longinus' on the Sublime* (Oxford: Clarendon Press, 1964), p. xvii.

eidolopoiesis, in which the speaker and audience alike are transported by a voice they mistake for the absent 'I'.[49] Longinus must be imagined reading out Sappho's Ode to Terentianus, momentarily inflamed by the figure of *auxesis* to the point where he speaks as Sappho, 'I fainted, sunk, and dy'd away'—the very point where the quotation (but not, apparently, the poem) interrupts itself. The impersonation is most passionate at the point where the alphabetic Sappho is forced to disappear, silenced by the mode of literate transmission, thus bringing voice to the 'I' at the very place where its extinction is recorded. It is necessarily a momentary triumph for Sappho's first person, for by a further irony Longinus is so inspirited by his impersonation that he returns to the text as a vigorous reader, anatomizing the figures that now, in the aftermath, no longer move him to any but a critical enthusiasm. In this anatomical frame of mind he reaffirms Sappho's exclusion to third person at the rim of his colloquy with his pupil. However, it is intriguing that her fragment should survive—live—nowhere but in his text, proof as it were of an invisible moment of transport when he did read her poem in the first person, and spoke (as Hawkesworth does for Cook, or Burke for Marie Antoinette) in the voice of the suffering 'I'.

[49] See D. A. Russell, *'Longinus' on the Sublime*, 69; and J.-F. Lyotard, *The Différend: Phrases in Dispute*, trans. George van den Abbeele (Manchester: Manchester Univ. Press, 1988), 20.

PART III

Readings

10

'Deformed he lay, disfigur'd':
Pope reads Blackmore's Job

I have already shown how, in his *Epistle to Bathurst*, Pope shunts the unacceptable particularities of excessive complaint, which he associates closely with the unregulated play of economic self-interest, to the side of Sir Balaam, an unregenerate modern Job, so that he can hiss in public the speculative losses over which he groans in private. His *Art of Sinking in Poetry* (1728), although a more complex set of satiric manœuvres directed at the production and reception of literary language, as opposed to the consumption of goods and credit, is impelled by the same hostility towards a particularizing excess, once again to be found embodied in a city knight who ventriloquizes the complaints of Job. Once again, it is an exercise in differentiation between public norms and private singularities that is troubled by a covert resemblance to the object under attack. Pope's struggle to disintricate his sense of subjective vulnerability from the judgements he directs against a culpable public manifestation of particularity is thrown in relief by studying the parallels that extend between Pope's desire to destroy the sublime of Sir Richard Blackmore's *A Paraphrase on the Book of Job* and his fascination, growing into disgust, with 'the Symptoms of an Amorous Fury'[1] he locates in the literary remains of Sappho. If Blackmore and Balaam strike Pope as the unhappy leftovers of Job's sublime, no less do the writings and person of Lady Mary Wortley Montagu strike him as the noisome detritus of Sappho's.

Sir Richard Blackmore published *A Paraphrase on the Book of Job* in 1700, issuing it again in 1716, a year after the first Jacobite rebellion. It is from this second edition that Pope draws more than a quarter of the quotations for his mock-Longinian treatise on the bathos, *The Art of Sinking*. The politics of the *Paraphrase* are those of an ardent Williamite

---

[1] The phrase is Bayle's, in his article on Sappho and Anacreon, where he defends Le Fevre's reading of it as a lesbian love-poem against Mme Dacier's estimate of it as an epistolary exercise, 'a Friend writing to a Friend'. She heads the fashion (followed by Addison in *Spectators* 223 and 229) for 'normalizing' the feelings expressed in Sappho's poetry. See Pierre Bayle, *An Historical and Critical Dictionary*, 4 vols. (London: C. Harper et al., 1710), iv. 2671 n. D. The 'fictions' spun out of the contested readings of Sappho among French critics during the seventeenth and eighteenth centuries suggest intriguing similarities with the British fondness for making fictions out of Job over the same period. See Joan de Jean, *Fictions of Sappho 1546–1937* (Chicago: Univ. of Chicago Press, 1989), 50–8. Pope comes the closest of any writer to conflating the fictionalization of Sappho with the fictionalization of Job.

Whig who wishes to praise the steadiness of the Hanoverian succession during its first crisis ('His Majesty's unrivalled Courage, and prudent Conduct [has] surmounted our fears of Foreign Enemies'). The Whiggism has its literary correlate in the author's wish to encourage a libertarian taste for novelty and independence ('We [are] all Copiers and Transcribers of Homer, Pindar, and Theocritus . . .' 'tis therefore to be wish'd that some good Genius . . . would . . . set up for an Original in Writing'). These are the politics and the taste exposed by Pope and Swift as the duncely underside of the growing fashion for the sublime, 'the gentle downhill way to the Bathos', 'the very *bottom* of all the Sublime'.[2]

Blackmore finds Job outstanding, both as a character and as literature, because of his resistance to a pitiless consensus about his condition. The victim not only of divine exactions but also of the 'exasperating Provocations' of a profane woman and three scandalizing men, Job preserves a matchless constancy, rebuking his tormentors in language that is 'sublime, majestick and astonishing' (pp. liv, lxi, xxxiii, xxxv). His lonely defence of his personal integrity, together with the principles of virtue, equity, and liberty it supports, against a canted orthodoxy of derived authority that scarcely disguises the malice it is used to satisfy, reminds Blackmore not only of George I, but also of himself: 'The Regard I have for the Interests of Religion, and my Zeal for the Safety of my Country, have extorted these Complaints from me' (p. vii). Blackmore offers his Job as a story that reverberates to the lonely vindication of Whig principles and the singular triumph of a Protestant succession. It also justifies an experiment in a style altogether original, replete with 'elevated Thoughts and splendid Expression' (p. xvii). He celebrates a double purgation of immemorial arbitrary rights: the indefeasible authority of monarchs that stifles individual liberty, and the peremptory regulations of the ancients that obstruct the sublime (p. xviii). He and Job exhibit between them the political and aesthetic advantages of liberty in a commonwealth, specifically of unrestricted words. 'For liberty of Speech so much I long | To vent my Woe, my Passion is so strong' (55). The inimitable sublime of Job's complaint is not defined by Blackmore—he is reluctant to submit 'the Opinion of Beauty and Ornament' to any 'fixt and unalterable Rule' (p. lxxvi)—but he translates its fine excess ('bold and rash' [p. lix]) into English by adding liberty to liberty: 'I have amplify'd the Text in many Places that appear'd more Poetical, and from General Heads I have descended sometimes to Particulars, the Enumeration of which, I believ'd would illustrate and enliven the Original' (p. lxxv). In the preface to his poems he adverts more succinctly to this principle when he says, in response to those who have suggested that he writes too freely and voluminously, 'I am unacquainted with the Definition of *Too Much*'.[3]

It is exactly this commitment to amplification unlimited by rule and definition that Pope identifies as Blackmore's most risible weakness. In the ninth chapter of the *The Art of Sinking* he tackles the question of imitation by ironically insisting that the function of 'a true Genius' is not to inhabit and reflect the glory of an original, but 'to bring it down, take off the Gloss, or quite discharge the Colour, by some ingenious Circumstance, or Periphrase'. He goes on, 'The Book of Job is acknowledg'd to be infinitely sublime, and yet has not our Father of the Bathos reduc'd it in every Page?' (39). He introduces Blackmore's translation of Job 29: 6 ('I washed my steps in butter') like this:

When Job says in short, He wash'd his Feet in *Butter*, (a Circumstance some Poets would have soften'd, or past over) hear how it is spread out by the Great Genius.

> With Teats distended with their milky Store,
> Such num'rous lowing Herds, before my Door,
> Their painful Burden to unload did meet,
> That we with Butter might have wash'd our Feet.

How cautious! and particular!   (34)

This and the following example are typical of Blackmore's habit of paraphrase and of Pope's method of critique.

In the Book of Job, are these Words, *Hast thou commanded the Morning, and caused the Day Spring to know his Place?* How is this extended by the most celebrated Amplifier of our Age?

> Canst thou set forth th'etherial Mines on high,
> Which the refulgent Ore of Light supply?
> Is the Celestial Furnace to thee known,
> In which I melt the golden Metal down?
> Treasures, from when I deal out Light as fast,
> As all my Stars and lavish Suns can waste.   (37)

Pope tirelessly identifies those images in the poem which are particularized as spillage, discharge, expenditure, or regurgitation. He lingers over verses where force or pressure threaten to puncture a body, and he often associates these breaches of the integument with the obstruction or thickening of light. Here for example Blackmore is ridiculed for ampli-

---

[3] Richard Blackmore, *A Collection of Poems* (London: W. Wilkins, 1718), p. xii.

fying verses akin in their laconic invocation of light to the *fiat lux* celebrated by Longinus and Boileau, until they are no different from a notice of a run on the bank.

Of the first seventeen examples of bathos in *The Art of Sinking*, all but two are from Blackmore; and of these, nine (two from *Prince Arthur* and seven from *Job*) are particularizations of the effects of light in the sky. Pope associates these swollen images of the firmament with bladders about to burst. The distich, 'Distended with the Waters in 'em pent, | The Clouds hang deep in Air, but hang unrent' reminds him of 'a Woman in great Necessity' (55); and indeed Blackmore's skies are frequently in this imminent or pregnant condition: and quite often they burst, like Job's boils. From Pope's point of view the plenitude of the vault of heaven is being reduced to the grossest and obscurest terms of material excess, and to a specifically feminine form of waste. Meanwhile the physical distress of the original Job is detailed to the point of burlesque. Here are Job and God cited by Pope as a pair of Hockley-hole wrestlers:

> Me in his griping arms th'eternal took,
> And with such mighty force my body shook,
> That the strong grasp my members sorely bruised,
> Broke all my bones, and all my sinews loosed.   (22)

Everything in Blackmore's poem threatens to break, bleed, leak, suppurate; so that when Pope gets to leviathan ('His motion works, and beats the oozy mud, | And with its slime incorporates the flood, | Till all th'encumbered, thick, fermenting stream | Does like one Pot of boiling Ointment seem' [54]), it is as if Blackmore is the poetic equivalent of this monster, sporting in the scum of a burst world.

Pope is not unfair in drawing attention to the frequency with which contents overflow containers in Blackmore's verse. His volcanoes 'spout their ruddy Vomit thro' the Air' (p. 5; *The Art of Sinking*, 40). Job's physical condition, with pus and gore seeping from the ulcers and scabs on his skin, is described with the specificity worthy of an eminent physician:

> The Putrefaction from my running Boils,
> In loathsome manner all my Vest defiles:
> Close to my Sores it sticks, as to my Throat,
> The narrow Collar of my seamless Coat.

Before enquiring more deeply into Pope's motives for attacking this technique of amplification, it is worth dwelling on Blackmore's motives for cultivating it, and writing in what seems (at least to Pope) to be a mindlessly literal fashion about divine and human affairs.[4]

Blackmore very deliberately positions his paraphrase between the extremes that are to govern the arguments of the Job controversy forty years later; namely, between the alternatives of reading the story of Job as an allegory or as a strictly factual history. On the one hand he refuses to read it as an allegory or fable: 'As to [this] Opinion, I think the Scriptures fully confute it, by asserting the Person and Patience of Job so plainly, that it leaves no room for any tolerable Evasion' (p. xx). On the other, he is not so wedded to a reading of 'nothing but real Facts' (p. xix) that he discounts the effects of poetic embellishment on factors such as the rapidities of the plot development, the prosopopoeias of God and Satan, and the elevated style of Job's speeches. He defines the book, therefore, as an original epic: a history of real events delivered in poetry instead of prose: 'And if there be any Facts in the Book, that seem improbable, 'tis owing to the Poetical manner of representing them' (p. xxviii). Doubtless it is the emphasis Blackmore places on *Job*'s status as an epic poem that invites Pope to name him 'the Homer of the Bathos' (25); however, there is room in Pope's own translations of epic for a less slighting comparison between Blackmore's particularities and Homer's. In his Preface to the *Iliad* and in his Postscript to the *Odyssey*, Pope frequently wonders about the specificity with which common activities such as killing and cookery are treated by Homer. 'The question is, how far a poet, in pursuing the description or image of an action, can attach himself to *little circumstances*, without vulgarity or trifling. What particulars are proper, and enliven the image; or what are impertinent, and clog it?' His answer to the question is speculative: 'Perhaps it may be with great and superior Souls', he observes, 'as with gigantick Bodies, which exerting themselves with unusual Strength, exceed what is commonly thought the due Proportion of Parts, to become . . . something near Extravagance. . . . It is owing to the same vast Invention that Homer's Similes have been thought too exuberant and full of Circumstances'.[5]

Blackmore offers his amplifications explicitly as this species of poetic representation, meant to preserve the same figurative buoyancy that

---

[4] 'The Physician, by the Study and Inspection of Urine and Ordure, approves himself in the Science; and in like sort should our Author accustom and exercise his Imagination upon the Dregs of nature. . . . The Circumstances which are . . . far-fetch'd, unexpected, or hardly compatible, will surprize prodigiously. These therefore we must principally hunt out; but above all, preserve a laudable Prolixity.' *The Art of Sinking*, 29, 33.

[5] Postscript to *The Odyssey of Homer*, ed. Maynard Mack, in *The Poems of Alexander Pope*, 10 vols. (London: Methuen, 1967), x. 387; Preface to *The Iliad of Homer*, vii. 13.

Pope detects in the exuberance of Homeric circumstances. They are not used to streamline or shape the historical material of the poem, which they rather distort or defamiliarize, as Blackmore points out. Whether he succeeds in this aim of ornamenting history, he nevertheless conceives of particularity as a mode of registering and exciting the passions which animate the actors in the poem, particularly Job. Blackmore assigns this importance to figures of amplification because, as he freely confesses, the history of Job is barren of events that might arouse an interest on their own account, consisting as they do of two 'sudden and surprizing' revolutions (p. xxiii) interspersed with provocations and complaints. 'I have . . . endeavour'd to prove,' he says, anticipating Lowth's claim for the epic status of Job, 'that the principal Character of the Poem may be as well unactive, and in a State of Suffering and Calamity.'[6] His refusal to read Job as sheer history backs on to his resistance to an allegorical interpretation, since both extremes suppose an importance—a story, a meaning—independent of the particulars of inactive suffering and calamity from which Job delivers his passionate complaints. It is specifically to these momentary intensities, divorced from their narratable and interpretable aspects, that Blackmore turns his attention as paraphrast and amplifier.

Although Blackmore suspects that the design of the poem may be 'to justifie the Divine Providence in suffering impious and flagitious Men to live in the undisturbed Enjoyment of all the Power and Plenty their Hearts can desire, while good and upright Men are often . . . expos'd to the scorn and outrage of their insulting Enemies' (p. lxi), it is clear from his emphasis that such contumelies are an injustice hard to justify. Besides, he notices that when God speaks he justifies himself solely in terms of his 'Dominion and Property' (p. lxi). Since the dispensations of providence are like history and allegory in not being interpretable in any equitable or plausible sense, and as there is no Mosaic Law to mediate between divine power and human conduct (p. xliv), Blackmore improves the agonistics of a passage of ancient history at the expense of theodicy. Consequently his book of Job illustrates nothing but the 'narrow and broken' view of providence to which its hero and its translator are alike restricted (p. lxvi). When Blackmore talks of his amplifications as supplying 'the Transitional and other Connexions, which according to their manner of Writing are omitted in the Original' (p. lxxx), he is not aiming to reduce the sublime to prose, or to structure the narrative according to some principle of divine or historical intelligibility. His object is to intensify ('illustrate and enliven') the pathos of

---

[6] Richard Blackmore, 'Of the Importance of the Action', in *Essays upon Several Subjects* (London: E. Curll, 1717), 49.

Job's predicament and to render in a form accessible to the English reader 'the true Súblime' of the oldest Hebrew verse (p. lxxxi). The addition of transitions and connections is not therefore designed to plump out an interrupted story into a coherent history, or to fill up the spaces between an otherwise occult providential series. These additions must be supposed to have the rhetorical function of arousing the mimetic intensity Longinus calls 'transport': that is, when imitators, translators, and readers confront an original genius, and 'are ravished and transported by a Spirit not their own'.[7]

There are three avenues leading to Blackmore's conception of the 'oriental' or primitive sublime as the figurative treatment of facts and circumstances. There is the aesthetic, in so far as Longinus points frequently to the circumstances of physical danger and bodily agony as a source of the sublime; then there is the political, in so far as the Whig refusal of arbitrary authority makes way for a singular and possibly extravagant account of private injury; and finally there is the scientific, in so far as Blackmore was trained like other 'barbaric experimentalists' to scrutinize the 'blatantly nonstandardized nonuniform example[s] of dashed and dotted dark nakedness' that served the Enlightenment and Alexander Pope as the model of impropriety.[8] I want to suggest that all three avenues place Blackmore in a triangular relation to his original and to his reader that conforms to the triangle which frames Sappho's enumeration of painful particulars in Fragment 31.

To take science, the third avenue, first: Steven Shapin and Simon Schaffer have shown how experimental philosophy in the late seventeenth century depended upon the production and array of 'matters of fact', a setting down of 'divers things with their *minute circumstances*' for the benefit of an absent spectator of the experimental scene whom they designate as the 'virtual witness'.[9] Whether in a picture or a verbal account, the priority was 'density of circumstantial *detail*' so that the viewer of an engraving or the reader of a reported experiment may retain, 'not a picture of the "idea" of an air-pump, but of a particular existing air-pump' (61–2). So peremptory is the demand for this sort of authentication, that a mouse is shown lying dead in Boyle's equipment; and Boyle himself is cited in the familiar anti-rhetorical tones of the Royal Society as claiming 'rather to neglect the precepts of rhetoricians,

---

[7] *On the Sublime*, ed. D. A. Russell (Oxford: Clarendon Press, 1964), xiii. 3.

[8] Barbara Stafford, *Body Criticism: Imaging the Unseen in Enlightenment Art and Medicine* (Cambridge, Mass.: MIT Press, 1991), 5, 319. The book is a moving account of how the anomalous and exorbitant particular makes head against systems and taxonomies during the eighteenth century.

[9] *Leviathan and the Air-Pump: Hobbes, Boyle, and the Experimental Life* (Princeton, NJ: Princeton Univ. Press, 1985), 60.

than the mention of those things, which I thought pertinent to my subject, and useful to you, my reader' (64).

Hobbes's objections to Boyle were in some respects identical with Pope's to Blackmore's poetry: he was making a breach in the plenum of knowledge by divorcing the matter of fact from the established rules of demonstration which permit it to be known logically as a philosophical truth or evidentially as an historical one (152, 102). His forsaking theory and principle to allege the sole authority of a witness is to create a vacuum not only within a machine but also within the systems of demonstration governing politics and natural philosophy. It opens up an unregulated space for *dissent* (102) based on nothing more stable than the elaborate and prolix production of supererogatory details. Hobbes anticipates Pope's neo-classical critique of the modernist grounds of Blackmore's amplifications, in so far as Pope limits the use of particulars only to 'those circumstances which contribute to form a full, and yet not a confused, idea of the thing' (Postscript to *The Odyssey* x. 387). But Hobbes goes one step further in understanding that minute circumstances offer no transparent view of the object, but constitute the figures of a rhetoric designed by the experimental scientist to allure the virtual witness, or 'you, the reader'—a branch of oratory with belief as its objective, not knowledge (325). To this extent, the producer of matters of fact and the virtual witness stand in the same relation to the pictorial or verbal representation as the sublime poet to the ravished reader: the transfer of a vivid impression is the exclusive concern of the person representing the scene, who may or may not be identical with the chief actor in the depiction but who is the creature and the agent of a strong feeling of identification. In any event the winning of belief in a transaction destitute of any authority or declension except the power of its details to make a probable and exciting image amounts, as far as Hobbes is concerned, to the usurpation of dominion over those who do believe it. Pope wants to think that Blackmore has no such figurative access to his reader's imagination, for he has conservative notions about the descent of power and authority; and besides, 'the low actions of *life* cannot be put into a figurative style without being ridiculous' (Postscript to *The Odyssey* x. 387).

If the scientific model of matters of fact depends on the excited participation by readers in a scene mediated to them by a transcriber who strongly identifies with a first person singular immersed in unregulated but probable circumstances, no less does the political model, as far as Blackmore is concerned. The isolation and danger in which 'good and upright Men' are often placed by their scornful and outrageous enemies make it hard for 'particular Persons . . . to vindicate themselves' (p. ix).

This situation suggests to Blackmore not only the parallel between Job and George I, who have both sustained their constancy in the volatile aftermath of a revolution,[10] but also the personal virtue and courage common to all the historical figures who have resisted the wiles of impious and flagitious men—Elizabeth I, Arthur, Alfred, William III. The title of an anonymous parody sums up Blackmore's sublime as just such an adversarial confrontation between arbitrary tyrants and noble individuals: 'The Flight of the Pretender: A Poem in the Arthurical, Jobical, Elizabethetical Style and Phrase of the Sublime Poet Maurus'.[11] These monumental epics indicate how heavily Blackmore invests in isolated heroes whose authority is won in perpetual conflict with the undifferentiated mass of their enemies (Jacobites, Danes, Spaniards, and comforters). It is specifically the recurrence of this individual resistance to the crowded forces of conservatism, history as the repetition of self-vindication and conscientious dissent in the face of manifold opposition, which stimulates Blackmore's imagination to amplify and particularize.

In a pamphlet recalling the assassination plot against King William of 1696, Blackmore defines history as a series of crises recurring in an identical pattern, replaying the antagonism of singular virtue and collective malice told in Job, the oldest story of all. Each involves an individual whose authority is about to be contested by a mob determined to restore an arbitrary government. In William's case, the 'People of Great Britain' are ready to embark on 'Publick Feuds and Animosities' which will damage the Revolution Settlement, and improve the opportunities of Jacobites and ex-monarchs determined to recover their indefeasible rights. Published in 1723, in the wake of the South Sea Bubble, Blackmore claims his narrative is 'as pertinent and seasonable in these Times, as . . . in those when [it] was written'.[12] In 1715, with Jacobite rioters burning an effigy of King William on a bonfire at Snow Hill, the context of certain metaphors of the preface to the revised edition of Job becomes recognizable as the recurrent crisis caused by public violence directed at an individual of integrity.[13] Public mischief is hydra-headed (p. v): combined with the criminal malcontents who are plotting to overthrow the constitution are the numberless depraved writers who have turned wit into an assassin's knife which they have 'plung'd into

---

[10] Job is overthrown by a revolutionary change in his fortunes, then redeemed by 'a no less sudden and surprizing Revolution'. *Paraphrase*, p. xxiii.

[11] London: Bernard Lintot, 1708.

[12] Richard Blackmore, *A True and Impartial History of the Conspiracy against William III* (London: J. Knapton, 1723), pp. vii, viii, xxv.

[13] Nicholas Rogers, *Whigs and Cities* (Oxford: Clarendon Press, 1989), 26. See also Gary Stuart de Krey, *A Fractured Society: The Politics of London in the first Age of Party* (Oxford: Clarendon Press, 1985), 257.

the Bowels of their Native Country' (p. vi). Virtue itself is wounded with 'cuts and deep gashes'; and both at Tyburn and in the theatre the agents of a monstrous and vicious collectivity glut their eyes on the 'Torments and dying Agonies' (p. x) of an isolated figure who, to Blackmore's eye, must look rather like the effigy of King William, or Job in the depth of his distress.

When Blackmore places Job before his readers he issues a challenge that has a direct bearing on his doubts about public responsibility and about the motives of social and political groupings in respect of suffering virtue. The challenge relies on his own belief in the efficacy of the rhetoric of amplification as a counterweight to social violence. The proclivity of spectators (and readers) in the mass for scenes of physical torment disqualify them from the transported identification with Job's particularized injuries, which are the cause and the end of Blackmore's composition of his *Paraphrase*. The attitude he desires from his reader *vis-à-vis* Job is not in any sense collective, or informed by social protocols or literary rules. He wants a relation as intimate and specific as that of the virtual witness to the experiment, or as his own to the body of King William, whom he served as personal physician.[14] He produces the body of Job, therefore, as an object of pathos as powerful as the corpse of William would have been, had his bowels been opened by a conspirator's knife; and he elaborates its defiled and broken condition in order to ask if it can be recognized:

> Deform'd he lay, Disfigur'd, Cover'd o'er
> With running Boyls, and undigested Gore.
> They sought him in himself, and scarce did know
> Their ancient Friend, disguis'd with so much Woe.   (10)

Should the readers, like the comforters, find nothing in Job's afflictions that rings a bell, and fail to seek his originality in themselves, then they merge with all the other crowds and cabals that are periodically driven to sacrifice the singular person of worth in the pursuit of some ambition that proclaims the law while flouting it, or that invokes providence for the fulfilment of the worst purposes and the most abandoned tastes.

Blackmore tries to interpose himself between Job and a hostile public by reproducing in his writing the office of physician he filled with William, standing as it were between the vulnerable body of the isolated hero and the various figurations of assassination which threaten it. The stance is identical with that of the engraver or transcriber of a scientific experiment, and the goal is the same, which is to win the reader's

---

[14] A service for which he was knighted in 1696, the year of the discovery of the plot against William's life.

identification with the chief figure in the represented scene by means of the rhetorical deployment of matters of fact. The important point is that the written interposition is *figurative*; for were it merely literal, as Pope suspects (or wishes to believe), Blackmore would be pandering to the scopophilia of the hydra-headed mob, which wants torment represented in detail as the legitimate effect of absolute power. He would likewise be failing to exert a poet's dissenting power over, and omitting to exchange its liberating energy with, 'you, the reader'. By amplifying, and being so cautiously particular, he arrays ruin and corruption in a rhetoric that is politically and historically legible as the cause of all 'good and upright Men' who resist popular, factional, and literary forms of tyranny. His dwelling on it at such length is his way of locating significance in events which, in the broader stream of history and providence, have none except their capacity to recur. Blackmore's way of finding Job in himself is to follow the figurative logic of the sprawl of uncontained material, and the flood of unrestrained liquid which dominate the images of his *Paraphrase*, until its expressive point is reached in the ink that flows from his own pen. But it is also implicitly a threat to the readers impervious to the invitation to see themselves in Job. In this respect Blackmore's rhetoric operates like the eloquence which Hobbes reproved in the representation of experiments, and which Hume is to recommend in orators, where 'swelling expressions' and images 'monstrous and gigantic' are used not to flatter the audience but to dominate it.[15]

The dynamics of this complex specular arrangement involve the dyad of the singular subject and his semblable transcriber that will, under the gaze of a reader reading in a spirit independent of a public desire for the subject's ruin, expand into a triad. This triad begs comparison with the arrangement of the lovers and the onlooker in Sappho's fragment 31, discussed in Chapter 9. How far Blackmore's concept of the sublime is derived from commentators such as Dryden and Dennis, and how far from his own reflections on the tenth section of *On the Sublime*, it is impossible to say. But his Job and Longinus' Sappho suffer a bodily reaction to misery that is represented by means of the 'ingenious and skilful Connexion . . . into one body' of the 'adherent Circumstances' of their physical condition.[16] Both exercises take place between the desire of winning a good reading and the risk of enshrining a bad one. The bad reader threatens to repeat the original cause of pain (Job will once again be set up as a mark for public scorn, and Sappho once again be reduced to dumb agony, because s/he will not recognize him/herself in the suffering subject). The good reader submits to the rhetorical force of the

[15] 'Of Eloquence', in *Essays Moral, Political and Literary*, 101.
[16] *On the Sublime* x. 1.

transcription, redoubling the resemblance already proclaimed between the sufferer and the chronicler in order further to authenticate the complaint. The combined effort of a victimized subject and an amplifying writer to produce a probable account of personal misery is now apprehended as genius and originality, by a reader whose excitement at the minute particulars so lavishly presented in the text liberates the voice of the first person lodged in the articulation of these adherent circumstances. This voice speaks out loud, as it were, both the theme and the vindication of stifled misery, by supplying the 'liberty of Speech' which Job and Sappho so passionately desiderate ('My voice was sunk, and died away'; see *Paraphrase*, 55).

This connection between Job and Sappho is strengthened by Blackmore's emphasis on the importance of writing to the project of a particular vindication. Just as the lover of Sappho's lover represents in his loving glance the impediment to Sappho's voice, so does the pitiless gaze of mobbed spectators, requiring agony that is maximally visible, represent for Blackmore the antithesis to the reverberative virtues of ink. Among the many anticipations of the dominant Whig aesthetics of the latter part of the eighteenth century is Blackmore's estimation of light as an irresistible destructive force. Like Burke's characterization of almighty power as a terrible beam before which 'we shrink into the minuteness of our own nature, and are, in a manner, annihilated'[17], Blackmore takes light to be the least modified form of God's arbitrary power, often associated with the images of swelling and discharge which he interprets almost always as a symptom of ruin. Sorrows swell and woes disembogue in the context of various metereological disturbances caused by the sun (26, 37). When God demands of Job therefore, 'How does the Light (I ask again) display | Its radiant Wings and spred the dawning Day?' (169), Job numbers up its effects as earthquake, drought, flood, lawlessness, servitude, and, in his own case, putrefaction (50–1, 57). In the most glittering of the execution scenes of the paraphrase, shafts of lightning, the 'bright Darts' of the Almighty, are hurled at Job as if he were a celestial St Sebastian:

> He sets me as a mark on rising ground;
> And his fierce Archers compass me around.
> My Gall, so deep, so mortal is the Wound,
> As well as Blood, flows out and stains the Ground.   (70)

Light creates and illuminates a scene of suffering which is then the object of crowds yearning to see it. Blackmore attaches flood metaphors to

---

[17] *A Philosophical Enquiry into our Ideas of the Sublime and Beautiful*, ed. James T. Boulton (Oxford: Basil Blackwell, 1958; rev. 1987), p. 68.

each stage: the victim is so deluged in tears (29) that he enquires whether his friends are keeping a watch over him as over a rising river (28); crowds eager to see how 'Wretches are expos'd to publick sight' (149) are compared to rivers and seas in a couplet placarded by Pope: 'A waving Sea of Heads was round me spred, | And still fresh Streams the gazing Deluge fed' (73; *Art of Sinking*, 35). And the problem, as Blackmore's Job sees it, is to control or staunch by means of articulate language the light-driven flood which the public longs to view: 'My struggling Thoughts which in my Bosom pent | Will make me burst, unless they find a Vent' (138).

This vent is supplied, and the frustrated discharge avoided, by liberated speech, couched in those bold and rash expressions of complaint that constitute the true sublime recommended by Blackmore to 'you, the reader'. However, to be voiced, these words must first be written. This is how the verses 19. 23–4 of Job are translated:

> O, that my Speech was written, that my Words
> Were Register'd, and kept in safe Records!
> O, that an Iron Pen's repeated stroke,
> Would grave deep Furrows in the Marble Rock!
> Let Letters fill them up of inlaid Lead,
> That all to come may my Profession read.   (83)

The effect of amplification here is rather like the clumsy and laborious traces of the chisel on the inscribed stones of country churchyards, which Wordsworth says are inseparable from the pathos of the message.[18] It gives Blackmore the opportunity to function as Job's *go'el*. Writing can staunch wounds by clotting the flow of blood, tears, or molten lead, and converting them into legible signs of very different construction from those the gazing public draw from his boils and ulcers:

> Tho' you produce my Sores and wrinkled Skin
> As Witnesses of some enormous Sin,
> Yet they can only testify the Weight
> Of those vast Woes, which my Complaints create.   (70)

To get from the shameful witnesses of wounds to the virtual witness of a good reader, Job needs an observer who can find in his defective outside enough of a self-reflection passionately to transcribe every circumstance attaching to it. Blackmore is this reader, a vindicator of 'particular Persons' (p. ix), who understands the importance of defects in binding heroes to their imitators: 'When the Examples of Virtue that

---

[18] *Essay on Epitaphs I, Prose Works*, ed. W. J. B. Owen and Jane Worthington Smyser, 3 vols. (Oxford: Clarendon Press, 1974), ii. 60.

are set before us, are discern'd to have a Mixture of Imperfection, we are provok'd and embolden'd to form ourselves according to such a Pattern, where there appears no Impossibility . . . of becoming like it' (p. xxxiv). He is also keenly aware of the advantages of writing. In praise of the pen, Blackmore sounds uncannily like Richardson, arguing that by means of the pen a dead person 'yet speaks, and while mould'ring in the Grave will inform the Ages in long Succession yet to come: For as the Pen annihilates immense intervening Space, so it removes interposing Ages'.[19] A wound is turned into an inscription by a double motion of the beholder of suffering. The beholder must recognize himself in an image singularly deformed and disfigured by pain—'perfectly deformed . . . most singular and odd', to borrow Adam Smith's definition of monstrosity.[20] Towards that frightful image, imminently leaking, the beholder lifts a pen, converting the threat of real putrefaction into figures of a monstrous exorbitance—amplification, pleonasm, hyperbole, periphrasis, tautology, or anadiplosis—rendered in ink, rather than in the discharge of lesions and ulcers.

In all respects Bildad, cast in the *Paraphrase* as the generic public scopophile, is the opposite of Blackmore. An enthusiastic supporter of the violence of decisive authority, Bildad justifies the ferocious disfigurement of Job as the first stage in a process of complete annihilation of the wicked. 'His Head and Limbs cut off shall lye around', he declares, all 'Marks and Monuments' of God's enemy shall be destroyed (79). The unmodified light of God ought to leave Job's shattered bits and pieces shrinking rapidly into nothing: no memorial, no inscription. Blackmore, the sedulous amplifier, makes his way between Job the private man and Bildad the public man to mitigate the damage with his pen. No matter how clumsy and prolix his assembling of the circumstances of disfigurement, Blackmore's project has the same sort of lenitive aim as Kierkegaard's complex transcriptions of Job; it is to make a poultice of text, and it carries him into the same relation to Job as leviathan, in whose figured deformities Job recognises the image of himself.

Blackmore's success may partly be reckoned from the abusive attention directed by his enemies at what they take to be his failure as a writer. Tom Brown is quick to spot the *Paraphrase* as a collision between Job, the patient, and Blackmore, the bad physician writing out prescriptions. In 'On Job newly Travestied' Brown has Job complain that his complaint has been so badly managed: 'Curs'd be the Wretch

---

[19] Richard Blackmore, 'Essay upon Writing', *in Essays upon Several Subjects*, 2 vols. (London: E. Curll, 1717), ii. 245.

[20] Adam Smith, *The Theory of Moral Sentiments*, ed. D. D. Raphael and A. L. Mcfie (Oxford: Clarendon Press, 1976), 198.

that taught him first to Write, | And with lewd Pen and Ink indulg'd his Spite'. Brown deliberately reverses the soothing effect of pen on violence that Blackmore has aimed at: 'Who can escape thy All-destroying Quill | When ev'n thy Cordials, and thy Praises kill?'[21] *The Art of Sinking* begins with the same denunciation of pen and ink in images and phrases typical of Scriblerian satire:

Poetry is a natural or morbid Secretion from the Brain. . . . I have known a Man thoughtful, melancholy, and raving for divers days, but forthwith grow wonderfully easy, lightsome and cheerful, upon a Discharge of the peccant Humour, in exceeding purulent Metre. Nor can I question, but abundance of untimely Deaths are occasion'd by want of this laudable Vent of unruly Passions; yea, perhaps, in poor Wretches, (which is very lamentable) for meer Want of Pen, Ink, and Paper! (13)

Like the extensive quotations from the *Paraphrase*, the purpose of comparing ink flowing through a pen to pus leaking from a boil is to insist on the desperate continuity of disfigurement with its representation in writing: the 'laudable Vent' as nothing but a gaping hole. The pen does not reverse or fix the flow of matter, it is its tributary and sewer. The confluence is even more vividly conceived by Tom Brown when he imagines Blackmore going on a professional visit to Charles Sedley to lance his syphilitic ulcers: 'I'll have no Paper spoil'd on my Disease. | The doctor cry'd, 'Tis true, th'Infection's such, | 'Twill certainly discolour't with a Touch' (Boys, 71). Consistent with confounding ink and writing with every other form of filthy discharge, Pope and his fraternity cite Blackmore's amplifications not as the rhetoricization of deformity, but as verse so dis-figured and literalized by incompetence that it spotlights and enlarges the worst aspects of Job's disease. Any resemblance between Job and Blackmore sprawling, leviathan-like, in curds of ointment is therefore infinitely to Job's disadvantage, who stands 'reduc'd in every Page' by such damaging applications of medical ink.

Pope's misreading of Blackmore's representation of Job is by far the most ingenious and searching. His favourite method of embarrassing Blackmore is, as I have shown, deliberately to misapply his imagery of light. Instead of the negative force capable of inflicting swellings and discharges, Pope construes light as the creative principle, scandalously abused and obscured by the elephantine gestures of a dunce. In lines written the same year as the publication of 'The Art of Sinking' (1727), entitled 'Verses to be placed under the Picture of England's Arch-Poet', he accuses Blackmore of turning Job into Balaam ('Made Job himself

---

[21] Cited in Richard C. Boys, *Sir Richard Blackmore and the Wits* (New York: Octagon Books, 1949; repr. 1969), 105, 116.

curse God and die') and his audience into apostates ('Made ev'ry Reader curse the *Light*') by virtue of the clumsiness and inertia of his lines. There is an interesting curvature to the accusation. The effect of Blackmore's writing on his hero and his reader is to turn them from light, the dictate of God, towards the darkness of the imprecation recommended to Job by his wife ('Curse God and die'). To be in this urgent or impatient condition that Pope calls 'great necessity' is to be like a woman; and if Blackmore's verse has any effect on people in this exigency, it is to make them turn against the light and towards feminine obscurity. The furthest Pope will go in granting Blackmore dominion over 'you, the reader', then, is in the form of a feminizing and scotomizing command—not a figurative or rhetorical triumph, but an oath that travesties and reverses, as most duncely excesses do in Pope's verse, the sublime excellence of the *fiat lux*.

Pope is not only engaging Blackmore on issues of good taste and poetic talent, then, but on the more fundamental question of what language is appropriate to the sublime. In his view the creation of light is expressive of all originary acts of political and poetic authority. Pope's political commitments after the 1715 were to the attainted Tories and neo-Jacobites, Atterbury and Bolingbroke, who had agitated and plotted in the interests of a Stuart succession and a *jus divinum*. His poetics are as consistent with his politics as are Blackmore's, quite on the opposite side. If the latter's model of the sublime is, in Addison's phrase, 'the mutilated Figure' of someone such as Sappho, 'quite dis-jointed and broken into pieces' (*Spectator* 229, 223), and if his conception of sublime language is the rhetorical figuration of ruin, Pope's is the peremptory and irresistible might of divine command, illuminating the plenum of a world where nothing is out of joint, and in which a collective audience owes passive obedience to unlimited authority. In proportion as Blackmore strays from the height of lucid illocution, so far, in Pope's opinion, does he collapse into the feminized 'dregs of nature' and the bathos of disfiguring particularity.

Pope's earlier poetry (including his translation of Homer) is not as adamant on this point as his mature work. The finest of his youthful inventions, the sylphs, are the iridescent correlates of female power, gleaming in dishevelled light. He has no difficulty in adapting the *fiat lux* to female commands that are, under more acceptable terms, the oaths of women in great necessity: 'At length great ANNA said—Let Discord cease! I She said, the World obey'd, and all was Peace'. Belinda supplies a comic example of the same performative: 'Let Spades be Trumps! she said, and Trumps they were'. Pope's ideal scientist, like his ideal woman, operates within the plenum of an authority exerting itself in commands immune to the unregulated manipulation of little circumstances: 'God said, Let NEWTON be! And all was Light'.[22]

A natural sensitivity to the effects of light allied with a fascination inherited from Boileau with all forms of words which create as well as name their referent (bold Longinus 'is *himself* that great *Sublime* he draws'[23]), accounts for Pope's lordly impatience with lesser forms of wordplay. Of his translation of the *Odyssey*, Joseph Spence remarks, 'There is one Case, which seems more particularly to lead Mr Pope into a glaring Stile: 'tis almost ever to be found in his Descriptions of Day, of Light, and of the Morning. . . . There is a great difference between giving one Light, and dazling ones Eyes'.[24] But dazzling imagery is the natural accompaniment of the actions of heroes and gods, who 'effect their designs with a *Touch*, with *Voice*, with a single *Thought*'. Spence quotes an example that falls into the familiar Longinian form of commandment: 'Let all be *Peace*,—He said, and gave the nod | That binds the Fates, the Sanction of the God'.[25] Laura Brown accounts for the appeal of the phrasing and imagery of the divine or royal sanction in Pope's poetry as a strategic pre-emption of Whig claims on the sublime. Quoting from the *Essay on Criticism* the lines distinguishing between ancient irregularity and modern heteronomy ('But tho' the Ancients thus their Rules invade, | (As Kings dispense with Laws themselves have made), Moderns beware!'), she observes,

The turn to an absolutist political metaphor is especially interesting here, because the eighteenth-century sublime, in its disregard for rules, tended to be associated with bourgeois notions of creative autonomy and individualism . . . Pope locates the most progressive or transitional point of his aesthetics in the most reactionary political theory available to him.[26]

In fact, the absolutism is not a metaphor so much as an instance of Pope's sublime of sanction and command. It leads to the superbia of the *Epilogue to the Satires*, when he answers to the charge of being too proud by a retort remarkable for its lack of irony: 'Yes, I am proud; I must be proud to see | Men not afraid of God, afraid of me'. In his letters he rated the price of occupying this higher region of sovereign light as the loss of figures, and of tropes such as irony: 'I see things more in the

[22] *Windsor-Forest*, ll. 327–28; *The Rape of the Lock*, iii. 46; *Epitaph. Intended for Sir Isaac Newton.*
[23] *An Essay on Criticism*, i. 680.
[24] Joseph Spence, *An Essay on Pope's Odyssey* (London: J. and J. Knapton, 1726–7), 6.
[25] *An Essay on Pope's Odyssey*, 118.
[26] *Alexander Pope* (Oxford: Basil Blackwell, 1985), 64–5.

whole. . . . But what I gain on the side of philosophy, I lose on the side of poetry: the flowers are gone'.[27]

Unlike Longinus' treatise, *The Art of Sinking* is a florilegium of dead flowers. Although they are pinned to scenes of wonder, confusion, loss, danger, and terror, they excite only laughter. The amplifications, paraphrases, tautologies, pleonasms, and other figures of excess are reduced by Pope to the dead level of the errant dunces who mistake them for the sublime. They are the transparent disguises of the pointlessness of sheer repetition and obsessive enumeration.[28] Thus the aposiopesis is 'an excellent Figure for the Ignorant, as, *What shall I say?* when one has nothing to say; or, *I can no more*, when one really can no more: Expressions which the gentle Reader is so good, as never to take in earnest' (46). Being a good deal more combative than the gentle reader, Pope turns every embellishment of great necessity into a flowerless literalism; which, in the case of violence, leaves suffering as suffering. 'If you have Occasion to mention a Number of Misfortunes, stile them "Fresh Troops of Pains, and regimented Woes" ' (62), he recommends, quoting Blackmore's Job (86), indicating behind the hopeless metaphor woes reduced to nothing but woes. Pope refuses to allow amplified complaint anything but the disfigurement—woe minus flower—of the original, for fear that he may recognize himself in an unflattering light, limping, for instance, like Blackmore, as Blackmore has leaked like Job.[29]

The history of Pope's dealings with Sappho are exemplary of his hardening attitude to the feminizing necessities of the Whig sublime he parades in *The Art of Sinking*. Her bodily privations are dramatically concentrated—'at a loss for her Soul, her Body, her Ears, her Tongue, her Eyes, her Colour, all of them as much absent from her as if they had never belonged to her' (*On the Sublime* x.3)—and represent a considerable threat to any gentle reader prepared to imitate her. In his translation of the Ovidian heroic epistle, *Sapho to Phaon* (1707), the physical symptoms of desire are dwelt upon as a prelude to the mutilated and fragmented condition that Sappho and her writings are destined to fall into after her plunge from the Leucadian rock. In his later adaptation of this epistolary complaint, *Eloisa to Abelard* (1716), the ruin of the desiring female, the 'craving void left aking in her breast', is projected as the literal wound to the groin of the man who has looked at her: Abelard

[27] *Epilogue to the Satires*, ll. 208–9. *Correspondence*, ed. Sherburn, iv. 190.
[28] Discussing Rowe's translation of Lucan, Cromwell remarks, 'He is so errant a Whig, that he strains even beyond his Author, in passion for Liberty, and aversion to Tyranny, and errs only in amplification'. And Pope responds, 'Indeed he amplifies too much'. *Correspondence*, i. 102–4.
[29] 'Never gallop Pegasus to death; | Lest stiff, and stately, void of fire, or force, | You limp, like Blackmore.' *Imitations of Horace*, Ep. I. i, ll. 14–16.

is castrated, 'a naked Lover bound and bleeding lies'.[30] Pope has a number of ways of rewriting this scene so that the threat of specular or readerly loss is contained. The most transcendent is the attenuation of *The Dying Christian to his Soul* (1712), which recruits Sappho's fragment 31 for devotional purposes, and where privations culminate in the liberation of the soul upwards towards the region of pure light—'I mount! I fly!'—and the body jettisoned without regret. The most crude is the *tu quoque* of his *Rondeau* (1710) which, he told Cromwell, 'I desire you show Sappho' (*Correspondence* i. 89).

> You know where you did despise
> (T'other day) my little eyes,
> Little legs, and little thighs,
> And some things of little size,
>   You know where.
> You, 'tis true, have fine black eyes,
> Taper legs, and tempting thighs,
> Yet what more than all we prize
> Is a thing of little size,
>   You know where.

Here the gazing male restores his shrunken bits by projecting their exiguity into the desired no-thing of the female, Abelard back to front as it were, or the 'laudable Vent' as the female hole. Pope's literary warfare with the other Sappho, Lady Mary Wortley Montagu, conforms to the structure of this *tu quoque*. She tells him his back is round, and he tells her that her hair is grey; and more besides. 'Sappho at her toilet's greasy task' secretly compounds (like Blackmore's leviathan) filth with ointment in a vain effort to plug her leaks and holes.[31]

In *Three Hours after Marriage* (1717) Phoebe Clinket gives her sublime piece, significantly entitled *The Universal Deluge*, to Sir Tremendous Longinus (i.e. John Dennis) for comments and suggestions. He proves to be an ungentle reader, editing and reducing her tragedy in the same way that Pope dis-figures the Whig sublime and Lady Mary. As Phoebe's text disintegrates, so does she, accompanying its destruction with a vigorous adaptation of Sappho's complaint: 'Ah, hold, hold', she cries as large chunks are being crossed out, 'I'm butcher'd, I'm massacred. For mercy's sake! murder, murder! ah!'[32] It aptly illustrates the disfigurement caused when the textual bridge between actual ruin and its figurative representation is blown up by a reader resistant to the 'too

---

[30] *Eloisa to Abelard*, ll. 94, 100.
[31] *To Ld. Hervey & Lady Mary Wortley*, ll. 2, 6. *Epistle to a Lady*, l. 25.
[32] John Arbuthnot, John Gay, and Alexander Pope, *Three Hours after Marriage*, in *Burlesque Plays of the Eighteenth Century*, ed. Simon Trussler (Oxford: Oxford Univ. Press, 1969), 112.

much' of amplification. Sir Tremendous's intervention into Phoebe's text is more like Pope's into Blackmore's or Sappho's than Dennis's into, say, Milton's or Pope's where, far from despising amplification in favour of the abrupt performative, he is very keen to identify the conditions for the successful cultivation of flowers.[33] Phoebe is made to exhibit a physical weakness incident to the astonishment and terror with which she aimed her (male) reader should, by means of her sublime tropes, be afflicted. It is not hard to believe that Pope's growing intolerance of amplification, interpreting it always as a threat or insult that has to be returned with a literalizing reading or a performative dismissal, has to do with the deplorable state of his own body and his appalling sensitivity to his weaknesses. What vulnerabilities might metaboles, hyperboles, pleonasms, tautologies, and all the other excessive figures and particularizing tropes of the sublime cause a man who began each day rather like Sappho, at a loss for his limbs until he was laced into a corset?

While 'Sappho' and Pope were still good friends, she sent him (in 1717) a translation of a Turkish love-poem written by Ibrahim Bassa. Her translation of the fourth stanza closely resembles fragment 31: 'I rub my face against the Earth, I am drown'd in scalding Tears—I rave! | Have you no Compassion? Will you not turn to look upon me?'[34] She explains to Pope the nature of the oriental sublime in terms that Blackmore had used the year before: 'I should have told you in the first place that the Eastern Manners give a great light into many scripture passages that appear odd to us. . . . They have what they called the Sublime, that is, a stile proper for Poetry, and which is the exact scripture stile' (i. 333). She sets up also the same triad as Blackmore and Sappho, offering her written translation as a medium through which the desired glance can be returned, and a voice be re-attached to the stifled and isolated complainant. In fact, this textual medium extends from her own pen all the way to 'scripture' itself, indicating a ground of comparison between secular and religious poetry far more implicated in bodies and figures than Pope's rendition of Sappho as a dying Christian. Faces marked by passion but made recognizable in the elaborate detail of their complaints will seem odd, she says, to 'us'—singular, that is, to the consensus of enlightened European opinion which she, in the first person

[33] See e.g. *The Grounds of Criticism in Poetry*, ed. Edward Niles Hooker, 2 vols. (Baltimore: Johns Hopkins Univ. Press, 1939), i. 353, where he argues that the authentic language of God is not sublime because it is not inflected with the passions and desires arising from human limitations and necessary for the production of figurative expressions: therefore only by means of a mediating figure such as prosopopeia, whereby a mortal creature impersonates the speech of God and imports human passion into it, can sublimity be achieved.

[34] *The Complete Letters of Lady Mary Wortley Montagu*, ed. Robert Halsband, 3 vols. (Oxford: Clarendon Press, 1965), i. 335.

singular, has already chosen to see in a different light, entering so far into oddity as to identify with a male passion for a female object and to be transported: 'You see I am pritty far gone in Oriental Learning' (i. 337).

Pope was not always so steady in his resistance to what Sappho's fragments, 'Sappho', and Blackmore's Job were holding out to him. When he compared Homer's repetitions and amplifications to heroic disfigurements, the '*Marks* and *Moles*' of 'gigantick Bodies', he was not frightened of seeing a deformed body reflected, even figuratively, in amplified descriptions.[35] Nor was he incapable of writing verse like Blackmore's. The year before *The Art of Sinking* appeared, Joseph Spence was doing to Pope's translation of the *Odyssey* what Pope was about to do to Blackmore's paraphrase of Job. Spence notices that instead of plain milk Polyphemus swallows the 'milky deluge', and that the shutting of a door is extended to this circumstantial length: 'The Door reclos'd; | The Bolt, obedient to the silken Cord, | To the strong Staple's inmost depth restor'd, | Secur'd the Valves'.[36] How particular! But when he decided that a poet's attachment to little circumstances could be construed as nothing but trifling and vulgarity, the disfigurement he visited on his enemies proved to be a vain avoidance of the moles, vents, and *paraleipomena* disfiguring his own body, and a self-tormenting rejection of the only consolation available for such deformities. Pope's refusal to own the 'dotted dark nakedness of the body' leaves him in well-lit isolation, crippled, and unredeemed by flowers. The illusion of omnicompetence is paid for with his alienation from what Burke calls the 'dominion of obscurity', inseparable from the wonder of the sublime: 'It is thus with the vulgar', says Burke, 'and all men are as the vulgar in what they do not understand'.[37] Hesitant in all larger bids for understanding, Blackmore understood at least this as he explored the compelling vulgarity of little circumstances.

[35] Preface to *The Iliad of Homer* vii. 19, 13.
[36] *An Essay on Pope's Odyssey*, 37, 27.
[37] *A Philosophical Enquiry*, 61.

11

'It is not so with me': Clarissa and the Regulation of Unprecedented Vehemence

Although Richardson appears to have had a brief flirtation with Jacobite politics in his early days, printing for Atterbury and his friends during the treason trials of 1723, his commitment to the Hanoverian succession during the forty-five was unwavering; and it has been common among readers of *Clarissa* to interpret Lovelace's aristocratic tyrannies as typical of extreme Tory prejudices against a 'trade-prospered' class and, contrariwise, to understand Clarissa's defence of her conscience and rights as the feminized declaration of Revolution principles.[1] A quick comparison of Richardson's attitudes with Blackmore's reveals a Whiggish symmetry in their judgements upon genius, originality, the sublimity of scripture, the depravity of a classical taste, and the wickedness of the times. In his correspondence with Young, Richardson refines the views that reach the public in *Conjectures upon Original Composition* (1759). Pope, for example, is an 'imitator of other *authors*' and therefore 'not the genius to lift our souls to *Heaven*': 'What originality is there in the works for which he is most famed?'[2] The property held by an original poet in his work ('quite his own') ensures its natural authenticity and tonic virtue, as opposed to the specious wisdom of a deist tract such as the *Essay on Man*, copied from Bolingbroke and saved from outright deism only by its *'Tinkering Editor'* (*Selected Letters*, 318). Such imitative practice is consistent with 'the present worse than sceptical age' and 'the general depravity' which it sanctions.[3] Original writing attains to the primitive wisdom of those treasures of morality, 'the Proverbs of Solomon, Ecclesiastes, the Books of Wisdom, and Ecclesiasticus', which Richardson promised Lady Bradshaigh to excerpt and to publish in a little book entitled, *Simplicity the True Sublime.*

---

[1] Tom Keymer, *Richardson's Clarissa and the Eighteenth-Century Reader* (Cambridge: Cambridge Univ. Press, 1992), 170–5; Christopher Hill, 'Clarissa Harlowe and her Times', *Essays in Criticism*, 5/4 (1955), 315–40.

[2] Richardson to Young, *Selected Letters of Samuel Richardson*, ed. John Carroll (Oxford: Clarendon Press, 1964), 333–4. See Edward Young, *Conjectures upon Original Composition* (London, 1759; repr. Leeds: Scolar Press, 1966), 12, 65.

[3] *Postscript to Clarissa, or the History of Young Lady*, 4 vols. (London: Dent, 1932; repr. 1965), iv. 559, 553 (based on the 3rd edn. of 1751).

However, in an age so abandoned to trifling 'that to make Wisdom looked upon as worth regarding, we must shew her with a Monkey's Grin', such enterprises are forlorn unless restricted to the uncorrupted taste of readers capable of relishing words sprung from the hearts of writers who live only to themselves, and who have contracted, in Young's phrase, 'full intimacy with the Stranger within'.[4]

Like Blackmore, Richardson also powerfully believes in writing as the purest conduit between an original author and the awakening conscience of the ductile reader. Richardson's extravagant claims for the familiar letter are based on the immediacy of this transaction. The letter instantly embodies the heart's impulses, disclosing '*Soul* and *Meaning*' without reserve or disguise because the pen 'expects, as I may say, to engross the writer's whole self' (*Selected Letters*, 68, 66). To raise epistolary communication to this order of self-evidence, so that the identity of the writer finds its undistorted image in the heart of the reader, is to place even more faith than Blackmore in the efficacy of 'Liberty of Speech' and the value of an original communication.

It is a surprise, therefore, to find that Richardson's Job, the scriptural centre-piece of *Clarissa*, is used to introduce a theodicy more akin to Pope's views about the suppression of the particulars of individual suffering than to Blackmore's amplifications of a singular complaint. It is an even greater surprise to find that Lovelace, the Tory Satan in this trial of virtue, seems more sharply sensible of what is involved in Clarissa's reinscription of Job than Richardson. There are five Meditations—fragments of scripture adapted to Clarissa's grievous case— transcribed in the novel, of which three consist largely in quotations from Job. Although Clarissa culls the most passionate of Job's exclamations, such as his longing for death, his curse against the days of his conception and birth, his refusal of spiteful consolation, and his desire that the charges against him might be written in a book or on a rock, Richardson is eager that these should not be mistaken as channels of a personal exasperation, and that they should be understood instead as citations of a general triumph over pain and despair. He has Belford explain that 'on every extraordinary provocation she has recourse to the Scriptures, and endeavours to regulate her vehemence by sacred precedents'.[5] The point is insisted upon in the thirty-two meditations— supposedly the full tally of Clarissa's scriptural excerpts—which

---

[4] *Selected Letters*, 222, 129. Sir Charles Grandison is a model of original morality, one whose heart and pen speak a self-identical first person: 'I live not to the world. I live to myself'. *Sir Charles Grandison*, ed. Jocelyn Harris, 3 vols. (Oxford: Oxford Univ. Press, 1972), i. 206. *Conjectures upon Original Composition*, 53.

[5] *Clarissa, or the History of a Young Lady*, ed. Angus Ross (Harmondsworth: Penguin, 1985), 1207.

Richardson circulated among his friends: 'It will be observed to the advantage of Clarissa's character, that she was led into even these execrations by Example, rather than by violence of temper, great as her afflictions were, and outrageous as the injury she had received'.[6] Even the most excessive complaint is harmonized to the example of patience, and Clarissa's imitation of it is likewise exemplary, 'serviceable to all such as labour under great afflictions and disappointments' (*Meditations*, 1).

Lovelace responds in quite the opposite way to Clarissa's imitations of her 'admired exclaimer' (1114). Job is an incitement to excessive complaints, not a regulator of them, 'else she would not have delivered herself with such strength and vehemence' (1148). He goes on to mark a strange equivalence between the singularity of the patriarch and her ventriloquization of his unexemplary and vehement declaration of the uniqueness of his case: 'Miss Harlowe, indeed, is the only woman in the world, I believe, that can say, in the words of her favourite Job (for I can quote a text as well as she), *But it is not so with me*.'[7]

Edward Young, in mutual collaboration with Richardson on the revisions of *Clarissa* and *Night-Thoughts*, was quite clear about the applicable doctrine of the text ('the history of Job . . . tells us the worst is supportable') and very keen to see the full set of *Meditations* inserted in the next edition, promising, 'It will much add to the verisimilitude, and pathos, and sublimity of the work'.[8] Although this suggestion, like so many vainly made by Richardson's readers, was ignored, Richardson's belief in the value of submission in adversity was as strong as Young's. In his abstract of the maxims and instructions delivered in *Clarissa*, he places under the heading of 'Consolation' the following terrifying lesson: 'If a person in calamity can consider herself as called upon to give an example of patience and resignation, she will find her mind greatly invigorated'.[9]

By the term 'verisimilitude' Young alludes to the nice adjustment of narrative, or fable, to moral. Of his *Night-Thoughts*, he boasted to Richardson, 'It differs from the common modes of poetry which is from long narratives to draw short morals. Here, on the contrary, the narrative is short, and the morality arising from it makes the bulk of the poem' (*Correspondence*, 349). Perhaps he felt that his friend's uncontrollable tendency to 'run into length', and to add three pages for every

---

[6] *Meditations Collected from the Sacred Books* (London, 1750; repr. New York: Garland, 1976), pp. v, 2.

[7] Cf. Job 9: 34–5: 'Let him take his rod away from me, and let not his fear terrify me: Then would I speak, and not fear him; but it is not so with me'.

[8] *The Correspondence of Edward Young*, ed. Henry Pettit (Oxford: Clarendon Press, 1971), 222, 342.

[9] *Letters and Passages Restored from the Original Manuscripts* (London, 1751), 229 (issued as the supplementary eighth volume of the second edition of *Clarissa* [1749]).

one he took out, needed this doctrinal counterweight to the narrative swellings. At any rate, he touches on a question crucial to Richardson's adaptation of the familiar letter to fiction, involving the ratio of narrative bulk to moral tendency. The material of the narrative consists firstly in those 'minute descriptions' which are necessary to the candour of an innocent correspondence; secondly in the minutiae that form the plots of a less than innocent letter-writer such as Lovelace; and finally in the matters 'circumstantial and minute' which are required to be emphasized in a probable representation of real life (42, 473, 1499). The aggregation of these little circumstances supply the basis of Richardson's rewriting of the book of Job as the story of Clarissa, intended to illustrate a moral of regulated vehemence. Instead of numbering up these particulars as the markers or figures of afflictions equal to Job's only in their unprecedented intensity (which is roughly the position adopted by Blackmore and Lovelace), he attempts to reconcile two conflicting positions. On the one hand he lays a claim to the unprecedented originality of a work pursued upon such a lengthy and detailed plan ('something that never yet had been done'[10]), whose loose sheets he is fond of calling the 'Original Manuscripts', and whose heroine is commonly referred to as inimitable, original to the point of oddity, as well as being a person of 'unexampled virtue'.[11] On the other, he insists on the derived and exemplary quality of the work, as if its sole function were to illustrate and enforce a prescription extrinsic to its own excellence—a law or truth already written down. 'Is Clarissa a mere Novel?' demands Philip Skelton under Richardson's authority. 'Whoever considers it as such, does not understand it. It is a system of religious and moral Precepts and Examples.'[12] Clarissa may be seized by 'resentments, strong resentments', but as her most passionate execrations are 'in humble imitation of the sublimest exemplar', she is never to be found outside the economy of the prescriptive system (1115, 1118). As Job comes into focus as guarantor of the very criteria of righteousness with which he was tormented, so is Clarissa more recognizable as a victim of consolation.

The question of how multiplying narrative circumstances relate to an exemplary teaching is deeply implicated in the question of how exactly Clarissa relates to Job. These questions raise yet another concerning the attitudes of Richardson and the more obedient of his readers to Clarissa herself as an example of providential government and poetic justice. Their imperturbable citation of the worst of injustices as agreeable to the

[10] *Postscript* to the 3rd edn., iv. 553.
[11] 1178. The 'shocking whimsy' of the coffin in the bedroom, standing there like a harpsichord, causes Belford to reflect that 'these great minds cannot avoid doing extraordinary things' (1305).
[12] *Clarissa: Preface, Hints of Prefaces, and Postscript*, ed. R. F. Brissenden (Los Angeles: Augustan Reprint Soc.), 7.

scheme of future rewards (as Clarissa puts it, perhaps not without chagrin, 'That I have not deserved the evils I have met with, is my Consolation'[13]) so resembles the mockeries of the comforters that it is impossible not to suspect that *Clarissa*, like so many rewritings of the book of Job, is condemned to repeat the conflicts of the original, not to resolve or interpret them. Even if Richardson transcends, as Young does not, the limitations of the comforters, is it not to take up God's position in the theophany, and to point majestically to the self-evident state of the thing? 'It may not be amiss to remind the reader, that so early in the work as pp. 332–3 the dispensations of Providence in her distress are justified by herself' (1498 n. d).

So often the clarity of the story and its lesson is affirmed not because of any consensus between the 'editor' and his reader, but because it is necessary to correct the puzzlement of the characters or to overcome strong readerly resistance to the systematic point, especially its requisite unhappy ending. Richardson is forced to intervene agonistically into his creation, indicating rather irritably the thing as it is precisely because it is not self-evident, and because narrative outcomes left to the candour of the general reader to determine have, he finds, 'neither art, nor nature, nor even probability, in them; and [are] moreover of very bad example'.[14] In this respect Job cannot be made to operate as a model of exemplary restraint. He imports into Richardson's novel all the unresolved conflicts of his own narrative, dramatizing and as it were authorizing a stand-off between, on the one hand, a system considered so irrefragable by its proponents that their summaries of it emerge as tautologies and, on the other, narrative material that is excessive in the sense both of representing unregulated vehemence in particulars and of appealing to readers to ignore or to test the self-evidence of doctrinal imperatives. Another way of putting this is to say that a competition develops between the tautologies of the system and the tautologies unfolded by the indiscipline of its narrative vehicle.

This conflict originates in Richardson's inability critically to distinguish between his ideal of the familiar letter and the literary tradition of the heroic epistle upon which his new species of writing abuts. He refuses to sacrifice his nostalgia for the paradisal simplicity of successful self-examination, where the pen's negotiation of presence and absence never impedes its sensitive function as the heart's oscillographic instrument. In this regime, to write is to reveal what never was hidden (namely, an identity whose wholeness has never been alienated or divided) in a spiritual labour whose benefit is always already felt, both by

---

[13] Cited by Richardson, *Letters and Passages*, 229.   [14] *Clarissa*, 3rd edn., iv. 553.

the whole self and the 'stranger' (whether s/he is construed as conscience or as the sympathetic reader), as profound familiarity. Clarissa's correspondence with Anna Howe, her 'sweet and ever-amiable friend—companion—sister—lover' (1357) may be compared with the clear and uninterrupted gaze that Sappho in fragment 31 longs to share with her lover. When the self is engrossed in this way it produces a strange shimmer which Terry Eagleton associates with tautology: 'Such transparency—the baffling enigma of that which is merely itself—is bound to appear socially opaque, a worthless tautology or resounding silence'.[15] He adds that the only lesson capable of being generated from this self-identity is circular, such as Anna Howe's reminder to Clarissa, 'Truth is truth, my dear!' (485).

Clarissa, like Sappho, has to find a way to her semblable friend through a mediating text, made necessary by an intervening male gaze that troubles the clarity of like compared with like. It has been pointed out frequently that writing is a textual supplement which, in completing the process of self-exposure, indicates an originary abatement of identity for which no amount of writing can ever compound. It supplies the place of what is missing, but only as a prosthesis, not as the desiderated element of self-identity. At the same time, writing is a technology of substitution, limited to standing in for what is distant or absent, so that it is incapable of rendering presently a subject that claims to be present to itself.[16] Tom Keymer is right to suggest that Richardson is keenly aware of the reserves, deceits, and indirections that breed in the gaps between the first person of the letter writer and the world s/he represents with a pen.[17] He argues that the invitation to intimacy extended by the epistolary address in fact challenges the reader to interpret its premeditations, elisions, and postponements in precisely the intrusive and violating fashion that Terry Castle cites as characteristic of Lovelace's interventions into Clarissa's textualized body.[18] From the moment Clarissa is unable to tell Anna Howe whether she loves Lovelace, instancing a 'conditional liking' instead of a present feeling, she turns away from the immediacies of self-delivery, and from the 'depth, extent, biass, and full sort of her mind' (*Conjectures*, 53), in order to study the art of a delayed communication (117), a promissory exercise whose limited disclosures she artlessly alludes to when she

---

[15] Terry Eagleton, *The Rape of Clarissa* (Oxford: Basil Blackwell, 1982), 75, 42.

[16] Eagleton points this out, *The Rape of Clarissa*, 42. See also William Beatty Warner, *Reading Clarissa* (New Haven: Yale Univ. Press, 1979), 54; Janet Gurkin Altman, *Epistolarity* (Columbus, Oh.: Ohio State Univ., 1982), 14; Terry Castle, *Clarissa's Ciphers* (Ithaca: Cornell Univ. Press, 1982), 145.

[17] *Richardson's Clarissa and the Eighteenth-Century Reader*, 19.

[18] *Clarissa's Ciphers*, 112.

informs Anna of her 'reserves of pens and ink' (366). These reserves are her only protection against a world of uncertain appearances and shocking circumstances (394), and the only support of a much-weakened subject position, eventually so uncertain that she demands: 'What is now my self?' (1022). They also implicate her in that world, and prevent her from answering her own question.

Although Richardson may be conscious of the difference between letters that declare the thing as it is, and those which function within difference itself by concealing and distorting a presence that has become merely notional, he finds it difficult to exploit or even articulate this difference because he lacks a perspective from which to account for it, and because he believes he has a method of recovering the original transparency of self-evidence without assigning difference any value beyond that of a binary opposition: *this* is eligible; *that* is not. He is so wedded to the ideal of language which speaks for itself of things which are themselves, that not only does he believe that presence and truth are only temporarily suspended during the crises endured by the virtuous, he also believes that the *rhetoric* of delay and absence, as opposed to the accidental or forced obliquities of the naturally straightforward, is the preserve of the vicious: something that occurs in his text but which he is not responsible for and which he need not justify in terms of his own practice of writing. In this respect at least he has a little in common with Tristram Shandy, who finds it hard to offer in a preface a purview of what he has written, postponing prefatory business dreadfully until he evolves something like Richardson's method of deictic argument, which he names 'dialectic induction'.[19] Richardson's difficulties with prefaces are notorious, driving him to rely upon ghosted work, including a preface to the first edition of *Clarissa* penned by no other than Pope's 'tinkering editor', William Warburton.

In that preface Warburton briskly divides the novel into two different modes of verisimilitude, roughly conformable to the two different modes of epistolarity recognized by Richardson. There is the fiction which economically deploys 'those lively and delicate impressions which Things *present* are known to make upon the minds of those affected by them' in order that the reader might find 'Directions for his *Conduct*, or Employment for his *Pity*' in viewing 'a Faithful Picture of *Nature* in *Private Life*'.[20] Then there is the fiction that makes a more extensive claim on the reader's attention by first of all running into an excess of particulars, and finally into monstrous improbabilities (pp. i–iii).

[19] *The Life and Opinions of Tristram Shandy, Gentleman*, ed. Melvyn New and Joan New, 3 vols. (Florida: Univ. Presses of Florida, 1978), i. 232.
[20] *Clarissa*, 7 vols. (London, 1748), i. pp. v–vi.

Richardson's reluctance to own such clearly expressed views, and his removal of them from subsequent editions, indicates no disagreement with them—after all, he utters and authorizes similar opinions in his private correspondence—rather, it suggests a horror of their bleak and schematized account of a practice he found it compromising to divide in this way, and from which he found it impossible ever securely to draw a full statement of purpose (that is, a reasoned account of the relation of the art of illusion to the production of moral truth) in the first person. He begs Warburton not to empty the reserves of pen and ink—'I could wish that the Air of Genuineness had been kept up, tho' I want not the letters to be *thought* genuine; only so far kept up, I mean, as that they should not prefatically be owned *not* to be genuine'—and in the process of this irresolute prevarication he undermines his own first person: 'How shall I take it upon myself? I must, if put to me, by Particulars, suppose it to be suggested me, at least, by some Learned Friend, so disguising as you may not be suggested to be the Person' (*Selected Letters*, 85).

There are three factors in play here that Richardson is failing to organize: the illusion of a genuine correspondence, which bears upon the reader's capacity for belief; the necessity of limiting that illusion, which bears upon 'directions for conduct' requiring, among other things, that fiction and truth finally not be confounded; and the problem of adequately drawing that line of limitation, which bears heavily upon his own sense of identity and his role as a moral agent. These three factors have a lively existence in the narrative action of *Clarissa* as well as overflowing into the dilemmas of its author, and they can be calibrated according to the necessity writers and readers jointly lie under of attending to little circumstances. For example, the purest kind of familiar letter plumbs the depth and bias of the mind in order to familiarize the self with that reflection or representation of itself which is only ever notionally a stranger. Here minuteness—Warburton's 'lively and delicate impressions'—indicates the range and confidence of the presiding self, with no hint of the division between 'you and yourself' which Anna Howe notices when Clarissa's eye has been diverted from self-examination to a consideration of the worldly Lovelace's merits (292). The data of this species of correspondence is all heart-directed, from the outside inward, and it either indicates or obtains for the first person an absolute competence with the pen, sentimentalized as 'writing your heart' or originalized as writing nothing but what is your own.

With the onset of reserve, the orientation of the letter changes radically. The first person singular is much more unstable both in judgement and expression. Once Clarissa has moved, along with her punctilio, out of doors, she finds it much harder to distinguish what is real from what is false, and she becomes increasingly unsettled by her failure to judge correctly. Until she escapes from Mrs Sinclair's house she is almost totally the creature of the supererogatory details of Lovelace's plots, and their abundant 'shocking circumstances' which will eventually form 'the particulars of my sad story' (394, 1418). In Lovelace's hands matters of fact are transformed into the chimerical fictions Warburton deprecates. Clarissa is amazed at their needless obliquity ('every step he took was a wry one, a needless wry one' [527]), until she realizes that she must respond in kind, with 'affectations and curvings from the plain simple truth' (484). Lovelace demands, 'Will not her *feints* justify mine? Does she not invade my province . . . and is it not now fairly come to *Who shall most deceive and cheat the other?*' (759).

Standing at the intersection of these proliferating circumstances, the credulous victim as well as the reluctant inventor of them, Clarissa finds out what it is to be a virtual witness and a practising narrator. She understands that the abundance of circumstances is a bid for mastery, 'to obtain a belief, and power over one' (171), and that resistance depends upon a circumstantial counter-narrative which itself causes the first person to dwindle to virtual status. She herself is reduced to performing the sincerity she once valued herself upon ('I thought it best . . . to appear not to doubt the sincerity of his confession, and to accept of it as sincere' [3rd edn., ii. 83]). As for Lovelace, he is 'a perfect Proteus . . . a perfect chameleon; or rather more variable than the chameleon' (3rd edn., ii. 82); and in meeting him eye to eye ('We are both great watchers of each other's eyes' [460]), Clarissa is contaminated with the same instability of identity. When she turns an eye towards her once-familiar self, she reports, 'I durst not trust my self with my own reflection' (337). The uncertainty of a first person who has lost moral agency is evident in Lovelace's careful reproduction of her repetitions and self-interruptions: 'I see, I see, Mr Lovelace, in broken sentences she spoke—I see, I see—that at last—at last—I am ruined' (881). Consequently her escape from his clutches is only partial, for her self-identity is left behind: 'Once more have I escaped—but, alas! *I*, my best *self*, have not escaped!' (974).

Richardson's recovery of Clarissa's authoritative first person depends upon the eviction of the negative coalitions of presence and absence which have weakened it. The presence of the lover and of the body, the desiring subject and the desired object, have always been a problem. Impulses are better embodied when 'ideally the beloved [is] Absent', and this purer absence can then reveal that presence as nothing 'but body' (*Selected Letters*, 68, 64). Hence Lovelace's exclusion from the deathbed scenes and Clarissa's growing disgust for her own person, which she focuses through the ornaments of her *vanitas*, the coffin, 'lined with white satin; soon she said to be tarnished by viler earth than any it could be covered by' (1306). Absence of mind, parents, and friends, which have variously required her to act as her own mediator, penning papers that have missed (as heroic epistles always do) their object of a happy reunion, is compensated now by her refusal of the responsibility of reporting her condition, or vindicating her actions. She appears to take leave of a narrative which she has scarcely patience to recall, by nominating Belford as her literary executor and regarding herself 'freed from the necessity of writing her own story' (1178). No longer obliged to negotiate disturbing presences and tormenting absences, her language attains a more than sepulchral authority ('Hear me . . . as one speaking from the dead' [1427]). At the same time, her identity and name are purged of all carnal associations in order that they may take their places within the allegory of her return to her father's house: 'She seems indeed', says Colonel Morden, 'to have been, as much as mortal could be, LOVE itself' (1422). As she is dying she arrives independently at a sense of her self as a kind of personification, a figure whose identity and agency are tautologously blended into self-presence, 'I am all blessed hope—hope itself' (1361).

Whether this transformation is credible or tolerable is the theme of much of Richardson's correspondence in the 1740s, in which he was called on to defend Clarissa's transcendence of all forms of narrative excess by a readership (referred to as 'the greater Vulgar' [*Selected Letters*, 87]), coarsely clamouring for her restoration in a comic ending and appalled by her attenuation in a tragic allegory of faith. Such readers were acting in defence of their own credulity, having willingly entered into a relationship with Richardson not unlike Clarissa's with Lovelace by succumbing to the 'Historical Faith which Fiction is generally read with'.[21] Even though they were capable of discriminating among the motives of the characters, and at a pinch risking disagreement with their author, the leading characteristic of the Richardsonian reader, at least in the opinion of Richardson's male friends, appears to have been passivity. Young refers to them as 'distressed Patients' who form the 'passive audience [that] tragedy requires' (*Conjectures*, 84). Rather more luridly, Joseph Spence compares the pangs endured by the reader during the 'enforcing' of the moral with 'the Incisions made by a kind Surgeon; who feels himself for every Stroke that he gives . . . to save

---

[21] 'The author of the novel of Clarissa Harlowe attempted to make his fictions interesting by . . . minute precision and exactitude in the detailed relations of all common circumstances.' Richard Payne Knight, *Analytical Enquiry into the Principles of Taste* (T. Payne: London, 1805), 283.

his Patients'.[22] Richardson himself seems to have believed that the raised imagination of the credulous reader spontaneously absorbs the example even of the most poignant or inflaming scenes. Finally, all dispute is settled with tautology: 'An example is an example; right is right; and wrong is wrong' (*Selected Letters*, 132).

But it is clear from Richardson's own experience that there is little equivalence between an example and a narrative, since the one completes the normative function of virtuous discourse, and is located and affirmed by a reader seeking the representation of identity guaranteed by the exemplary first person; whereas the other is naturally excessive and diminishes the agency of reader and narrator alike, as is evident in the very letter where Richardson desires Warburton to impersonate the first-person editor of letters 'aimed to be exemplary' in so far as 'they should not prefatically be owned *not* to be genuine' (85). Can he even be aware of the damage he does to the steadiness of his own judgements when he confesses to Lady Bradshaigh, 'It is not fair to say—I, identically I, am any-where, while I keep within the character'? (*Selected Letters*, 286). How can an I which is not an I deduce from its 'own' operations an example which is simply and unproblematically an example? The system and the vehicle tend inevitably in two contrary directions. The narrative of *Clarissa* dramatizes this fundamental incompatibility between the supposed integrity of the identical subject and the protean unsteadiness of the first person who generates the story designed to test and prove it. Clarissa and Lovelace represent and probe this difference; Richardson succumbs to it whenever he protects the delusions of art in the name of an example he dare not own in the first person. If the novel is exemplary of anything it is not the conveniently binarized oppositions of truth and falsehood, exemplarity and excess, right and wrong, spirit and body, but of the contagious power of the art of obtaining belief, which infects all methods designed to bind it, and resists all efforts to extract from it a determinate lesson or positive truth. Its particularity provokes an anomie that evidently, in Richardson's case, blinds him to the implausibility of his dream of simplicity and identity because it implicates him in the effects of a narrative excess so deeply that he can never 'prefatically' get clear of them. The example declares, in short, that there is no example that is not also exemplary of this.

The closest Richardson gets to an account of the difference between his desire for interpretative symmetry and a narrative practice that

---

[22] *Clarissa: Preface, Hints of Prefaces etc.*, 10. The analogy between experimental anatomy and Richardson's mode of appealing to the sensibility of his readers has been handled again recently by Ann Jessie van Sant, *Eighteenth-Century Sensibility and the Novel* (Cambridge: Cambridge Univ. Press, 1993), 53.

overwhelms all normative discourse, is in his reflections on Clarissa's transcriptions of Job, and in a short excursus on the degree of probability obtained by the adjustment of the small circumstance to the greater fact in a credible narrative. Of the latter he observes, 'Attentive Readers have found, and will find, that the Probability of all Stories told, or of Narratives given, depends upon small Circumstances; as may be observed, that in all Tryals for Life and Property, the Merits of the Cause are more determinable by such, than by the greater Facts; which usually are so laid, and taken care of, as to seem to authenticate themselves'.[23] The greater fact is assigned the status of a self-evident truth, whereas the small circumstance allows room for manœuvre and discretionary rhetoric. Although it is not clear from what Richardson writes that the array of small circumstances necessarily serves the cause of truth embodied in the greater fact, he seems to be assuming that particularity functions as the auxiliary of generality, making what was cognitively certain also probable to the imagination. Whether this is how small circumstances are used, or how they ought to be used, is not clear; but if it were a general rule of forensic eloquence, then Richardson would have begun to solve the problem of the antagonism between narrative and example along lines similar to Young's alignment of fable and moral.

He tries again with Clarissa's transcriptions from the book of Job, where he discovers the sole value of imitation to lie in the transformation of what otherwise would be a passionate and reprehensible execration into an exemplary quotation. Her impersonation of Job's curses means she does *not* curse: rather, she instances the fault of impatience in the very act of sidestepping it. Her use of Job's story is to drain it of every excess by reducing the symptoms of uncontrolled passion to representations: turning the *circumstances* of a failure of self-control into the sign of the *greater fact* of self-control. A similar interpretation of the book of Job was currently on offer in the spate of commentaries that followed Warburton's treatment of it as an allegory in the *Divine Legation*. John Garnett, the bishop of Clogher, wished to suggest that the dialogues are an elaborate performance, undertaken upon forensic principles, intended to represent the extremes of impatient expostulation as an exemplary argument for patience: 'The business is, from this representation of him, to acquit Job of, what God acquits him not, impatience and impiety'.[24] God is not God, of course, but Elihu impersonating him, and challenging Job to the contest: ' "Come on then;

---

[23] *Clarissa, Preface, Hints of Prefaces etc.*, 5. See Alexander Welsh, *Strong Representations* (Baltimore: Johns Hopkins Univ. Press, 1992), 70.

[24] John Garnett, *A Dissertation on the Book of Job*, 2nd edn. (London, 1751), 14 (preface). The 1st edition was published in 1749, the same year as the 2nd edition of *Clarissa*.

suppose me for once to be God; I will act the part of God" ' (*Disser-tation* [preface], 11). Although Garnett concedes that he is reading Job as an allegory, he stresses that its development as a 'forensic drama' keeps it 'a picture of human life' (preface, 14), rather than the personi-fication of various abstract attributes—'the properties of elements, the faculties of mind, and the virtues and vices, in forms and persons' (9). It is 'a composition, which, to all appearance, exhibits the life and story of one person at the same time that in fact it is intended to convey the life and story of another' (10). The small circumstance is always aligned as the auxiliary of the greater fact. Job in his particularities therefore speaks as counsel for 'the impatient Jew' (247): his actual boils are to be understood as expressive of 'the judicial proceedings of providence against a people for their sins' (93). Garnett never wants to lose sight of this real substantial connection between the particular instance and the general case, nor of the rhetorical force of small circumstances in render-ing the representation of excess probable as well as morally compelling. Although he mocks as fanciful Warburton's interpretation of Job's wife as the personification of 'pagan impieties and idolatrous practice' (121–2), Garnett's technique of allegorizing across a horizon of material and temporal existence—rather than making vertical connections between the material and the abstract—is recognizably Warburtonian.

The value to Richardson of such an argument is that it binds the energy of small circumstances, which otherwise would escape in the strangely subjectless, amoral, and self-engendering particularity typical of Lovelace's plots, and invests it strictly in the exemplary greater fact. The name of the bare circumstance, whose only larger function would be to coalesce with other circumstances into the aggregate of an un-principled narrative, is used instead to designate the general object of apodictic certainty: the thing itself. By a species of emphatic iteration the individual term introduces the greater fact: Job is really 'Job', a boil is a 'boil', a wife is idolatry. This combines the extravagant narrative de-mand for the 'circumstantial and the minute' with the restraint of 'lively and delicate impressions' without sacrificing the aim of giving, in Warburton's words, 'a Faithful Picture of Nature in Private Life' (Pref-ace, pp. v–vi). This is the reasoning behind Richardson's claim that Clarissa execrates by example, and is vehement only in a regulated way: the greater fact enfolds the outrageous particular in an interpretative web that keeps precedent and purpose, prescription and fulfilment, always in touch.

The finest critique of these arguments in favour of an auxiliary par-ticularity in service to an exemplary and self-authenticating end is sup-plied by Lovelace's commentary on Clarissa's imitation of Job. This is best approached via his remarks on small circumstances. Basically he reverses Young's distinction in favour of the moral system by maintaining that the greatest power and pleasure is to be had from a story that perpetually substitutes its means for its end, its narrative density for its exemplary point. Lovelace sees running into length as hedonistically and rhetorically necessary. Rhetorically it is important to multiply details, because a story based on tautology will not command the reader's belief: 'I never forget the *minutiae* in my contrivances. In all *doubtable* matters the *minutiae* closely attended to and provided for are of more service than a thousand oaths, vows and protestations made to supply the neglect of them' (473). Aesthetically it is more pleasing to have *minutiae* begetting *minutiae*, until the focus of interpretation is lost, because the witty roundabouts of invention afford endless bustle and surprise, whereas the arrival at a destination is always tedious: '*Preparation* and *expectation* are, in a manner, everything: *reflection*, indeed, may be something . . . but the *fruition*, what is there in that?' Although Lovelace proposes seduction as exemplary, designed to prove the truth of woman's frailty that she may be 'a more eminent example to her sex' (869), he is bored by any sign of such an outcome and fascinated by any postponement of it. To deceive oneself about the truth of something one is perfectly convinced of is as pleasing as to deceive others. Lovelace quotes Swift to this effect (700).

At the simplest level he is doing no more than reciting the rake's creed, fetched from Ovid and Montaigne, on the voluptuous enjoyments of indirection and delay, which are themselves closely implicated in textual and epistolary difference. At another he is setting up a series of experiments, being an ardent proponent of 'practices and experimentals' as opposed to the 'whipped syllabub' of speculative and theoretical knowledge (538; 3rd edn., iii. 216), the results of which he closely details for the benefit of his virtual witness, Belford. At another he is developing an addiction for certain scenes of anger and distress, such as the fire scene or the penknife scene, whose appeal lies not in any classic delineation of virtue in distress, nor in any monitory or erotic promptings, but solely in the performance of passion, which he pursues again and again sheerly for the 'sake's sake' (817), watching fear, contempt, despair embodied in hair, flesh, drapery, and eyes.[25] At another he is discovering the strange

---

[25] Ann Jessie van Sant argues that Lovelace's impersonation of Satan and his metaphors of experiment are perfectly adapted to one another and, in bringing virtue to the touchstone, provide Richardson with the 'means of articulating his own novelistic intention' (*Eighteenth-Century Sensibility*, 66). I am suggesting, on the contrary, that as Satan, Lovelace has an interest in the unexemplary qualities of a spectacle of suffering, and that as an experimental scientist he has (like Robert Boyle) an interest in the subversion of plenary systems caused by the rhetoric of particularity.

sensation of being the predicate of his own subject, of drifting from his already unstable first person into the second or third persons—character, audience, or creature—of fictions which he is ceasing to invent for any purpose beyond the pleasure of invention. The Sinclair, Fretchville, and Tomlinson stories accumulate details which require the corroboration of other details, dispersing the purposes of their inventor, who himself concedes that they multiply in the room made by his disabled will: 'I am a machine at last, and no free agent' (848). At all levels Lovelace is deserting the prescriptive, final, or general aspect of an activity for the provisional satisfaction he takes in its specific and concrete adjuncts, which in turn constitutes the sole grounds of pursuing or justifying further activity—grounds that he no longer entirely controls, but for whose fruitlessness he craves. He delays because he has delayed, he watches because he has watched, he tells stories because he has told stories before.

The incremental pressure of the small circumstances involved in delaying, watching, and narrating evacuates all interpretative and preceptual valency from the scene, making a hollow in the system of verisimilitude where the greater fact ought to have been. This hollow is penetrated only by the dissident desire that it might recur endlessly at precisely the same order of intensity. Certainly his response to Clarissa's passionate gestures and exclamations is uninflected by any sense of prior or posterior importance in the form of models, precedents, types, or portents. It is not an impulse to allegorize but to particularize which drives him to declare that 'in every attitude, in every humour, in every gesture, [she] is beauty beautiful' (641). His 'present-tense manner' focuses 'peculiarly' upon the peculiarity—that is, the extravagant actuality—of scenes which never fail to immobilize him and to make him forget himself: 'All my purposes suspended for a few moments, I knew neither what to say, nor what to do' (882, 880). He 'recollects himself', and renews his subjective commitment to seduction or rape, only as an alibi for further scenes of delicious self-forgetting. If he has cheated Clarissa out of her 'self' (840), he is as frequently persuaded by her vehemence out of his own. The question of the regulation of this vehemence is related to the dynamics of the mutual cheat, involving the joint dispersal of subjectivity amidst narratives whose sole accomplishment is the renewal of narrative possibilities. This in turn leads to the unfolding of the exemplary tautology—truth is truth, the example is the example—into phrases such as the 'sake's sake', 'the narrative of narratives', and 'beauty beautiful' (817, 767, 641), which are not intended to express the distillation of particularity into a general form, or to draw vehemence into the pale of a precedent, but on the contrary to celebrate the risks, passions, fugitive probabilities, and the power to be enjoyed within a non-normalizable and self-justifying practice.[26]

The nature and the scene of this enjoyment is to be analysed by Burke a few years later when he turns, as Richardson turns in his postscripts, to the problem of why we find tragic spectacles satisfying. The reason we might enjoy the dismembering of Damiens, suggests Burke, is not owing to any ethical desire to lessen his pangs but to the simple appetite of the human organism ('the mechanical structure of our bodies') to view with delight ('and that no small one') the 'circumstances of real distress' (*Enquiry*, 44–5). That is to say, the bare desire to witness distress is not significative nor constitutive of an active, willing subject, but the result of a phylogenetic need. The delight procured by satisfying it is modified by subjective factors only when it takes on a reflexive density—when, instead of being a passive but delighted spectator of a deed 'we would by no means chuse to do', we *choose* instead to look at the choiceless spectators of it. It is a critical difference between *delight*, which is passively implicated in the unmodified circumstances of a scene of distress, and *choice*, which exercises itself at two removes from the circumstances in the redoubling of the gesture of delight, namely by looking at looking. This is a sight of sights in the same sense that Lovelace's is a narrative of narratives: the pleonasm denotes not a rarefaction of practice at some essential or formal level of excellence determinable by an objective criterion, but a way of applying extra purchase upon an activity that enters no pleas in the courts of ethics or reason, but always simply circulates between the points of compulsion, desire, and agency—what we have to do, what we want to do, what we choose to do. The choice, and the temporary stabilization of the subject position acquired by exercising it within this circuit of practical possibilities, are measurable by the degree of self-reference. By looking at looking we see beauty beautiful, or perhaps sublimity upon sublimity; at any rate, it is not the self-evidence of beauty or sublimity that these reflexive formulations denote, but the power that oscillates rapidly and non-transitively between the virtual subjects populating the circuit.

Revising the traditional concept of power as transitive and as operating in non-circular modes, Niklas Luhmann observes that it is precisely in self-reference that it is discovered and obtained: 'Power has to be seen as selection based on selection'. He points to the eighteenth century as a period disturbed by the complexity of these reflexive selective pro-

---

[26] Niklas Luhmann notes that the revision in the codes of love in the eighteenth century was accompanied by a phrasing very similar to Lovelace's. Love and its associated values can no longer be scrutinized for a wider social valency, therefore 'frivolity can only be enjoyed as frivolity, feeling only as feeling, virtue only as virtue'. *Love as Passion*, 110.

cedures, of which the discourse of taste is vividly symptomatic: 'New, risky, and one might say "unsocial" selective procedures were liberated: *curiosity* became a legitimate motive for pursuing knowledge, *profit* became something like income without a contractual base (i.e. without social legitimation), *raison d'état* became a political maxim, and *impassioned love* became a sufficient basis for choosing a partner' (*The Differentiation of Society*, 267). The virtual subject of Burke's *Enquiry*, the 'I' briefly capable of taking a grip on a scene by observing how observers observe it, practises power in its socially unlegitimized mode because self-reference complicates and empowers the subject without bringing it under prescriptive restraint. Lovelace, circulating within the vacuum created by his narrative roundabouts, and encountering in a reflexive way the circumstances of Clarissa's distress, is just such a social anomaly, subscribing to no value independent of the justification arising from what he does. Thus he compares himself to a prince who proceeds 'from infraction to infraction, from robbery to robbery' (1437), one whose absence is dreaded as absence (521), and who observes his victim moving 'from step to step, from distress to distress' (1344).

His favourite self-referential activity is to look, like Burke's metaspectator, at looking. Once he has inducted Clarissa into the art of returning a gaze, he and she function interchangeably as each other's spectacle and spectator. 'Have I not told you that my beloved is a great observer of the eyes?' he asks; and she confirms it, 'We are both great watchers of each other's eyes' (876, 460). In drawing her into this specular arrangement, he sidesteps the judgements Richardson would like to make about him and his victim, namely that he exhibits the pertinacity of a skilled encroacher moving towards his goal of seduction, and that she displays the constancy of an embattled heroine acting in defence of virtue. Lovelace has no interest in this sort of long-term vision of the competence of the self-identical subject; as for Clarissa, she is fast losing it. Really all of Lovelace's desires are satisfied in the momentary intensities of each ocular performance. The equivocation on eye and I is apt, for it suggests both the indeterminate agency of the subject and the means by which power is transferred from one 'I' to the other. The sharpness of the glance alone decrees who shall be most rapidly self-recollected, and who therefore shall most confidently speak in the first person at that moment to the other self-forgotten and powerless party. When the eye falls, or turns in upon itself, the 'I' hesitates and dwindles: 'I see, I see . . . I see that I am ruined' (881). Clarissa is ruined only if she imports into the reflexive exchange of glances an exotic standard of impermeable values: that is to say, if she harks back to the ideal of original self-delivery located by Richardson in female familiar letters, or if she somehow anticipates the spiritual recuperation he is going to make out of the exiguities of her death-bed. Otherwise she is an equal player with Lovelace, as likely to astonish him as he is to terrify her, and well equipped to keep performance and narrative in endless agitation. Lovelace's eventual reliance on force restores the same exotic principles of end and example to primacy, and explodes the narrative of narratives. It is important to remember at this point that it is not a man or a woman I am referring to, but the dynamics of narrative practice.

Job enters the story at this critical juncture, when Lovelace has breached his own reflexive system, and when Clarissa is apparently hastening towards an exemplary end. It is generally agreed that his purpose is to shepherd Clarissa out of a narrative structure that never deserved and can no longer accommodate her, into a meditative frame of mind conformable to the reflections Young sent down to Richardson in the post: 'such exalted sentiments and expressions [as] will adorn her last hours, when above the world, and above the resentments she acknowledges'.[27] Job is the greater fact behind the particular circumstances of Clarissa's outbursts, the precedent and model that regularizes vehemence. Job is Richardson's method of giving 'an uncommon Turn and Appearance, to common Calamities' (*Selected Letters*, 87). This interpretation survives in the most recent consideration of Job and Clarissa: 'Having virtually abandoned the effort to document her life in epistolary narrative, she discovers in biblical wisdom a form that replaces "minute particulars" of circumstantial realism with a luminous and cogent symbolism, and this makes a newly emphatic medium in which to define her wrongs and vent her grief'.[28] It is also assumed that in taking leave of the narrative, Clarissa falls into a state of speechless misery which Job supplements with his own words and his own story: 'The scriptural passages Clarissa chooses have a metacritical function . . . they comment, hermetically, on her own linguistic exploitation, and the essential uselessness of words, except as tools of violence'.[29] Rita Goldberg makes a surprisingly positive claim for this supplement, arguing that Job is the frequent object of didactic references in Puritan literature.[30] In various ways, these interpretations all preserve Job as Clarissa's precedent and exemplar, the greater fact to her small

[27] Young, *Correspondence*, 217.
[28] Tom Keymer, 'Richardson's Meditations: Clarissa's *Clarissa*', in *Samuel Richardson: Tercentenary Essays*, ed. Margaret Doody and Peter Sabor (Cambridge: Cambridge Univ. Press, 1989), 94.
[29] Castle, *Clarissa's Ciphers*, 130.
[30] *Sex and Enlightenment: Women in Richardson and Diderot* (Cambridge: Cambridge Univ. Press, 1984), 67–8.

circumstances of resentment, an authority for what she says, a type of her suffering, a promise of her redemption, an epitome of her story, or a way out of it.

When Lovelace quotes Job at Clarissa's quotations of Job he seems to be making a very different point. In typically reflexive form he is saying that her imitation produces a negative originality, a particular state of privation out of range of the precedents and regulations enclosed within the absent attribute (that which is not so with either of them but which presumably is so with everyone else). It is the second time he has lodged a claim like this. On the first occasion he has received the ten distracted papers, scrawled and torn by Clarissa after the rape, together with the letter where, beside herself and bereft of a consistent first person, Clarissa begs that she can be hidden from his sight forever. Lovelace tells Belford he can make no copy of the letter: 'For my life I cannot; 'tis so extravagant. And the original is too much an original to let it go out of my hands' (889). Having transcribed the tenth paper, which consists in fragments of poetry, he takes heart: 'I see there is method and good sense in some of them, wild as others of them are; and that her memory, which serves her so well for these poetical flights, is far from being impaired' (894). The phrase, 'an original which is too much an original' is not reflexive in the manner of 'looking at looking', since it denotes her total abdication from the narrative of narratives in a gesture so extreme that it fails to empower him with the choices usually annexed to this kind of doubling. Sheer originality is the spectral other, inane or mad, of the self-presence of the familiar letter; it is the contradictory property of non-identity, the 'all her own' of someone not herself. It is perhaps to be compared with the original distraction which is the theme of Sappho's fragment 31, or the disorientation and despair which afflicted Cook when he found himself a first person at the limit, or the speechless misery in which Warburton was to end his life, or the unredeemed lamentations of Job.

Here in the letter demanding that she be hidden away, and only here, does Clarissa demand an exit from the narrative; which is why Lovelace seizes on the tenth paper as a sign of her returning spirits, for there she adapts the text to her circumstances, using fragments to represent her ruin, disjointing poetry to speak of self-disjunction. It is as if Damiens were to give the metaspectator as good as he got, or as if the death-song of Smith's dying Indian were to turn cleverly on the pain of giving pain, or the spectacular pleasure of viewing disappointed spectators. Originality acquires this communicative buoyancy only by self-reference, which of course prevents it from being positively original, since it is mediated through a text or a figure that doubles it, such as

Hawkesworth's impersonation of Cook's first person, or Sappho's textualization of the circumstances of her distraction; and besides, it is a privative condition that is being doubled. This is not to say, however, that the mediation blurs the effect of singularity, or that it sets up a precedent to regulate the vehement expression of singularity; its only purpose is to link the isolated position of the weakened subject to the circuit of power so that the intensity of singular experience can recur. This requires that extravagance be turned outwards in a legible form, for the benefit of those that have eyes to see.

When Lovelace quotes Job at Clarissa's quotations of Job he is responding to this power, reading Clarissa as she has read Job: not as a supplement, that is, nor as a decipherable sign or as an interpretable allegory, but as a narrative bridge between one intensity and another. In locating the element of originality in her imitation, he grasps what she has grasped in the course of her quotations, which is the difference between the ideal of self-presence ('there is none like him in the earth, a perfect and an upright man' [Job 1: 8]) and the resource of someone who is desperate: 'Oh that my words were now written' (19: 23). This is the very difference Richardson is forced to skirt, and it revolves through the same phases of self-loss ('thine eyes are upon me, and I am not' [7: 8]) and the recovery of the subject as the unpredicated residue of a negative statement ('it is not so with me' [9: 35]) that configures Clarissa's experiences within the text of Job, and gives her the power of returning the glance of the figure of power, 'Whom I shall see for myself, and mine eyes shall behold' (*Meditations*, 5; Job 19: 27). In Job she is not finding words for her speechlessness, or using his story as a recapitulation of her own, or demanding a release from the narrative of narratives, or acquiring a representative status as sufferer. She is beyond the need of a supplement because she is beyond any positive concept of identity, having been broken in pieces with words, precipitated as a negative being, and reconstituted as fragments of text. If Lovelace's specialty is looking at looking, she is developing the self-referential form of writing, presenting her citations of Job as a counter-script which will eventually fix Lovelace in the position of its reader, the subordinate eye in *her* narrative, and one whom she will behold for herself.

On the way to this new phase in their power relations, Clarissa takes notice, in Job's words, of the harshness of writing which interprets suffering as a sign of providential order: 'Why hast Thou set me as a mark against Thee. . . . He hath made me a byword of the people' (1192; Job 7: 20, 17: 6). When she complains that she cannot justify herself without condemning herself (1163; Job 9: 20) she alludes to the trap of a positive, interpretative language that cannot render suffering in any exemplary form that is not opprobrious to the sufferer. She regards her own story as fraught with this risk, either from the side of personal chagrin ('But my injuries being recent, and my distresses having been exceeding great, *self* would crowd into my letter' [976]) or from the side of theodicy ('I am quite sick . . . of an earth in which *innocent* and *benevolent* spirits are sure to be considered as *aliens*' [1020]). Like Cook, she is aware that the only first-person account she is capable of delivering would be misinterpreted; so she stands between the abundance of shocking circumstances which compose her story ('all the particulars of my sad story' [1018]) and the desire of telling it in a satisfactory way, 'Oh that my words were now written! Oh that they were printed in a book!' (1125). It is precisely here, between an unintelligible providence and a first person doubtful of presenting an adequate narrative, that Hawkesworth locates Job as expressive of the pure force of circumstance, uninterpretable according to any rule of providence, and points to Richardson as the novelist who has learned to exploit that force in a story.[31] Richardson uses the fifth *Meditation*, supposedly transcribed after the letter in which Clarissa concedes that 'self' keeps her from making her circumstances known, to indicate that she is still isolated by her regulated vehemence from the common sense of elevated sentiments to which these circumstances must conform ('Then would I speak . . . But it is not so with me' [*Meditations*, 11]). For his part Lovelace uses the same Joban exception to affirm an unexemplary singularity that is nevertheless eminently narratable—'She has now a tale to tell, that she may tell with honour to herself' (943)—and Clarissa alights on his letters, 'his strangely-communicative narrations' of plots he wickedly called *providences*,[32] as the fittest medium for releasing its particulars from the constraint of morals and sentences.[33]

Quite the reverse of her author, she finds a way of giving a particularizing turn to uncommon calamities by supplying Job's desideratum: 'Oh

---

[31] 'The relation of little circumstances requires no apology, for it is from little circumstances that the relation of great events derives its power over the mind.' *Pamela* is 'remarkable for the enumeration of particulars in themselves so trifling, that we almost wonder how they could occur to the author's mind'. That these circumstances fall into no immediately intelligible pattern should not make us repine: 'Shall we, says Job, "receive good from the hand of God and shall we not receive evil?"' *An Account of the Voyages*, i. pp. vii; xix.

[32] *Clarissa*, 3rd edn., iii. 98; iv. 77 (p. 1175).

[33] In one of the most interesting of the 'beautiful suckers' to 'rise from the immortal root' of *Clarissa* (Young, *Correspondence*, 337) is Mary Brunton's *Self-Control*, a novel evidently committed to the doctrine held forth in the title, but one which the author finds it very difficult to wind round to an economic and verisimilar conclusion. The greater the difficulties the more lavish and romantic the route taken by the plot, until it leaves the heroine stranded in a lonely hut in the wilds of Canada. It seems appropriate at this moment of personal crisis and narrative excess that the heroine, Laura Montreville, should begin to paraphrase Clarissa's quotations of Job: 'O that Thou wouldst hide me in the grave . . . My soul is weary of my life' (Job 14: 14, 10: 1). Mary Brunton, *Self-Control* (London: Pandora, 1986), 415–17.

that mine adversary had written a book' (1164). Lovelace takes up his place as her Hawkesworth, or (and here is the true Whig orientation of his commitment to *minutiae*) her Blackmore: a *go'el*, a reader-redeemer, voicing her script just as she, in the depths of her misery, has voiced Job's. As her narrative takes shape by his mediation, he of course gets closer to Job, and begins to paraphrase him on his own account: 'In fine, I am a most miserable being. Life is a burden to me. I would not bear it upon these terms for one week more, let what would be my lot' (1340; Job 7: 16). But because Lovelace's letters are appropriated to Clarissa's narrative, and to the printing of her book, he is condemned to redeem her without ever recovering the narrative power that comes from self-referential practice. She proves this with a further quotation from Job. In the letter as it were from the dead, where her writing takes on the monitory style of an adversarial tomb inscription, she instructs him to tremble and reform, for, 'Thus is it written, "The triumphing of the wicked is short, and the joy of the hypocrite but for a moment"' and so on (1427). Instead of instructing Lovelace, this compilation of mocking sentences drawn from the comforters Zophar and Bildad (Job 20: 5, 18: 11) is Clarissa's attempt to break him in pieces with the very consolations that she and Job have had to endure. It is a case of mockery upon mockery. She is using the power of her narrative initiative not to make an exemplary point but to force a scene to recur at the level of its original intensity. If she cared to, she could distinguish his sense of unprecedented isolation and exasperation with a further quotation, by pointing out that Mr Lovelace is the only person in the world of whom it might be said, in the words of his and her favourite exclaimer, 'But it is not so with me'.

12 *The Strangled Sublime: Fielding's Representation of the Barely Possible*

If his protestations are anything to go by, Fielding sets even more store by pictures of exemplary self-restraint in his fiction than Richardson. He begins *Joseph Andrews* with the 'trite but true Observation, that Examples work more forcibly on the Mind than Precepts'.[1] In the dedication of *Tom Jones*, he defines *example* as 'a kind of picture, in which virtue becomes as it were an object of sight'.[2] And in *Amelia* he proposes the heroine as an 'excellent example to all mothers'.[3] He is led by at least two considerations to this reliance upon example as a more probable method of instruction than the recitation of sententious observations. The first is the widely available empirical truth that precepts will not persuade people to moderate their behaviour, because they have first often failed to convince the pedagogues, magistrates, and maxim-mongers who are fondest of quoting them. Fielding has a rare talent for revealing the wise and just in dereliction of the very rules and directions they have just delivered, such as Squire Allworthy talking resentfully of those who harbour resentment, and Mrs Bennet despising only the folk who find others despicable.[4] The second is his wide reading in the law, which taught him the deterrent value of exemplary punishment to the community at large. In his *Enquiry into the Causes of the late Increase in Robbers* (1751), he mentions with approval Machiavelli's and Hale's arguments in favour of making an example of malefactors, how it forges 'the Chain of Justice', which ought not to be weakened by acts of mercy. He then outlines his own idea of an ideal execution, where 'The Terror of the Example is the only Thing proposed, and one Man is sacrificed to the Preservation of Thousands'.[5]

Good and bad examples, then, offer visible and credible inducements to right thinking and virtuous action by entwining chains of fictional

---

[1] *The History of the Adventures of Joseph Andrews*, ed. Martin C. Battestin (Oxford: Clarendon Press, 1967), 17.

[2] *The History of Tom Jones, a Foundling*, ed. R. P. C. Mutter (Harmondsworth: Penguin, 1966), 37.

[3] *Amelia*, ed. Martin Battestin (Oxford: Clarendon Press, 1986), 167.

[4] *Tom Jones*, 85; *Amelia*, 311.

[5] *Enquiry*, ed. Malvin Zirker (Connecticut: Wesleyan Univ. Press, 1988), 166.

circumstances and chains of justice within narratives which dramatically confirm the moral he would rather not simply recite. This appears to be Fielding's contribution to the principle of poetic justice so prominent in systems of neo-classical verisimilitude, where private and particular interests are harmonized with public standards of virtue by means of a probable series of events framing an exemplary picture. It appears also to depend on his legal training, especially in the field of evidence, where connected circumstances (the 'Train of Circumstances'[6]) are assumed to lead juries to the truth with an irresistible persuasive power. Nevertheless, Fielding's comic talent for exhibiting the weakness of precepts often extends to examples themselves, whose singularity is frequently so marked, private, and ungeneralizable as to skirt, and sometimes quite to diverge from the public norms of right and justice they were meant to enforce. I aim to argue that the meshing of the plausible example with the useful moral, driven by the circumstantial chain of a narrative, is one that seldom occurs smoothly in Fielding's fiction or, for that matter, in his reflections upon the law, and for the same reason: namely, that his imagination is dogged by the counterfactuals—the odd particulars, unruly exceptions, and barely possible other cases that refuse to be connected or put into train—which are provoked by his very insistence on the exemplarity of tidy fables. The more he wants to enforce an example, the more he is overwhelmed by the recalcitrant particularity of circumstances.

There are two chapters in *Joseph Andrews*, counterparts, as Fielding calls them, which display in twin tableaux the problems he meets in trying to represent the circumstances of distress as probable examples. These problems are keyed to a tripartite division of the sublime that he makes in respect of the language of complaint. The two chapters are the tenth and eleventh of the third book, following the tragic scene of Fanny's abduction by the servants of the 'roasting squire', which has ended with her being dragged out of the inn, 'crying and tearing her Hair'. No sooner has she been removed than the poet and the player (accomplices in Fanny's fate) begin a discussion of the difficulties of writing and staging scenes of pathos in the modern theatre. Meanwhile upstairs, Parson Adams tries to moderate Joseph's passionate outcries with seasonable Christian advice about patience and submission.

Far from the upper tableau providing the example that the precepts from below require for their illustration, however, the simultaneous demonstrations of the theory and the practice of distress seem to be guided by a contrast between the real and the artificial that Fielding is

---

[6] See Alexander Welsh, 'Burke and Bentham on the Narrative Potential of Circumstantial Evidence', *New Literary History*, 21/3 (1990), 615.

often tempted to explore. The bathos of false sentiment is justified at the lower level because it is so remote from the sounds of real grief that come from above. It would seem to be consistent with this contrastive arrangement that the rules of dramatic representation discussed by the player and the poet should be plainly otiose with regard to the tragic timbre of complaint from upstairs. In fact, both tableaux fail in the same way. There is a an element of real distress at the lower level, just as there is a futile reliance upon precepts at the upper. In neither scene is there a satisfactory accommodation of the circumstances of excessive emotion to the rules governing a probable representation of it. The clergyman and the poet are equally incapable of sustaining discourse fit to tame the wildness of passion; rather the opposite. If Joseph could learn to contain his distress, he would exhibit both the example of Christian patience which Adams recommends, and also the figure of the model tragic hero, breathing disdain of life, which the player finds so movingly represented by Otway, and which the poet believes he has mastered in his last play. But this is impossible, because to broach the question of example is instantly to agitate feelings that are beyond the limit of controlled exhibition.

It is not owing to any defect of will that the performances of Joseph and the player fail to match expectations of moral and artistic economy. The arguments chosen by their companions are so heavily larded with contingencies and hypotheses that they provoke a recurrence of distress in its most disorderly and least exemplary form. Adams strays from the immediate fact of Fanny's loss into the possible circumstances that may surround it and flow from it. 'You have lost the prettiest, kindest, loveliest, sweetest young Woman . . . by whom you might have promised yourself many little Darlings. . . . You have not only lost her, but have reason to fear the utmost Violence which Lust and Power can inflict upon her.' Having decorated the general case with these possibilities, he switches his line of speculation to the chance of having Fanny restored unravished, which is apparently as possible as any other outcome and may, or may not, depend upon the degree of patience shown by Joseph.[7] That is to say, he musters all the circumstances that his imagination can attach to this emergency, with no provision for their consistency, in order to affirm that each is consonant with providence and therefore necessary. He is in effect outlining a Leibnizian theodicy by means of an array of possibilities to which he attaches an epistemic rather than an aleatory significance, reducing them to the order of

---

[7] On the question of equipossibility in eighteenth-century theories of probability, especially in relation to Leibniz's theodicy, see Ian Hacking, *The Emergence of Probability* (Cambridge: Cambridge Univ. Press, 1975; repr. 1991), 122–33.

knowledge rather than to the actual nature of things. Adams interprets all possibilities and chances not as fortune or luck, but as links in a probable train of circumstances which he has determined is *a priori* for the best. This reinforces Joseph's already strong sense of the peculiar injustice of his suffering and of the caprice of the agency causing it. The harder the clergyman argues for the probability of a providence that encompasses all possibilities, the more the distress of his catechumen is quickened to its original intensity.

The poet produces on the player the same effect as Adams on Joseph as he forces him to recollect the bare possibilities which silenced the production of the play: if the player had not forgotten the lines, if the lines had not been so bad, if there had not been a cabal in the pit and the upper gallery bent on damning the performance, and if the actors had not been pelted with oranges throughout the last act, then the play would have been done justice, and greeted as the perfect representation of distress which (according to the poet) it certainly is. There are so many possibilities listed in defiance of this supposedly probable outcome, that effectuality plainly lies on the side of the contingencies rather than of the formal causes to which the poet appeals. The dialogue ends in acrimony because the player, agitated by memories of the multifarious chances which put his distress beyond the mediation of language and gesture, passionately recalls the pangs he then suffered: 'I think the Performers did the Distress of it Justice, for I am sure we were in Distress enough . . . we all imagined it would have been the last Act of our Lives'. Just as Joseph is incapable of representing these disturbing possibilities in a way which is not affected by his own feelings, and not destructive of Adams' interpretations of them, so the player is advanced by possibilities to a peculiarly authentic performance which does justice to distress only at the expense of the system of poetic justice invoked by the poet.

The numerous contingent particulars of distress, while blocking the delivery of the Christian and the tragic sublime, prompt the following alternatives in the agitated party: he is moved either to quote lines that are more apt to his circumstances, as Joseph quotes Macduff's lament from *Macbeth*, and as the the player quotes Lee and Otway; or he persists in the agonized silence to which Joseph succumbs at the end of Adams's speech, and into which the player falls when he is so disconcerted by the flying oranges that he is 'put out', as he says, and left speechless. Altogether, then, there are three avenues open for the representation of distress, none of them compatible with each other. There is the exemplary management of grief according to Christian or heroic ideals of self-restraint; there is the passionate quotation of a dramatic model of suffering that seems equal to the present exigency; and there is the disorderly transport that spends itself in ignorance of prescription or precedent. These three avenues correspond to the three variants of Fielding's sublime.

Upstairs, at the level of Adams's advice to Joseph, where conduct is supposed to be exemplary and where all events are necessary, is to be found the sublime implementation of doctrines of stoicism and self-restraint. These were to be proposed again by Fielding in the memorandum he composed after the death of his daughter Charlotte, *Of the Remedy of Affliction for the Loss of our Friends* (1743), where he expands Adams's Christian gloss on Cicero and Seneca in order to to find some sense in what he called 'A Train of melancholy Accidents scarcely to be paralleled'.[8] Although this consolation failed to save Fielding from grief 'approaching to Frenzy' when his wife died the following year, just as it had failed to save Joseph from wild impatience two years before, nevertheless he cites this Romano-Christian standard as 'the true Sublime in Human Nature', and told James Harris that in Valerius Maximus he had found 'the truest Sublime I ever met with'.[9]

Downstairs, at the level of the bladdered nonsense of the poet, Fielding locates the false sublime of heroic tragedy and of Longinus, which he is fond of burlesquing, first of all in the excesses of his Scriblerian mock-tragedies, and later, in his novels, in the self-important exclamations of forlorn lovers.[10] The supererogations of Otway and Lee can be heard in Lady Booby's tormented reflections on love ('I will have those pitiful Charms which now I despise, mangled in my sight' [327]) and in Miss Mathews's paean of vengeance: 'Murder! Oh!'tis Music in my Ears' (43), as well as in Booth's vapid and apparently spontaneous quotation from *The Mourning Bride*, 'Who calls the wretched thing that was Alphonso?' (84). Clearly Joseph's impersonation of Macduff belongs to this category of the false sublime because, like all examples of bathos, it reduces the representation of excessive emotion to a jejune announcement of its unparalleled intensity, or to a tired and schematic extrava-

---

[8] *Daily Post*, 5 June 1742; cited in Martin Battestin, *Henry Fielding: A Life* (London: Routledge, 1989), 339.

[9] *Miscellanies*, ed. Henry Knight Miller (Connecticut: Wesleyan Univ. Press, 1972), i. 12; Letter to Harris, 24 Nov. 1744, cited in Battestin, *Fielding: A Life*, 386.

[10] 'What can be so proper for tragedy as a set of big-sounding words, so contrived together as to convey no meaning? which I shall one day or other prove to be the sublime of Longinus'. Preface, *The Tragedy of Tragedies* in *Eighteenth-Century Plays* (Dent: Everyman, 1954), 168. The joint foundation of Fielding's literary principles in Scriblerian satire and Aristotle's poetics makes him especially alive to the bad economy of the transports recommended by Longinus. For a fine analysis of sublime transport applicable to Fielding's Aristotelian views, see Marc Shell, *The Economy of Literature* (Baltimore: Johns Hopkins Univ. Press, 1978), 90–105.

gance. This sublime is ambitious, in the player's words, 'to outdo the inimitable', but it cannot succeed.

Just to the expressive side of the dumbness of acute distress there is a possibility of imitating the inimitable that is neither tame nor routine. It occurs whenever a character replays an unparalleled impatience such as Job's while being unaware of the parallel. When he cries out to his teacher, 'O you have not spoken one Word of Comfort to me yet', Joseph carries the force of the Joban original within the sharpness of a present grief not by a feat of memory or allusion, but by an intuition of the uninterpretability of his afflictions, their inexplicable uniqueness which paradoxically recalls a precedent. The unwitting parallel is confirmed by the narrator in the companion scene to this one, in which Adams is informed that his son has been drowned and briefly he inhabits the same intuition of singularity, only to recover and to renew his lessons on the schooling of pain, according to a doctrine which he has himself signally failed to prove: 'The Patience of Joseph, nor perhaps of Job, could bear no longer; he interrupted the Parson, saying, "It was easier to give advice than to take it." ' (266). I will term this recurrence of an inimitable intensity the 'put out' or strangled sublime, and suggest that to achieve maximum effect it needs to be set off by the failure of a precept or an example.

Fielding's strangled sublime belongs to the unprecedented imitations of Job found in other mid-century reactions to the possibilities which lie on the other side of probability and interpretation. In effect Joseph asserts, along with Clarissa, David Hume, Walter Shandy, and Job, that it is not so with him, that his affliction is pointlessly and exclusively his own, and that any narrative which seeks to render it probable and significant is an insult. Along with Blackmore he is also discovering that history (even a personal history) is made up of painful interruptions that may recur at the same level of intensity at any time. He is therefore sceptical of time's power to heal a grief by softening the image of it. He does not believe that the mind will become forgetful of past misfortunes or 'callous to future Impressions of Grief'.[11] In short, he enters a state of mind that ought not to be narratable according to the principles of exemplarity laid down by its narrator. The same gulf that divides experience from the rules of representation in the twin tableaux opens up between Joseph's first-person testimony and the third-person record of it. Recent work on Fielding's *Amelia* has explored the fundamental contradictions that impede its working out as a probable train of cir-

---

[11] Mrs Bennet to Amelia, whom she is concerned not to tire 'with Repetitions of Grief'. *Amelia*, 271.

cumstances, and which trap characters and story alike in cycles of repetition, as if neither were capable of learning from experience, or of processing information and adapting themselves to a necessary outcome.[12]

In other fictions of Job it has become clear that a delegate, or *go'el*, is required to ventriloquize the complaint of the first person if its improbability and uniqueness is not to block its delivery. But in Fielding's novels it seems that the narrative voice delegates not for individual distress but for the instructors—Adams, Allworthy, Harrison—who want to universalize it by suppressing the surplus affect of untrained circumstances and contingent particulars. When the teacher himself proves incapable of living up to his own doctrine, it can only be assumed (so far in this argument) that Fielding's taste for comedy outstrips the pace of his neo-classical vehicle, and that he leaves the moral of the story to wallow in uncertainties while he pursues the anomalies of actual practice, as he does in *Amelia* to the detriment of his declared aim of teaching the 'Art of Life' by just representations of scenes of domestic distress. In all of Fielding's novels, however, his narrators seem exceptionally alert to the contradictions arising from this sort of learned ignorance. Allworthy's failures in the practice of the law are underlined, and so is the impossibility of realizing the standards of personal and political probity demanded by Harrison. As for Adams, his paradoxical hospitality to counterfactuals is given a happy topographical twist by his storyteller when he reports, 'He came to a Place, where by keeping the extremest Track to the Right, it was just barely possible for a human Creature to miss his Way. This Track however did he keep, as indeed he had a wonderful Capacity at these kinds of bare Possibilities' (125). How is it that a character devoted to the large views of Christian explanation can be embarrassed by bare possibilities, and why is it that his exemplary narrator can be so clear-sighted about his blindness to them?

Part of the answer is to be found in Geoffrey Hawthorn's claim that the force of any explanation is proportionate to the number of counterfactuals that it necessarily implies. If things could not have been different, why be so vehement in assigning their causes? It is not for nothing that eighteenth-century treatises of probability try to naturalize this surplus by talking about the *doctrine* or the *law* of chance.[13] Adams's habitual use of providentialist interpretations of events stands in a direct ratio to his capacity for bare possibilities. His weakness for theodicy is

[12] See e.g. John Bender, *Imagining the Penitentiary* (Chicago: Univ. of Chicago Press, 1987), 139–200; and Terry Castle, *Masquerade and Civilisation* (London: Methuen, 1986), 177–252.

[13] See Abraham de Moivre, *The Doctrine of Chances* (London: W. Pearson, 1718).

exactly proportionate to the chances in his life which it cannot explain, such as narrow tracks, forgotten horses, and missing children. 'Possibilities increase under explanation', Hawthorn maintains, 'to decide how plausible any such possibility, causal or practical, is, is not in any strong or simple sense a theoretical matter'.[14]

When we ask what kind of matter this is in Fielding's work, there are two related answers. The first answer is that it is a juridical matter, in so far as there is a dialectic operating between the chances that escape from the citation of a law (or a rule or a principle), and the desire of students of chance to find a law of sortilege. This is the dialectic of the epistemic as opposed to the aleatory ordering of possibilities, into which the law introduces itself as a branch of knowledge capable of arranging contingent particulars into a probable train of circumstances, susceptible to judgement and to sentence. Centrally at issue in the adversarial legal contests of the British courts, as Elaine Scarry points out, is 'the making real of the counterfactual'.[15] Fielding is never tired of pointing out that in law a fact has no value until it is assigned its place within the circumstantial train. But in a court of law, the prosecution's narrative must be shown by the defence to be a collection of loose facts and bare possibilities, and vice versa. Hence the peculiar volatility of the plot of a trial, in which facts and values are highly relative until a final narrative is formed, believed, and acted upon. But the price of constructing it is the expulsion of all the unattached facts that are now stigmatized as extraordinary and unthinkable. However, in the reiterations of the exemplary narrative that accompany the rituals of sentencing, confession, and Last Dying Words, the unthinkable returns as various outrageous and unexemplary acts that call into question the value of the official train of circumstances.

The other answer to the question of possibilities is that it is an aesthetic matter, involving the subject in an experience of unprecedented and unlimited intensity. If such an experience is to be represented, the narrator's commitment to an exemplary third-person narrative must be supposed to be replaced, or at least weakened, by a mimetic or sympathetic relation to the first person that restricts or interrupts the regulatory function of storytelling. This is, in fact, the basis of Fielding's delegations, but it depends upon the dialectic of law and chance to work. Distress must be sharpened and variegated by the very justifications that would shape and explain it; the narrative of an individual's

---

[14] Geoffrey Hawthorn, *Plausible Worlds: Possibility and Understanding in History and the Social Sciences* (Cambridge: Cambridge Univ. Press, 1991), 123.

[15] *The Body in Pain: The Making and Unmaking of the World* (Oxford: Oxford Univ. Press, 1985), 299.

plight, running parallel with the work of justification and explanation that it records, such as the poet's and Adams's in the twin tableaux, must interrupt itself, as they do, just when it promises to explain too much. Such a narrative, moreover, must be able to recognize in its failure to acquire knowledge—that is, in its own failure knowledgeably to represent the failure to know—a sublime *aisthesis* valuable not on its own account, or in itself, but by virtue of its resistance to the forces of interpretation, explanation, and justification.

When Fielding invents or recalls a complaint that achieves a high level of improbability, he often associates it with one of two possibilities: either the doubtful ending of *The Beggar's Opera*, or a scene of female grief. In the twin tableaux of *Joseph Andrews* he is fiddling with the enigma of the split ending of Gay's comedy, trying to set it in different keys. He is fascinated by the outrageous reflexive shuffle with which Gay's player and poet disperse the tragic moral of this Newgate pastoral, already imperilled by the burlesque of Senecan *topoi* leading up to Macheath's execution. Their casual decision to end the opera as a comedy, with a reprieve and a maxim that values chances above just narratives, removes the necessity of poetic justice. At the very moment when Macheath becomes particular, and starts to snivel, when the sublime of self-restraint and the sublime of extravagant theatricality is breaking down into the sublime of the put-out and the strangled, the play interrupts itself with a bare possibility, followed by a song bidding welcome to the multitude of incalculable chances. In its last act the play traverses the same gap between formal precepts and aleatory compensations negotatiated by Hume in his essay on 'The Sceptic', when he turns from reflections on the necessity of sorrow to amuse himself with the hazards of the backgammon board.

For Fielding, the author of such solemn pieces as *Examples of the Interposition of Providence in the Detection of Murder* (1752), such a shift must constitute a trivialization of poetic justice; but for Fielding, the comic narrator of the unexemplary failure of exemplary projects, it illustrates perfectly the dialectical interplay of the explanatory and the unaccountable. He is fascinated by an interruption that allows equipossibility to supervene in the blockage of a third-person train of circumstances. The aleatory element is allowed to disperse the epistemic order of facts, and to introduce into the structures of tragedy and the law the unthinkable other case—not out of principle, but just to see what happens. Such an interruption makes room for everything that interests Fielding about the failure of example, and the strangled sublimity which is then disclosed.

When he wept for his dead wife, Fielding owned he 'blubbered like a Woman' (Battestin, 386); and when he set out on his last voyage and said goodbye to his children for the last time, he notes, 'I submitted entirely to [Nature], and she made as great a fool of me as she had ever done of any woman whatsoever'.[16] Amelia complains passionately against her husband's departure for the wars, 'the *woman* still prevailing' (103); and when Booth himself becomes excessively distressed, he owns, 'These Sensations are above me, they convert me into a Woman' (333). Females who have gone beyond the government of patience Fielding calls 'Jobs in Petticoats' (*Amelia*, 345), and their agonies of grief generally 'exceed the Power of Description' (346) and proceed 'beyond my Power of Description' (316). The original of many of these scenes of unrepresentable distraction are the two complaints made by Charlotte Fielding and recorded by her husband in the *Remedy*, both exhibiting her terror at the repeatability of intense pain. The first was made after the birth of their daughter: 'Good God! have I produced a Creature who is to undergo what I have suffered!' Her second, after the death of the infant: '[My] Child [will] never know what it [is] to feel such a Loss as [I now] lament' (224). These complaints are heard again in *Amelia* when the mother intended by her author to be an example to all other mothers exclaims in her misery, 'It is too much, too much to bear', (491) and asks pardon of her children for bringing them into a world where the repetition of limitless suffering cannot be prevented.

The simplest way of identifying a pattern of delegation here is to observe how the feminization of grief extends to males who are, like Joseph (the mirror-image of Fanny) or Parson Adams (a man whose cassock is made to serve for a petticoat) or Fielding himself, feminized by his last illness, driven beyond explanation into the extremity of 'too much'. The 'woman' is everything exorbitant to systematic explanation, a passionate surplus provoked by unparalleled accidents which can scarcely be spoken of, and never adequately described or explained. She is sister to the felon of Macheath's kidney, poised upon a strangled complaint against the law. But a simple marginalization of distress fails to exploit the dialectic of explanation and bare possibility that Hawthorn asks us to consider—a dialectic which takes the question of delegation into a complex and restricted engagement with narratives of justification, of which the strangled sublime (the minimal parallel that can be run with the unparalleled) is the fruit. The points of contact beween these contradictory pairings come more clearly into view if the

---

[16] *Jonathan Wild and The Journal of a Voyage to Lisbon* (London: J. M. Dent, 1932), 201.

woman and the criminal are brought together within the angle of the tree.

In *Jonathan Wild* (1743), a piece straddling the categories of fiction and criminal history, the narrator experiments with two very different endings, both played out at the gallows' foot and both exploiting the model of *The Beggar's Opera*. The first involves the unlucky Heartfree, about to be put to death for a crime he has not committed, and his wife, who has survived abduction and threats of rape in Africa only to return to her husband's execution. The second involves Wild and the Newgate Ordinary, who accompanies the unrepentant criminal in his reflections upon death and attends him to his end at Tyburn. These mirrored scenes recapitulate the contrasts of the twin tableaux in *Joseph Andrews*. Heartfree takes up Adams's role of comforter and preceptor, telling Friendly, 'I will bear all with Patience', and consoling his wife with the promise of their reunion in heaven; meanwhile Mrs Heartfree runs frantic, crying, 'Tell me, some Body who can speak, while I have my Senses left to understand, what is the Matter'.[17] For his part, the Ordinary takes on the poet's role, responsible for the staging of a tragedy whose performance fails in every respect to exemplify the moral system he is using to justify it. Wild is driven to the same degree of consternation as the player, put out by the missiles flung by an angry crowd, retaining only enough presence of mind to rob his comforter of a corkscrew before being put to a death that is, on account of that theft alone, exemplary of nothing. Clearly Heartfree and the Ordinary are bracketed as failed preceptors, unable to sustain the first order of the sublime; and Mrs Heartfree and Wild, both considerably put out and possessed of a strong intuition of the uninterpretability of their afflictions, occupy the same scarcely representable condition belonging to the third order of Fielding's sublime, where the barely possible supplants the exemplary picture.

The second order of the sublime, involving the citation of dramatic precedents, is the preserve of the narrator himself in this instance, who goes to *The Beggar's Opera* for precedents. After the reprieve is cried and Heartfree is restored to his wife's arms, he excuses himself, 'Lest our Reprieve should seem to resemble that in *The Beggar's Opera*, I shall endeavour to shew [the reader] that this Incident, which is undoubtedly true, is at least as natural as delightful; for we assure him we would rather have suffered half Mankind to be hanged, than have saved one contrary to the strictest Rules of Writing and Probability' (205). It is the same boast that is going to be made, rather more plausibly, in *Tom*

---

[17] *The Life of Jonathan Wild the Great* (London: A. Millar, 1754), 202.

Jones, where various alliances are made between notions of probability and scenes of hanging.[18] Here it functions as a counterpart to what the narrator says when no reprieve arrives for the great man, Wild. Then he urges the sacrifice of the strictest rules of writing and probability to ensure that rogues hang. The historian is invited to 'indulge himself in the Licence of Poetry and Romance, and even do a Violence to Truth, to oblige his Reader with a Page . . . which could never fail of producing an instructive Moral' (255).

The irony of these two positions is controlled by a double feint at history and at fiction. The facts of Wild's story are all true, whereas the extravagant coincidences of Heartfree's are manifestly false. However, the bare possibility of a reprieve which would render Wild's improbable is the very chance that makes Heartfree's true. That is to say, in the sphere of history the entry of a bare possibility transforms the narrative into fiction, either by virtue of its own incredibility or by the necessity the historian then lies under of erasing it with 'the Licence of Poetry and Romance'; but in the sphere of fiction the opposite is the case, and the truth of poetic justice is supposedly confirmed by an event whose possibility is so bare the narrator must explicitly distinguish it from the interruption at the end of Gay's play. On both Wild's side and Heartfree's the narrator is introducing equipossible events in order to make the dialectic of explanation and its counterfactuals serve the cause of probability and the law. He naturalizes chances by forcing them either to contribute to the probability of an example, or to retrieve an example they have interrupted. The narrator is aiming for a reflexive sublation of the dialectic that would lead from over-ambitious explanation to self-interruption.

In this experiment he achieves something rather like Swift's redrafting of Ebenezer Elliston's last words, where a bad example is repaired by a fact which is not true. Fielding's oscillation between history and romance suggests that history is correct only if it is adjusted by a fiction

---

[18] For example, 'We had rather relate that he was hanged at Tyburn (which may very well be the case) than forfeit our integrity, or shock the faith of the reader' (*Tom Jones*, 678). The improbable repentances of heroes in the last acts of modern comedies are, suggests the narrator, to be compared with those at Tyburn, 'a place which might, indeed, close the scene of some comedies with much propriety, as the heroes in them are most commonly eminent for those very talents which not only bring men to the gallows, but enable them to make an heroic figure when they are there' (366). There is a very detailed discussion of this scene, exploring its connections with *The Beggar's Opera*, in Bender, *Imagining the Penitentiary*, 151–7. In it he argues that Fielding arranges the conflict between Wild and Heartfree 'as a combat between variant novelistic accounts of material circumstance,' with Wild representing the distorted presentation of evidence and the 'good magistrate', who acquits Heartfree, using the clear and panoptic processing of real facts which is to become the narrative ideal of *Amelia*. But as the most fascinating part of Bender's argument turns on the uncanny resemblances between Wild and Fielding as thief-takers, it seems hard to find a distinction which will survive these obliterated differences. See also Susan P. McNamara, 'Mirrors of Fiction within *Tom Jones*: The Paradox of Self-Reference', *ECS* 12/3 (1979), 372–90.

transcending the lies which history tolerates. His priority is to appropriate all the surplus possibilities that might interrupt a narrative of justice
between the moment of sentence and the moment of strangulation, and
to make them serve the law they might otherwise weaken.[19] This is
certainly Swift's aim, and in so far as Fielding shares it, he opposes the
equipossibility of *The Beggar's Opera*, whose effect on the criminal
classes has been to denarrativize criminal history, in order to exploit
romance as an ornament of chance and particularity, and to endorse a
maxim concerning lucky interruptions from which 'villains are encouraged to hope for impunity', as Fielding's supporter Martin Madan
points out, prompting them to exhibit in real life 'a most mischievous
example, of hardness and obduracy'.[20]

It is, however, impossible to make or reverse an equation between
probability and possibility that restores the authority of good examples,
as Fielding is already aware. Once you play the game of equally likely
outcomes, as Adams plays it unwittingly with Joseph or as Fielding here
reflexively plays it with the reader, you sacrifice the right to an ending
which is necessarily exemplary and superior to another. Fielding's interruptions of his hanging scenes with conjectures about the arrival and
non-arrival of reprieves may be breaches of probability he knows already he cannot avoid, in which case they have less to do with recovering a good example than with exploring the narrative potential of bare
possibilities. In which case it is more likely that he intends these
rewritings of *The Beggar's Opera* to shift the concept of example itself
outside the boundaries of probable narrative, so that he can experiment
not with its restoration to a sphere of public credit and significance, but
rather with its usefulness within the restricted mode of representation
that delegation requires. Macheath, Joseph, Amelia, Mrs Heartfree, and
Wild are all 'put out', in the grip of intuitions and feelings which place
them beyond common forms of discourse and impart to their performances, no matter how artificially or ironically introduced, the unparalleled quality of the strangled sublime. How is it possible to be
paralleled?

The distinction the narrator seems to draw between the circumstances

[19] 'All the Avenues to Tyburn appear like those to a Wake or Festival. . . . And as the Looks and
Behaviour of the Spectators so well bespeak them to be assembled to see some Shew or Farce, those
who are to exhibit the Spectacle seem brought thither only as the Performers of such ridiculous
Drama. Some indeed, as in the Case of all Players, perform their Parts beyond others, have much
more Mirth in their Countenances, and of Jest in their Mouths, and do consequently entertain the
good Company better than their Companions; but even among those who fall shortest of such Merit,
there are very few who do not preserve the Appearance of Indifference at least, and tho' all cannot
force a Laugh, there is scarce one who doth not refrain from Tears, and from every other Mark of
Fear or Contrition.' *Covent-Garden Journal*, 55.
[20] *Thoughts on Executive Justice* (London: J. Dodsley, 1785), 67–8.

of the Heartfrees and those of Wild's incarceration and execution is one that makes no difference. Mrs Heartfree's frantic request for an interpretation of the bare possibilities which are about to ruin her life beg comparison with the symptoms of Wild's fear, obliquely held forth in his clumsy questions about an afterlife and in his unconvincing repudiation of female terrors. At the gallows they are both isolated, with Mrs Heartfree the object of cruelly salacious jokes, and Wild the target of abuse and missiles. Like the player in *Joseph Andrews*, they are convinced they are embarked upon the last act of their lives, and neither they nor their mediators, including the pious Heartfree, the pragmatic Ordinary, and the ironic narrator, can arrange the train of circumstances around these crises in a credible and instructive way. In other words, Mrs Heartfree and Wild find out what it is to be a woman. When juridical mercy relieves Mrs Heartfree's feelings, and stern justice despatches Wild to his fate, this resemblance is not weakened. All the explanations capable of distinguishing the two have already been tried and seen to fail, and the narrator's jokes about the rules of history and romance merely strengthen the impression that he has no plausible way of realizing counterfactuals.

The narrator's capacity for delegation has to be interrogated, therefore, not through the distinction between mercy and justice, but through the intensities arising from the obliteration of that very distinction, to which the narrator's irony has contributed in some measure. There must be supposed to be a potential intensity at the level of narration equal to that caused to the characters in the story by the interruption of the law. The narrator's recurrent failures in introducing and exemplifying standards of normative conduct indicate a symptomatic interest in this phenomenon. If Fielding is exploiting Hawthorn's dialectic not to bring it within the scope of the normative, but simply to widen the play of possibilities and to realize counterfactuals on behalf of those likely to be silenced for the sake of example, it is equally possible with all other possibilities that the narrator's irony is the very medium of delegation, the bridge from third to first person.

To examine a little more closely the scene of Fielding's last farewell, where he himself confessed to acting like a woman, is to discover how the parallels between his unparalleled circumstances and Wild's become, as John Bender has pointed out, particularly close.[21] Paralysed by dropsy and suffering considerable pain, Fielding was swung aboard his Lisbon-bound ship like a hanged man, and he recalls in the *Journal* how, as his useless body was slowly winched up the side of the vessel, the sailors and

---

[21] *Imagining the Penitentiary*, 151–7; see also Battestin, *Henry Fielding*, 438, 500, 577.

watermen witnessing this 'spectacle of horror' insulted and mocked his torment (202). Raised on machines that exalt them in the air so that they can present clearer targets for outrageous insults and inhuman jokes, Fielding and Wild experience shortly before their deaths the ingratitude of a public insensible of the efforts and sacrifices of health each has made for its defence. In both cases the defence of the capital's streets has involved a gang, and a thief-taker with sufficient information judiciously to prune the criminal population—until he is pruned himself. In that moment of shameful and unjust isolation, as each beholds a circle of faces devoid of pity and a thicket of fingers pointing scorn and obloquy, Wild and Fielding are evidently impressed, as are Mrs Heartfree, Clarissa, and Job, with the scantiness of available explanations for what is happening to them.

The experience of an isolation made horrible by the victim's inability to see in it even a sacrificial logic is not new to Fielding. He had felt it himself when the trains of melancholy accidents surrounding the deaths of his daughter and his first wife resisted for a while all parallels. He is drawn to speculate most deeply about it whenever the criminal and female sides of the strangled sublime culminate in questions about trains of circumstances. If the agony of a woman is caused or exacerbated by the law, especially by the law's need to rely upon circumstantial evidence, then he will want to write about it. His contribution to the celebrated case of Mary Blandy, who was convicted and hanged for parricide in 1752 on circumstantial evidence, provides an interesting example of the fervency of Fielding's interest in this aspect of exemplary justice, and his keenness to delegate for the unspeakable female woes it entails. Although Blandy was to die in exemplary form, crying, 'Good People, take Warning by me to be on your Guard against the Sallies of any irregular Passion',[22] Fielding wished to enter the debate on very different terms. 'Here a Woman was adjudged guilty of the most enormous of all Crimes before Conviction,' he complained, 'stigmatized, and hung up as an Example of black Iniquity, at a Time when her Trial is near approaching.'[23] He fights against the presumption of her guilt by asking the reader to consider her feelings as a woman isolated, threatened with death, and very possibly innocent of the charges laid against her. During his magistracy Fielding made considerable efforts to put the best face on evidence against women, no matter how damning, and to bring them down safely from the bleak eminence of the juridical example where they were likely to be hung up. Battestin gives an

[22] *Miss Mary Blandy's own Account of the Affair between her and Mr Cranstoun* (London: A. Millar, 1752), 63.
[23] *Covent-Garden Journal*, 10.

account of his assiduity on behalf of a Mrs Molloy, and a young woman accused of robbing a man called Fagan, and a Frenchwoman denied by her husband, all of whom appeared guilty or in some way compromised.[24] Here is Fielding as it were crying reprieves as fast as he can for the benefit of a succession of women who strike him as replicas of Mrs Heartfree in so far as they are tormented by the law for what is possibly—even barely possibly—not their fault. Because they are to suffer on a presumption and not the proof of guilt, Fielding steps in to untrammel them from the iniquities of the exemplary narrative, and from the train of circumstances which, according to the rules of evidence, makes such a presumption probable.[25]

No delegation is more remarkable, and no reprieve more vehemently argued for, than Fielding's pamphlet, *A Clear State of the Case of Elizabeth Canning* (1753). It concerns a young woman who disappeared for several weeks, and who, when she showed up, told an amazing story of abduction, imprisonment, and starvation in a disorderly house at Enfield Wash, on the outskirts of London. Many people found the story hard to believe, for not only was her account strenuously contradicted by her supposed abductors and their alibis, but also crucial motivations and corollaries were missing from it—why was she not raped, or forced to see company, instead of being starved; why did it take her so long to escape, and how had she the energy to accomplish it? In the end she was transported for perjury (see Zirker, pp. xciv–cxiv). Fielding, who had heard her testify under oath and was much impressed by her candour, set himself the task of answering these objections in a double critique of the principles of evidence and verisimilitude.

He begins by conceding that according to the three levels of presumption in regard to circumstantial evidence—violent, probable, and light[26]—Canning's story excites only a light presumption of its truth, since it is 'a very extraordinary Narrative . . . consisting of many strange Particulars, resembling rather a wild Dream'.[27] He seeks to distinguish therefore between the *evidentia rei* ('Circumstances which arise from the Nature of the Fact itself' [292]), such as the fact of her absence and the undeniable signs of starvation on her body ('Her Limbs were all

---

[24] See also Zirker, p. xcix.

[25] 'When the fact itself cannot be proved, that which comes nearest to the Proof of the Fact is, the Proof of the Circumstances that necessarily usually attend such Facts, and these are called Presumptions.' Geoffrey Gilbert, *The Law of Evidence* (London: W. Owen, 1760), 160.

[26] I am indebted here and elsewhere in this chapter to the investigation of the connection between circumstantial evidence and narrative fiction conducted in Alexander Welsh, *Strong Representations* (Baltimore: Johns Hopkins Univ. Press, 1992), 20 *et passim*. Compare Gilbert, *The Law of Evidence* (London: W. Owen, 1760), 160: 'Presumptions are twofold, violent, or only probable, for the light and rash Presumptions weigh nothing'.

[27] Zirker, 288.

emaciated, and the Colour of her Skin turned black' [291]), and the story itself, the *historia rerum gestarum*,[28] whose wildness presents a barrier to belief. He argues as follows in support of the credibility of a bare possibility regardless of the narrative train in which it appears:

It may yet become a proper Object of our Belief, from the Weight of the Evidence; for there is a Degree of Evidence by which every Fact that is not impossible to have happened at all, or to have happened in the manner in which it is related, may be supported and ought to be believed.

This argument is the juridical equivalent of Gay's comic song about chances; and, like the song, it is intended to recall extreme suffering to a representable form by allowing the barely possible an equivalence with other modes of probability. It has something in common with the distinction used by Richardson while drawing parallels between the presentation of evidence and the particulars of a good story; namely, between the small circumstances which accumulate interest and belief as they coalesce into a narrative, and the greater fact which stands alone, self-evident. 'The Probability of all Stories told, or of Narratives given, depends upon small Circumstances; as may be observed, that in all Tryals for Life and Property, the Merits of the Cause are more determinable by such, than by the greater Facts; which usually are so laid, and taken care of, as to seem to authenticate themselves.'[29] This is Richardson's version of the difference between the *historia rerum gestarum* and the *evidentia rei* which, as far as he is concerned, diminishes in proportion as a probable narrative and an undeniable fact prompt the same degree of belief in a jury or a readership. Fielding has called attention to the facts—the woman's absence, the signs of starvation—and he turns with greater zeal to the small circumstances, which he wants to detach from a narrative which so many people have been unable to believe. He wants to give these incidental details a prominence and self-evidence similar to what Richardson accords the greater fact. And in the case of Elizabeth Canning the small circumstance which stands out for Fielding in the most startling fashion is the mince-pie, the sole resource of 'a poor little Girl whom the many have already condemned' (286): 'Nor will I quit this Case without observing the pretty Incident of the minced Pye, which . . . possibly saved this poor Girl's Life' (310). He isolates this confection, which Canning had in her pocket and which was allegedly her only sustenance during the time of her captivity, offering it both as a thing of wonder and as a proper object of belief.

---

[28] See Laurent Stern, 'Narrative versus Description', in *New Literary History*, 21/3 (1990), 562.
[29] *Clarissa*, Preface, Hints of Prefaces, etc., 5.

Once he has achieved this abstraction of the small circumstance from the wild narrative that would discredit it, Elizabeth Canning's sufferings and his own partiality for defending them from disbelief know no bounds. Hers is a case deplorable and desperate (286), her misery unprecedented (295), and she 'the most unhappy and injured of all human Beings' (311). As for himself, he expects a higher tribunal than public opinion to vindicate the motive 'which raises me to the Protection of injur'd Innocence' (286). And as for the multitude which has resisted her story, he asks whether its disbelief is not owing to a common failure to imagine unparalleled wretchedness, and whether this failure does not add insult to injury:

An innocent young Creature, who hath suffered the most cruel and unheard of Injuries, is in Danger of being rewarded for them by Ruin and Infamy; and what must extremely aggravate her Case, and will distinguish her Misery from that of all other Wretches upon Earth is, that she will owe all this Ruin and Infamy to this strange Circumstance, that her Sufferings have been beyond what Human Nature is supposed to be capable of bearing.[30]

Like Parson Adams, Elizabeth Canning has a wonderful capacity for bare possibilities.

Fielding is forced to concede, however, that setting Canning's experience beyond the range of probability, and turning it into a marvel of the barely possible in order that it might be generally believed, is a hopeless task. Regardless of his fine motives, he is bound to prove that unequivocal gestures of mercy fail in much the same way as unequivocal acts of justice: namely, from lack of public support. To maintain that a bare possibility should be believed simply because it is so remote from the appearance of truth, drives Canning's case into the same paradox of fictionality that he has elaborated in *Jonathan Wild*, but without the advantage of self-reference. To locate her travails within the strangled sublime, it is necessary that they be presented as equipossible with their opposite, just as they are in Fielding's rewritings of *The Beggar's Opera*. Indeed, he ends his treatment of the case with a proposition of equal possibility: Elizabeth Canning is either the 'most unhappy and injured of

---

[30] Zirker, 310. The same problem of injustice upon injury (*tort* upon *dommage*) has recently been theorized by the French philosopher Jean-Francois Lyotard, *The Différend: Phrases in Dispute*, trans. George van den Abbeele (Manchester: Manchester Univ. Press, 1988). He calls it the *différend* and, like Elizabeth Canning's aggravated case, it occurs when, 'the plaintiff is divested of the means to argue and becomes on that account a victim. . . . A case of *différend* between two parties takes place when the 'regulation' of the conflict which opposes them is done in the idiom of one of the parties while the injustice suffered by the other is not signified in that idiom'. And like Fielding, Lyotard relates the silence of an idiomless injury to the sublime: the challenge of a feeling in excess of all modes of presentation. See J.-F. Lyotard, 'The *Différend*, the Referent, and the Proper Name', and David Carroll, 'Rephrasing the Political with Kant and Lyotard: From Aesthetic to Political Judgements', in *Diacritics* 14/3 (Fall, 1984), 5, 83.

all human Beings' or she is the most consummate liar he has ever dealt with, 'a Monster of Iniquity' (311). But this is a rhetorical challenge to public incredulity, not a truly dialectical enquiry into alternatives.

His critics responded quite literally to the challenge by supposing that Elizabeth Canning was indeed a monster, and Fielding her gull. Affirming that her tale was indeed a waking dream, and 'a piece of contradictory Incidents, and most improbable Events', John Hill wondered not at the marvellous mince-pie but at Fielding's impudence in defending the truth of testimony on the grounds of its improbability.[31] In a very lucid assault upon Fielding's position, Allan Ramsay makes a point which Fielding had already travestied in *Jonathan Wild* and which he was explicitly denying now, but which nevertheless was a pillar of the law of evidence:

> To bring a fact within the compass of possibility, there is nothing required but that it should not contradict itself; but to make it probable, it is likewise required that it should not be contradictory to ordinary experience; for in proportion to the several degrees in which it is removed from common experience, it acquires an appearance of falshood, and to entitle it to belief, must be supported by evidence apparently true, to as great or greater degree than the fact which it means to prove, is apparently false. This . . . is the general and leading principle in all enquiries concerning probable evidence.[32]

As Gilbert says, 'If the Fact be contrary to all Manner of Experience and Observation, 'tis too much to receive it upon the Oath of one Witness'. But it is Fielding's point that unparalleled suffering has no other route to take; and in offering one of the slightest circumstances of Canning's story as a miracle worthy of belief, he was also breaching another leading principle of probable evidence, namely, that 'the Law requires the highest Evidence that the Nature of the Thing is capable of'.[33] If he sets aside all principles of evidence in an attempt to present the bare possibility of extremest misery, to whom, apart from himself, will he be presenting it?

Although Fielding enters a case such as Canning's in the spirit of equity—that is, to correct the law when it is deficient by virtue of its universality[34]—his passionate defence of women isolated by the legal process and by the general standards of narrative probability is too prone to failure, specifically the failure credibly and knowledgeably to explain its own grounds, to be construed as delegation. However, it is equally mistaken to suppose that Fielding is contributing ingenuously towards the practice of equity, and marking little circumstances with the

---

[31] John Hill, *The Story of Elizabeth Canning Considered* (London: M. Cooper, 1753), 16, 8.
[32] *A Letter Concerning Elizabeth Canning* (London: A. Millar, 1752), 5–6.
[33] Gilbert, *The Law of Evidence*, 150, 15.   [34] Blackstone, *Commentaries*, i. 61.

same attention as liberal theorists of the law such as Romilly and Godwin. His intervention into the notorious case of Bosavern Penlez, who was hanged for theft in 1749 on circumstantial evidence, shows how easily he could appear on the other side, and argue strenuously against mercy and bare possibilities. Fielding did everything in his power to ensure the conviction and efficient execution of this young man who in many respects shared the background and the bad luck of the hero of Fielding's own *Tom Jones*, published the same year. The riots in the Strand which led to Penlez's alleged offence (the theft of some linen from Peter Woods' brothel) were such, he argues, 'as called for some Example, and . . . the Man who was made that Example, deserved his Fate'.[35] He rides roughshod over Penlez's steady refusal to confess to any crime ('[He] could not, or would not give any other Account' [46]); and justifies the law's casual determination to hang Penlez and to reprieve John Wilson (a rioter taken in similar circumstances) by means of a groundless 'Distinction between an Object of Mercy and an Object of Justice' (54). He is therefore indignant that the law's victim is acquiring a posthumous reputation as a hero, 'instead of remaining an Example to incite Terror' (3). It falls to Penlez's anonymous apologists to take up the theme that Fielding reserves apparently only for female defendants. Penlez's epitaph ends with a mock entreaty remarkably similar to the lost moral of *The Beggar's Opera*: 'Learn hence to respect the Laws— even the most oppressive'.[36] The author of a pamphlet in his defence paints a picture of a patient Heartfree, sacrificed to 'the Form and Letter of the Law'.[37] In a rare surge of pathos, the *Newgate Calendar* reports, 'It is not in language to describe how much [Penlez] was pitied by the public'.[38]

This is not the only occasion when Fielding's haste to have a man condemned and made an example of overrode questions of equity. In 1749 he crossed the border of legality itself in defence of his Bow Street gang, refusing to receive any information against John Berry and Stephen McDaniel, men well known for conspiring to arrange the crimes for which they then arrested and charged their victims—offences they were finally convicted of in 1754, when Fielding could no longer shield them.[39] Rather than ascribe Fielding's harshness in these instances and

---

[35] *A True State of the Case of Bosavern Penlez* (London, 1749), 52.

[36] Published in *The Gentleman's Magazine*, (Oct. 1749), 465; cited in Zirker, p. xlii.

[37] *The Case of the Unfortunate Bosavern Penlez* (London, 1749), 48–52. For a good account of the Penlez case see Peter Linebaugh, 'The Tyburn Riot against the Surgeons', in *Albion's Fatal Tree*, ed. Douglas Hay *et al.* (Harmondsworth: Penguin, 1975), 89–100. The most authoritative treatment of the case as it affected Fielding is now Zirker's, pp. xxxiii–lii.

[38] *The New Newgate Calendar, or Malefactors' Bloody Register*, 5 vols. (London, 1779), iii. 240.

[39] Ruth Paley, 'London Thief-Takers', in Douglas Hay and Francis Snyder (eds.), *Policing and Prosecution in Britain 1750–1850* (Oxford: Clarendon Press, 1989), 334.

the Penlez case to his political ambitions or his penological principles,[40] which is bound to leave irreducible the contradiction between his notions of justice and mercy, it is more interesting to view his alternation between them as a dialectic of opposite possibilities, a repetitious mode of self-interruption requisite for the restricted representation and delegation of the strangled sublime. Canning and Penlez are two sides of the same equipossible outcome, as are Heartfree and Wild, and the tragic moral and the comic maxim of *The Beggar's Opera*. They are the wretch of today and the happy man of tomorrow, drawing prizes and blanks in 'the lottery of justice';[41] they are the value-free alternatives which occur when a fact is measured not by its likely truth but by the counterfactual resistance it excites; they constitute the cheveril glove of non-probative law, alternating endlessly, as Bentham says, between that which is false and that which is false, from history as fiction to fiction as history, in search of some limited engagement with unparalleled intensity.[42]

Fielding's fascination with equipossibility encourages the conclusion that his investment in the public example made of Penlez is no more principled than his interest in the bare possibility of Canning's case. He is neither explaining nor justifying, although he may use the language of explanation and justification. He accords as little significance to 'the instructive moral' secured by the licence of poetry as he does to the maxim of chance supported by small circumstances, since each depends on the other and has no existence without its counterpart. That is to say, each narrative is interrupted at the level of basic generic expectations of probability, being adequate neither as history nor fiction. His investment lies instead with the degree to which faulty narrative or discursive failure may be mimetic or representative of agonized intensity. Insert a false circumstance into history (the reprieve) or leave history to depend on a small circumstance that is trying to behave like a greater fact (the mince pie), and the narrator inherits the effects of an interesting breach of probability, capable of being combined with reflexive self-interruption to reproduce the intensity of the strangled sublime. It is of no abiding concern to Fielding whether it is explanation or pity, a nod in the direction of justice or mercy, which prompts this dialectic, as long as it provides the opportunity for paralleling the unparalleled. Fielding is always at his best when he swings between two equal possibilities in order to seize a perspective upon a human predicament not generally within the capacity of language to describe.

---

[40] Battestin, 473, 485–6; Zirker, 1.
[41] Leon Radzinowicz, *A History of English Criminal Law* (London: Stevens and Sons, 1948), i. 330.
[42] *Theory of Fictions*, ed. C. K. Ogden (London: Routledge and Kegan Paul, 1932), 121.

Two years after Penlez was despatched, Fielding entered into a theory of exemplary punishment with his tract, *An Enquiry into the Causes of the late Increase of Robbers*. For all its formal appearance it is, like all of Fielding's law-work, a disquisition upon the calculation of chances. He musters every legal argument he can think of to minimize the chances of the defendant's escape from the law, and to remove the 'enchanting Alternative' that sustains criminals through the legal process; namely, 'a Possibility, at least . . . of retrieving all their former Hopes' (93). He strongly recommends the introduction of circumstantial evidence in the shape of criminal witnesses such as Berry and McDaniel, whose temptation to perjury will supposedly be removed by the reflection that they have 'a better Chance of convicting the Guilty' (162). There will be no pardons or reprieves to disturb the necessity of punishment for the guilty. Though 'it is of the very Nature of Hope to be sanguine, and it will derive more Encouragement from one Pardon, than Diffidence from twenty Executions' (165), Fielding is lengthening the odds against such optimism. Nor will the scene of execution present the consoling opportunity for displays of hardihood, because it will be as isolated and terrible as possible. *An Enquiry* presents in broad strokes the plan for ensuring that rogues hang which Fielding first draws out in *Jonathan Wild*, down to the licence taken from poetry to ensure that conviction and execution will be united by 'every Circumstance of Probability' (160). The only difference is that it is, like his pamphlet on Penlez, apparently written without irony. Horace, Montaigne, and Shakespeare are Fielding's authorities for the superior terror of deaths offstage or fenced about with ritual; and in an argument that anticipates the sublime of obscurity, loneliness, and privation which Burke will elaborate six years later, Fielding concludes, 'Nothing can, I think, be imagined . . . more terrible than such an Execution' (171).

As Wild to Heartfree, and Penlez to Canning, so is *An Enquiry* to the *Remedy*. It is a consolation in reverse: a manual designed to eradicate possibility from a fatal narrative of probable circumstance, so that the malefactor may be strangled in the most exemplary way. How sublime this death may be, is another question. Just as the emollient sentiments of the *Remedy* define a condition of unlimited distress which Fielding graphically describes as 'tearing the Heart, the Soul from the Body' (*Remedy*, 215), so here he strips every shred of comfort from the criminal about to face death, defining the last degree of being put out as a project of public utility and education. When he protests that this is all in pursuit of example ('more for example, and to prevent evil, than to punish') and rejects mercy on Machiavelli's grounds 'that examples of justice are more merciful than the unbounded exercise of pity' (166–7), it prompts one to wonder exactly what he means by example: whether he is once again arguing firmly on the side of justice, defining a public sacrifice along Paley's or Madan's lines; or whether, having presented execution as a branch of aesthetics, he is not exploiting the mimetic possibilities of the strangled sublime.

Although most theorists of example agree that the victim is unlucky in being selected for a punishment out of proportion to the crime, they see the deficiency in equity outweighed by the advantage the society enjoys from such a sacrifice to its laws. For this advantage to be secured, two things are necessary. First of all the criminal has to participate in the narrative, rising to meet the challenge of poetic justice either by a heartfelt confession or, in remarkable instances of self-transcendence, by allegorizing the role to be played. The Reverend Robert Foulkes told his audience, before he was turned off for child-murder, 'You see in me what Sin is'.[43] This matching of the narrative of confession with the narrative of the death-sentence is precisely what Fielding declares never happens at Tyburn. Secondly, the spectacular nature of the punishment can never be ignored. Indeed, in his commentary on the *Enquiry*, Martin Madan dramatically invokes all the stages of a criminal trial, ending with the scaffold, where 'the wretches are led forth to suffer, and exhibit a spectacle to the beholders, too aweful and solemn for description'.[44] Even Burke's arguments in favour of an obscure sublime leave the execution of the state criminal to take place in the light of day, and Paley's on behalf of private executions are designed to maximize the spectacular effect even of hidden violence upon the public sensibility.[45] Fielding is alone in abstracting the scene of punishment completely from the public view, and in making it accessible to the public mind not by exotic cruelties, nor by any elaborate ceremony, but solely via the imagined extreme distress of someone about to die without pity or hope. Access to this terror is obtained, that is to say, not by a spectacular crowning (like Madan's) of a public and probable narrative of guilt, in which the ideal victim is willingly participating, but by the intuition of a lonely and subjective terror provoked by the interruption of a public narrative and the obstruction of a public sight-line.

As this intuition cannot arise from the adequacy of a public account,

[43] Charles Johnson, *A General History of the Lives and Adventures of the most famous Highwaymen, Murderers, Street-Robbers etc.* (London, 1734), 316–17; cited in Lincoln B. Faller, *Turned to Account: The Forms and Functions of Criminal Biography in Late Seventeenth and Early Eighteenth Century England* (Cambridge: Cambridge Univ. Press, 1987), 61.

[44] *Thoughts on Executive Justice*, 29.

[45] He mentions the proposal of 'casting murderers into a den of wild beasts, where they would perish in a manner dreadful to the imagination, yet concealed from the view'. *The Principles of Moral and Political Philosophy*, 548.

it must proceed from the counterfactuals excited by the failure of such an account. It must coincide, therefore, with the keenest sense of the lack of any narrative or explanation adequate to the bare possibility of what is being endured in the first person. However odd it may seem, Fielding's *Enquiry* delegates for that emergency in the same way as his comic applications of the *Remedy* in his fiction; that is, by dividing the subject from the predicate of public discourses, and by releasing as discontinuous possibilities the very circumstances that were supposed to unite in a probable explanation. It doesn't matter where Fielding the moralist or penologist positions himself in this process, for the joint failures of language and spectacle to discover their legitimate object, which here he hails as the point of his innovation, outline two extreme and antagonistic possibilities: either state power has found the final solution to criminal intransigence by transcending probability in order to function as the immanent Subject of all executed sentences; or the isolated subject—the individual criminal—having reluctantly acquired priority as the keenest sensibility in this process, is the first person in a sentence that means quite literally nothing to him. When Fielding says of it, 'Nothing can, I think, be imagined . . . more terrible than such an Execution' (171), in whose person does he speak, as the Subject of state, or as the lonely victim? Does he measure the terror from the outside or the inside? The axis of delegation is the first person ('I think'), controlling two irreconcilable possibilities, each without a predicate in the form of a probable and visible narrative. When Mr Allworthy talks resentfully of those who indulge in extreme resentment he explores exactly the paradox of contingent self-substitution which Fielding develops in the *Enquiry*.

If private and singular feelings can erupt from the ruin of examples designed to make public and universal sense, it is worth wondering why Fielding bothers with such a word as 'example' at all. Of the authorities cited in the *Enquiry*, Montaigne and Machiavelli are the most germane to his reorientation of exemplary discourse towards the self. Victoria Kahn shows how Montaigne uses the singular judgements of taste to destroy the validity of examples while still seeming to use them.[46] The wonderful exceptions made by the palate to all rules and precedents of correctness wins his interest, not least because in affirming a certainty that cannot be known or declared within any system of knowledge, taste is 'exemplary' of the self-destructive propositions of Montaigne's own Pyrrhonism. It is something akin to Montaigne's aesthetics of the fragment and the interruption which informs Machiavelli's negative

[46] Victoria Kahn, *Rhetoric, Prudence, and Scepticism in the Renaissance* (Ithaca, NY: Cornell Univ. Press, 1985), 135.

examples of example, according to John Lyons,[47] for he makes the example perform as well as treat of an interruptive, particular, and unprecedented act of policy or terror whose fascination lies in its specific internal dynamic, not its general applicability to the world. Like any aesthetician, Machiavelli is searching for an operating discourse between the particular and the universal that will do justice to this intensity. The instance of Torquatus, who killed his son to urge the Romans to victory, presents in the guise of a model 'only the extreme and extraordinary nature of such violence' (Lyons, 52). This estimate of example as the representation of the unparalleled event corresponds with Michel de Certeau's reading of the *Discourses* as constitutive of a shift from history as the predicate of an immanent Subject to history as a practice, an indeterminate and infinite effect of the actual 'subject in action'.[48] Machiavelli removes historiography from the self-evidence of the universal affirmative proposition, where subject and predicate are one, to the status of the contingent proposition, where the relation between the two is asymptotic, 'involving a progression to infinity'.[49]

When Montaigne's essay, 'To philosophise is to learn to die', is cited in the *Enquiry* to show how the terror of dying alone 'makes an Impression on the Mind, especially on the Minds of the Multitude' (170), the two aspects of example are straddled: the subjective intensity and the attempt at a public lesson. And when Fielding cites *The Prince* on the value of exemplary punishment, he likewise tries to combine personal distress with public utility. Yet Montaigne insists that any lesson he teaches is designed to privatize death, to make it all his own work, the fruit of the subject in action: 'a Death involved within itself . . . and all my own' (*Essays*, iii. 220). And for his part, Machiavelli sees violent death on the scaffold as a close transaction between two agents, whose point is blunted by mercy not because it makes an exception but because it universalizes the question: 'Exorbitant mercy has an ill effect upon the whole universality, whereas particular Executions extend only to particular persons'.[50] It is not any obtuseness on Fielding's part that inclines him to mistake his authorities for true examples of the exemplary when really they are only casual apologists of

[47] 'Claiming to write a text on a new science, Machiavelli attempts to fragment the continuum of history into a new, discontinuous collection of illustrative instances. . . . Therefore the contemplation of example in history may have a purely theoretical or even aesthetic value.' John D. Lyons, *Exemplum: The Rhetoric of Example in Early Modern France and Italy* (Princeton, NJ: Princeton Univ. Press, 1989), 35–6. See also Timothy Hampton, *Writing from History: The Rhetoric of Exemplarity in Renaissance Literature* (Ithaca, NY: Cornell Univ. Press, 1990), 193–7.

[48] Michel de Certeau, *The Writing of History*, trans. Tom Conley (New York: Columbia Univ. Press, 1988), 7.

[49] G. W. Leibniz, 'On Contingency', *Philosophical Essays*, ed. and trans. by Roger Ariew and Daniel Garber (Indianapolis: Hackett, 1989), 28.

[50] *Works of the Famous Nicholas Machiavel* (3rd edn.; London: A. Churchill, 1720), 221.

the particular. It is only by making that mistake repeatedly, exploding the universality of example again and again, that he can advance the dialectic of faulty explanations and disorderly counterfactuals. By interrupting himself into an intuition of the bare possibilities of the strangled sublime, he brings the subject of unparalleled intensity into range of the subject who acts by writing, fashioning out the failure of a probable and public narrative a restricted representation of impressions that are singular and, at the same time, joint. This, I think, is what he means by example.

13 *Conclusion: Job and the Epitaph*

Nowhere is the book of Job more frequently or more variously reproduced in the eighteenth century than on tombstones, vaults, and mausoleums. Its popularity as a source of epitaphic sentiments is reflected in James Hervey's *Meditation upon the Tombs* (1746), where the author marks almost every pause before the dead with a quotation from Job, ranging from the common choices for graveyard inscription ('Here even the Wicked cease from troubling' and 'This is the House appointed for all Living') to rather more vociferous passages, such as 'I shall never more see Good in the Land of the Living'.[1] Similar inventories are to be found in Robert Blair's *The Grave* (1786) and in George Wright's *Pleasing Melancholy: or a Walk among the Tombs* (1794). The strong association between graves and the book of Job is owing to the verses beginning, 'O that my words were written', in which Job imagines that he might continue his complaint by having it carved on a rock and positioned between his dead body and his reader. With this vision of an epitaph Job presents the alternatives of reading as practice and as interpretation. As practice the words on the stone will work a change upon the relations of the writer both to the reader and to the world: they are implicated in what is about to happen. As a challenge to interpretation, the words present the reader with a code that has to be cleared; only then will the literal terms reveal a hidden message as prophecy or typology. Job's writing is read, then, either as one in a series of illocutionary events delivered in the first person which personally affect the reader, and which tie the future to an unsettled issue in the past; or as a figured promise of a general and equitable future which relies on a communitarian spirit and a forgetting of past injuries.

The same alternatives are presented by graveyard inscriptions. In the form of a name, a date, and a short summary of a life that has ended, they offer the reader a number of facts, inflected with varying degrees of pathos and optimism, capable of being treated either as the literal and self-evident testimony of a real person given to another, or as an exemplary fable whose moral is to be found out by interpretative effort. In literal language, the dead speak of their mortality as an unsettled injury, and with varying degrees of aggression appeal to the reader's interest in

[1] James Hervey, *Meditations among the Tombs* (London: J. Rivington, 1746), 49, p. vi, 17.

recognizing and not forgetting this ('I was what you are', 'When thou readst the state of me | Think on the Glass that runs for thee'[2]). In this favourite form of the *tu quoque*, the dead promise the living access to that endless series of intensities which has already been seen to be characteristic of the sublime and of certain kinds of sympathetic interchange in the eighteenth century. In this sequence, each succeeding generation is destined to inhabit the unrelative experience of the last, including the miracle of dying, and to complain about it. The words on a gravestone are a machine for producing this mimesis, and for instigating the substitution of reader for victim which Job calls redemption.

The sort of redemption secured by interpretation, however, supplants the seriality of one-to-one exchanges with a chiliastic vision that reduces the importance of the particular details and personal injury in proportion as it delivers a message of universal significance. 'I know that my Redeemer lives, | What comfort this assurance gives. | Reader, may you to this attain, | This soul-reviving knowledge gain.'[3] Such knowledge is to be gained by scrutinizing what the monument does not say, or what it has lost owing to the obliteration by time and weather of the techniques of anamnesis. Only when its particulars are erased, and it betokens nothing but forgetfulness, does it become readable as an exemplary spectacle—of vanity, decay, frailty, and mortality—whose meaning ceases to be current as a first-person complaint. It remains only as an occasion for a collective statement of faith. The material sign in the stone is detached from the past emergencies, discontinuities, and intensities which have caused it to be carved, so that it may be transferred to an allegory of a just and general future. The reader who deciphers this kind of redemption mediates between a sign and a code, whereas the reader who acts as the redeemer mediates between a script and a voice, between the dead and the living.

I want to conclude this study by setting Job inside a short history of the epitaph that is partial to these distinctions. I want to consider the practice of redemptive reading as constantly engaged in a struggle to preserve susceptibility towards private intensities, in opposition to the tendency of interpretative redemption to supplant them with communitarian or universal expectations that reduce the probability of personal complaints. But I will emphasize that, in this struggle, practical reading defends a particularity so various and disjointed that it risks disorientation, and even terror, so extreme that they threaten even the

[2] Erwin Panofsky, *Tomb Sculpture* (London: Thames and Hudson, 1964), 64; Thomas Dingley, *History from Marble*, 2 vols. (London: Camden Society, 1867), ii. p. ccxlix.

[3] George Wright, *Pleasing Melancholy: or a Walk among the Tombs* (London: Chapman and Co., 1793), 166.

limited, serial redemption of one-to-one mimesis. It risks short-circuiting the link between writer and reader, causing a build-up of energy that blocks the transfer of intensity from one to the other, and prevents the paralleling of the unparalleled upon which the series depends. In this respect the epitaph describes the same rim of fundamental disorder as the sublime, and its reader is as prone to succumb to it. I will propose two images and an instance of this sublime rupture from the later eighteenth century: *The Dead Soldier* (1789) by Joseph Wright of Derby; *Job Reproved by his Friends* (1777) by James Barry; and the tomb that is partly the subject of a collection of poems entitled *Sorrows sacred to the Memory of Penelope* (1796) by Sir Brooke Boothby. Each arrives at a limit to the possibilities of complaint, which even incorporated readings of the book of Job (attempted by Boothby and Barry) are unable to extend. As Barry and Boothby both have direct links with the politics and aesthetics of Burke, it will be possible to measure the blockage of the series against the standards of spectatorial and readerly practice set by Burke in the *Enquiry* and the *Reflections*, and to judge how far a revolution in the political sphere disturbs the vocality of complaint in the private. And as this question revolves in each case around the figure of a female, it reintroduces under the new agenda of tomb sculpture the 'nice and womanish' side of Job's impatience identified by Calvin. I want to end by showing how Wordsworth confronts in the French Revolution a terror that is in danger of becoming too private, and how by means of epitaphic precedents, he is able to interpret this intensity conformably to moral ideas of society, history, and pedagogy, and to sidestep the violence that belongs to the transferred intensities of a delegated redemption.

In the Job controversy commentators such as Grey, Lowth, and Peters try to preserve the strength of Job's complaint, treating it as an extension of his desired epitaph, now transcribed and studied as a book. They respond to the specificities and particularities of the life it commemorates, and they entail upon themselves the harsh duties of the reader-redeemer who is bound, by the very nature of the *go'el*'s task, to stand in an adversarial relation to the forces abroad that are hostile to the good name of their client. The Warburtonians, who represent these forces, wish to blot whatever is particular or unparalleled from the chronicle of Job, in order to spell out an exemplary fable from the patriarch's anger and distress. They transform the literal or historical account of suffering into an allegory that is successfully deciphered only when it removes all trace of a real and private Job, and installs in his place a figure who represents national causes and who provides the medium of public messages. They turn him from the source of an improbable complaint into the channel of a credible narrative.

It is easy to observe this oppositional pattern in the genre of tomb-meditation. The inheritors of Young's platitudinous apothegms concerning the negligibility of suffering and death construe the bad writer or reader as one devoted to a vain, egotistical, and circumstantial misery, or to a false self-sufficiency. 'Those bold insurances of deathless fame, | Supply their little feeble aids in vain,' Blair reminds those readers tempted to rely on the durability of alabaster and verse.[4] Looking straight at Job, Hervey makes the same point: 'Characters cut with a Pen of Iron, and committed to the solid Rock, will ere long cease to be legible' (*Meditations*, 48). The mother so abandoned to grief for her dead son that she believes she will no longer see good in the land of the living, and thinks only of raising a pillar to him as David raised one to Absolom, has neglected the primary duty of all parents, which is to the future, not the past. She ought to be cultivating 'the Morals, and secur[ing] 'the immortal Interests of their Children', not planning a monument (*Meditations*, 17). Similarly, George Wright's dying cleric who catches the mortalist heresy from Job ('If a man die, shall he live again?'), has failed to instruct himself and his flock in the Christian truth of the message of the redeemer.[5] This is a message freed from the restrictions of a material labour and assigned instead to ideal agents, as Hervey makes clear when he apostrophizes Christ as redeemer: 'Inscribe the Memory of thy matchless Beneficence, not with Ink and Pen, but with that precious Blood. . . . Trace it not with Hammer and Chizel, but with that sharpened spear which pierced thy blessed Side' (*Meditations*, 43). The dead become legible and useful to the public in proportion as their personal bids for a life in the reader's memory are seen to fail, and to crumble into a blurred *vanitas*: 'And what would these dumb Monitors inform me of?' asks Hervey, looking at the lettered paving stones of the church and relishing their anonymity, 'Why, that beneath their Little Circumferences were deposited such and such Pieces of clay, that once lived, and moved, and talked' (*Meditations*, 9). If ruin, not inscription, is to be the sign that is to be interrogated (stones 'ruind so that to the viewers eye, | In their owne ruines they intombed lie'[6]), it is important that such monitors be dumb. Hervey has no interest in listening to the 'haggard Skeleton', should it acquire the power to open its 'stiffened Jaws, and, with a hoarse tremendous Murmur, break this profound Silence' (63). Blair plays the part of Hamlet to his skull, demanding in

---

[4] *The Grave* (London, 1786), ll. 188–89.   [5] *Pleasing Melancholy*, 15.
[6] John Weever, *Ancient Funerall Monuments* (London, 1631; repr. Theatrum Orbis Terrarum: Amsterdam and New Jersey, 1979), p. 4.

mockery, 'Tell us what 'tis to DIE?—Do the strict laws | Of your society forbid your speaking | Upon so nice a point?' (ll. 440–2).

In his *Essays on Epitaphs*, Wordsworth restores to these dumb monitors the privilege of articulate, private, and urgent particularity that the priority of a publicly legible sign displaces. He insists that the address from the dead to the living is not a proud or public writing, but a 'loving solicitation', delivered often in the first person singular, so as to 'personate the deceased, and represent him as speaking from his own tombstone'.[7] It is not a laborious fable or a flattering narrative that brings the dead into communion with the living, but 'the affections which . . . are for the most part secret; the tears . . . and the sighs . . . [which are] a labour of privacy' (*Essays* ii. 64). As may be expected from someone used to reading the Bible in its Lowthian sense, he reinstates decisively not only the value of private grief but also the salience of the minute particular: 'For the occasion of writing an Epitaph is matter of fact in its intensity, and forbids more authoritatively than any other species of composition all modes of fiction' (ii. 76). He affirms no less definitely a continuity between these matters of fact in their intensity and the slow and laborious effort of cutting their record in the rock (ii. 60). Together they form a 'substance of individual truth' which makes its way from one heart to another, transmitting at full strength 'these primary sensations' to 'the inner cell of the mind to whom [they are] addressed' (ii. 70).

In his *Essay on Sepulchres* William Godwin pursues a similar line. He laments the short life of gravestones and tombs and the dumbness this forces on the dead. At Thetford Abbey he looks at the ruined memorials of the Howards and the Mowbrays ('All now was speechless') not as a lesson but as a substantial loss.[8] He insists that there is a real presence in a grave—'the dust that is covered by his tomb, is simply and literally the great man *himself*'—which ought properly to be commemorated. 'Do not fear to remember too much', he advises; and he quotes Ezekiel, ' "Let these dry bones live." ' (67, 105, 78). When the resting-places of the dead are marked with wooden crosses and slabs, such memorials will operate as moving pledges of the truth of history, and as overtures to sentimental conferences with the simple and literal remains beneath them. 'I want to repair to the place where [Milton] *now dwells*. Some spirit shall escape from his ashes, and whisper to me things unfelt before' (77).

While stressing the particular and personal nature of this communion,

---

[7] William Wordsworth, *Essays upon Epitaphs in the Prose Works*, ed. W. J. B. Owen and Jane Worthington Smyser (Oxford: Clarendon Press, 1974), ii. 59–60.
[8] William Godwin, *Essay on Sepulchres* (London: W. Miller, 1809), 43.

neither Wordsworth nor Godwin is blind to the civic benefits of giving the dead a voice. Godwin imagines England mapped not according to the situation of gentlemen's seats or of post-roads, but along the coordinates of cemeteries and churchyards, which would provide an atlas 'of a very different measure of utility' from the usual (115). While aiming not to disturb the privacy of the grave, Wordsworth is aware that the community is served by an exchange of sentiments in its vicinity. It is a traffic made for the common benefit, 'concerning all and for all' (ii. 69), whose themes of mortality and 'the vanity of those affections which are confined to earthly objects' (ii. 60) are so feelingly touched upon that they 'profitably chastise' the villager or traveller who reads them. Like Godwin, Wordsworth intends to reconcile private claims with public benefits without sacrificing the simple, literal, and intense matter of fact they both identify as the idiom of the deceased. They are unambitious for grand narratives, fictions, and allegories; but they do expect moral improvement to flow from these conferences between a deceased first person and an appreciative community. They stand between the raw seriality of practical redemptive reading and the bland public allegories favoured by Hervey, Blair, and Wright.

Their defence of a minimum standard of public utility is commensurate with a dim recognition of what may be unsettling or excessive in the reading of a memorial. Godwin concedes that mnemotechics may cause the fear of remembering too much and of labouring, with Borges's Funes the Memorious, under the despotism of a memory that forbids the forgetting of anything. The accumulation of literal details not only prevents their abridgement, but also the material fact itself generates tautologies which are peculiarly insignificant given the feelings they are supposed to arouse: 'the dust is simply and literally the *great man himself*', 'what the grave encloses is himself' (67, 18). This is the quality referred to by Wordsworth as 'a substance of individual truth', having the power to 'fasten the mind with absolute sovereignty upon itself' (*Essays on Epitaphs* ii. 66, 81), but having trouble, like Hegel's force of the spirit working in stone 'to realise itself for itself', with the recalcitrance of its material.[9] Hence the traces of the 'slow and laborious hand' in the 'very form and substance of the monument' (*Essays*, 60), which is analogous to other difficulties with epitaphs, such as 'this monotonous language of sorrow' in which the core of individual truth is obliged to manifest itself (66).

Monotony participates with other repetitious or serial phenomena of the grave. Hervey complains of an effect not unlike the infinite

---

[9] *Phenomenology*, 423–4; see Jacques Derrida, *Margins of Philosophy*, trans. Alan Bass (Chicago: Univ. of Chicago Press, 1982), 97 n. 25.

array of pillars in Burke's *Enquiry*: 'No sooner turned from one *Memento* . . . but a second, a third, a long Succession of these melancholy Monitors crowd upon my Sight' (*Meditations*, 25). George Wright quotes an epitaph that turns the *tu quoque* into the mathematical sublime: 'Oft have I stood as you stand now, | To view the graves as you view mine; | Think, thou must soon be laid as low, | And others stand to gaze at thine' (*Pleasing Melancholy*, 167). The quotation of the quoted epitaph of Gray's *Elegy*, found by Wordsworth inscribed on William Taylor's headstone in Cartmel churchyard and recorded in the tenth book of *The Prelude*, hints at a seriality which often, in the verse of epitaphs themselves, takes the form of a punning or a stuttering echolalia.[10] Wordsworth draws attention to the memorials that pun on the fate in a name, the *nomen* as *omen* in surnames of pilgrims called Palmer (ii.74). Weever cites an epitaph that puns on the name of Sir Thomas More: 'If I had usd with More regard, | The More that I did give, | I might have made more use and fruit | Of More while he did live'.[11] Debra Fried has a fine example of an inscription that rings the changes on the *tu quoque* itself: 'Shall we all die? | We shall die all: | All die shall we— | Die all we shall'.[12] Panofsky records a motto from the tomb of Margaret of Austria at Brou which combines this sort of palindrome with a pun: 'Fortune Infortune Fort Une' (*Tomb Sculpture*, 75).

The unending series or the core tautology which gives rise to this chiming or echoing language has its origin in the ancient laments set up by women at the graveside. In its most articulate form it emerges as the figure of stychomythia in Greek tragedy, expressive of woes upon woes such as those commemorated by the chorus of Aeschylus' *The Persians*, and adapted for modern use by the dowager queens in Shakespeare's *Richard III*. At its most primitive it is the ululation of female despair, *otototoi*.[13] It is as close to vocality as the dead can get, and it enacts in its play upon identical syllables the mimesis of intensity which the dead bequeath the living: the same thing again and again. If Hervey's haggard skeleton were to let loose its hoarse tremendous murmur, it would achieve the monotony of a series of homophones. The grinning skull corresponds to various icons of femininity traditionally associated with funerary rituals and monuments, notably the gorgoneion, or Medusa-head often carved on tombs and façades, whose grimace represents

[10] *The Prelude* (1805), ed. Ernest de Selincourt, corr. Stephen Gill (Oxford: Oxford Univ. Press, 1970), x. 495–99.
[11] *Ancient Funerall Monuments*, 824.
[12] Debra Fried, 'Repetition, Refrain, and Epitaph', *ELH* 53/3 (1986), 615.
[13] Gail Holst-Warhaft, *Dangerous Voices: Women's Laments in Greek Literature* (London: Routledge, 1992), 132, 148.

'some terrible noise',[14] and whose petrifying power ensures the substitution by the astonished reader or viewer for the stone-girt dead.

In its manifestations as the Keres, Erinyes, Gorgons, Sirens, Sphinxes, and Harpies of funerary iconography and mortality myths, the feminine force attendant upon the dead strikes the spectator merely as unspeakable or disgusting. These figures, with their talons spread, their teeth chattering, and their mouths distorted by the groans and shrieks of tortured men (Vernant, 95, 124), register the pressure of the political and social needs to silence the noise of female mourning. The *conclamatio* of bare-breasted women, often carved on the friezes of sarcophagi such as the Meleager Tomb or the Sarcophagus of the Mourning Women (Panofsky, 20–35),[15] presents the same threat to the Greek *polis* that the death-song presents to an Indian tribe: namely, of the impossibility of the dead sleeping in peace. They sing and shout of the scandalous appetite for revenge, and the unavoidable seriality of fatal intensities. Just as the tortured and disfigured Indian, sacrificed to the manes of the slain of the captor-tribe, remembers and promises the same torments that are presently killing him, so do the clamouring women commemorate the unappeasable injury of death by embarking upon the barbarous extravagance of an inconsolable private grief, unsettling in the process, like Iphigenia, the boundary drawn by the law between a personal or familial exigency and a duty to the state. 'As long as he can, he whoops and out-braves the enemy, describing his own martial deeds against them, and those of his nation, who he threatens will force many of them to eat fire in revenge of his fate.'[16] 'Why hide what keeps whirling in my mind and shaking it?'[17] The dead, as Hegel says, find in women their instruments of vengeance; for its part, the community or state 'can only maintain itself by suppressing this spirit of individualism'.[18]

There are gradations of suppression. The maternal figure of the Sphinx and the Harpy, or of the mother who is the special object of demonic care, such as Clytemnestra, shades off into the less threatening immobility and silence of a metamorphosis such as Niobe's. The tragedies of Aeschylus and Euripides transform the eldritch shrieks of female lament into a public performance and a civic song (Holst-Warhaft, 124, 160). The sexual allure of the sirens, who beguile sailors to their deaths by singing them their epitaphs (Vernant, 105), is figured

---

[14] Jean-Pierre Vernant, *Mortals and Immortals* (Princeton, NJ: Princeton Univ. Press, 1991), 116; on the *gorgoneion* see Panofsky, *Tomb Sculpture*, 25.

[15] See also Marina Warner, *Monuments and Maidens* (London: Picador, 1985), 283.

[16] James Adair, *The History of the American Indians* (London: Charles and Edward Dilley, 1775), 391.

[17] Holst-Warhaft, *Dangerous Voices*, 148.   [18] *Phenomenology*, 286–8.

as the warning sign of the tomb's semi-pulchritude, fair without and foul within ('*sepulchra, id est, semipulchra*'), no longer a temptation to self-destruction but a legible and public 'externall helpe to excite, and stirre up our inward thoughts'.[19]

Although the savagery of female mourning can destroy the orderly rituals of sepulture even at the pinnacle of civilization—John Warton mentions the immeasurable distress of the daughters and relict of the atheist Mr Sambrook, who sought to clamber into the grave while 'the church-yard resounded to their screams'[20]—there is a definite reduction of the bare-breasted, grieving woman to the scale of a public statement about death that corresponds to civic ideals of common sense and common purpose. On the great tombs of the early modern period, such as Bernini's, the winged and breasted Harpy who once suckled the souls of the dead has been transformed into the figure of Charity, a nursing mother, who participates with Faith and Hope in the allegory of redemption. This makes way for the variations played on the allegorical attributes of the female form so popular in late-eighteenth-century and early-Romantic tomb sculpture, all easily recuperable as the idealized tableau of family grief whose focus is the mother.[21] Flaxman's monument to Viscountess Fitzharris (1816–17) represents the mother reading the Bible to her two children, one curled up at her breast, the other standing at her knee, indicating that the naturalization of the allegorical figure need not be made at the expense of its exemplary function.[22] Nicholas Penny suggests it is hard to decide whether the representation of the mourning figure on late-eighteenth-century tombs is an idealized image of an actual female relative, or a personified attribute; but one way or another, she will contribute to a scene that is 'a paradigm of narrativity'.[23] More recently, it has been argued that the feminine presence, even when recruited for the most public-spirited ends, never perfectly suppresses the contests between the present and the past, the living and the dead, and the private and the public, that anciently she urges with such fierce monotony.[24]

Wright of Derby's *The Dead Soldier* was exhibited at the Royal Academy in 1789 and was an instant success. There are five surviving

[19] Weever, *Ancient Funerall Monuments*, 9.
[20] Warton, *Death-bed Scenes and Pastoral Conversations*, i. 108.
[21] Brian Kemp, *English Church Monuments* (London: Batsford, 1980), 125.
[22] David Irwin, 'Sentiment and Antiquity: European Tombs 1750–1830', in *Mirrors of Mortality*, ed. Joachim Whaley (New York: St Martin's Press, 1981), 144–5.
[23] Nicholas Penny, *Church Monuments in Romantic England* (New Haven, Conn.: Yale Univ. Press, 1977), 69; Garrett Stewart, *Death Sentences: Styles of Dying in British Fiction* (Cambridge, Mass.: Harvard Univ. Press, 1984), 5.
[24] Priscilla E. Muller, *Goya's Black Paintings* (New York: Hispanic Society of America, 1984), 153; Peter M. Sacks, *The English Elegy* (Baltimore: Johns Hopkins Univ. Press, 1985), 15; Joshua Scodel, *The English Poetic Epitaph* (Ithaca: Cornell Univ. Press, 1991), 331.

versions, and James Heath and J. L. Phillips made good business from prints of Heath's 1797 engraving. It seems to sit comfortably between the line of sentimental depictions of female loss Wright had been exploring in *Maria* (1781), *The Indian Widow* (1783–5), *Penelope Unravelling her Web* (1783–4), and *Romeo and Juliet* (1787–9), and the iconography of tomb sculpture on which *The Dead Soldier* draws and to which in turn it contributes. Wright borrows *The Indian Widow* from Canova's figure of Charity on the tomb of Clement XIV,[25] and *The Dead Soldier* inspires Richard Westmacott's *The Distressed Mother*, a classic funerary composition exhibited at the Royal Academy in 1822, together with such memorials as that to Anna Greaves (1819) in Watersperry Church, which reverses the positions of father and mother and has the infant suckling at a cold bosom.[26]

Despite the fact that *The Dead Soldier* (Fig. 3), like so many Royal Academy paintings, has a literary source, it makes very little sense narratively or allegorically. Langhorne's poem *The Country Justice* is claimed to provide a tale for the picture by assigning the causes of the behaviour of the local tramp—the father dead on a remote battlefield, and the mother's grief presaging the vagrancy of 'the child of misery baptiz'd in tears'[27]—yet the image is still enigmatic. How has the soldier died? Has he staggered back from the battle fatally wounded, to expire at the feet of his family? Has a stray bullet hit him while he was tenderly leaning over them? In any event, why is a domestic scene set so close to a battle? Richard Payne Knight suggests that it is the accumulation rather than the interrogation of these circumstances that improve the pathos of 'Mr Wright's Soldier's Tent' and give it the local colour ('minute precision and exactitude in the detailed relations of all common circumstances') upon which all sentimental relations depend.[28] Ronald Paulson is happier with a representation of attributes that borders on allegory ('She may be identified as the widow or she may be only an allegorical figure, but she fills, in the little drama of family and gender, the role of a wife'[29]). On the other hand, John Bender reads Wright's work from this period as exhibiting the absorptive qualities identified by Michael Fried in contemporary French painting, which breach the

[25] Robert Rosenblum, *Transformations in Late Eighteenth-Century Art* (Princeton, NJ: Princeton Univ. Press, 1967), 45.

[26] See Nicholas Penny, *Church Monuments*, and Irvine Loudon, *Death in Childbirth* (Oxford: Clarendon Press, 1992). For a fuller account of Wright of Derby's debts and contributions to tomb sculpture see Ronald Paulson, *Breaking and Remaking: Aesthetic Practice in England 1700–1780* (New Brunswick, NJ: Rutgers Univ. Press, 1989).

[27] John Langhorne, *The Country Justice: A Poem* (London: T. Becket, 1774), 17.

[28] *Analytical Enquiry into the Principles of Taste* (London, 1805), 305, 283.

[29] *Breaking and Remaking: Aesthetic Practice in England 1700–1800* (New Brunswick, NJ: Rutgers Univ. Press, 1989), 245.

comfortable sentimental relation of viewer to painful subject.[30] The inescapably erotic lighting of the woman's bosom, however, and the child's indisputable role in fastening the viewer's eye upon it, indicates a wider entry-point for the gaze than absorptive tableaux generally supply. Is this erotic appeal the necessary effect of narrative breakdown, such as occurs (Norman Bryson maintains) when the body's history and customary speech are silenced in favour of the voyeuristic pleasures supplied by its postures and attitudes?[31] Or is it that the nursing mother is supplying a new icon for fresh political and social agendas?[32]

The fact that all these questions and suggestions are buoyant, and that no answer deals decisively with the issues they raise, indicates the difficult and indeterminate relation of the viewer's eye to Wright's picture. In some respects, it conforms with the pattern of his more famous pieces, such as *An Experiment on a Bird in the Air Pump* (1768), *Miravan Breaking Open the Tomb of his Ancestors* (1772), and *A Blacksmith's Shop* (1771), where a conflict is depicted between a project of public utility and a personal sense of loss. A battle, an imperial tomb, a machine for making a vacuum, and a forge stand as the object of a collective effort which leaves one or more of its witnesses sightless as they turn away in pain from the process, with their hands or arms in front of their eyes. Because Wright is always very interested in effects of chiaroscuro, the lighting of the conflict bears on its outcome, the public project generally being the source or focus of light, while the darkness gathers up the defeated spectators, who retreat to it in the act of shielding their eyes. There is another common element linking the female victims of light, and that is their *décolletage*. In the *Air Pump*, the dresses of both children are worn quite deeply off the shoulder. In *An Iron Forge* (1772) and *An Iron Forge viewed from without* (1773), the women standing to the right of the trip hammer have their shoulders bare; so do *Maria* (1781) and *The Corinthian Maid* (1782–85). *The Indian Widow* (1785) is naked to the waist, and so is the curiously epicene figure of Telemachus in *Penelope Unravelling her Web* (1785).

In *The Dead Soldier* the elements of chiaroscuro, a hidden face, and an exposed breast are combined in a classically conceived mourning scene, such as those Wright copied into his Roman sketchbook.[33] It is

---

[30] John Bender, *Imagining the Penitentiary: Fiction and the Architecture of Mind in Eighteenth-Century England* (Chicago: Univ. of Chicago Press, 1987), 238.

[31] Norman Bryson, *Word and Image* (Cambridge: Cambridge Univ. Press, 1981), 91–5.

[32] On the 'moral politics of the bosom' see Simon Schama, *Citizens* (Harmondsworth: Penguin, 1989), 147; and Nicholas Roe, *Wordsworth and Coleridge: The Radical Years*, 126–30.

[33] Inscribed 'J. Wright, Feb.y 1774', British Museum, Dept. of Prints and Drawings, case 199 n; no. a 16.

possible that the erotic prominence of the breasts was suggested to him by Poussin's *Rinaldo and Armida* (Fig. 4), sold in London at Christie's the year before (1788), and destined to provide Mary Wollstonecraft with bosom-centred associations of desire and mourning.[34] The significance of the naked breast to Wright, however, seems to have more in common with the unregulated transports of the Greek original than with subsequent developments. He produced *The Dead Soldier* between two lengthy and severe bouts of depression. In 1783 he complained to William Hayley of 'ill-health for these sixteen years past (the core of my life) [which] has subjected me to many idle days, and bowed down my attempts towards fame and fortune'.[35] Ten years later he wrote to John Phillips of his despair of ever seeing the engraving of *The Dead Soldier* finished, adding 'I am now wounded at so many points, I despair of ever being well again' (Bemrose, 94). In letters to his sister Nancy, prone like himself to find her 'honest heart' agitated by the world's contrarieties, the symptom of distress is a 'ruffled bosom', in its natural state 'formed for peace and sweet repose' (Bemrose, 34). The major portion of his *œuvre* between these attacks of depression deals with ruffled bosoms, or with bosoms bare in order to indicate consternation or grief, the result (as he told Nancy) of a world 'made up of good and ill'. And he conceived of *The Dead Soldier* as a dramatic image of bosom-ruffling contrariety, for 'It is related that Wright said before he painted the "Dead Soldier", that he would depict the greatest possible sorrow, yet there would be a smiling face in the picture' (Bemrose, 70).

The baby's is a Cupid's smile that does not complicate or intensify so much as interrupt or deflect the viewer's sympathetic interest in the greatest possible sorrow. The spectator's function as delegate or redeemer is blocked by a swerve of the eye that is no less the gesture of its viewer than it is the afflicted widow's and the baby's. The gaze moves from the smile to the bosom, from the bosom to the dead soldier, from the dead soldier to the fallen mobcap, and so back to well-lit breasts too voluptuous to warrant the immemorial iconography of the ruffled bosom, or even the poignancy of mingled sorrow and joy which Wright seems to have had in mind. There is only a turning away from a turning away that leaves the widow as it were doubly alone in an unreadable tableau. Her grief is an unrelative private event, deliberately removed

[34] Maria, the heroine, has been separated from her nursling child and placed in a madhouse. Her fellow-prisoner Darnforth is attracted by her mind and 'her well-proportioned, and even almost voluptuous figure', now fuller than ever owing to her tragic circumstances. When they share their first moment of rapturous sympathy, it is as if, 'by a powerful spell, we had been transported into Armida's garden'. *The Wrongs of Woman: or Maria, A Fragment*, ed. Gary Kelly (Oxford: Oxford Univ. Press, 1976), 101.
[35] William Bemrose, *The Life and Works of Joseph Wright A.R.A.* (London: Bernrose and Sons, 1885), 61.

from the public sphere of allegory and narrative, but at the same time bereft of a deputizing eye that might ensure the passage and repetition of its intense matters of fact. In this respect the soldier's wife presents a memorandum of a very private grief, and an image of a bosom so singularly ruffled there is no sharing its pangs: 'It is not possible in this world to comprehend a state so perfectly miserable; all one can say, to give some idea of it, is this:—'Tis a ghastly solitude, by the separation it finds itself in from all union and society; 'tis a dreadful desolation, by the want of all consolation; 'tis a cruel rupture, which violently rends the soul from every object of its love'.[36]

Just such an uncontrollable experience of loss was to be endured by Wright's friend, Sir Brooke Boothby, when his daughter Penelope died of meningitis in 1791, at the age of six. On her tomb, a block stele surmounted by a life-size representation of the child, carved by Thomas Banks in Carrara marble (Fig. 5), Boothby inscribed a number of fragments in Italian, Latin, and French, together with two pieces of English: a verse of Job (3: 26)—'I was not in safety, neither had I rest, and the trouble came'—and a simple statement: 'She was in form and intellect most exquisite. The unfortunate parents ventured their all on this frail Bark, and the wreck was total'.[37] Like Godwin, Boothby is under no illusions about what remains of his child ('a little senseless dust'); so the eloquence of the monument is devoted not so much to commemorating the dead Penelope, as to recording the agony of those who have lost her. The writer stands on the same side of the grave as the reader, that is to say, promising the sort of useful proximity of sufferer and redeemer at which the verse from Job might be understood to glance. The sequel, however, indicates very little comfort for Boothby from this quarter.

He expands the tomb inscriptions into a sonnet sequence expressive of the isolation of intense grief, of the irrelevance of consolation, and of the illegibility of the various memorials he has constructed. He detaches his complaint from its object: Penelope is never to know a grief like his, for 'she from woes like mine was ta'en away' (Sonnet iv); he detaches it also from its audience, introducing the *Sorrows* to the reader with the wish, 'Mayest thou never experience the sorrows they describe' (5). It ought to come as no surprise to him, therefore, to find that such a singular pain can find no relief in common sense and those 'vain precepts, which the unwounded breast | Dictates, at ease, to sufferings never known' (Sonnet iv). To the proposition that thousands every day sustain the loss of a

---

[36] Elizabeth Rowe, *Friendship in Death: In Twenty Letters* (London, 1740), 78.
[37] These are transcribed (and translated) in Sir Brooke Boothby and Anna Seward, *Monumental Inscriptions in Ashbourn Church, Derbyshire* (Parkes: Ashbourn, 1806).

child, he responds, 'Obdurate Comforter! shall others' woe, | Soften the bitter anguish I endure!' (Sonnet xxi). Amidst a number of Joban exclamations ('Did I not weep for him that was in pain!' 'Mine eyes are weary of the sun'), he promises, 'All that on earth remains, shall ne'er avail, | To stop unfailing tears and endless sighs' (Sonnet x). These remnants include the tomb Banks has made, Fuseli's picture of Penelope being gathered into heaven by an angel, and a locket with the child's hair set in crystal. None of these things conveys to his mind anything but an unimprovable idea of ruin. The exquisite accuracy of the marble figure reminds him of the simple and literal matter of fact that of her most radiant and expressive gestures 'a little senseless dirt alone remains' (Sonnet xii). Fuseli's picture cannot cheat 'these weary eyes'; and the lock of hair ('last relic of an angel face') is as insignificant and as inanimate as the living creature was warm and intelligent.

These empty signs join with the allegorical poverty of the *Sorrows* to denarrativize Penelope's death, and to present it as nothing but a colossal interruption. Like the sculpture, personified agencies are cold and pointless: 'The steps of Grace, and Beauty's radiant bloom, | Are but mementoes of the mouldering tomb' (Sonnet xxi); and like the tomb they advertise nothing but death and decay: 'Come then, cold crystal, on this bosom lie, | Till Love, and Grief, and fond Remembrance die' (Sonnet xvii). When Boothby tries to find a moral in his suffering, as in Sonnet xviii, where he wonders if the Joban sequence that leads from happiness to foreboding, and from foreboding to loss, might not be reversed, the argument fails. His mind cannot advance: either it comes up sharply against the literal and simple senseless dirt in the vault, or it circles among tautologies: Penelope was 'young in her youth, and graceful in her grace' (Sonnet i). In the Preface to his *Fables and Satires* he had pointed out that the dramatized maxims of an Aesopean fable are designed for 'the generality of mankind, and for daily occasions'. Exceptional experiences are beyond such regulation: 'Extraordinary persons do not need them; and extraordinary circumstances are therefore exceptions to common rules'.[38] He defines his own extraordinary position in a sonnet sequence which, like the tomb, the picture, the locket, and all the other empty signs of consolation, can communicate no idea and no intensity to anyone but himself. It is an exclusively self-memorializing technique, which the other artefacts merely variegate. Boothby has turned himself into inscription and reader, but at the cost of redemption. His function is endlessly to remind himself of a loss he cannot forget, and to supply the proof of a fact he once deprecated: namely, that

---

[38] Sir Brooke Boothby, *Fables and Satires* (Edinburgh: George Ramsay, 1809), p. xxiii.

excessive feelings breed from themselves, mourning is born of mourning as 'anger generates anger and intemperance begets intemperance'.[39]

In the *Sorrows*, Boothby describes himself in the classic funerary pose in which Wright painted him in 1781, lying by a stream where 'soft murmurs soothe the shadowy bower' (Sonnet ix). In the picture he holds a copy of Rousseau's manuscript, published by Boothby the previous year, which intervenes between the viewer and the pensive figure to justify and redeem his melancholy. The book deals with the difficulties of bringing the anguish of a feeling heart into the public sphere, and with an egoism whose tendency is to trigger again the very pangs it details: 'Tandis que je force mes yeux à suivre les lignes, mon coeur gémit et soupire'.[40] It is Rousseau's familiar complaint, soothed by the expected adjustment between the particularities of the feeling heart and the virtues instinctive in the generality of humankind. 'Les passions douces et primitives qui naissent immédiatement de l'amour de soi' (31) vibrate with 'tous les premiers mouvemens de la nature [qui] sont bons et droits' (26). Boothby is the medium of this vibration, having (as he puts it in a sonnet predating the *Sorrows*), 'taught the tear | To glisten in his eye for other's pain'.[41] Wright's picture shows Boothby as reader successfully mediating, softening, and incorporating the ills of life, and offering the viewer the identical opportunity of reading well, and agreeably to his belief that 'Suspended woe to ecstasy can warm, | Or gild with transient beam the darkest fate' (*Sorrows*, 43).

The revolution in Boothby's opinions on the gilding of darkest fates coincides with his published disagreements with Burke on the subject of the French Revolution. It is apropos Burke's excessive rhetoric in the *Reflections* that Boothby (presently 'free from all anxiety' and untroubled by premonitions of what is to happen five months later) observes that 'anger generates anger and intemperance begets intemperance'.[42] He associates this passionate extremism with the sort of political absolutism which he understands Burke to be palliating, both in the *Reflections* and in *An Appeal from the New to the Old Whigs* (1791). Power unhindered by abstract principles and 'great and general truths'[43] is self-breeding. 'It is of the essence of power to encrease by its own force,' he observes, and quotes Pope to the effect that it 'grows with our growth, and strengthens with our strength' (*A Letter*, 77). It isolates

---

[39] Sir Brooke Boothby, *Observations on the Appeal from the New to the Old Whigs* (London: John Stockdale, 1792), 80.

[40] *Rousseau Juge de Jean-Jacques* (Lichfield: J. Jackson, 1780), 16.

[41] *Sorrows Sacred to the Memory of Penelope* (London: W. Bulmer, 1796), 55.

[42] *Observations*, pp. iii, 80.

[43] Sir Brooke Boothby, *A Letter to the Right Honourable Edmund Burke* (London: J. Debrett, 1791), 6.

its monopolists, for kings, 'having no equal, they can have no friend nor no competitor' (*A Letter*, 25). It transforms its votaries, such as Pitt the Younger, into undistracted lovers of the self: 'a minister chaunting forth his own praises in a canticle known to be of his own inditing, echoed back by thanking himself for his own exploits' (*Observations*, 238). Its characteristic is 'a narrow selfish egotism, where every man feels himself one central point of his own little circle of luxuries and conveniences, and holds a stupid indifference to the public concern' (*A Letter*, 99). And with an irony impossible for Boothby to control, he asks Pitt not to 'forget that the day must come when all his glories, will be comprised in the narrow compass of an epitaph' (*Observations*, 218).

For the French to be denied the right of ending their suffering under this species of self-bred oppression, Boothby would have to suppose a society destitute of moral ties, and blindly moving without the guides of historical precedent. Under these privations a revolution becomes a monstrous and unthinkable event, and the agency of the mass of the people an inconceivable momentum—as he takes Burke to be saying that indeed both are. But he insists that revolutions, like the sociable impulses of sympathy, gild the darkest fates by combining individuals in acts of resistance to the iniquities of power, vindicating the people in a 'most magnificent spectacle . . . [of] a great and generous nation, animated with one soul, rising up as one man to demand restitution of their natural rights' (*A Letter*, 26). This is not a wild usurpation of power, Boothby insists, but 'a grand precedent' for a redrawn contract and a healthy state (*A Letter*, 111). It is the equivalent in the public sphere of medicines in the private: 'A revolution is the only true specific' (*A Letter*, 10).

'I and my family are, thank God, in good health,' he declares at the end of the *Observations*, tempting providence once again, 'and when any of us are ill, we use . . . known and tried remedies' (274). But when the words thunder in his ears, 'Thy child is gone' (Sonnet ii), none of these remedies avails to reduce the inconceivable and unparalleled agony of such a change. Boothby's mind, in Wordsworth's phrase, fastens with absolute sovereignty upon itself; he has no choice but to become an absolutist and egoist in his grief, a monarch without competitor in the realm of unlimited anguish, a William Pitt of pain, revolving in the vicious circles of tautology and self-generation an intensity he is incapable of passing on. He enters a condition without precedent or remedy, where his extraordinary circumstances are indifferent to common rules. He mourns a daughter whose qualities ('young in her youth, graceful in her grace') are analogues of a mind that fastens upon itself, encouraging anguish to breed anguish as power breeds power: that is, sovereignly and without competitor or restraint. The castigation of Pitt's political egoism boomerangs upon the parent who grieves because he grieves: He is 'a father chaunting forth his own grief in a canticle known to be of his own inditing, echoed back by the immiseration of himself in his own misery'.

Burke had already analyzed the politics of Boothby's crisis, and shown why someone as susceptible as he to extraordinary circumstances was tempting providence a third time in declaring he would live and die in 'the old-fashioned despised principles of Whiggism' (*A Letter*, 116). According to Burke, the spokesman of Old Whigs, extraordinary circumstances arise when individuals, claiming to have access to the voice and the rights of the People, produce an authority and precedent for revolution, and seek to 'methodize anarchy; to perpetuate and fix disorder'.[44] The rhetoric of extraordinary circumstances is a convenient way of disguising personal injuries as public injustices, and proposing local circumstances as reasons for a general usurpation. Such complaints echo the banalities of patriotism, 'idle lamentation of the calamities of their country',[45] but they are also very dangerous. Burke had parodied them in his mock-patriotic piece, *A Vindication of Natural Society* (1756), but was obliged to take a much more serious view of them forty-five years later. The agitation of grievances and the fomenting of disorder can beget that 'foul, impious, monstrous thing, wholly out of the course of moral nature', a revolution.[46] The *Reflections*, as J. G. A. Pocock has recently emphasized, passionately defend the structure of British political practice against 'a force utterly new in European and perhaps human history—the energies of mind set free from any social or historical discipline whatever'.[47] This force, notionally defined and empowered by certain fundamental rights, is what Boothby undertakes to defend in his two pamphlets written against Burke. In his view, the People exists as a collective party to a contract, armed with a precedent for revolution by virtue of the Glorious Revolution and the American Revolution. When 'the great mass of the people,' 'this vast and unwieldy machine', suffers more than is tolerable from the self-growth of power, it must call itself into action to cure 'this great and grievous disease' with 'the only true specific'. (*A Letter*, 17, 10)

In *The Appeal* Burke makes two points about this notion of revolution that recall the dynamic of his sublime. First, he argues that power is not susceptible to any force derived from the moral intelligence of

---

[44] *An Appeal from the Old to the New Whigs* (London: J. Dodsley, 1791), 10.

[45] Edmund Burke, *Thoughts on the Causes of the Present Discontents* (London: J. Dodsley, 1770), 1–3.

[46] *An Appeal from the Old to the New Whigs*, 10.

[47] J. G. A. Pocock, 'The Devil has Two Horns', *London Review of Books* 16/4 (24 Feb. 1994), 11.

human beings. 'I know of no sanction to any contract, actual or virtual, against the will of prevalent power' (*An Appeal*, 121). Like the illimitable power of God in the *Enquiry*, power in the state cannot be modified by resistance (look at Lucifer), only by the screens and veils which obscure the light of power, and transform it into images which, in his political works, Burke associates with use, custom, and the fictions of common law: 'Dark and inscrutable are the ways by which we come into the world' (*An Appeal*, 122). When these ways are questioned and overturned under the government of the new empire of light and reason, collectivity disappears for all practical purposes (and in the absence of principles these are the only ones that count). The People survive not even as a New Whig theory; they disintegrate into 'a number of vague loose individuals, and nothing more' (125). To prevent this atomization of society, and to preserve the obscure customs and politic veils which give power at least the appearance of gentleness, Burke unfolds the tautology of power as a force modifiable by the virtualities arising from practice, not as a criterion immune from politics: 'For there is no medium besides the medium itself. That medium is not such, because it is found there; but it is found there, because it is conformable to truth and nature' (*An Appeal*, 112). The same reflexive alertness to the practical possibilities of an untheorized mediation between power and the public, which he analyzes in the *Enquiry* as the choice arising from looking at looking, and in the *Reflections* as the eye's adjustment to the oblique beams of royal power, is here proposed as the only real and lasting instrument of political amelioration.

When Boothby is overtaken by the revolution in his private life which is, despite his forebodings, an unparalleled and unrelative event against which there is no appeal, he is without the redeeming medium of the Old Whig, and bereft of the rights and principles of a New Whig. His voice contracts to the range and repetition of a loose individual denied the opportunity of transferring his intensities to his reader, or of universalizing them as a public narrative. He inhabits an anarchy which cannot be methodized and which combines the extremes of absolute sovereignty and revolutionary usurpation. His cries reverberate among disjointed particulars which are nothing but themselves ('a little senseless dirt'), loose and individual, and with savage monotony they echo the indefeasible tautologies of an exceptional grief. In his last sonnet he talks of natural life as an aggregation of pains which 'the cultured intellect' is destined to feel to their 'exquisite extent' precisely because they cannot be ordered or methodized. As for the restraint of social laws, he can instance only the terror of 'War's horrid art; commerce in man that deals; | Dread superstition's threats, and torture's racks and wheels'

(Sonnet xxiv). With uncanny accuracy Boothby catches the tone and literalizes the irony of Burke's mimicry of Bolingbroke in his *Vindication*, where the apologist of natural society asks us to 'take a Review of the Dungeons, Whips, Chains, Racks, Gibbets, with which every Society is abundantly stored, by which hundreds of Victims are annually offered up to support a dozen or two in Pride and Madness, and Millions in abject Servitude'.[48] For Boothby, the analogy between universal abjection and the exquisite torments of private grief is now utterly uncomfortable, an oppression or a usurpation equally incapable of remedy, a nightmare of foul and monstrous circumstances.

The combination of an in-turned misery, a female figure, and a burst of patriot oratory is perfectly represented in James Barry's aquatint, *Job Reproved by his Friends*, which he dedicated to Burke. The picture shows Job plunged in grief, while in the background his dead children are being carried home. In the left foreground Eliphaz is pointing a moral and teaching a lesson, in opposition to Job's wife, who from the centre of the composition directs her vigorous complaint to heaven. The imbecility of grief so heavily marked in Job's countenance compares with Barry's other two notable studies of extreme misery, his aquatints of *Philoctetes* (1777) and of *King Lear and Cordelia* (1776). Eliphaz takes up the same position *vis-à-vis* Job as Zenocrates to the figure of Polemon in *Job*'s companion piece, *The Conversion of Polemon* (1778) (Fig. 7); and the general resemblance of these two counsellors is explained by a remark of Barry's to Fox, to the effect that Zenocrates is based upon 'ye general figure of Mr. Edmund Burke'.[49] The face of Job's wife, on the other hand, owes much to the aquiline profile of William Pitt the Elder, which Barry was to delineate again in *William Pitt, Earl of Chatham* (1778) (Fig. 8) and in the figure of Pericles in the large Society of Arts piece, *Crowning the Victors at Olympia* (1777–84) (see Pressly, 81).

The history of 'Independent Barry'[50] and his relations with Burke, whose protégé he was from 1765 until 1774, when a disagreement about how to arrange sittings for a portrait put an end to cordial exchanges, forms a fascinating tale of abnormal sensitivity, of a patron's advice neglected and his warnings ignored by a man notorious for his thin skin and his obsessive defence of his own honour and originality. Burke's advice to Barry in the matter of painting was to avoid the false sublime of magnitude ('Any madman can describe a giant striding from

---

[48] *A Vindication of Natural Society* (London: M. Cooper, 1756), 39.
[49] Barry to Fox, 5 October 1800, Beinecke Library; cited in William L. Pressly, *The Life and Art of James Barry* (New Haven, Conn.: Yale Univ. Press, 1981), 81.
[50] A sobriquet invented for him by William Blake; see Pressly, 1.

London to York'), and instead to attend to the particulars: 'Minute and thorough knowledge of anatomy, and practical as well as theoretical perspective . . . is all the effect of labour and use in *particular* studies, and not in general compositions'.[51] In the matter of personal conduct he warned him against too freely accommodating the fancy that he alone of all men possessed integrity:

That you have had just subjects of indignation always, and of anger often, I do no ways doubt; who can live in the world without some trial of his patience? But believe me, my dear Barry, that the arms with which the ill dispositions of the world are to be combated, and the qualities by which it is to be reconciled to us, and we reconciled to it, are moderation, gentleness, a little indulgence to others, and a great deal of distrust of ourselves. (*The Works of Barry* i. 156)

To enforce his warning he made a short but accurate forecast of Barry's life as a modern Job, commencing with his return from Rome:

By degrees you will produce some of your own works. They will be variously criticised; you will defend them; you will abuse those that have attacked you; expostulations, discussions, letters, possibly challenges, will go forward; you will shun your brethren, they will shun you. In the mean time gentlemen will avoid your friendship, for fear of being engaged in your quarrels: you will fall into distresses, which will only aggravate your disposition for farther quarrrels; you will be obliged for maintenance to do any thing for any body; your very talents will depart, for want of hope and encouragement, and you will go out of the world fretted, disappointed, and ruined.[52]

For his part, Barry was resolved to preserve the character of Job, posing the question, 'What am I?' and coming up with this answer: 'I saw from the beginning that I was hated . . . and hated for the very dispositions I relied upon to recommend me . . . I found myself of that stubborn disposition either to conquer or perish in [the cause of resistance]' (*The Works of Barry* i. 207, 170). The world which he is resisting he characterizes as a vast game of chance, 'a great chasm of doubt and disbelief' in which it is impossible to find 'a remedy and a balsam for . . . the disappointment of baffled ambition, pride, avarice, and of all the other pursuits, where the hopes of multitudes of men finish in disappointment, ruin, and chagrin'.[53] His resistance is to enshrine in art, particularly in the vast canvases he painted for the Society of Arts, the highest ideals of artistic composition and civic virtue. During the French Revolution, he reminded the public of these great principles by publishing etchings based on *Elysium* and *Crowning the Victors*, in which he draws a series of

---

[51] *The Works of James Barry Esq.* 2 vols. (London: J. M'Creery, 1809), i. 264, 88.

[52] *The Works of Barry*, i. 156.

[53] *An Inquiry into the Obstruction to the Acquisition of the Arts in England* (1774), in *The Works of Barry* ii. 288.

radical parallels between ancient and modern systems of political liberty and indicates how the polity might be restored to health by committing itself fully to principles of religious toleration and republican government. In this enterprise he salutes only those radicals as isolated as himself (such as 'the long-to-be-lamented Mary Wolstonecraft'[54]), until he is left quite alone to relish the paradox of the patriot so ardent in the pursuit of virtue that he loses his constituency. 'Could any one have believed,' he writes to the Earl of Buchan shortly before his death, 'that so singular an example of a man whose exertions on the publick service God had crowned with a success so unique could have been so long left struggling, without any protection from the baneful envy & malignity which such exertions must necessarily exite.'[55] It seems consistent with the aggressive vulnerability of such a singular and unique phenomenon as Barry, that the only reward of his public service was to have his front garden filled with dead cats and other noisome refuse, and, when he was dying and needed to lie down, to find his front door keyhole blocked up with pebbles (Pressly, 198).

Barry presents more acutely and publicly the same contradictions between civic business and private misery that are to be found in Wright's paintings of the 1780s and in the political and poetical discourses surrounding Boothby's commission of a tomb for his daughter Penelope. What distinguishes his choice of a female figure from theirs is that Job's wife is androgynous, vocal, and (by implication at least) political. Her posture might be interpreted as a sign of Barry's enduring commitment to radical principles, as well as to radical women such as Wollstonecraft, notwithstanding the many rebuffs he received for his implicit faith in them. Is she the most finished embodiment of public spirit in female form, the final reconciliation of individual exigency with the principles of public utility? John Barrell has argued along these lines, descrying a horizon beyond the petty opposition of the public to the ideals of Barry the artist-hero, where the 'civic theory of history painting [is adapted] in such a way as to enable it to represent and foster what [Barry] understands to be the properly egalitarian nature of mass society'.[56] In the pictures and aquatints produced between 1776 and 1778, however, the place of principle, and of the pedagogy it must sustain if principle is to provide a basis of community, is very insecure; and its

[54] 'Her honest heart, so estranged from all selfishness, and which could take so deep and generous an interest in whatever had relation to truth and justice . . . would find some matter for consolation, in discovering that the ancient nations of the world entertained a very different opinion of female capabilities from those modern . . . degrading notions of female nature.' *A Letter to the Dilettanti Society*, in *Works of Barry* ii. 594.

[55] Letter from Barry to the Earl of Buchan, 21 Dec. 1804; cited in Pressly, 190.

[56] John Barrell, *The Political Theory of Painting from Reynolds to Hazlitt* (New Haven, Conn.: Yale Univ. Press, 1986), 217.

insecurity is bound up with Barry's conflicted relationship with his patron, Burke.

To the companion pieces of *Job Reproved* and *The Conversion of Polemon* there ought to be added a third, *Ulysses and a Companion fleeing from the Cave of Polyphemus* (1776) (Fig. 9), where Barry himself is represented as the companion, and Burke, his finger raised in warning or admonition, takes the part of Ulysses. With its daring insertion of modern personalities into an ancient story, Barry strengthens a hint already present in the other two aquatints which was to be fully developed in the Society of Arts pictures. In *Commerce, or the Triumph of the Thames*, for instance, he shows heroes from modern history, such as Raleigh, Drake, and Cook, collaborating with personifications, such as the Thames, Europe, and Africa. Here the mixture of allegory and history enacts his belief in the relevance of ancient principles to present enterprises. But in *Job Reproved* and its related pieces it is, on the contrary, the troubled relation between advice and conduct which is being dramatized. Lear and Philoctetes, for example, are given no advice worth heeding: underneath *King Lear and Cordelia* is inscribed Lear's death-song, addressed to Edgar and Kent, the futile moralizers of his case, 'Howl, howl, howl, howl,—O, you are men of Stone | Had I your tongues and eyes, I'd use them so, | That heaven's vault should crack' (see Pressly, 266). Although Zenocrates'/Burke's advice to Polemon/Charles Fox may succeed in reclaiming a libertine, Ulysses/Burke is teaching his companion/Barry how to play a trick, where it is not principle but cleverness and discretion that count. It is a scene that sums up Barry's own feelings about the advice Burke had been giving him, where the emphasis is placed squarely on an easy adjustment of conscience and honour to the demands of social practice, and on an analogous reconciliation of the vulgarity of little circumstances with the grand outlines of the sublime. In *Job Reproved* the cruel pointlessness of Eliphaz's counsel is underlined by the lethargy with which Job receives it and by the jabbing finger with which it is enforced, to reappear in *Polemon*, and later in Blake's version of the Job story (derived from Barry's), where the comforters line up behind their pointing fingers like Goya's firing squad.

This leaves Job's wife, whose distress, somewhat modified by the indignation of her own pointing finger and her patriot profile, presents an intriguing alternative to the pragmatism of Burkean instructions. Is she singing her husband's death-song, or taking up the *conclamatio* of the grieving female? Is she loudly repeating the same word, like Lear, or developing the see-saw figure of stychomythia? The finger suggests not; rather that she is introducing a moral or a principle, but in a radically different manner from Eliphaz. Barry means the viewer to assume that she is speaking with the same superb carelessness of petty consequences as Pitt, who was as disdainful of the present advantage as Burke (according to Barry at least) was attentive to it. An outline of Barry's estimate of Pitt's eloquence is to be found in the epitaph being inscribed by Britannia on the pyramid that forms the background to his bust in the aquatint *William Pitt*. There it is recorded that

The Secretary stood alone, modern degeneracy had not reached him, Original, and unaccommodating; the features of his character had the hardihood of Antiquity.—his august mind over-awed Majesty. . . . No state chicanery, no narrow system of vicious Politics, no idle contest for ministerial victories, sunk him to the vulgar level of the great; but overbearing, persuasive and impracticable, his object was England, his Ambition fame.   (Pressly, 271)

Job's wife is saying, then, that Job's integrity, like his anguish, is impermeable and without a competitor; and that so far from compromising with his circumstances to own a fault or to palter for forgiveness, he will, through her, impracticably and sovereignly proclaim his originality and hardihood for as long as she has breath for both of them. In short, Job is James Barry, his principles justified before God by Pitt, disguised as an outraged woman, in opposition to Burke/Eliphaz, whose chicanery and pragmatic vulgarity masquerade as sound advice.

Although Wright's and Boothby's unredeemed extremity ends up in a private terror comparable to the intensities of other singular subjectivities, despotically revolutionary or absolutely monarchical, it might be supposed that Barry has avoided such isolation by finding his *go'el* in Pitt, or at least in the inscribed stone of his epitaph, which speaks for the marginalized artist as well as the incorruptible statesman. But to suppose this requires a naïve estimation of Pitt's public spirit of which Barry alone is capable. His reading of Pitt's proud patriot disclaimers of private interest univocalizes their extravagance just as Boothby's intense loneliness causes him to literalize the ironies of Burke's mock-patriotic *Vindication*. We saw in Chapter 5 that principle always comes first in Pitt's list of topics, and last in order of his imperatives. The blend of hauteur and impudence that distinguishes equally his behaviour in power and out of it is proof not of an unswerving obedience to the calls of public spirit, but of a politics evolved out of the tactical use of political language itself. The habitual self-instantiation of the patriot orator as the marginalized embodiment of ancient virtue— 'I am traduced, aspersed, calumniated from morning to night'[57]—is produced as a self-evident disqualification from public office that works

---

[57] Horace Walpole, *Memoirs of George II*, ed. John Brooke, 3 vols. (New Haven, Conn.: Yale Univ. Press, 1941), ii. 78.

as one of the most effective instruments in acquiring one. The austerities and despairs of the loose individual are the factitious themes of those provisional narratives which, as J. C. D. Clark has pointed out, help to unfold the tautology of politics as politics amidst the common pursuit of local tactical advantages, both in the Commons and the Court.[58] This necessarily renders the patriot's actions 'like himself' only after a manner of speaking, since the resemblance is never so entire as not to serve a political end, or not to ornament the political version of the legal fiction.

Pitt operates perfectly in accordance with Burke's doctrine that 'there is no medium besides the medium itself' (*An Appeal*, 112) by ensuring that his sublime genealogies of principle never harm his interests at the level of the vulgar private interest, and never introduce an ideal so divorced from practice that it would demand a pointless sacrifice to claim it. Barry fails to understand this, mortgaging himself to imperatives he understands to be absolute, whose sublimity (as far as he is concerned) is without the alloy of particularity, and whose inscription therefore resists all acts of redemption, since the attempt to read Pitt as the subject of antecedent intensities, and to locate himself as the parallel of his unparalleled patriotism, in fact ends up as a categorical statement of an impracticable idealism that is peculiarly, sovereignly, and unrepeatably Barry's own, strictly without a parallel. He is destined to read only himself in others in proportion as he believes himself engaged in projects of civic virtue, broadly defensive of the commonwealth of patriots or Barrell's egalitarian mass society. Although a correspondent in the *General Advertiser* accused him of writing panegyrics 'by HIMSELF to HIMSELF',[59] this is exactly the reflexive faculty for looking at looking through a medium which is only a medium which Barry is the least likely of his contemporaries to command.

He sets out frozen in the absolute gestures which Boothby and Wright are forced eventually to adopt, proud of the originality of his character. His reading of Job can vindicate only the singularity of his own case, and reproduce (as Burke foretells) the very isolation of which the patriarch complains. Whatever solace Job expects from the epitaph carved in the rock, Barry sedulously removes it—every shred of it—not by returning to the false counsel of Eliphaz, nor by entering too deeply into the primitive iterations of female mourning, but by believing that a candid appeal to principle is on its own sufficient to justify a life.[60]

[58] *The Dynamics of Change: The Crisis of the 1750s and English Party Systems* (Cambridge: Cambridge Univ. Press, 1982), 16.

[59] *General Advertiser*, 19 Jan. 1778; cited in Pressly, *Works of James Barry*, 88.

[60] Burke scorns the impracticality of such appeals: 'It is surely no very rational account of a man's life, that he has always acted right; but has taken special care, to act in such a manner that his endeavours could not possibly be productive of any consequence.' *Thoughts on the Present*

The ninth and tenth books of *The Prelude* summarize the difficulties faced by the loose individual when tackling the infoliate tautologies of power. Wordsworth considers the French Revolution under a number of headings—history, femininity, patriotism, law, power, pedagogy—only to find that its aggregation of unrelative, or what he defines as self-sanctioning, events (x. 615) twists the logic of each explanatory category into a vicious circle, and leaves each fancied exemplary instance without a precedent or an application, including the first person who wishes to bring reason and example to bear upon a scene where 'all things were to me | Loose and disjointed' (ix. 106–7). He solves these difficulties by subjecting the revolution to the same transformation he had already effected in his nature poetry. He turns his theme into a 'larger grave-yard', to adapt Geoffrey Hartman's phrase, so that 'the division between revolution and cemetery is hardly felt'.[61] With that done, he can read it as an epitaph, and decode a message of redemption that is no longer blurred by the monotonous savageries of Robespierre's usurpation. By 'monumentalizing' the terror of unprecedented violence, as David Bromwich has indicated, Wordsworth can reintroduce the reciprocal conversion of a social and a personal good that compensates his earlier enthusiasm for the Revolution, 'reconstructing a humanity which the poet feels he has lost in a heartless agreement to do good on behalf of humanity'.[62]

At the heart of Paris, and at the beginning of the Terror, Wordsworth positions himself against the multitude of self-sanctioned events as the grieving viator: 'a woeful time, . . . most woeful for those few, | They had the deepest feeling of the grief, | Who still were flatter'd, and had trust in man' (x. 387–9). Hence the poet's certainty in grief, whatever other certainties he lacks: 'Yet did I grieve' (x.146). But the inscription he studies makes no sense, either as an imagined volume, 'being written in a tongue he cannot read' (x. 52), or as the literal stone he picks up from the ruins of the Bastille ('I look'd for something that I could not find, | Affecting more emotion than I felt' [ix. 70–1]), because he finds it hard to identify with the mass formations thrown up by the Revolution. After perfunctory experiments with the themes of patriotism ('I thus did soon | Become a Patriot, and my heart was all | given to the People'), and Gothic fancies ('many gleams of chivalrous delight' [ix. 503]), and after introducing but failing to thematize the image of the

Discontents, in *The Writings and Speeches of Edmund Burke*, ed. Paul Langford (Oxford: Clarendon Press, 1981), ii. 314.

⁶¹ Geoffrey H. Hartman, *The Unremarkable Wordsworth* (Minneapolis: Univ. of Minnesota Press, 1987), 34.
⁶² David Bromwich, 'Burke, Wordsworth, and the Defense of History', in *A Choice of Inheritance* (Cambridge, Mass.: Harvard Univ. Press, 1989), 69, 73.

grieving woman ('the Magdelene of le Brun . . . fair face | And rueful, with its everflowing tears' [ix. 78–80]), he returns to intensities that have all the dreariness of his celebrated 'spots of time', without any of their visionary uplift. The September Massacres strike out of him the same monotonous rhythm of an ancient lament: 'Year follows year, the tide returns again, | Day follows day, all things have a second birth' (x.72–3). It sounds like the background to the 'dull and heavy slackening' of the sixth book, following the weird oblivion of his crossing of the Alps, where he passes 'woods decaying, never to be decay'd' and hears winds thwarting winds, and 'the rocks that mutter'd close upon my ears, | Black drizzling crags that spake' (vi. 557–63). In these monotonies can be heard the skeleton's hoarse tremendous murmur, or the reverberative cry of primitive woe, delivered by Wordsworth in pleonasms, never more insistently than when he reacts to the pointlessness of serial slaughter, 'Head after head, and never heads enough' (x. 335).

The subject position corresponding to these pleonasms is extremely isolated: a voice hopelessly conducting its defence before unjust tribunals (x. 377), the target of 'unintelligible chastisements' (x. 415), and an outcast, at home neither in France nor England, 'like an uninvited Guest | Whom no one owned' (x. 272). But it is important to notice that it is an isolation not without parallel among the victims of Robespierre's tyranny. There is a strong identification with Louvet, Robespierre's forlorn accuser who tries to turn the tide of slaughter back upon its agents and pays the price of failure with his head; and with Madame Roland, who understands what crimes are committed in the name of liberty. At this point the detached first person avoids the extreme isolation of Boothby and Barry by nursing a dream of vengeance for the atrocities being committed, and ardently desiring that Moloch's regent be 'levell'd with the dust' (x. 469). These uneasy bursts of passion unnerve him because they obliterate the genealogies of love and duty that ought to constitute the subject: 'In the depth | Of those enormities, even thinking minds | Forgot at seasons whence they had their being' (x.346–8). In this state of amnesia, the first person loses a sense of community but enters into a terrible but intense sympathy with power: 'great my joy in vengeance', he cries when he hears that Robespierre is dead (x. 416, 540).

This excited relation of the loose individual to the absolute tyrant brings Wordsworth as close as he will ever get to the unsentimental function of the *go'el*, the vindicator of a particular suffering who responds with active intensity to the cry from the grave. The cost of this vengeful entry into the series of fatal usurpations is the derangement of the train of circumstances that makes history an intelligible and moral tale. His sense of a publicly legible chronicle overthrown, Wordsworth has uncanny presentiments of Kierkegaard's 'recollection forwards' when 'the fear gone by | Press'd on me almost like a fear to come' (x. 62–3). He is so deeply engaged in disjointed and self-sanctioning events he feels they make a mockery of history, 'the past and that to come' (ix. 172). By conglomerating so many violent particulars, and so many transient records and pamphlets, the Revolution prevents even eye-witnesses from doing justice to it, or from repairing the broken lines of descent connecting the society of the past to a civil future.

His efforts to remedy the breakdown in history with stories of the poets and chivalric fictions of patriotic deeds are doomed to fail because they are proposed as anodyne alternatives to a politics in which Wordsworth, the vindicator operating in sympathy with power, is actively and violently implicated. He can emerge from the problem only on the problem's own terms, which are those of the serial act of vengeance committed to redeem a dead innocent. Revenge comes to him in the afternoon of the day he spends visiting Cartmel Churchyard, for it is a few hours afterwards that he hears of Robespierre's death. Although he greets the news with vengeful joy, he marks the moment with the memory of his dead teacher, quickened that morning when he read the quotation of the quoted epitaph from Gray on Taylor's stone. The inscribed stone sends a message from the past to the future that is not effaced by violence, nor singularized or serialized by its pleonastic vehicle (quotation upon quotation). History and community are returned to the grieving traveller under the auspices of a dead teacher whose authority re-harmonizes the elements of poetry, chronicle, and principle that make the past flow sequentially and justly towards the future. That this reconciliation of the individual and the social is won by vengeance is a fact not ignored, but assuredly not to be repeated. David Bromwich believes that Wordsworth learned from Burke how to soften the brutality of power: 'In terror, | Remembered terror, there is love and peace'.[63] Through the medium of memory revolutionary matters of fact lose their intensity, and acquire instead the loving solicitude and the communitarian point of reference of the rural epitaph, whose commemoration of the instructive amity shared by the living and the dead is based upon the forgetfulness of particular pains and injuries. This is where the reading of epitaphs in the spirit of a *go'el*—which is the spirit of individual contention and opposition demanded by Job of his vindicators in the eighteenth century—ends.

---

[63] *The Borderers* iii. 5. ll. 1468–9; cited in Bromwich, *A Choice of Inheritance*, 73.

Bibliography

PRIMARY TEXTS

ADAIR, JAMES, *The History of the American Indians* (London: Charles and Edward Dilly, 1775).

AKENSIDE, MARK, 'The Pleasures of the Imagination', in *The Poems of Mark Akenside* (London, 1772).

ALISON, ARCHIBALD, *Essays on the Nature and Principles of Taste*, 2 vols. (Edinburgh, 1812).

ANON., *Impartial Remarks upon the Preface of Dr Warburton* (London: H. Cooper, 1758).

ANON., *The Case of the Unfortunate Bosavern Penlez* (London, 1749).

ANON., *The History of the Press-Yard* (London, 1717).

ANON., *A Farther Defence of the Ancient Philosophers Concerning their Doctrine and Belief of a Future State* (London: John Jackson, 1747).

Annual Register for the Year 1773 (London: J. Dodsley, 1774).

ARBUTHNOT, JOHN, *Of the Laws of Chance* (London: Benjamin Motte, 1692).

BAILLIE, JOHN, *An Essay on the Sublime* (London, 1747; repr. Los Angeles: Clark Library, 1953).

BANKS, JOSEPH, *The Endeavour Journal of Joseph Banks 1768–71*, ed. J. C. Beaglehole, 2 vols. (Sydney: Public Library of New South Wales and Angus and Robertson, 1962).

BARRY, JAMES, *The Works of James Barry Esq.*, 2 vols. (London: J. M'Creery, 1809).

BATE, JULIUS, *An Essay on the Third Chapter of Genesis* (London: James Bettenham, 1741).

BAYLE, PIERRE, *An Historical and Critical Dictionary*, 4 vols. (London: C. Harper *et al.*, 1710).

BEATTIE, JAMES, *Dissertations Moral and Critical* (London, 1783; repr. Stuttgart: Friedrich Frommann, 1970).

BELLAMY, DANIEL, *A Paraphrase on the Book of Job* (London, 1748).

BEMROSE, WILLIAM, *The Life and Works of Joseph Wright A.R.A.* (London: Bernrose and Sons, 1885).

BENTHAM, JEREMY, 'Of Laws In General', in *Collected Works*, ed. J. H. Burns and H. L. A. Hart (University of London: Athlone Press, 1970).

—— 'A Comment on the Commentaries', in Burns and Hart (ed.), *Works*.

—— *Theory of Fictions*, ed. C. K. Ogden (London: Routledge and Kegan Paul, 1932).

BLACKMORE, SIR RICHARD, *A Collection of Poems* (London: W. Wilkins, 1718).

—— *The Creation: A Philosophical Poem* (London: S. Buckley, 1712).

—— *Essays upon Several Subjects* (London: E. Curll, 1717).

—— *A Paraphrase on the Book of Job* (2nd edn., London: Jacob Tonson, 1716).

—— *A True and Impartial History of the Conspiracy against William III* (London: J. Knapton, 1723).

BLACKSTONE, WILLIAM, *An Analysis of the Laws of England* (Oxford: Clarendon Press, 1756).

—— *Commentaries on the Laws of England*, 4 vols. (Oxford: Clarendon Press, 1765).

BLACKWELL, THOMAS, *An Enquiry into the Life and Writings of Homer*, 2 vols. (London, 1735).

BLAKE, WILLIAM, *The Complete Poetry and Prose of William Blake*, ed. David V. Erdman (Berkeley, Calif.: University of California Press, 1982).

BLAIR, HUGH, 'A Critical Dissertation on the Poems of Ossian', in *The Poems of Ossian*, trans. James Macpherson, 3 vols. (London, 1805).

—— *Lectures on Rhetoric and Belles Lettres*, 3 vols. (London, 1787).

BLAIR, ROBERT, *The Grave* (London, 1786).

BOILEAU-DESPREAUX, NICOLAS, *Traite du sublime ou du merveilleux* (Paris, 1674; repr. New York: Scholars' Facsimiles & Reprints, 1975).

Book of Job, trans. MARVIN H. POPE (New York: Doubleday, 1965).

BOOTHBY, SIR BROOKE and SEWARD, ANNA, *Monumental Inscriptions in Ashbourn Church, Derbyshire* (Ashbourn: Parkes, 1806).

BOOTHBY, SIR BROOKE, *Fables and Satires with a Preface on the Aesopean Fable* (Edinburgh: George Ramsay, 1809).

—— *A Letter to the Right Honourable Edmund Burke* (London: J. Debrett, 1791).

—— *Observations on the Appeal from the New to the Old Whigs* (London: John Stockdale, 1792).

—— (ed.), *Rousseau juge de Jean-Jacques* (Lichfield: J. Jackson, 1780).

—— *Sorrows Sacred to the Memory of Penelope* (London: W. Bulmer, 1796).

BOUGAINVILLE, LOUIS-ANTOINE, CHEVALIER DE, *Voyage autour du monde*, 2 vols. (Paris: Saillant et Nyon, 1772).

BOUGAINVILLE, LEWIS DE, *A Voyage Round the World*, trans. Johann-Reinhold Forster (London: J. Nourse, 1772).

BROSSES, CHARLES DE, *Histoire des Navigations aux Terres Australes*, 2 vols. (Paris, 1756).

BROUGHTON, HUGH, *Iob: to the King* (London, 1610).

BROWN, JOHN, *An Estimate of the Manners and Principles of the Times* (London: L. Davies and C. Reymers, 1757).

BRUNTON, MARY, *Self-Control* (London: Pandora, 1986).

BURKE, EDMUND *An Appeal from the New to the Old Whigs* (London: R. Dodsley, 1791).

—— *A Philosophical Enquiry into our Ideas of the Sublime and Beautiful*, ed. James T. Boulton (Oxford: Basil Blackwell, 1958; revised 1987).

—— 'Reflections on the Revolution in France', in L. G. Mitchell (ed.), *The*

Writings and Speeches of Edmund Burke, vol. viii (Oxford: Clarendon Press, 1989).

—— *Thoughts on the Causes of the Present Discontents* (London: J. Dodsley, 1770).

—— *A Vindication of Natural Society* (London: M. Cooper, 1756).

BURNEY, FRANCES, *The Early Diary of Frances Burney 1768–1778*, ed. A. R. Ellis, 2 vols. (London: George Bell, 1907).

CALVIN, JOHN, *Sermons of Master Iohn Calvin, upon the Booke of IOB*, trans. Arthur Golding (London, 1574).

CAMPBELL, GEORGE, *The Philosophy of Rhetoric* (1776), ed. Lloyd F. Bitzer (Carbondale, Ill.: Southern Illinois University Press, 1963).

CHAPPELOW, LEONARD, *A Commentary on the Book of Job with a Paraphrase*, 2 vols. (Cambridge, 1752).

CHARLEVOIX, P. F. de, *Journal of a Voyage to North America*, 2 vols. (London: R. and J. Dodsley, 1761).

CHUBB, THOMAS, *Posthumous Works*, 2 vols. (London, 1748).

CHURCHILL, CHARLES, *The Poetical Works of Charles Churchill*, ed. Douglas Grant (Oxford: Clarendon Press, 1956).

COLERIDGE, SAMUEL TAYLOR, *Biographia Literaria*, ed. J. Shawcross, 2 vols. (Oxford: Clarendon Press, 1907).

—— *Miscellaneous Criticism*, ed. T. M. Raysor (Cambridge University Press, 1936).

COOK, JAMES, *The Voyage of the Endeavour 1768–1771*, ed. J. C. Beaglehole (Cambridge: Hakluyt Society, 1955).

—— *The Voyages of the Resolution and the Adventure 1772–1775*, ed. J. C. Beaglehole, 2 vols. (Cambridge: Hakluyt Society and Cambridge University Press, 1961).

CONDILLAC, ÉTIENNE BONNOT DE, *An Essay on the Origin of Human Knowledge*, trans. Thomas Nugent (London: J. Nourse, 1756).

COSTARD, G., *Some Observations on the Book of Job* (Oxford, 1747).

—— *Two Dissertations* (Oxford, 1750).

The Critical Review, or Annals of Literature, vol. xxxvii (London: A. Hamilton, 1774).

DALRYMPLE, ALEXANDER, *An Account of Discoveries in the South Pacific Ocean previous to 1764* (London, 1767).

—— *An Historical Collection of Voyages and Discoveries in the South Pacific Ocean*, 2 vols. (London, 1770–71).

—— *A Letter from Mr Dalrymple to Dr Hawkesworth* (London, 1773).

—— *Observations on Dr Hawkesworth's Preface to the Second Edition* (London, 1773).

DAMPIER, WILLIAM, *A New Voyage Round the World* in *A Collection of Voyages*, 4 vols. (London: J. and J. Knapton, 1729).

DENNIS, JOHN, *The Critical Works of John Dennis*, ed. Edward Niles Hooker, 2 vols. (Baltimore: Johns Hopkins University Press, 1939).

DINGLEY, THOMAS, *History from Marble*, 2 vols. (London: Camden Society, 1867).

EDEN, WILLIAM, EARL OF AUCKLAND, *Principles of Penal Law* (London: B. White, 1771).

Edinburgh Magazine and Review (Edinburgh, 1773).

FERGUSON, ADAM, *An Essay on the History of Civil Society* (Edinburgh: A. Millar and A. Kincaid, 1767).

FORSTER, JOHN REINOLD [*sic*], *Observations made during a Voyage round the World* (London: G. Robinson, 1778).

FORSTER, GEORGE, *A Voyage round the World in the Sloop Resolution 1772–1775* (London: B. White *et al.*, 1777).

—— *A Reply to Mr Wales's Remarks* (London: B. White, 1777).

FIELDING, HENRY, *Amelia*, ed. Martin Battestin (Oxford: Clarendon Press, 1986).

—— *An Enquiry into the Causes of the late Increase in Robbers*, ed. Malvin R. Zirker (Connecticut: Wesleyan University Press, 1988).

—— *The Covent-Garden Journal*, ed. Bertrand A. Goldgar (Connecticut: Wesleyan University Press, 1988).

—— 'Examples of the Interposition of Providence in the Detection and Punishment of Murder', in Zirker (ed.), *An Enquiry*.

—— *The History of the Adventures of Joseph Andrews*, ed. Martin Battestin (Oxford: Clarendon Press, 1967).

—— *The History of Tom Jones, a Foundling*, ed. R. P. C. Mutter (Harmondsworth: Penguin, 1966).

—— *The Life of Jonathan Wild the Great* (London: A. Millar, 1754).

—— *Jonathan Wild [and] The Journal of a Voyage to Lisbon* (London: Dent, 1932).

—— *Miss Mary Blandy's own Account of the Affair between her and Mr Cranstoun* (London: A. Millar, 1752).

—— *Of The Remedy of Affliction for the Loss of our Friends in Miscellanies*, vol. i, ed. Henry Knight Miller (Oxford: Clarendon Press, 1972).

—— *Of the True State of the Case of Bosavern Penlez* (London, 1749); repr. in Zirker (ed.), *An Enquiry*.

—— *The Tragedy of Tragedies*, in *Eighteenth-Century Plays* (Dent: London, 1954).

—— *The Voyages of Mr Job Vinegar*, ed. S. J. Sackett (Los Angeles: Augustan Reprint Society, 1958).

GARNETT, JOHN, *A Dissertation on the Book of Job* (London, 1751).

GAY, JOHN, *The Beggar's Opera* in *Eighteenth-Century Plays* (London: Dent, 1928).

The Gentleman's Magazine, vol. 43 (London, 1773).

GERARD, ALEXANDER, *An Essay on Genius* (London, 1774; repr. New York: Garland Publishing, 1970).

—— *An Essay on Taste* (London, 1759; repr. Menston: Scolar Press, 1971).

GIBBON, EDWARD, *An Essay on the Study of Literature* (London, 1764; repr. New York: Garland, 1970).

—— *Journal to January 1763* (London: Chatto and Windus, 1929).

—— 'Critical Observations on the Sixth Book of the Aeneid' (1770), in Patricia

B. Craddock (ed.), *The English Essays of Edward Gibbon* (Oxford: Clarendon Press, 1972).

GILBERT, GEOFFREY, *The Law of Evidence* (London: W. Owen, 1760).

GODWIN, WILLIAM, *A History of the Life of William Pitt, Earl of Chatham* (London, 1783).

—— *An Enquiry concerning Political Justice*, 2 vols. (London: G. and J. Robinson, 1793).

—— *An Essay on Sepulchres* (London, W. Miller, 1809).

—— *Things as They Are: or, The Adventures of Caleb Williams*, ed. David McCracken (London: Oxford University Press, 1970).

GOLDSMITH, OLIVER, *The Life of Henry St John, Viscount Bolingbroke* (London: T. Davies, 1770). ·

—— *The Collected Works of Oliver Goldsmith*, ed. Arthur Friedman, 5 vols. (Oxford: Clarendon Press, 1966).

GREY, RICHARD, *An Answer to Mr Warburton's Remarks on the Book of Job* (London, 1744).

HALE, MATTHEW, *The History of the Common Law of England* (London: J. Walthoe, 1713).

HARTLEY, DAVID, *Observations on Man, his Frame and Duty and his Expectations*, 2 vols. (London, 1749; repr. Gainsville, Fla.: Scholars' Facsimiles & Reprints, 1966).

HAWKESWORTH, JOHN, *An Account of the Voyages for making Discoveries in the Southern Hemisphere*, 3 vols. (London: W. Strahan and T. Cadell, 1773).

—— *The Adventurer*, 2 vols. (London: J. Payne, 1753).

—— (trans.), *The Adventures of Telemachus* (London: Harrison and Co., 1784).

—— *Almoran and Hamet: An Oriental Tale* (London: Harrison and Co., 1790).

—— *Oroonoko* [Hawkesworth's corrected version of Thomas Southern's drama based on Aphra Behn's novel] (London: C. Bathurst, 1775).

HAWKINS, WILLIAM, *Tracts in Divinity*, 3 vols. (Oxford, 1758).

HEGEL, GEORG WILHELM FRIEDRICH, *Aesthetics*, trans. T. M. Knox, 2 vols. (Oxford: Clarendon Press, 1975).

—— *Lectures on the Philosophy of Religion*, ed. Peter C. Hodgson, 2 vols. (Berkeley, Calif.: University of California Press, 1987).

—— *Phenomenology of Spirit*, trans. A. V. Miller (Oxford University Press, 1977).

—— *Philosophy of Right*, trans. T. M. Knox (Oxford: Clarendon Press, 1942).

HERDER, J. G., *The Spirit of Hebrew Poetry*, trans. James Marsh, 2 vols. (Vermont: Edward Smith, 1833).

HERVEY, JAMES, *Meditations among the Tombs* (London: J. Rivington, 1746).

HERVEY, JOHN, *Miscellaneous Thoughts* (London: 1742).

—— *The Publick Virtue of Former Times and the Present Age Compared* (London: J. Roberts, 1732).

HILL, JOHN, *The Story of Elizabeth Canning Considered* (London: M. Cooper, 1753).

HOBBES, THOMAS, *Leviathan*, ed. A. R. Waller (Cambridge: Cambridge University Press, 1935).

HOME, HENRY, LORD KAMES, *Elements of Criticism*, 2 vols. (Edinburgh, 1774).

—— *Historical Law-Tracts*, 2 vols. (Edinburgh: A. Millar, 1758).

HUME, DAVID, *Dialogues Concerning Natural Religion*, ed. Norman Kemp Smith (New York: Bobbs Merrill, 1947).

—— *Essays Moral, Political, and Literary*, ed. Eugene F. Miller (Indianapolis: Liberty Classics, 1987).

—— *The Letters of David Hume*, ed. J. T. Greig, 2 vols. (Oxford: Clarendon Press, 1932).

—— *A Treatise of Human Nature*, ed. Ernest C. Mossner (Harmondsworth: Penguin, 1969).

—— *An Enquiry Concerning Human Understanding*, ed. L. A. Selby-Bigge (Oxford: Clarendon Press, 1975).

HURD, RICHARD, *Two Tracts of a Warburtonian* (London, 1789).

—— *Remarks on Mr David Hume's Essay on the Natural History of Religion* (London: M. Cooper, 1757).

JOHNSON, SAMUEL, *The Lives of the Poets*, ed. George Birkbeck Hill, 3 vols. (Oxford: Clarendon Press, 1905).

—— 'The Vanity of Human Wishes', in *Samuel Johnson*, ed. Donald Greene (Oxford: Oxford University Press, 1984).

—— *Works*, 16 vols. (New York, 1903).

KANT, IMMANUEL, 'The Failure of all Philosophical Attempts towards a Theodicy', in *Kant*, ed. Gabrielle Rabel (Oxford: Clarendon Press, 1963).

—— *Critique of Judgment*, ed. James Creed Meredith (Oxford: Clarendon Press, 1952; repr. 1973).

—— *Essays and Treatises on Moral, Political, and Various Philosophical Subjects*, 2 vols. (London: William Richardson, 1789).

KIERKEGAARD, SØREN, *Repetition: An Essay in Experimental Psychology*, trans. Walter Lowrie (New York: Harper Row, 1941).

KING, WILLIAM, *An Essay on the Origin of Evil*, trans. Edmund Law, 2 vols. (London, 1732).

KILVERT, FRANCIS (ed.), *A Selection from Unpublished Papers of William Warburton* (London: John Bowyer Nichols, 1841).

LAFITAU, PIERRE, *Mœurs des Sauvages Ameriquains*, 2 vols. (Paris: Charles Hocherau, 1724).

LANGHORNE, WILLIAM, *Job: A Poem* (London, 1750).

LANGHORNE, JOHN, *The Country Justice: A Poem* (London: T. Becket, 1774).

LE CLERC, JEAN, *Twelve Dissertations out of Genesis* (London, 1696).

LEIBNIZ, GOTTFRIED WILHELM, *Philosophical Essays*, ed. and trans. Roger Ariew and Daniel Garber (Indianapolis: Hackett, 1989).

—— *Theodicy*, trans. M. M. Huggard (London: Routledge and Kegan Paul, 1951).

LESSING, GOTTHOLD EPHRAIM, *Laocoon*, trans. Edward Allen McCormick (New York: Bobbs-Merrill, 1962).

LONGINUS, *On Great Writing*, trans. G. M. A. Grube (New York, Bobbs-Merrill, 1957).

'Longinus' on the Sublime, ed. D. A. Russell (Oxford: Clarendon Press, 1964).

Dionysius Longinus on the Sublime, trans. William Smith (London, 1739; repr. New York: Scholars' Facsimiles & Reprints, 1975).

The Works of Dionysius Longinus, trans. Leonard Welsted (London, 1712; repr. 1724).

LOWTH, ROBERT, *Isaiah: A New Translation*, 2 vols. (Edinburgh: George Caw, 1807).

—— *Lectures on the Sacred Poetry of the Hebrews*, trans. G. Gregory, 2 vols. (London: J. Johnson, 1787).

—— *A Letter to the Author of The Divine Legation of Moses Demonstrated* (Oxford, 1765).

—— *A Letter to Dr Warburton* (London, 1760).

MACHIAVELLI, NICCOLO, *The Works of the Famous Nicholas Machiavel* (3rd edn., London: A. Churchill, 1720).

MACKENZIE, HENRY, *Julia de Roubigne: a Tale* (London: W. Strahan and T. Cadell, 1777).

MADAN, MARTIN, *Thoughts on Executive Justice* (London: J. Dodsley, 1785).

MIDDLETON, CONYERS, *A Letter from Rome* (London: R. H. Evans, 1812).

MOIVRE, ABRAHAM DE, *The Doctrine of Chances* (London: W. Pearson, 1718).

MONKHOUSE, WILLIAM BROUGHTON, *Journal of a Voyage in the Endeavour*, BM Add. MS 27889, ff. 83–94.

MONTAGU, LADY MARY WORTLEY, *The Complete Letters of Lady Mary Wortley Montagu*, ed. Robert Halsband, 3 vols. (Oxford: Clarendon Press, 1965).

MONTAIGNE, MICHEL DE, *The Essays of Montaigne*, ed. W. Carew Hazlitt, trans. Charles Cotton, 3 vols. (London: George Bell, 1892).

The Monthly Review or Literary Journal, 49 and 57 (London: R. Griffiths, 1774–78).

NIETZSCHE, FRIEDRICH, *The Will to Power*, trans. Walter Kaufmann and R. J. Hollingdale (New York: Vintage, 1968).

The New Newgate Calendar, 5 vols. (London, 1779).

PAINE, THOMAS, *The Rights of Man*, ed. Henry Collins (Harmondsworth: Penguin, 1969; repr. 1983).

PALEY, WILLIAM, *The Principles of Moral and Political Philosophy* (London: R. Faulder, 1785).

PARRY, RICHARD, *A Defence of the Bishop of London's Interpretation of Job* (Northampton, 1760).

PATRICK, SIMON, *The Book of Job Paraphrased* (London, 1697).

—— *A Consolatory Discourse to Prevent Immoderate Grief* (London, 1676).

PAYNE KNIGHT, RICHARD, *Analytical Enquiry into the Principles of Taste* (London, 1805).

PETERS, CHARLES, *A Critical Dissertation on the Book of Job* (London, 1757).

—— *An Appendix to the Critical Dissertation* (London, 1760).

PHILOCRITICUS CANTABRIGIENSIS [pseud.], *A Treatise on the Improvements in the Art of Criticism* (London, 1748).

POPE, ALEXANDER, *The Correspondence of Alexander Pope*, 5 vols. ed. George Sherburn (Oxford: Clarendon Press, 1956).

—— *An Essay on Man*, ed. Maynard Mack (London: Methuen, 1950; repr. 1958).

—— *Poems*, ed. John Butt (London: Methuen, 1963).

—— *The Art of Sinking in Poetry*, ed. Edna Leake Steeves (New York: King's Crown Press, 1952).

—— Postscript to 'The Odyssey of Homer' and Preface to 'The Iliad of Homer', in Maynard Mack (ed.), *The Poems of Alexander Pope*, 10 vols. (London: Methuen, 1967), vols. vii and x.

PRIESTLEY, JOSEPH, *A Course of Lectures on Oratory and Criticism* (London, 1777; repr. Menston: Scolar Press, 1968).

PREVOST, ANTOINE-FRANCOIS, *Histoire générales des voyages* (Paris, 1745).

The Public Advertiser, 11912–39; 14 June to 21 July 1773.

QUARLES, FRANCIS, *Job Militant* (London, 1624).

[RAMSAY, ALLAN], *A Letter Concerning Elizabeth Canning* (London: A. Millar, 1752).

REYNOLDS, SIR JOSHUA, *Discourses on Art*, ed. Robert R. Wark (San Marino, Calif.: Huntington Library, 1959).

RICHARDSON, SAMUEL, *Clarissa, or the History of a Young Lady*, 7 vols. (London: Samuel Richardson, 1748).

—— *Clarissa, or the History of a Young Lady*, 4 vols. (London: Dent, 1932; repr. 1965).

—— *Clarissa, or the History of a Young Lady*, ed. Angus Ross (Harmondsworth: Penguin, 1985).

—— *Clarissa: Preface, Hints of Prefaces, and Postscript*, ed. R. F. Brissenden (Augustan Reprint Society No. 103: Los Angeles, Calif., 1964).

—— *The Correspondence of Samuel Richardson*, ed. Anna Laetitia Barbauld, 6 vols. (London, 1804).

—— *Letters and Passages restored from the Original Manuscripts* (London: Samuel Richardson, 1751); issued as the supplementary eighth volume of the second edition of Clarissa (1749).

—— *Meditations Collected fron the Sacred Books* (London: Samuel Richardson, 1750; repr. New York: Garland, 1976).

—— *Selected Letters of Samuel Richardson*, ed. John Carroll (Oxford: Clarendon Press, 1964).

—— *Sir Charles Grandison*, ed. Jocelyn Harris, 3 vols. (Oxford: Oxford University Press, 1972).

RILKE, RAINER MARIA, *The Notebooks of Malte Laurids Brigge*, trans. John Linton (London: Hogarth Press, 1972).

ROMILLY, SIR SAMUEL, *Observations on the Criminal Law in England* (London: T. Cadell and W. Davies, 1810).

ROUSSEAU, JEAN JACQUES, *Rousseau juge de Jean-Jacques*, ed. Sir Brooke Boothby (Lichfield: J. Jackson, 1780).

—— *Lettre de J. J. Rousseau à Monsieur de Voltaire* (Paris, 1759).

ROWE, ELIZABETH, *Friendship in Death: In Twenty Letters* (London, 1740).

Sandwich Papers, National Maritime Museum, F.36.29.

SANDYS, GEORGE, *A Paraphrase upon the Divine Poems* (London, 1638).

SAPPHO, *Poetarum Lesbiorum fragmenti*, ed. Edgar Lobel and Denys Page (Oxford: Clarendon Press, 1955).

SCHILLER, FRIEDRICH, *On the Sublime*, trans. Julius A. Elias (New York: Frederick Ungar, 1966).

SEWARD, ANNA, and BOOTHBY, SIR BROOKE, *Monumental Inscriptions in Ashbourn Church, Derbyshire* (Ashbourn: Parke, 1806).

SHERLOCK, THOMAS, *The Works of Bishop Sherlock*, 5 vols. (London, 1830).

SHERLOCK, WILLIAM, *A Discourse Concerning the Divine Providence* (London: William Rogers, 1694).

SMITH, ADAM, *The Theory of Moral Sentiments*, ed. D. D. Raphael and A. L. Mcfie (Oxford: Clarendon Press, 1976).

SMITH, WILLIAM, *Dionysius Longinus on the Sublime* (London, 1739; repr. New York: Scholars' Facsimiles & Reprints, 1975).

SPENCE, JOSEPH, *An Essay on Pope's Odyssey* (London: J. and J. Knapton, 1726–27).

STERNE, LAURENCE, *Letters of Laurence Sterne*, ed. Lewis Perry Curtis (Oxford: Clarendon Press, 1935; repr. 1965).

—— *The Life and Opinions of Tristram Shandy, Gent.*, 3 vols., ed. Melvyn New and Joan New (University Presses of Florida, 1978).

—— *A Sentimental Journey through France and Italy*, ed. Gardner D. Stout (Berkeley, Calif.: University of California Press, 1967).

St James's Chronicle and British Evening Post, 1916, 15–17 June, 1773.

ST. JOHN, HENRY, VISCOUNT BOLINGBROKE, *A Familiar Epistle to the Most Impudent Man Living* (London, 1749).

—— *Letters on the Spirit of Patriotism* (London: A. Millar, 1752).

—— *Letters on the Study and Use of History*, 2 vols. (London: A. Millar, 1752).

—— *Reflections upon Exile* (London: Alexander Murray, 1870).

—— *Some Reflections upon the present State of the Nation* (London: A. Millar, 1753).

SWIFT, JONATHAN, *The Poems of Jonathan Swift*, ed. Harold Williams, 3 vols. (Oxford: Clarendon Press, 1937; repr. 1958).

'Testament of Job' in *The Old Testament Pseudepigraphia*, ed. James H. Charlesworth, 2 vols. (New York: Doubleday, 1983).

TILLARD, J., *A Reply to Mr Warburton's Appendix* (London, 1742).

TOWNE, JOHN, *Remarks on Dr Lowth's Letter to the Bishop of Gloucester* (London: L. Davies and C. Reymers, 1766).

VOLTAIRE (FRANÇOIS MARIE AROUET), *Œuvres Complètes* (Paris: La Société Littéraire-Typographique, 1785).

—— *Candide ou l'optimisme*, ed. René Pomeau (Oxford: Voltaire Foundation, 1980).

WALES, WILLIAM, *Remarks on Mr Forster's Account of Captain Cook's Last Voyage* (London: J. Nourse, 1778).

WALPOLE, HORACE, *Memoirs of George II*, ed. John Brooke, 3 vols. (New Haven, Conn.: Yale University Press, 1985).

—— *Correspondence*, ed. W. S. Lewis, 10 vols. (New Haven, Conn.: Yale University Press, 1941).

WARBURTON, WILLIAM, *The Alliance Between Church and State* (London: Fletcher Gyles, 1736).

—— *A Critical and Philosophical Commentary on Mr Pope's Essay on Man* (London: John and Paul Knapton, 1742).

—— *A Critical and Philosophical Enquiry into the Causes of Prodigies and Miracles as related by Historians* (London: Thomas Corbett, 1728).

—— *The Divine Legation of Moses Demonstrated*, 3 vols. (London: Thomas Tegg, 1846).

—— *Appendix* to *The Divine Legation of Moses Demonstrated*, 9 vols. (London, 1758).

—— *The Doctrine of Grace*, 2 vols. (London: A. Millar, 1763).

—— *Remarks on Several Occasional Reflections* (London, 1744).

—— *Remarks on Mr David Hume's Essay on the Natural History of Religion* (London: M. Cooper, 1757).

—— *A View of Lord Bolingbroke's Philosophy* (London, 1756).

—— *The Works of William Warburton*, 14 vols. (London: T. Cadell and W. Davies, 1811).

—— *A Letter to the Editor of the Letters on the Spirit of Patriotism* (London, 1749).

WARTON, JOHN, *Death-Bed Scenes and Pastoral Conversations*, 3 vols. (4th edn., London: John Murray, 1830).

WATSON, RICHARD, *An Apology for the Bible in a Series of Letters Addressed to Thomas Paine* (Cork: A. Edwards, 1796).

WEBB, PHILIP CARTERET, *A Letter to the Reverend Mr Warburton* (London, 1742).

WEEVER, JOHN, *Ancient Funerall Monuments* (London, 1631; repr. Amsterdam and New Jersey: Theatrum Orbis Terrarum, 1979).

WELSTED, LEONARD, *The Works of Dionysius Longinus* (London, 1712).

WOLLSTONECRAFT, MARY, 'An Historical and Moral View of the French Revolution', in *Mary Wollstonecraft: Political Writings*, ed. Janet Todd (London: W. Pickering, 1993).

—— *The Wrongs of Woman: or Maria, a Fragment*, ed. Gary Kelly (Oxford: Oxford University Press, 1976).

WORDSWORTH, WILLIAM, *The Prelude* (1805), ed. Ernest de Selincourt, corr. Stephen Gill (Oxford: Oxford University Press, 1991).

—— *The Prose Works of William Wordsworth*, ed. W. J. B. Owen and Jane Worthington Smyser, 3 vols. (Oxford: Clarendon Press, 1974).

—— *William Wordsworth*, ed. Stephen Gill (Oxford University Press, 1984).

WORTHINGTON, WILLIAM, *An Essay on Man's Redemption to which is annexed A Dissertation on the Design of the Book of Job* (London, 1743).

WRIGHT, GEORGE, *Pleasing Melancholy: or A Walk among the Tombs* (London: Chapman and Co., 1793).

YOUNG, EDWARD, *A Letter to Mr Tickell Occasioned by the Death of the Right Honourable Joseph Addison, Esq.* (London, 1719).

—— *The Complaint, or Night-Thoughts* (London: J. Dodsley, 1742; A. Millar, 1750).

—— *The Complaint, or Night-Thoughts*, ed. Stephen Cornford (Cambridge: Cambridge University Press, 1989).

—— *Conjectures upon Original Composition* (London, 1759; repr. Leeds: Scolar Press, 1966).

—— *Correspondence*, ed. Henry Pettit (Oxford: Clarendon Press, 1971).

—— *A Paraphrase on Part of the Book of Job* (London, 1719).

SECONDARY TEXTS

ABBEELE, GEORGE VAN DEN, *Travel as Metaphor: Montaigne to Rousseau* (Minneapolis: University of Minnesota Press, 1992).

ABBOTT, JOHN LAURENCE, *John Hawkesworth: Eighteenth-Century Man of Letters* (Madison, Wis.: University of Wisconsin Press, 1982).

ABRAMS, M. H., *The Mirror and the Lamp* (Oxford University Press, 1953).

ADORNO, THEODOR W. and HORKHEIMER, MAX, *The Dialectic of Enlightenment*, trans. John Cumming (London: Allen Lane, 1973).

AIZENBERG, EDNA, *Borges and his Contemporaries* (Columbia, Mo.: University of Missouri Press, 1990).

ALBRIGHT, W. F., 'Some Canaanite-Phoenician Sources of Hebrew Wisdom', *Supplements to the Vetus Testamentum*, 3 (1960).

AL-FAYYUMI, SAADIA BED JOSEPH, *The Book of Theodicy*, trans. L. E. Goodman (New Haven, Conn.: Yale University Press, 1988).

ALTIERI, CHARLES, 'Plato's Performative Sublime and the Ends of Reading', *New Literary History*, 12/2 (1985), 251–73.

ALTMAN, JANET GURKIN, *Epistolarity* (Columbus, Oh.: Ohio State University Press, 1982).

AMORY, HUGH, 'Henry Fielding and the Criminal Legislation of 1751–1752', *Philological Quarterly*, 50 (1971), 175–92.

ARAC, JONATHAN, 'The Media of Sublimity,' *Studies in Romanticism*, 26 (1987), 209–20.

ARMSTRONG, NANCY, *Desire and Domestic Fiction: A Political History of the Novel* (Oxford: Oxford University Press, 1987).

BARKER-BENFIELD, C. J., *The Culture of Sensibility* (Chicago: Chicago University Press, 1992).

BARRE, M. L., 'A Note on Job 19: 25,' *Vetus Testamentum*, 29 (1979), 107–10.

BARRELL, JOHN, *The Political Theory of Painting from Reynolds to Hazlitt* (New Haven, Conn.: Yale University Press, 1986).

BARRELL, JOHN and GUEST, HARRIET, 'Contradictions in the Long Eighteenth-Century Poem', in *The New Eighteenth Century*, ed. Laura Brown and Felicity Nussbaum (London: Methuen, 1987).

BARRELL, JOHN (ed.), *Painting and the Politics of Culture: New Essays on British Art 1700–1850* (Oxford: Oxford University Press, 1992).

BATTESTIN, MARTIN C., *Henry Fielding: A Life* (London: Routledge, 1989).

—— *The Providence of Wit* (Oxford: Clarendon Press, 1974).

BEATTIE, J. M., *Crime and the Courts in England 1660–1800* (Oxford: Clarendon Press, 1986).

BENDER, JOHN, *Imagining the Penitentiary: Fiction and the Architecture of Mind in Eighteenth-Century England* (Chicago: University of Chicago Press, 1987).

—— 'Prison Reform and the Sentence of Narration in *The Vicar of Wakefield*', in *The New Eighteenth Century*, ed. Laura Brown and Felicity Nussbaum (London: Methuen, 1987).

BELL, IAN A., *Literature and Crime in Augustan England* (London: Routledge, 1991).

BLACK, JEREMY, *Pitt the Elder* (Cambridge: Cambridge University Press, 1992).

BLOOM, HAROLD, *The Anxiety of Influence* (Oxford: Oxford University Press, 1973).

—— 'Freud and the Poetic Sublime', in *Freud: A Collection of Critical Essays*, ed. Perry Messel (New Jersey: Prentice-Hall, 1981), 211–31.

BOGEL, FREDERICK, *Acts of Knowledge: Pope's Later Poems* (Lewisburg, Pa.: Bucknell University Press, 1981).

BOURDIEU, PIERRE, *Distinction: A Social Critique of the Judgement of Taste*, trans. Richard Nice (Cambridge, Mass.: Harvard University Press, 1984).

—— *Outline of a Theory of Practice* (Cambridge: Cambridge University Press, 1977; repr. 1990).

BOX, M. A., *The Suasive Art of David Hume* (Princeton, NJ: Princeton University Press, 1987).

BREWER, JOHN, and STYLES, JOHN, *An Ungovernable People: The English and their Law in the Seventeenth and Eighteenth Centuries* (London: Hutchinson, 1980).

BREWER, JOHN, *Party Ideology and Popular Politics at the Accession of George III* (Cambridge: Cambridge University Press, 1976).

—— *The Sinews of Power: War, Money, and the English State 1688–1783* (London: Unwin Hyman, 1989).

BROOKE, JOHN, *The Chatham Administration* (London: Macmillan, 1956).

BROMWICH, DAVID, *A Choice of Inheritance* (Cambridge, Mass.: Harvard University Press, 1989).

BROWN, LAURA, *Alexander Pope* (Oxford: Basil Blackwell, 1985).

—— and Nussbaum, Felicity, *The New Eighteenth Century* (London: Methuen, 1987).

BROWN, MARSHALL, 'The Urbane Sublime', in *Modern Essays on Eighteenth-Century Literature*, ed. Leo Damrosch (Oxford: Oxford University Press, 1988), 426–54.

BRYSON, NORMAN, *Word and Image* (Cambridge: Cambridge University Press, 1981).

BUTLER, MARILYN, *Burke, Paine, Godwin and the Revolution Controversy* (Cambridge: Cambridge University Press, 1984).

—— 'Revolving in Deep Time: The French Revolution as Narrative', in *Revolution and English Romanticism: Politics and Rhetoric*, ed. Keith Hanley and Ramon Selden (Sussex: Harvester Wheatsheaf, 1990), 1–22.

CAILLOIS, ROGER, *Pierres* (Paris: Gallimard, 1966).

CAPLAN, JAY, *Framed Narratives: Diderot's Genealogy of the Beholder* (Minneapolis: University of Minnesota Press, 1985).

CARUTH, CATHY, 'The Force of Example: Kant's Symbols', *Yale French Studies*, 74 (1988), 17–37.

CASTLE, TERRY, *Clarissa's Ciphers* (Ithaca, NY: Cornell University Press, 1982).

—— *Masquerade and Civilisation* (London: Methuen, 1986).

CAYGILL, HOWARD, *Art of Judgement* (Oxford: Basil Blackwell, 1989).

CHRISTENSON, JEROME, *Practicing Enlightenment: Hume and the Formation of a Literary Career* (Madison, Wis.: University of Wisconsin Press, 1987).

CLARK, JONATHAN, *The Dynamics of Change: The Crisis of the 1750s and English Party Systems* (Cambridge: Cambridge University Press, 1982).

—— *English Society 1688–1832: Ideology, Social Structure and Political Practice during the Ancien Régime* (Cambridge: Cambridge University Press, 1985).

—— *The Language of Liberty 1660–1832* (Cambridge: Cambridge University Press, 1994).

COCKBURN, J. S. (ed.), *Crime in England 1550–1800* (Princeton, NJ: Princeton University Press, 1977).

COOKE, G. A., *A Text-Book of North Semitic Inscriptions* (Oxford: Clarendon Press, 1903).

COOPER, ALAN, 'Narrative Theory and the Book of Job', *Studies in Religion*, 11 (1982), 35–44.

COURTINE, JEAN-FRANÇOIS et al., *Du Sublime* (Paris: Éditions Belin, 1988).

CRUDEN, ALEXANDER, *A Complete Concordance to the Holy Scriptures* (London: J. Rivington, 1834).

DE BOLLA, PETER, *The Discourse of the Sublime* (Oxford: Basil Blackwell, 1989).

DE CERTEAU, MICHEL, *The Practice of Everyday Life*, trans. Steven Rendall (Berkeley, Calif.: University of California Press, 1984).

—— 'Travel Narratives of the French to Brazil', *Representations*, 33 (1991), 221–6.

—— *The Writing of History*, trans. Tom Conley (New York: Columbia University Press, 1988).

DEGUY, MICHEL, 'Le Grand-Dire: Pour contribuer à une relecture du pseudo-Longin', *Poetique*, 58 (1984), 197–214.

DE JEAN, JOAN, *Fictions of Sappho 1546–1937* (Chicago: University of Chicago Press, 1989).

DELEUZE, GILLES and GUATTARI, FELIX, *Anti-Oedipus*, trans. Robert Hurly, Mark Seem, and Helen Lane (London: Athlone Press, 1983).

DE LUCA, VINCENT, 'Blake and the Two Sublimes', in *Studies in Eighteenth-Century Culture* 11, ed. Harry C. Payne (Madison, Wis.: University of Wisconsin Press, 1982).

DE KREY, GARY STUART, *A Fractured Society: The Politics of London in the*

First Age of Party (Oxford: Clarendon Press, 1985).

DE MAN, PAUL, 'Autobiography as Defacement', *MLN* 94 (1979), 919–30.

—— 'Hegel on the Sublime', in *Displacement: Derrida and After*, ed. Mark Krupnick (Bloomington, Ind.: Indiana University Press, 1982).

—— 'Hypogram and Inscription', *Diacritics* 11/4 (Winter, 1981), 17–35.

—— 'Phenomenality and Materiality in Kant', in *Hermeneutics*, ed. Gary Shapiro and Alan Sica (Amherst, Mass.: University of Massachusetts Press, 1984).

DENING, GREG, *Mr Bligh's Bad Language* (Cambridge: Cambridge University Press, 1992).

—— *The Bounty: An Ethnographic History* (Melbourne: Melbourne University Press, 1983; repr. 1989).

DERRIDA, JACQUES, 'Economimesis', *Diacritics* 11/2 (Summer, 1981), 3–25.

—— *Glas*, trans. John P. Leary and Richard Rand (Lincoln, Nebr.: University of Nebraska Press, 1986).

—— *The Margins of Philosophy*, trans. Alan Bass (Chicago: University of Chicago Press, 1982).

—— *The Truth in Painting*, trans. Geoffrey Bennington and Ian McLeod (Chicago: University of Chicago Press, 1987).

DÉTIENNE, MARCEL, *Les Savoirs de l'écriture en Grèce ancienne* (Presses Universitaires de Lille, n.d.).

DOODY, MARGARET ANN and SABOR, PETER (ed.), *Samuel Richardson: Tercentenary Essays* (Cambridge: Cambridge University Press, 1989).

DHORMÉ, PAUL, *Le livre de Job* (Paris: Victor Lecoffre, 1926).

DOUGLAS, MARY, *Implicit Meanings: Essays in Anthropology* (London: Routledge and Kegan Paul, 1975).

DRIVER, G. R., *Semitic Writing: From Pictograph to Alphabet* (London: British Academy, 1948).

EAGLETON, TERRY, *The Ideology of the Aesthetic* (Oxford: Basil Blackwell, 1990).

—— *The Rape of Clarissa* (Oxford: Basil Blackwell, 1982).

EDEN, KATHY, *Poetic and Legal Fiction in the Aristotelian Tradition* (Princeton, NJ: Princeton University Press, 1986).

EGERTON, JUDY, *Wright of Derby* (London: Tate Gallery, 1990).

ERDMAN, DAVID V. (ed.), *The Poetry and Prose of William Blake* (New York: Doubleday, 1970).

ESCOUBAS, ELIANE, 'Kant ou la simplicité du sublime', *PO&SIE*, 32 (1985), 112–25.

FALLER, LINCOLN, *Turned to Account: The Forms and Functions of Criminal Biography in Late Seventeenth- and Early Eighteenth-Century England* (Cambridge: Cambridge University Press, 1987).

FERGUSON, FRANCES, *Solitude and the Sublime: Romanticism and the Aesthetics of Individuation* (New York: Routledge, 1992).

—— 'The Sublime of Edmund Burke, or the Bathos of Experience', *Glyph*, 8 (1981), 62–78.

—— 'Legislating the Sublime', in *Studies in Eighteenth-Century Art and Aes-*

thetics, ed. Ralph Cohen (Berkeley, Calif.: University of California Press, 1985), 131–44.

—— Commentary on Suzanne Guerlac's 'Longinus and the Subject of the Sublime', *New Literary History*, 12/2 (1985), 291–7.

FISH, STANLEY, 'Spectacle and Evidence in *Samson Agonistes*', *Critical Inquiry*, 15 (1989), 556–86.

FOUCAULT, MICHEL, *Discipline and Punish*, trans. Alan Sheridan (New York: Vintage Books, 1979).

FOX, MICHAEL V., 'Job 38 and God's Rhetoric', *Semeia*, 19 (1981), 53–61.

FRASER, DAVID, *Joseph Wright of Derby* (Derby: Derby Art Gallery, 1979).

FRIED, DEBRA, 'Repetition, Refrain, and Epitaph', *ELH* 53/3 (1986), 615–25.

FRIED, MICHAEL, *Absorption and Theatricality: Painting and the Beholder in the Age of Diderot* (Berkeley, Calif.: University of California Press, 1980).

FRY, PAUL, 'The Absent Dead: Wordsworth, Byron, and the Epitaph', *Studies in Romanticism*, 17 (1978), 413–33.

—— *The Reach of Criticism* (New Haven, Conn.: Yale University Press, 1983).

FURNISS, TOM, 'Edmund Burke: Bourgeois Revolutionary in a Radical Crisis', in Peter Osborne (ed.), *Socialism and the Limits of Liberalism* (London: Verso, 1991).

—— 'Rhetoric in Revolution: The Role of Language in Paine's Critique of Burke', in *Revolution and English Romanticism: Politics and Rhetoric*, ed. Keith Hanley and Ramon Selden (Sussex: Harvester Wheatsheaf, 1990), 23–48.

GENTILI, BRUNO, *Poetry and its Public in Ancient Greece* (Baltimore: Johns Hopkins University Press, 1988).

GIRARD, RENÉ, *Job the Victim of his People*, trans. Yvonne Freccero (London: Athlone Press, 1987).

GOLDBERG, RITA, *Sex and Enlightenment: Women in Richardson and Diderot* (Cambridge: Cambridge University Press, 1984).

GOURNAY, JEAN-FRANÇOIS (ed.), *La Justice en Angleterre du xvi au xix siècle* (Presses Universitaires de Lille, n.d).

GREENBLATT, STEPHEN, *Marvelous Possessions: The Wonder of the New World* (Chicago: University of Chicago Press, 1991).

GUERLAC, SUZANNE, 'Longinus and the Subject of the Sublime', *New Literary History*, 12/2 (1985), 275–89.

GUILLORY, JOHN, *Cultural Capital: The Problem of Literary Canon Formation* (Chicago: University of Chicago Press, 1993).

HABERMAS, JURGEN, *The Structural Transformation of the Public Sphere* (Cambridge, Mass.: MIT Press, 1989).

—— *Theory and Practice*, trans. John Viertel (Boston, Mass.: Beacon Press, 1973).

HACKING, IAN, *The Emergence of Probability* (Cambridge: Cambridge University Press, 1975; repr. 1991).

HAMPTON, TIMOTHY, *Writing from History: The Rhetoric of Exemplarity in Renaissance Literature* (Ithaca, NY: Cornell University Press, 1990).

HARTMAN, GEOFFREY, *The Unremarkable Wordsworth* (Minneapolis: University of Minnesota Press, 1987).

—— *The Taming of Chance* (Cambridge: Cambridge University Press, 1990).

HAVELOCK, ERIC, *The Literate Revolution in Greece* (Princeton, NJ: Princeton University Press, 1982).

—— *Preface to Plato* (Oxford: Basil Blackwell, 1963).

HAWTHORN, GEOFFREY, *Plausible Worlds: Possibility and Understanding in History and the Social Sciences* (Cambridge: Cambridge University Press, 1991).

HAY, DOUGLAS, 'Property, Authority, and the Criminal Law', in *Albion's Fatal Tree*, ed. Peter Linebaugh *et al.* (New York: Pantheon Books, 1975).

HAY, DOUGLAS and SNYDER, FRANCIS, *Policing and Prosecution in Britain 1750–1850* (Oxford: Clarendon Press, 1989).

HEBDIGE, DICK, 'The Impossible Object: Towards a Sociology of the Sublime', *New Formations*, 1 (1987), 47–76.

Hentzi, Gary, 'Sublime Moments and Social Authority in Robinson Crusoe and Journal of the Plague Year', *Eighteenth-Century Studies*, 26/3 (Spring 1993), 419–34.

HERRNSTEIN SMITH, BARBARA, *Contingencies of Value* (Cambridge, Mass.: Harvard University Press, 1988).

HERTZ, NEIL, *The End of the Line: Essays on Psychoanalysis and the Sublime* (New York: Columbia University Press, 1985).

HILL, CHRISTOPHER, 'Clarissa Harlowe and her Times', *Essays in Criticism* 5/4 (1955), 315–40.

HIPPLE, WALTER J., *The Beautiful, the Sublime, and the Picturesque in Eighteenth-Century British Aesthetic Theory* (Carbondale, Ill.: Southern Illinois University Press, 1957).

HOLST-WARHAFT, GAIL, *Dangerous Voices: Women's Laments in Greek Literature* (London: Routledge, 1992).

IGNATIEFF, MICHAEL, *A Just Measure of Pain: The Penitentiary in the Industrial Revolution 1750–1850* (London: Macmillan, 1978).

IRWIN, DAVID, 'Sentiment and Antiquity: European Tombs 1750–1830', in *Mirrors of Morality*, ed. Joachim Whaley (New York: St Martin's Press, 1981).

JACOBS, CAROL, 'On Looking at Shelley's Medusa', *Yale French Studies*, 69 (1985), 163–79.

JOHNSON, CLAUDIA L., '"Giant HANDEL" and the Musical Sublime', *Eighteenth-Century Studies*, 19 (1986), 515–33.

KAHN, VICTORIA, *Rhetoric, Prudence, and Skepticism in the Renaissance* (Ithaca, NY: Cornell University Press, 1985).

KAY, CAROL, *Political Constructions* (Ithaca: Cornell University Press, 1988).

KEMP, BRIAN, *English Church Monuments* (London: Batsford, 1980).

KEYMER, TOM, *Richardson's Clarissa and the Eighteenth-Century Reader* (Cambridge: Cambridge University Press, 1992).

KEYNES, J. M., *A Treatise on Probability* (London: Macmillan, 1921).

KING, PETER, 'Decision-makers and Decision-making in the English Criminal Law 1750–1800', *Historical Journal*, 27 (1984), 25–58.

KINK, JAMES K., 'Impatient Job: An Interpretation of Job 19: 25–27', *Journal of Biblical Literature*, 84 (1965), 148–52.

KINNIER WILSON, J. V., 'A Return to the Problems of Behemoth and Leviathan', *Vetus Testamentum*, 25 (1975), 1–14.

KITTLER, FRIEDRICH, *Discourse Networks 1800/1900*, trans. Michael Metter and Chris Cullens (Stanford, Calif.: Stanford University Press, 1990).

KNAPP, STEVEN, *Personification and the Sublime: Milton to Coleridge* (Cambridge, Mass.: Harvard University Press, 1985).

KRAMNICK, ISAAC, *Bolingbroke and his Circle: The Politics of Nostalgia in the Age of Walpole* (Cambridge, Mass.: Harvard University Press, 1968).

KRISTEVA, JULIA, *Black Sun: Depression and Melancholia*, trans. Leon Roudiez (New York: Columbia University Press, 1989).

LACOUE-LABARTHE, PHILIPPE, 'La vérité sublime', *PO&SIE*, 38 (1986), 83–116.

LAMB, JONATHAN, 'Exemplarity and Excess in Fielding's Fiction', *Eighteenth-Century Fiction*, 1/3 (1989), 187–207.

—— 'Longinus, the Dialectic, and the Practice of Mastery', *ELH* 60 (1993), 545–67.

—— 'The Job Controversy, Sterne and the Question of Allegory', *Eighteenth-Century Studies*, 24/1 (1990), 1–19.

—— 'The Subject of the Subject and the Sublimities of Self-Reference', *Huntington Library Quarterly*, 56/2 (1993), 191–207.

—— *Sterne's Fiction and the Double Principle* (Cambridge: Cambridge University Press, 1989).

LEHMANN, JAMES, '*The Vicar of Wakefield*: Goldsmith's Sublime, Oriental Job', *ELH* 46 (1979), 97–121.

LEIGHTON, ANGELA, *Shelley and the Sublime* (Cambridge: Cambridge University Press, 1984).

LEVINAS, EMMANUEL, *Totality and Infinity*, trans. Alphonso Lingis (Pittsburg: Duquesne University Press, 1969).

LEVINE, JOSEPH M., *The Battle of the Books* (Ithaca: Cornell University Press, 1991).

LIEBERMAN, DAVID, *The Province of Legislation Determined: Legal Theory in Eighteenth-Century Britain* (Cambridge: Cambridge University Press, 1989).

LINDBERG, BO, *William Blake's Illustrations of Job* (Abo: Abo Akademi, 1973).

LINEBAUGH, PETER, (ed.), *Albion's Fatal Tree* (New York: Pantheon Books, 1975).

—— *The London Hanged: Crime and Civil Society in the Eighteenth Century* (Harmondsworth: Allen Lane, 1991).

LIVINGSTON, DONALD, *Hume's Philosophy of Common Life* (Chicago: University of Chicago Press, 1984).

LIU, ALAN, 'Local Transcendence: Cultural Criticism, Postmodernism, and the Romanticism of Detail', *Representations*, 32 (1990), 75–113.

LLOYD, DAVID, 'Kant's Examples', *Representations*, 28 (1989), 34–54.

LUHMANN, NIKLAS, *Essays on Self-Reference* (New York: Columbia University Press, 1990).

—— *The Differentiation of Society* (New York: Columbia University Press, 1982).

—— *Love as Passion: The Codification of Intimacy*, trans. Jeremy Gaines (Cambridge, Mass.: Harvard University Press, 1986).

—— *Political Theory and the Welfare State*, trans. John Bednarz (Berlin: Walter de Gruyter, 1990).

—— *A Sociological Theory of Law*, trans. Elizabeth King-Utz and Martin Albiero (London: Routlege and Kegan Paul, 1985).

—— *Trust and Power* (Chichester: John Wiley, 1979).

LYONS, JOHN D., *Exemplum: The Rhetoric of Example in Early Modern France and Italy* (Princeton, NJ: Princeton University Press, 1989).

LYOTARD, JEAN-FRANCOIS, *The Differend: Phrases in Dispute*, trans. George van den Abbeele (Manchester: Manchester University Press, 1988).

—— *Lessons on the Analytic of the Sublime*, trans. Elizabeth Rottenberg (Stanford, Calif.: Stanford University Press, 1994).

—— *Libidinal Economy*, trans. Hamilton Grant (Bloomington and Indianapolis: Indiana University Press, 1993).

—— 'The Sign of History', in Derek Attridge, Geoff Bennington, and Robert Young (eds.), *Poststructuralism and the Question of History* (Cambridge: Cambridge University Press, 1987), 162–80.

—— 'The Sublime and the Avant-Garde', *Artforum*, 22/8 (April 1984), 36–43.

—— 'Le sublime, à present', *PO&SIE* 34 (1985), 97–116.

—— *Just Gaming*, trans. Wlad Godzich (Minneapolis: University of Minnesota Press, 1985).

MARIN, LOUIS, 'The Body-of-Power and Incarnation at Port Royal and in Pascal', in *Fragments for a History of the Human Body*, ed. Michael Feher, 3 vols. (New York: Zone, 1989), 412–47.

MARSHALL, DAVID, *The Figure of Theater* (New York: Columbia University Press, 1986).

—— *The Surprising Effects of Sympathy* (Chicago: University of Chicago Press, 1988).

MARSHALL, P. J. and WILLIAMS, GLYNDWR, *The Great Map of Mankind* (Cambridge, Mass.: Harvard University Press, 1982).

McKEON, MICHAEL, *Origins of the English Novel* (Baltimore: Johns Hopkins University Press, 1987).

McNAMARA, SUSAN, 'Mirrors of Fiction within *Tom Jones*: The Paradox of Self-Reference', *Eighteenth-Century Studies*, 12/3 (1979), 372–90.

MITCHELL, W. J. T., *Iconology: Image, Text, Ideology* (University of Chicago Press, 1986).

MONK, SAMUEL HOLT, *The Sublime in Eighteenth-Century England* (New York: MLA, 1935).

MORETTI, FRANCO, *Signs Taken for Wonders: Essays in the Sociology of Literary Forms*, trans. Susan Fischer, David Forgacs, and David Miller (London: Verso and New Left Books, 1983).

MORRIS, DAVID B., *The Religious Sublime* (University of Kentucky Press, 1972).

MULLAN, JOHN, *Sentiment and Sociability* (Oxford: Clarendon Press, 1988).

MULLER, PRISCILLA E., *Goya's Black Paintings* (New York: Hispanic Society of America, 1984).

MUSSELWHITE, DAVID, 'Reflections on Burke's *Reflections 1790–1990*', in *The Enlightenment and its Shadows*, ed. Peter Hulme and Ludmilla Jordanova (London: Routledge, 1990), 142–62.

NANCY, JEAN-LUC, 'L'Offrande sublime', *PO&SIE*, 30 (1984), 76–103.

NEMO, PHILIPPE, *Job et l'excès du mal* (Paris: Grasset, 1978).

NEW, MELVYN, 'Sterne, Warburton, and the Burden of Exuberant Wit', *Eighteenth-Century Studies*, 15/3 (1982), 245–74.

NICOLSON, BENEDICT, *Joseph Wright of Derby: Painter of Light*, 2 vols. (New York: Paul Mellon Foundation, 1968).

O'BRIEN, CONOR CRUISE, *The Great Melody* (London: Minerva, 1992).

ODELL, DANIEL W., 'Young's *Night-Thoughts* as an Anwer to Pope's *Essay on Man*', *SEL* 12 (1972), 481–501.

PAGDEN, ANTHONY, *European Encounters with the New World* (New Haven, Conn.: Yale University Press, 1993).

—— '*Jus et Factum*: Text and Experience in the Writings of Bartolome de las Casas', *Representations*, 33 (1991), 147–62.

PANOFSKY, ERWIN, *Tomb Sculpture* (London: Thames and Hudson, 1964).

PAULSON, RONALD, *Breaking and Remaking: Aesthetic Practice in England 1700–1800* (New Brunswick: Rutgers University Press, 1989).

—— *Representations of Revolution* (New Haven: Yale University Press, 1983).

PEASE, DONALD E., 'Sublime Politics', *Boundary 2*, 12/13 (1984), 259–79.

PENNY, NICHOLAS, *Church Monuments in Romantic England* (New Haven, Conn.: Yale University Press, 1977).

PLAISANT, MICHÈLE, 'Le Juste, le justicier, la justice poétique dans *The Vicar of Wakefield*, *Bulletin de la société d'études anglo-americaines des xvii et xviii siècles*, 24 (1987), 63–75.

POCOCK, J. G. A., *The Ancient Constitution and the Feudal Law* (Cambridge: Cambridge University Press, 1957; repr. 1987).

—— 'The Devil has two Horns', *London Review of Books*, 16/4 (24 February 1994), 10–11.

—— 'Early Modern Capitalism—the Augustan Perception', in *Feudalism, Capitalism and Beyond*, ed. Eugene Kamenka and R. S. Neale (Canberra: Australian National University Press, 1975).

—— *The Machiavellian Moment* (Princeton, NJ: Princeton University Press, 1975).

—— *Virtue, Commerce, Society* (Cambridge University Press, 1985).

POLAND, LYNN, 'The Bible and the Rhetorical Sublime', in *The Bible as Rhetoric*, ed. Martin Warner (London: Routledge, 1990).

POTKAY, ADAM, 'Classical Eloquence and the Polite Style in the Age of Hume', *Eighteenth-Century Studies*, 25/1 (1991), 31–56.

PRESSLY, WILLIAM, *The Life and Art of James Barry* (New Haven, Conn.: Yale University Press, 1981).

QUINTERO, REUBEN, *Literate Culture: Pope's Rhetorical Art* (Newark, Del.:

University of Delaware Press, 1992).

RADZINOWICZ, LEON, *A History of English Criminal Law* (London: Stevens and Sons, 1948).

RICHETTI, JOHN J., *Philosophical Writing: Locke, Berkeley, Hume* (Cambridge, Mass.: Harvard University Press, 1983).

RICHEY, WILLIAM, 'The French Revolution: Blake's Epic Dialogue with Edmund Burke', *ELH* 59/4 (1992), 817–37.

RIFFATERRE, MICHAEL, 'Prosopopeia', *Yale French Studies*, 69 (1985), 107–23.

ROE, NICHOLAS, *Wordsworth and Coleridge: The Radical Years* (Oxford: Clarendon Press, 1988).

ROGERS, NICHOLAS, *Whigs and Cities* (Oxford: Clarendon Press, 1989).

ROSS, JAMES, 'Job 33: 14–30: The Phenomenology of Lament', *Journal of Biblical Literature*, 94 (1975), 38–46.

ROWOLD, HENRY, '*Mi hu! Li hu!* Leviathan and Job in Job 41: 2–3', *Journal of Biblical Literature*, 105 (1986), 104–9.

ROSENBLUM, ROBERT, *Transformations in Late Eighteenth-Century Art* (Princeton, NJ: Princeton University Press, 1967).

SACKS, PETER M., *The English Elegy* (Baltimore: Johns Hopkins University Press, 1985).

SAINT GIRONS, BALDINE, *Fiat lux: une philosophie du sublime* (Paris: Éditions Quai Voltaire, 1992).

SANDERS, PAUL (ed.), Twentieth-Century Interpretations of the Book of Job (Princeton, NJ: Prentice-Hall, 1968).

SCARRY, ELAINE, *The Body in Pain: The Making and Unmaking of the World* (Oxford: Oxford University Press, 1985).

SCHAMA, SIMON, *Citizens* (Harmondsworth: Penguin, 1989).

SCHOR, NAOMI, *Reading in Detail: Aesthetics and the Feminine* (London: Methuen, 1987).

SCODEL, JOSHUA, *The English Poetic Epitaph* (Ithaca: Cornell University Press, 1991).

SHAPIN, STEVEN and SCHAFFER, SIMON, *Leviathan and the Air-Pump: Hobbes, Boyle and the Experimental Life* (Princeton, NJ: Princeton University Press, 1985).

SHAPIRO, BARBARA, *Probability and Certainty in Seventeenth-Century England* (Princeton, NJ: Princeton University Press, 1983).

SHAPIRO, GARY, 'From the Sublime to the Political', *New Literary History*, 12/2 (1985), 213–36.

SHELL, MARC, *The Economy of Literature*, (Baltimore: Johns Hopkins University Press, 1978).

SITTER, JOHN, *Literary Loneliness in Mid-Eighteenth Century England* (Ithaca: Cornell University Press, 1982).

STAFFORD, BARBARA, *Body Criticism: Imagining the Unseen in Englightenment Art and Medicine* (Cambridge, Mass.: MIT Press, 1991).

—— *Voyage into Substance* (Cambridge, Mass.: MIT Press, 1984).

STERN, LAURENT, 'Narrative versus Description', *New Literary History*, 21/3 (1990), 355–74.

STEWART, GARRETT, *Death Sentences: Styles of Dying in British Fiction* (Cambridge, Mass.: Harvard University Press, 1984).

SVENBRO, JESPER, *Phrasikleia: anthropologie de la lecture en Grèce ancienne* (Paris: Éditions La Découverte, 1988).

TATE, ALAN, *The Man of Letters and the Modern World* (New York: Meridian Books, 1955).

THOMPSON, E. P., *Whigs and Hunters* (Harmondsworth: Penguin, 1975).

TRUSSLER, SIMON, *Burlesque Plays of the Eighteenth Century* (Oxford University Press, 1969).

TUR-SINAI, N. H., *The Book of Job: A New Commentary* (Jerusalem: Kiryath Sepher, 1957).

VAN SANT, ANN JESSIE, *Eighteenth-Century Sensibility and the Novel* (Cambridge: Cambridge University Press, 1993).

VERNANT, J.-P., 'Dim Body, Dazzling Body', in *Fragments for a History of the Human Body*, ed. Michael Feher, 3 vols. (New York: Zone, 1989), i. 21–38.

—— *Mortals and Immortals* (Princeton, NJ: Princeton University Press, 1991).

—— *Myth and Thought among the Greeks* (London: Routledge and Kegan Paul, 1983).

WARNER, MARINA, *Monuments and Maidens* (London: Picador, 1985).

WARNER, MARTIN (ed.), *The Bible as Rhetoric* (London: Routledge, 1990).

—— *Philosophical Finesse* (Oxford: Clarendon Press, 1989).

WARNER, WILLIAM BEATTY, *Reading Clarissa* (New Haven, Conn.: Yale University Press, 1979).

WEISKEL, THOMAS, *The Romantic Sublime* (Baltimore: Johns Hopkins University Press, 1976).

WELLEK, RENÉ, *A History of Modern Criticism 1750–1950: The Later Eighteenth Century* (Cambridge: Cambridge University Press, 1981).

WELSH, ALEXANDER, 'Burke and Bentham on the Narrative Potential of Circumstantial Evidence', *New Literary History*, 21/3 (1990), 607–27.

—— *Strong Representations* (Baltimore: Johns Hopkins University Press, 1992).

WHITE, HAYDEN, 'The Politics of Historical Interpretation', in *The Content of the Form* (Baltimore: Johns Hopkins University Press, 1987).

WIMSATT, W. K., and BROOKS, CLEANTH, *Literary Criticism: A Short History* (New York: Knopf, 1957).

YAEGER, PATRICIA, 'Toward a Female Sublime', in *Gender and Theory: Dialogues on Feminist Criticism*, ed. Linda Kauffman (Oxford: Basil Blackwell, 1989).

ZERILLI, LINDA M. G., 'Text/Woman as Spectacle: Edmund Burke's "French Revolution"', *The Eighteenth Century: Theory and Interpretation*, 33/1 (1992), 47–72.

ZIMMERMAN, 'Tristram Shandy and Narrative Representation', *The Eighteenth Century: Theory and Interpretation*, 28/2 (1987), 127–47.

ZIZEK, SLAVOJ, *The Sublime Object of Ideology* (London: Verso, 1989).

ZUCKERMAN, BRUCE, *Job the Silent: A Study in Historical Counterpoint* (Oxford: Oxford University Press, 1991).

Index